Shriram
Bharatiya Kala Kendra

Kendra's epic production 'Ramlila', which has been performed since 1957 for forty unbroken years. ▶

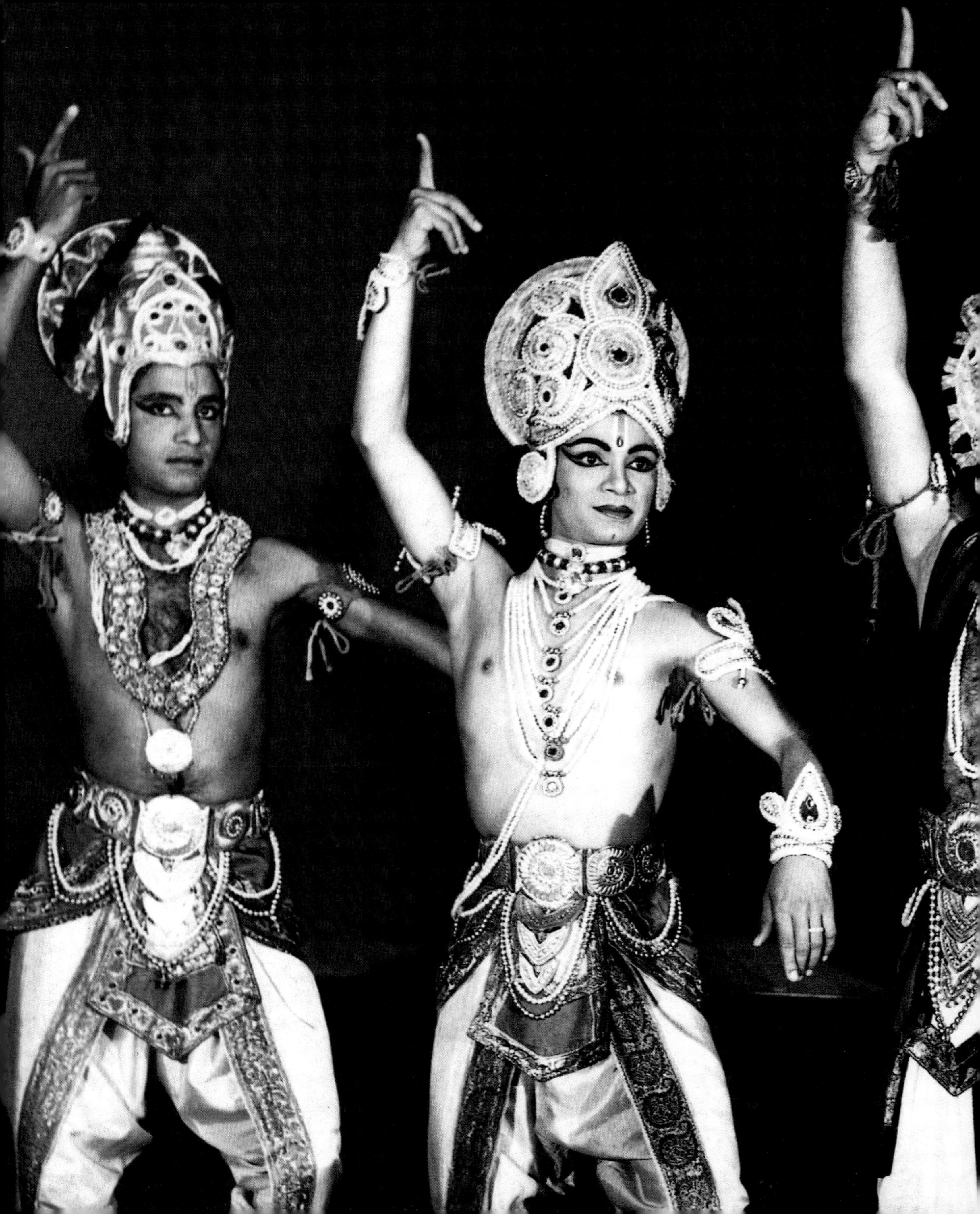

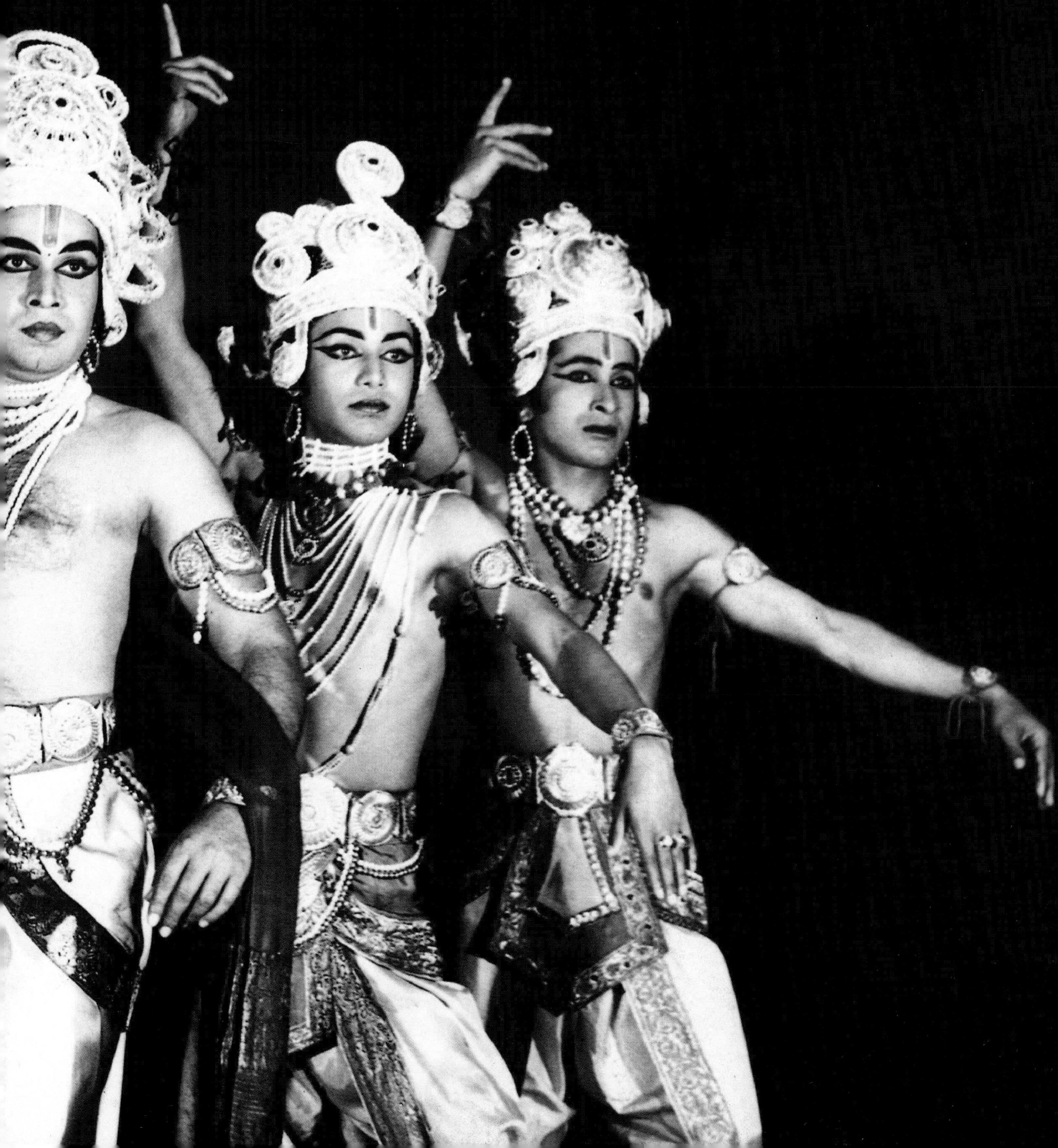

BASED ON
ARCHIVAL MATERIAL
FROM THE
MOHAN KHOKAR
DANCE COLLECTION

Shriram Bharatiya Kala Kendra
A History

SUMITRA CHARAT RAM REMINISCES

❖

ASHISH KHOKAR

❖

Lustre Press
Roli Books

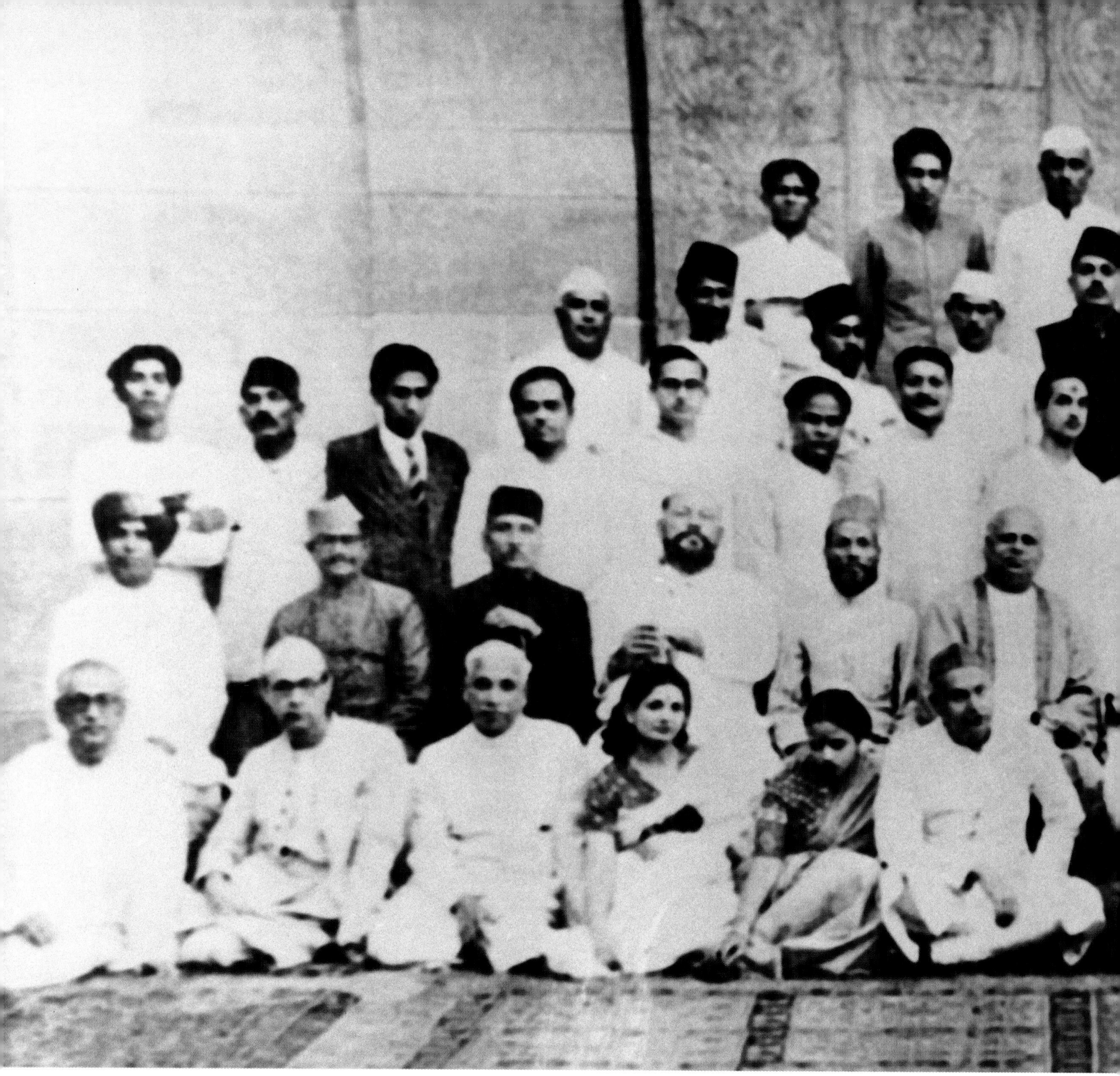

A historic occasion—the 1951 Conference of Music hosted by the Shriram Bharatiya Kala Kendra, in which the who's who of the music world participated. Seated row-wise. ***From bottom (right to left/seated on ground):*** *Nirmala Joshi, Kamala Lal, Brinda Lal, Dr. Sen, Shivraj Bahadur, Pt. Haksar, Sumitra Charat Ram, Sheila Bharat Ram, Hansraj Gupta, Pt. Shungloo.* ***Second row (left to right):*** *Ustad Nissar Khan, Ahmad Jaan Tirakkwa, Ustad Hafiz Ali Khan, Ustad Mushtaq Khan,*

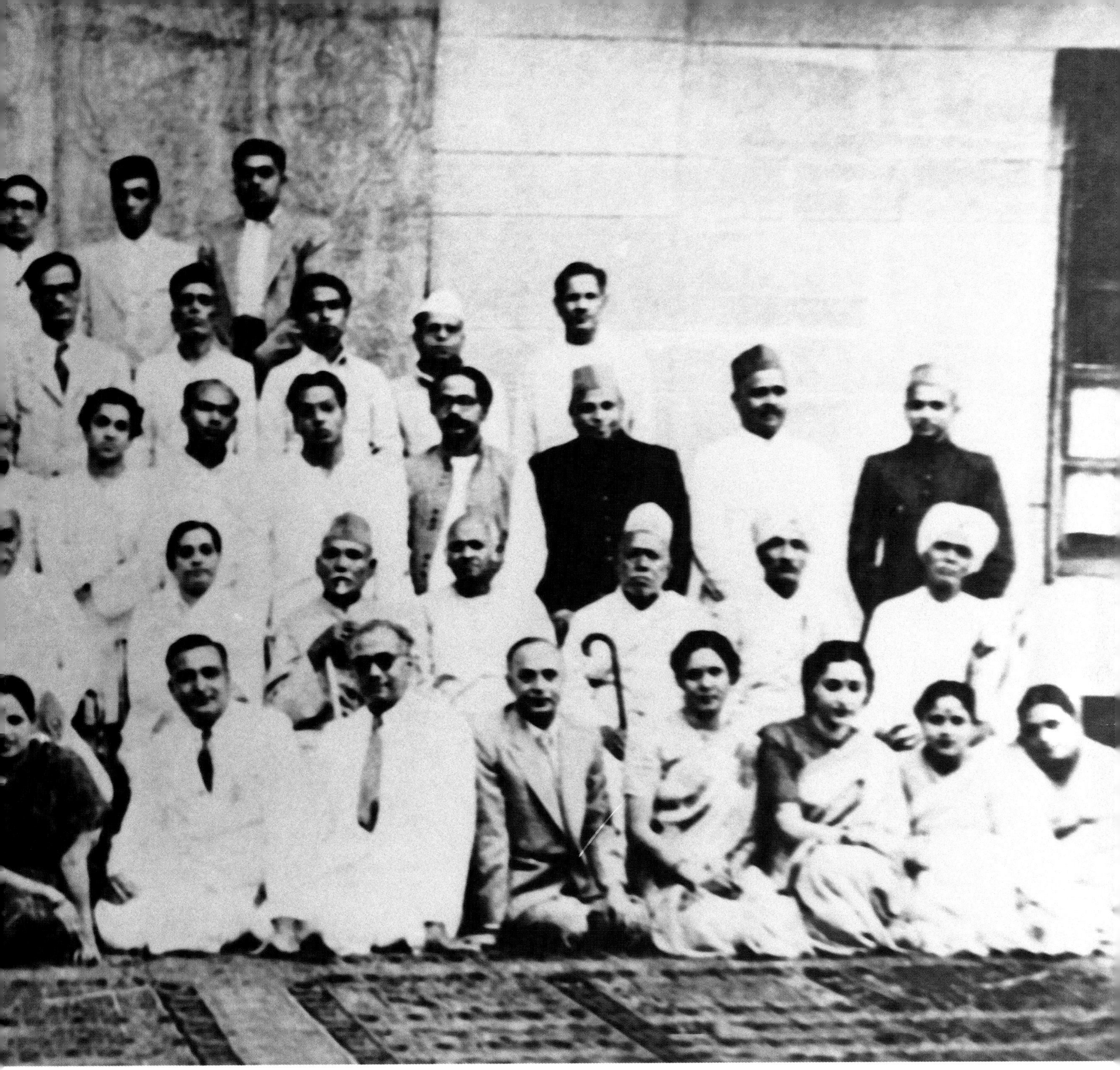

Pt. Omkarnath Thakur, President of India Rajendra Prasad, Kesarbai Kelker, Ustad Allaudin Khan, Kante Maharaj. ***Third row (left to right):*** *Pt. Uma Shankar Mishra, Raikumar Moitra, Ustad Bismillah Khan, Krishan Maharaj, Ravi Shankar, Ali Akbar Khan, Vilayat Khan, Vinayakarao Patwardhan, D.V. Paluskar.* ***Fourth row (left to right):*** *Ustad Bade Ghulam Sabri among others.* ***Last row (standing):*** *Second from left, Pt. Vinay Chandra Maudgalya with other staff members.*

SUMITRA CHARAT RAM
AND
ASHISH KHOKAR
HUMBLY DEDICATE THIS BOOK TO
THE ARTISTS OF INDIA

Contents

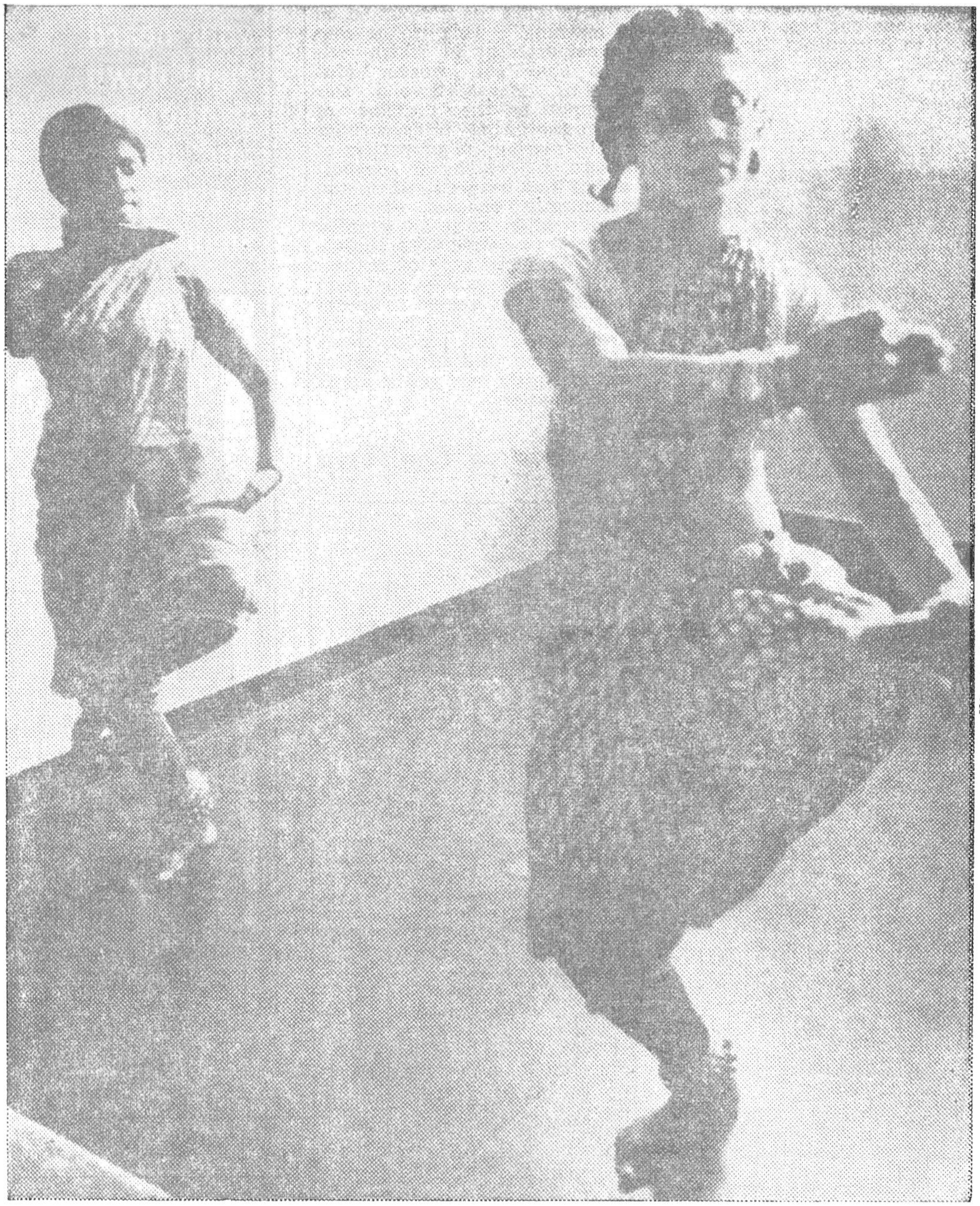

Dance performance at the Bharatiya Kala Kendra, Delhi.

FROM BACK TO TH GLITTE

Breaking the barriers of caste and gious enclaves, Delhi's Bharatiya Kala It has not only come of age, but achieved greatest names in music, dance and dra and success.

THE messenger boy who dreams of becoming a matinee idol on the silver screen is perhaps asking for moon. By and large, influence and the "right contacts" still count with producers in the filmdom of Bombay, notwithstanding good looks, dash and histrionic talent. But on the stage, the "legitimate theatre" right here in New Delhi, there are instances like that of a shoeblack boy who works at the sets both for cultural organisations putting up dance, music and drama shows as well as for the TV during his spare time. An organisation which employed a man as a peon and then trained him to participate in a ballet which has done about 900 rounds in different parts of the country and abroad, the Bharatiya Kala Kendra, is perhaps not alone in drawing upon the common man for its cast. But it has consciously tried to discover talent from the street and harness it for presentation on the boards against the glittering footlights of theatres in different parts of the country.

The organisers count off many such notable instances. Besides Mool Chand, peon-turned-dancer, there is the case of Lakshminarayan appointed to iron costumes who has risen to be stage assistant in the Kendra's Ballet unit. A small time Delhi 'durzee' (tailor), Karan Singh is today a sought after expert costume designer, and has made costumes for players in the major productions of the Indian National Theatre and other cultural organisations. Harish, grandson of a cook working with one of the Kendra's organisers, literally danced his way from an Anand Parbat labour colony where he was entertaining a street audience dressed up like a Kumaonese girl. The Bharatiya Kala Kendra gave him a stipend for three years. Today Harish is a valued staff member earning a salary of Rs 350 per month.

A little Harijan girl whose father worked in the home of a senior army officer similarly attracted notice for her nimble performances in back-verandahs. Today, the young lady of 24 is an accomplished ballet dancer. She is continuing her vocation, though married. That art and charm can sometimes break the rigid barriers of caste is a heartening factor as demonstrated by the case of this young dancer.

But the path of art is not one strewn with roses. Ghasi Ram, the shoeblack boy, who did part-time jobs to paint the backdrops for TV and the stage as well as singing with groups, and has tried desperately to abandon shoe-shining to assume the more "respectable" nomenclature of artiste, sadly admits that there is more money in shoe-shining than in painting sets or group singing and doing bit parts for the stage. Yet he would naturally like to climb up the social ladder not merely for his own sake but that of his son whom he is trying to give schooling and for whom he has visions of a white-collar job. He would like to bury his past as a shoe-shine.

Manual labour just does not have the respectability it should but all the stigma one can imagine. The world of the shoeshine and the sweeper is a different, isolated one even if he earns as much or more than say a lower division clerk or a bus conductor or a police constable. The world of art cannot divorce itself from genuine talent and talent is not the preserve of the well-to-do or the upper class or the high caste alone. But talent can wither away unseen. It can remain undeveloped without training and direction. The role of organisations like the Bharatiya Kala Kendra cannot, therefore, be underestimated in bringing to light talent among the poor and, in some cases, the socially ostracized.

New shelter

With independence and the democratisation of the arts the old system of patronage disappeared. While this helped in accelerating the liberation of the arts from the narrow confines of an outmoded system it could not fully provide the country's artistes, particularly the young, with the necessary encouragement and help.

It is in the fitness of things that a section of the country's well-to-do elite, who happen to be enlightened enough to appreciate the arts, should supplement official effort to develop them and help provide a new shelter for budding artistes.

With its base in the Capital, what came to be known as the Bharatiya Kala Kendra was established in 1952 by a small circle of music-lovers who named it "Jhankar.
was to organise mu
festivals and semi
for its members.

Soon the need fo
training centre f
music and dance v
a college of music
was started in 1955.
ing centre has ha
character of its ow
to raise a new ge
performing artistes
tants by following
of "Guru-Shishya."

Its home, at 5-B
a little house, hu
activity, where s
country's top maes
field of music and
ed. The most
among them were
Khan and Shambh
now both dead.
started with the
vocal as well as
music and Kathak
Raj Bahadur, Sun
Ram, Nirmala Jos
Haksar, C. B. Rao,
rat Ram, Ravi Sha
Devi, Mr Rajaman
Chief Justice of
Kamla Devi Chatto
Prof. Humayun K
among those associa

Besides Shambh
and Hafiz Ali Khan,
the Kendra as 'g
were other well-kn
who gave of their
Kendra's students.
cluded the late
Khan Dagar and
Vilayat Husain Kha
der Prasad. Am
names connected w
the late Mustaq Hu
Birju Maharaj,
Khan Dagar, Wa
Purushottam Das,
Khan, Latif Khan,
dra Vedi, Sidhes

THE VERANDAH

RING STAGE

nunity in search of talent on the streets and in the backyards of presti- idra can look back with satisfaction that it has done a job – and done it well. h more. Today, the Kendra has a truly national character with some of the issociated with its work, PROMILLA KALHAN tells the story of its struggle

A centre for the arts and a home for artists is born. Noted columnist Promila Kalhan platformed the activities of the Kendra through this spread which appeared in the Hindustan Times *dated September 16, 1973, on the occasion of the completion of more than two decades of the Kendra's service to the arts and artists of India.*

bject certs, ainly

gular ssical , and dance rain- stinct rying n of xecu- ystem

Road, with the the work- nding Ali haraj, endra g of ental Shiv harat . N Bha- Naina rmer dras), and were th it. haraj oined there tistes o the in- uddin Lal, Sun- other are: Khan, uddin Khan, Ali Chan- Devi,

Ishtiaq Hussain Khan, Debabrata Chowdhary, Hashmat Ali Khan and Mayadhar Rout.

There are about 70 students, including foreigners, at present receiving training in vocal music (khayal), instrumental music (sitar) and Orissi dance at the Kendra. Some of the outstanding ex-students of this institution are: Laxaman Bhatt Tailang (vocal), Sulochana Yajurvedi (vocal), Nimai Chand Baral (vocal), Rita Kothari (vocal), Aloka Panikar (Orissi dance), Amjad Ali Khan (sarod), Nupur Roy Chowdhary and Ghulam Sadiq Khan (vocal).

Kathak revival

A noteworthy achievement of the Kendra has been the revival of Kathak dance. The Kendra made serious effort to revive and restore it to its original grace and dignity. The puppet section of the Kendra which has since closed down produced several interesting folk ballets. Mrs Indira Gandhi, who was president of the Kendra in the early days, according to the organisers, was impressed by the skill of its artistes who turned out masks and costumes sitting in the basement of a house on Kasturba Gandhi Road. She encouraged them in their pursuit.

The Ramlila Ballet, now in its 16th year, has staged around 900 shows. A number of directors, including Narendra Sharma, Inder Razdan, Bhagwan Das Verma, Jyotirindra Moitra and Sushil Das Gupta, have been connected with it. Mrs Sumitra Charat Ram, a trustee of the Kendra, is the moving spirit behind the organisation. Her efforts have gone a long way in the Kendra

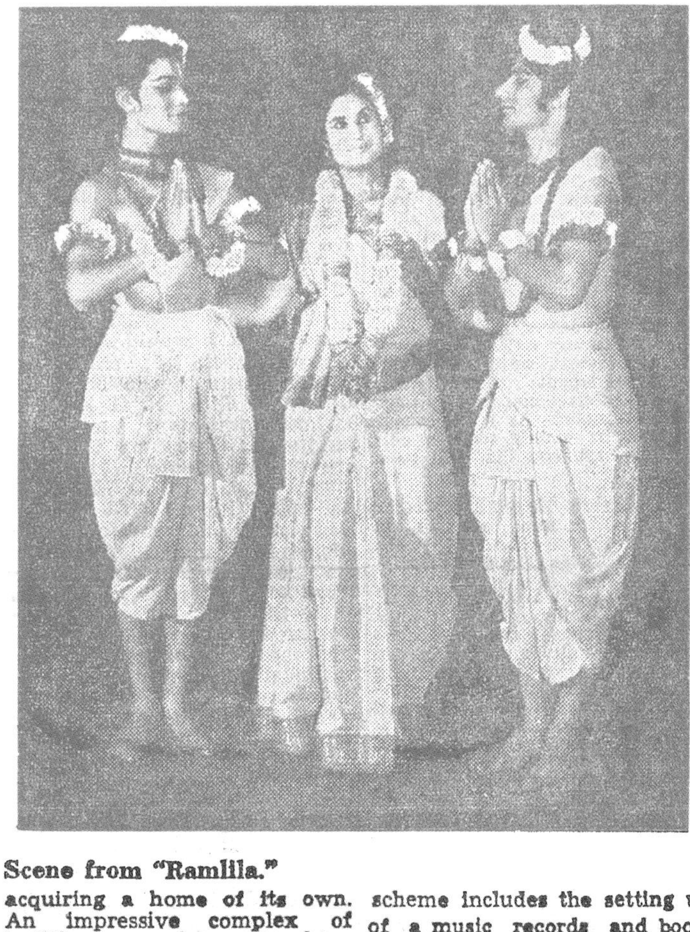

Scene from "Ramlila."

acquiring a home of its own. An impressive complex of buildings comprising a teaching block, residential flats and hostel and the Kamani Auditorium now houses the Kendra's staff and students and provides its own forum for its activities. There are at present 34 students staying in the hostel, 12 of whom are foreigners.

The Kendra's expansion scheme includes the setting up of a music records and book library with adequate listening facilities, a documentary film library, facilities for holding lecture-demonstrations on music and dance not only at the Kendra itself but also on visits to educational institutions. It also proposes to bring out publications on the contemporary performing arts.

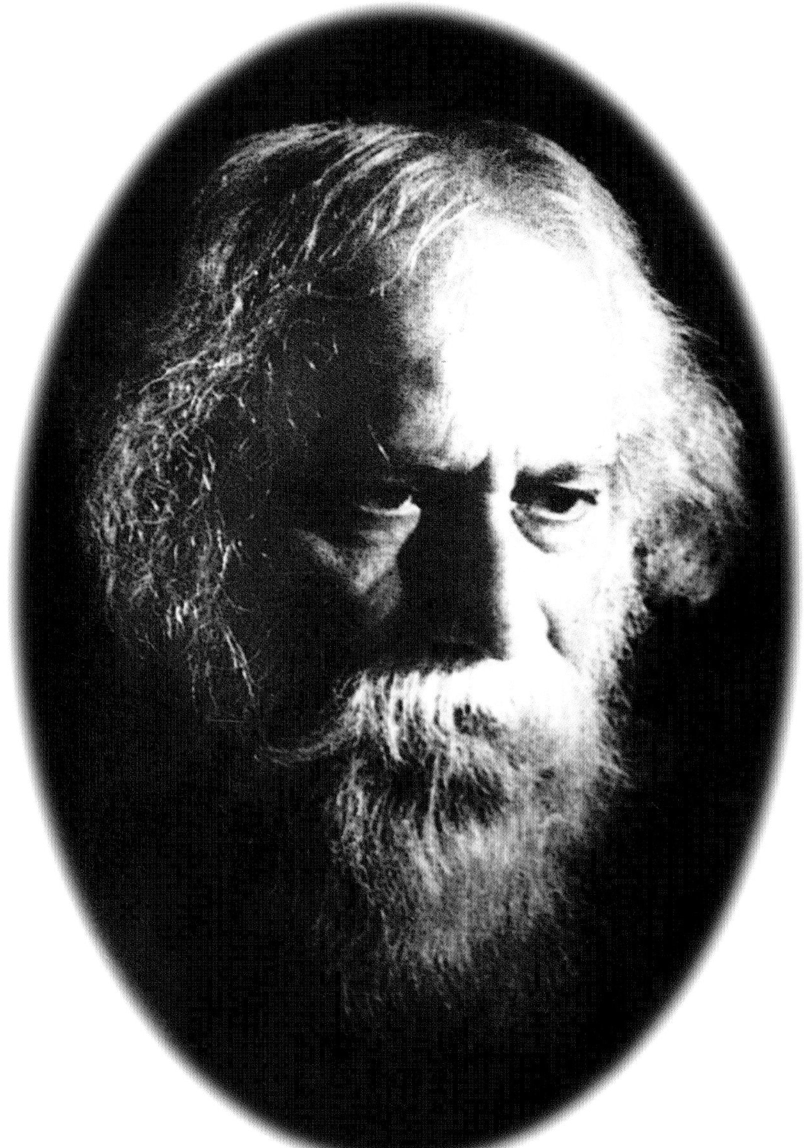

Rabindranath Tagore

Acknowledgements

There are the countless artists, associates and activists who have shared their memories and memorabilia. The best way to acknowledge their inputs is to profile them, since no compilation of their work and worth exists. This compilation, in the second portion of the book, is by no means exhaustive but it is a beginning, especially since the government-run cultural agencies do not even have correct profiles of such artists.

Specifically, I am beholden to Dr. Karan Singh (former Maharaja of Kashmir, Union Minister for Education, Culture and Tourism, former Ambassador to USA, a scholar and a philosopher) for readily agreeing to write the Foreword. His readiness showed his faith in my modest abilities.

Without the inputs of the Mohan Khokar Dance Collection, this book would have been poorer, for his collection is the single largest resource for archival compilation, reference and research. Jehanara Wasi, helped editorially and exclaimed with delight that the manuscript she received for editing was rather clean. It was so, because my wife, Betsy Hall, my in-house editor, had cleaned it up. Ratnottama Sengupta, my other 'in-house editor' (of *The Times of India* which I serve as the dance critic), went through the manuscript for content editing. If this work holds, it is thanks to their collective inputs, not mine. Jehanara Wasi also helped with the chapterisation and indexing. And it was left to Ashok Srinivasan to give the entire draft a final touch.

Shobha Deepak Singh's indomitable will prevailed and she insisted that I author this compilation. She stuck through thick and thin, against ups and downs of the four years this compilation took. Her colour photos in the centre-section add beauty to the book.

Sankar Ghose, that efficient, erudite Man Friday of the Shriram Industrial Enterprise Limited helped in the initial stage and Bhupinder Sachedva of Printways and his computer girls, Harpreet and Anju, set the initial pre-editing manuscripts.

Pramod Kapoor of Roli Books readily stepped in to publish it. His faith in my ability must most certainly be misplaced but he still prodded on extending full cooperation and expertise. The final product is his doing and I am extremely grateful to him and his team.

The Sangeet Natak Akademi generously helped with whatever little material they had on artists and Govind Vidyarthi, Aloka Panikar, Rekha Shankar, Kumudini Lakhia and Thakur Harnarain Singh provided material help in the form of old photographs and memorabilia.

Above all, the three women in my life—my guru, my mother and my wife, guided, supported and helped in every way to make this humble homage to the arts and artists of India, possible.

Ashish Khokar

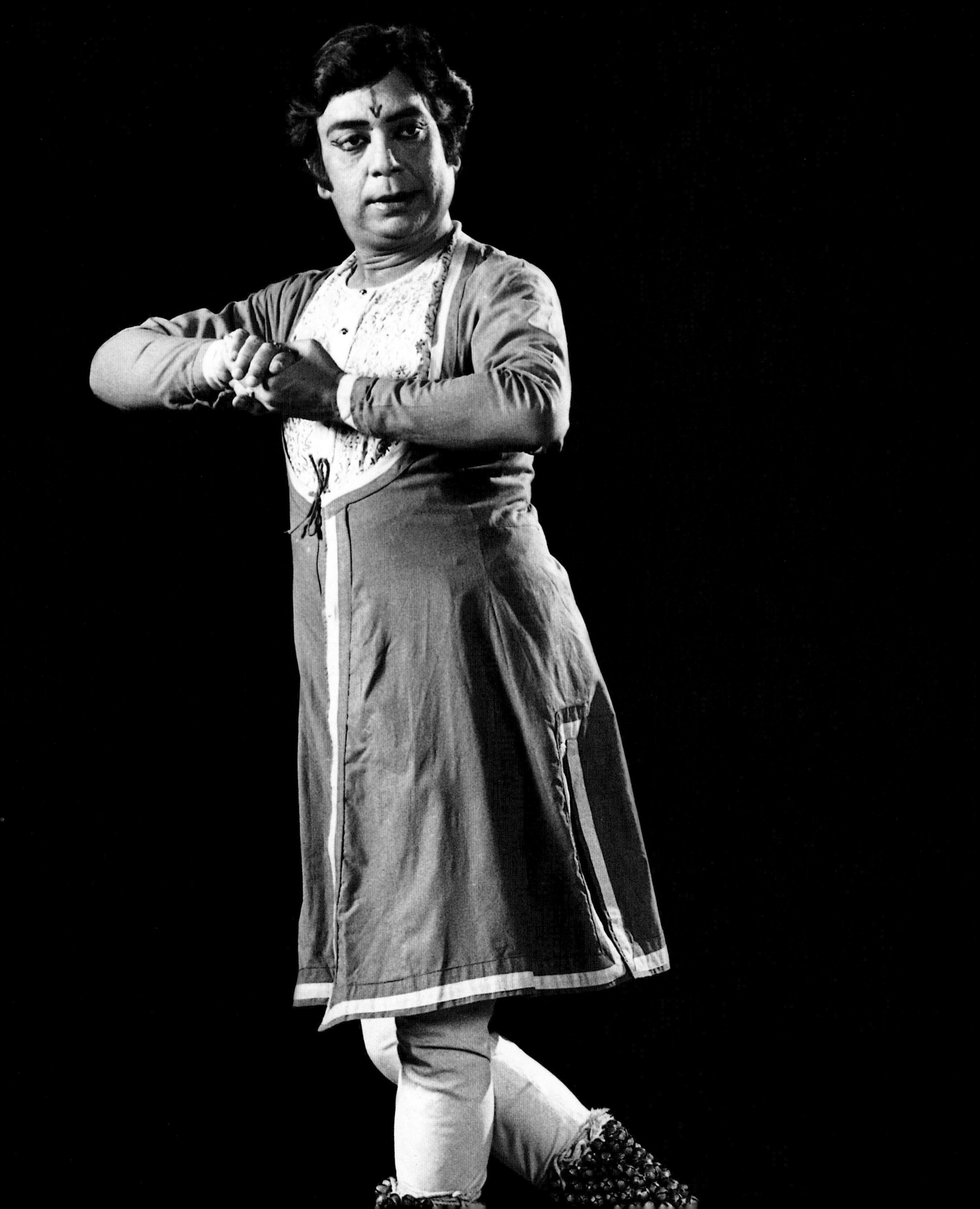

Foreword

In a world torn by dissension and disharmony, the creative arts have a significant role to play in refining our consciousness and opening our awareness to the deeper levels of rhythm and harmony. In India, perhaps more than in any other civilisation, music and dance is looked upon as a divine gift and a potent means for spiritual development. The astounding concept of Shiva Nataraja, Lord of the Cosmic Dance, who dances the universe into being, dancing sustains it and finally, dancing subsumes it in the vast aeons of time, while giving the individual soul at every moment the opportunity to break into divine consciousness, is surely one of the marvels of human civilisation. Similarly Lord Krishna playing the flute on the banks of Yamuna represents the eternal call of the divine consciousness which beckons the individual soul to respond in love and devotion.

One of the most positive and remarkable developments in India over the last half century since Independence has been the dramatic revival of art and culture, specially classical music and dance. Previously these areas depended largely upon the patronage of the princely order for their survival, and indeed the unbroken tradition of Hindustani and Karnatic music has always been a matter of great pride for us. With the advent of freedom and the passing of the feudal order, it was essential that the gap should be filled. This was, in fact, achieved in two ways. Firstly, through All India Radio and, much later, Doordarshan, classical artists were given encouragement and opportunities for growth, for which we owe a debt of gratitude to the first Minister for Information and Broadcasting in Pandit Jawaharlal Nehru's cabinet, Dr. B.V. Keskar. The second was the growth of voluntary organisations dedicated to foster the performing arts, and here the Shriram Bharatiya Kala Kendra, set up by Shrimati Sumitra Charatram, has played an outstanding role in the capital over the last five decades.

◀ *The king of Kathak today—Birju Maharaj initially made his presence felt in a career in dance at the Kendra, where he was projected as a principal dancer and later, teacher.*

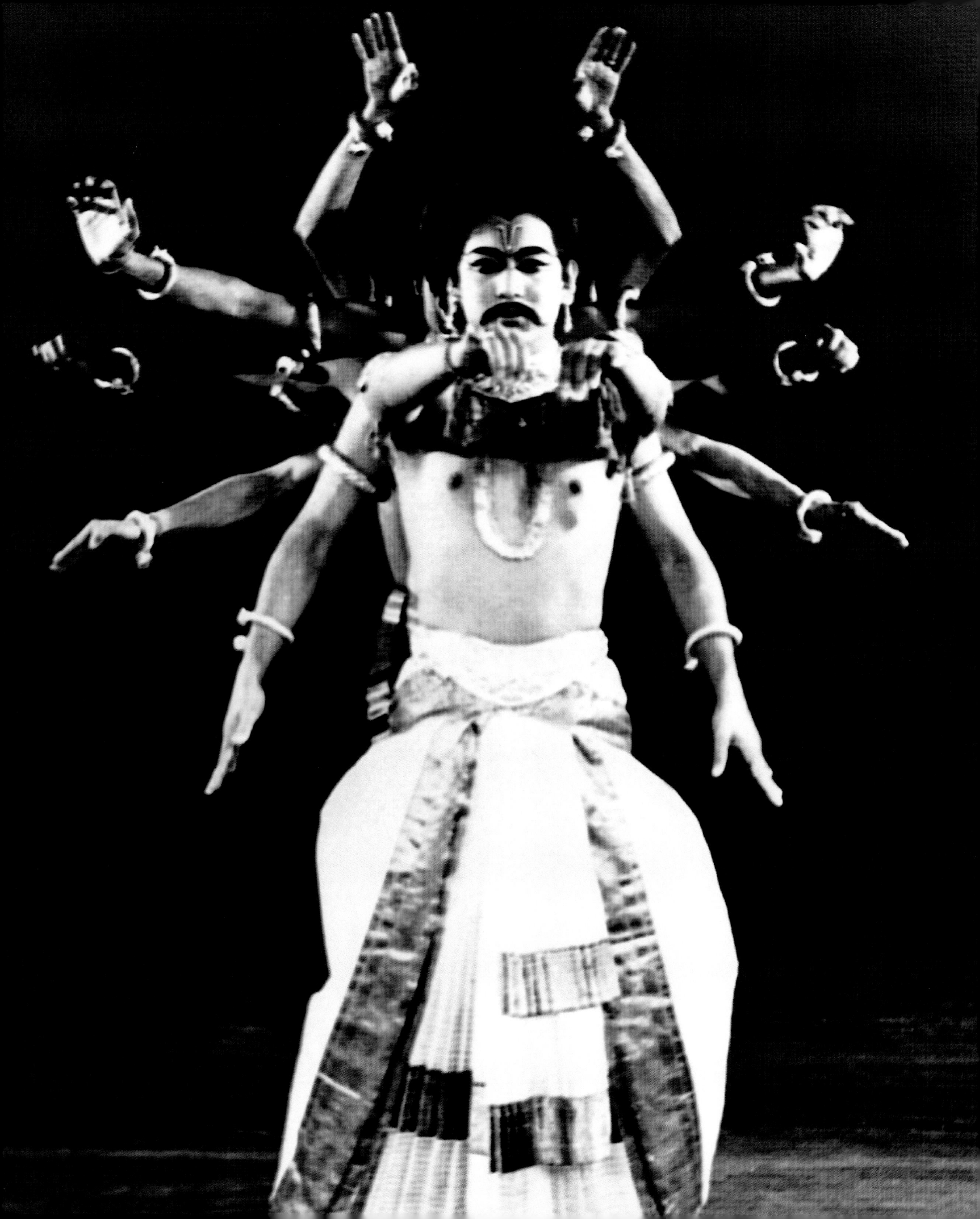

The vision and energy of a single person usually lies behind any great achievement. Sumitraji's single minded devotion to this institution, later supported by her daughter Shobha has been largely responsible for a unique spectrum of cultural activities in Delhi which includes classical and folk dances in many styles, dance dramas and classical music. Some of our greatest contemporary artists and intellectuals have participated in the varied activities of the Shriram Bharatiya Kala Kendra and I have personally enjoyed many such performances down the corridors of time over the last half century.

The entire odyssey needed to be recorded and documented in a manner that would present to the interested public a comprehensive overview of its activities, based largely upon Sumitraji's own recollections and reminiscences. This task has been ably undertaken by Sumitraji with the help of the talented young writer and critic Ashish Khokar. His painstaking research, especially in compiling over a hundred profiles of artists will be a useful record for all times to come. This book is coming out on the occasion of the 50th anniversary of the founding of the Kendra which has left such a significant mark on the cultural fabric of the capital. It will be read with interest and pleasure by all those involved in the marvellous world of dance, drama and music, in the broader movement of cultural renaissance and the restatement of the undying spirit of India that has persisted from the very dawn of history and, despite all the negativities of our public life, has retained its vigour and inspirational power.

Karan Singh

◀ *Bhushan Lakhandari undertook stellar roles in the productions of Kendra.*

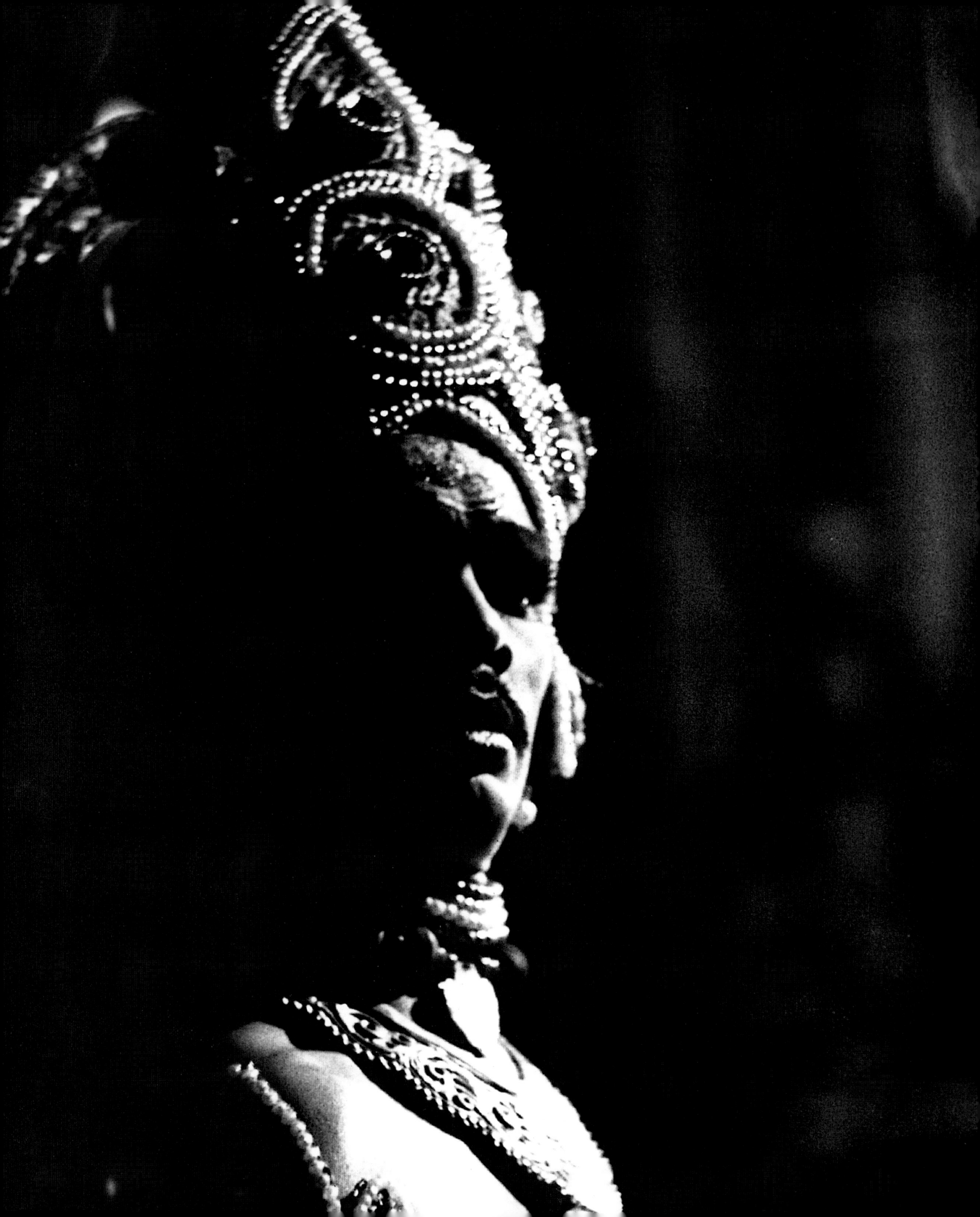

Author's Note

The history of the arts and artists of India in the twentieth century is at best confined to individual memory, not factual compilation. This has happened largely because the early historians of this century were reconstructing and recapturing the spirit and glory of ancient India and its traditions. It became more important to record five thousand years of Indian history than record the immediate history of the arts and artists. This book has been compiled with the specific purpose of remembering our immediate past. This book relates to efforts on the part of individuals, institutions and individuals who became institutions. One such is Sumitra Charat Ram.

As a student, and later a teacher of Indian History at the University of Delhi, I often marvelled at the process of recording of history. Sourcing became an important aspect. There were primary and secondary sources; literary and numismatic. In the creation of history, its reconstruction became an equally important task, if not more.

Constructing and commenting on recent history is another matter altogether, for the sources are several and for the better part, alive. Thus, after collection of material and its collation, cross-checking becomes critical. Memories become faded when they are not jaded and often emotions take over facts. This is what I learnt most as I trudged on this journey of reconstructing the art and cultural history of Delhi through the persona of Sumitra Charat Ram.

Sumitra Charat Ram is an unusual subject, for she displays reluctance at being the subject. Repeatedly, she requested that nothing adulatory be written or put on record. An extensive exercise of contacting over a hundred artists-associates thus became counter-productive in her eyes because she feared all they would heap on her would be praise, or worse, flattery.

The first task was to assure her that she was incidental, even if she was the central focus of this book. Largely owing to her philosophical nature, she could understand this dichotomy but often she would be reticent if she felt she was being spotlighted. Over a four year period, starting from June 2, 1994, through Jan 2, 1998, she shared her inner joys and concerns.

She cherished and relived her dreams and desires. For me—for the reader, ultimately—she created that vision, that depth which helped her create a leading institution of not only Delhi, but of India. Her memory is amazingly

◀ *Veladuyanathan Nair in a pensive mood in the Kendra's evergreen production 'Ramlila'.*

clear and crisp and despite her eighty plus years; she recaptured events and happenings as if they had happened yesterday. Her elder brother, Dharam Vira, who is over ninety, served as principal source for recounting family history and Sumitra Charat Ram's early childhood days. His memory and observation remain sharp and astute and in his recollection of small details, he showed a dispassionate concern.

India's history is long and ancient, but India as a country is young and new. If 1947 is taken as the cut-off point for purposes of national identity (and history), then 1947 is also the cut-off point for Sumitra Charat Ram creating cultural history. It was on this momentous occasion that she decided willy-nilly to step into the world of the arts and culture. This happened at the night-long soirée organised by her on the occasion of the birth of India. This night sowed the seeds of creation for fifty long years of artistic work, spanning three generations of artists and five glorious decades of work. Today, if the Kendra celebrates its fifty years, it is that modest and humble beginning it remembers. Although the Kendra technically came into being in 1952, it was this event in 1947 that led to the formation of the Jhankar Music Circle in Feb '49 which was a precursor to the Kendra. It is that seed sown in 1947 which grew to become a mighty oak.

Sumitra Charat Ram recalls these years of search and research; seeking and solace; substance and soul with a memory which is sharp and succinct. Her recollections have helped reconstruct the cultural history of Delhi. And for her culture is not merely the arts but a way of life. In her being, pages of history flutter as if they were canvases of thoughts upon which the indelible ink of experience had registered for itself the permanence of memory which becomes history.

History bequeaths credibility to remembrance. Mere memory becomes personal; tinctured with facts, memory celebrates life and in the process becomes history. In Sumitra Charat Ram's long and eventful innings, she has seen history being made.

Today, Delhi stands proud as the artistic and cultural capital of India but this process has taken over fifty years in independent India. Several players came and created their own areas of excellence; several forces contributed to its making. This book briefly captures that spirit and those who contributed to Delhi's growth as a city of cultural activities and this book records the origins, growth and development of the Shriram Bharatiya Kala Kendra.

The Shriram Bharatiya Kala Kendra is no ordinary institution for it has nurtured the arts and artists for a long, consistent and continuous period. It has helped establish talents, supported creative work and served in the upkeep of the national heritage. By doing so, it created new arenas of artistic interest while preserving old traditions. Through its numerous dance-drama productions, the Kendra celebrated Indian mythologies and through its various teaching faculties, it created new talents in the field of dance and music. The artists helped the Kendra and the Kendra in turn helped the artist community. If a group needed support, the Kendra lent its artists, costumes or even a production. In that, the Kendra helped foster a spirit of sharing and caring among the artist community, which is sorely missing today.

Where the Kendra focussed its attention most was in the propagation, of the classical dance style of Kathak. In the mid-thirties, efforts at platforming this neglected form had been undertaken by gurus in different parts of the country. In 1936, Guru Mohanrao Kalyanpurkar with Guru Sundar Prasad started his school in Bombay. In 1939, the Marris College of Music in Lucknow (today known as the Bhatkande Sangeet Mahavidyalaya) also initiated measures for its propagation. In the forties, Guru Gowri Shankar initiated the Pracheen Nritya Kendra which dovetailed with the efforts of Madame Menaka's Nrityanilayam in Khandala. In the fifties, the M.S. University of Baroda proved to be the first university in the country to offer a degree course in dance, of which Kathak was an important part.

By being among the first serious institutions in Delhi, other than the Sangeet Bharati where Pandit Achchan Maharaj taught in the late forties, the Kendra laid the foundation for its national appreciation. By having on its faculty the best gurus of Kathak—Vidwan Shambhu Maharaj, Pt. Sunder Prasad, Birju Maharaj, Bansi Lal, Devi Lal — amongst others, the Kendra provided pioneering support to this form and helped in its revival. Likewise by inviting the best gurus of Orissi such as Guru Deba Prasad Das, Guru Harekrishna Behera and Guru Mayadhar Raut to teach Orissi and Guru Krishna Chandra Nayak for Mayurbhanj Chhau both these forms got a shot in the arm by the support and platform it received from the Kendra.

As the Shriram Bharatiya Kala Kendra enters its fiftieth year, it can look back on a lifetime of devoted involvement with and to the arts. It can see for itself the fruits of seeds sown decades ago grown into fulsome trees of artistic and creative talents. Most importantly, it can rest assured that it has left its mark on the cultural history of India, especially Delhi. In a way, the story of the Kendra is the story of Sumitra Charat Ram.

Ashish Khokar

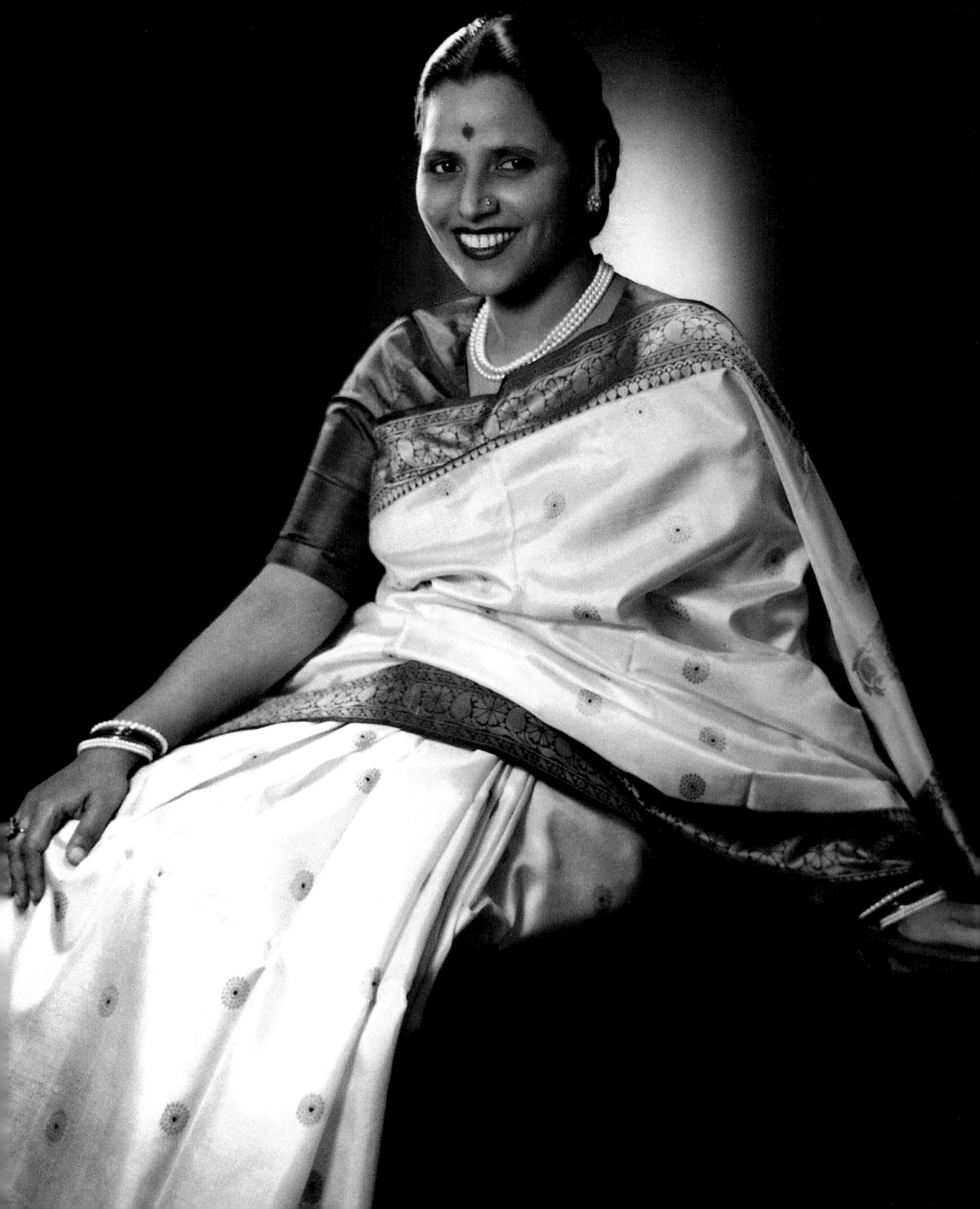

Prologue

When I look back on a lifetime which has been fulfilling and inspiring, I wonder how I came to create an institution—the Shriram Bharatiya Kala Kendra—with little design or intent. I had no ambition of establishing a centre for the arts, much less an institution to perpetuate my name. If anything, it was providence.

I was born into a family where the core cultural tenets of India were maintained. Culture to me does not merely mean song and dance or the finer things of life, but a refined way of living. In the family into which I was born, traditional lore and values were inculcated. It was through the celebrations of our traditional festivals and myths that the best of our heritage came to expression. I feel that India's real culture lies in its villages. If it was true some decades ago, it is even more true today. Village India represents a certain closeness to Mother Nature.

We often mistake cultural institutions to mean a training centre for various arts. While that is part of the truth, the other more important aspect is creating people who are sensitive and refined, who can appreciate beauty and substance and who value values. I have often wondered why I got to do this. Did God plan for me to be the tool or instrument of his desire? I never wanted to cherish or celebrate myself. In fact, I have always believed in teamwork. I often jokingly tell my youngsters that I am a person with limited qualities or talent but the one thing which they can learn from me is to absorb my utmost faith in teamwork.

It is this *mantra* of team-spirit in every sphere that I look back upon when I think of nearly fifty years of working in the field of the arts and culture. I cherish the memory of hours of rehearsals, preparations and productions. I enjoy the nuances of those times, when the great names of today worked as one family without any feeling of one-upmanship or constraints. So many artists came into contact with us and because of their affection and devotion, we felt a certain bond of friendship. I do not wish to single out any one artist but in these fifty years the growth and development of the Shriram Bharatiya Kala Kendra as a leading cultural institution of not only Delhi but of the country, is in no small measure due to the devoted and unflinching support and contribution of hundreds of artists.

Without artists there can be no art institution. In the case of the Shriram Bharatiya Kala Kendra, the artists alone made this institution and in return,

◀ *Sumitra Charat Ram—the initiator of the institution.*

Bharatiya Kala Kendra

Presents

NATIONAL DANCE FESTIVAL

H.T : *Sponsored by* 3.11.55

SANGEET NATAK AKADAMI

AT THE

ART THEATRE

(INDIAN INDUSTRIES FAIR)

From 2nd Nov. to 10th Dec., 55 at 6 P.M.

ARTISTS PARTICIPATING:—

Bala Saraswati, Shanta Rao, Rita Chatterji, Roshan, Shambhu Maharaj, Guru Kunju Kurup, Manipuri Troupe, Uday Shankar, Orissa: Chhau and Odissi, Sm. Hima, Krishna Nayyar, Chathunni Panikkar, Kuchipuri Dancers Mrinalini Sara Bhai, Narendra Sharma, Birju Maharaj, Saraikela Chhau, Assam Jhumura,

3rd and 5th Nov., 55	Smt. BALA SARASWATI
6th and 7th Nov., 55	MANIPURI TROUPE
8th and 9th Nov., 55	Smt. SHANTA RAO

TICKETS AVAILABLE AT

Pandit Bros., Gaylord, D.C.M. Store, C. Place, Regional Tourist Office, Queensway, New Delhi, D.C.M. Store, Chandni Chowk and at the gate.

Tickets 10|- 5|- & 2|-.

"All ticket holders for the National Dance Festival are not to pay any entrance fee for the Fair. There is a separate Theatre gate for the Inauguration."

the institution, perhaps, helped them flower. I first give credit to the countless years of work by so many creative talents whose insights and inputs, dedication and service made this institution what it is—a Kala Kendra, or centre for the arts. In the five decades of its existence, several productions on Indian mythology and heritage have been mounted, hundreds of students trained in the classical art of music and dance, numerous special events organised and major festivals celebrated. Today when I look back on the fifty years of work, I feel a certain calm. This comes from a spirit within which tells me that the journey has been fruitful.

I have never sought public attention, much less publicity, for my work, which for me was more pleasure than work. Often I have refused commenting in the media, largely because I am convinced that I did nothing exceptional. This documentation of the fifty years of the Kendra is only to record the greatness of the artists who shaped and made the institution. I reiterate, I do not wish to celebrate myself through it but the artists who helped me make this institution.

This book is a record not only of the Kendra but also of Delhi, in this century: how it grew from a small settlement to a large town, from a capital to a metropolis, culturally. It records the advent of other institutions and in the process may help the readers and audiences of today to realise the dimensions and outreach of this important field of human endeavour. I am indebted to countless people who have contributed their time and energies in the shaping of this book. It is my wish that the readers of this documentation find it an informative insight into a slice of recent history, especially of Delhi's growth as the cultural capital of India.

All these years, I have consciously avoided being the centre of attention but after prodding from my family, both the immediate and the larger one comprising numerous well-wishers and artists, I have agreed to record and share these memories of more than fifty years of relishing and cherishing the world of the arts and artists. I am grateful to Ashish Khokar for helping me fulfil this responsibility.

Sumitra Charat Ram

◀ *In 1955, the Kendra organised the first National Dance Festival sponsored by the Sangeet Natak Akademi and the participating artists included most of the noted and well-known names of the dance world.*

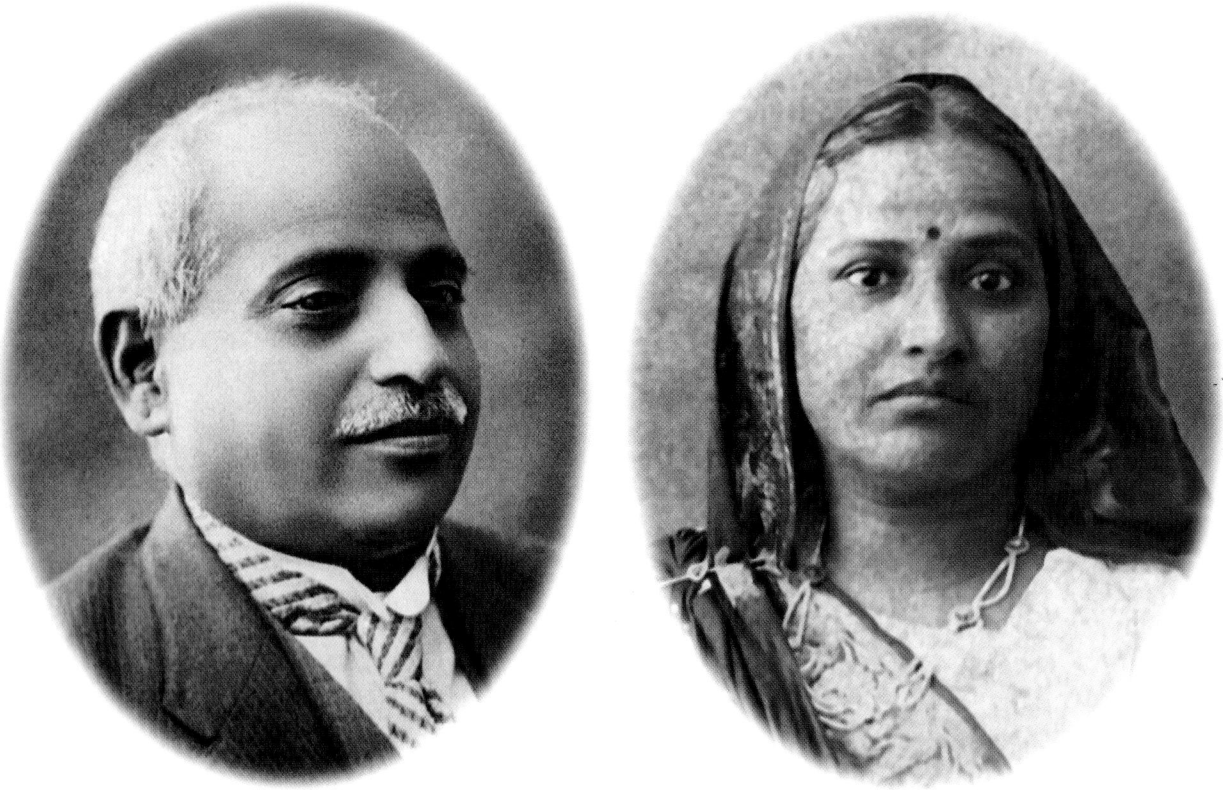

Portraits of parents who inculcated basic Indian cultural values in their children: Raja Jwala Prasad and Rani Bhagyawati.

Advent

Meerut, 1914: In the household of Raja Jwala Prasad and Rani Bhagyawati, on the night of Diwali, November 17, a special light illumined all. This light came in the form of a baby girl born to them. The eldest brother, Dharam Vira, remembers having returned home after having made the customary courtesy call on all the family elders on the occasion of Diwali, and being given the news of this special gift—a younger sister named Sumitra. Sumitra had five older siblings: three brothers—Dharam Vira, Kanti Vira and Satya Vira and two sisters, Yashoda and Sushila.

Raja Jwala Prasad came from a family of landed gentry and his propitious deeds had earned him the eternal gratitude of his people, who had named the cluster of villages surrounding his lands in Bijnore district of Uttar Pradesh as Dharamnagari or the 'land of good deeds'. Rani Bhagyawati, his wife contributed by helping village women in acquiring some skills and by inculcating in them a need for self-reliance. That the region flourished and attracted developmental work could largely be attributed to the generosity of the Raja Jwala Prasad family. That both Muslims, who had a sizeable presence in the area, and Hindus, participated in each other's festivals and family gatherings, reflected a certain sense of well-being and welfare which the genial personality of the Raja fostered.

Raja Jwala Prasad was a man of rank and stature by birth, fortified by the high position he was appointed under the British as the Chief Engineer of Canals and Irrigation of U.P. (then called the United Provinces). He was the first Indian to be so appointed and he served the office with dignity, devotion and distinction. His duties often necessitated the setting up of camps on site, wherever work so demanded. The family maintained a winter base in Lucknow and a summer base in Nainital, where, as was the custom in those days, the entire administration under the British moved to the cooler climes of the Kumaon Hills. At the time Sumitra was born in Meerut, her father was stationed there on an important assignment.

After her birth in Meerut, Sumitra's early years were spent in the Amethi Kothi, Benaras, situated on the banks of the holy river Ganga. Raja Jwala Prasad had been requested by Pandit Madan Mohan Malaviya to help oversee the construction of his Benaras Hindu University. An Arya Samajist, Raja Jwala Prasad was an enlightened man believing in education and equality of women. He desired that his children be given the best education. Sumitra was thus sent to the best schools, first in Nainital and later to the boarding school in Allahabad where her elder brother studied.

At Allahabad, in school in the mid-twenties, Sumitra's world enlarged and opened up as never before. She became acquainted with her brother's friends. Among these were budding poets, writers and future civil servants who looked after her as their own sister. Among her seniors were Mahadevi Verma, later to become a national poet. In a school production on Shahjehan Maladevi Verma was cast as Shahjehan and Sumitra as Sipar, his grandson. Often, Mahadevi Verma would jokingly say, 'Where is my grandson?' In yet another production, Sumitra played the role of the child Krishna.

It was part of the upbringing in India of those days that traditional festivities became the bedrock for teaching and learning the nuances of music and dance, prose and poetry. Occasions such as Teej, the festival coinciding with the monsoons, and Holi, the festival of spring, provided not only visual colour but became a platform for observing and absorbing songs like *Kajri, tappa, dadra*, even *ghazals*. Births and weddings provided additional opportunities. In those days, private music and poetry sittings called *mushaira* and dance coupled with vocal accompaniment called *mujra* were occasions for social interaction and entertainment.

Having been brought up initially in Lucknow which was the seat of Islamic culture, Sumitra was then exposed to the best of Hindu culture at Benaras and Allahabad. Visiting Parsi theatre companies in these towns opened the doors to another world, another culture in those days when religion did not play a divisive role but acted as a cementing bond. As a youngster, Sumitra was brought up in this environment, where they were told to respect both cultures, if not all.

Allahabad was the centre of political activity in pre- Independence days. In the patriotic climate of those days, it was popular to participate in processions and sing patriotic songs. The popular newspapers of the day, *Aaj* in Hindi and *Leader* in English, were replete with news of the struggle for Independence. By sheer coincidence, Sumitra was exposed to this patriotic fervour which was soon to grow and envelop the entire country in the struggle for freedom from foreign rule. Young Sumitra saw history being made.

Early Experiences

Raja Jwala Prasad had helped plan and supervise the construction of the Benaras Hindu University. The founder, Pandit Madan Mohan Malaviya, once chided the Raja that although he had helped construct the university, he had not sent any of his children to study there. By then, most of Sumitra's older brothers had already been educated at various universities in England and her sisters, married off. The Benaras Hindu University held a special appeal to Sumitra for it offered music as a subject. When the time came, she happily opted to study at the university for the twin prospects of learning music and studying under renowned writers and litterateurs, delighted her.

'The university life those days was very different from what it has become today. It is difficult for our children today to know what simple joys lay in having picnics where we roasted white-skinned baby brinjals or of taking a boat across the river to see the 'Ramlila'. These outings became a source of much mirth and gaiety which cannot be substituted today with any amount of noisy party-scenes or outings in five star hotels. Our lives were simple and unaffected; so were the times.'

At the Benaras Hindu University, luminaries such as Hari Oudh, Ramcharan Shukla, Shyama Sundar Das and Jaishankar Prasad taught on the faculty. The last was in the process of writing his tome, *Kamayani,* and the insights of such teachers helped young Sumitra see mythology and legends in a new light. She recalls that 'literature was taught in such a manner that we were first made to understand the *bhava* or feeling of the subject then the subject itself. Literature was taught in a lively manner and at college socials we would often create and compose couplets which would contain elements of gentle leg-pulling'.

'The Benaras Hindu University had a great effect on me,' reminisces Sumitra fondly. It was here that she was exposed to higher learning, it was here that her cultural values were formed. On the occasion of the Foundation Day of the University, which coincided with Basant Panchami, all the students were attired in yellow and Bismillah Khan Sahib played the *shehnai* at dawn. The setting was mesmerising: the banks of the river Ganga, the campus of the Benaras Hindu University, the morning dew and Khan Sahib's *shehnai* !

But above all, Benaras gave Sumitra a dream which some day was to become a magnificent reality. It was here that the 'Ramlila' tale was projected by the Maharaja of Benaras with pomp and show. Different scenes took place in various villages. One village 'became' Awadh for Rama's birth and his wedding took place in Ramnagar, across the river in Benaras.

Sumitra's local guardian was A.D. Pandit, the Collector of Benaras and a friend of her brother Dharam Vira, who had joined the Indian Civil Service by then. A.D. Pandit undertook the guarantee that she would be taken care of and thus the group set off across the river. Although the 'Ramlila' proved to be entertaining, it still had a rural approach to costumes and ornamentation. Sumitra enjoyed witnessing it for she saw how devoted the audiences were, some having come from distant villages. For them it was not merely a story, a piece of entertainment, but a depiction of the tale and legend of Lord Rama.

Sumitra had a weakness for the *Ramayana*, partly because of a habit cultivated at home. Before retiring every night, her father asked her to read a few *chaupies* (passages) from the epic. To escape this onerous task, often Sumitra would feign sleep but her father was wise to her tricks and did not accept any such excuses. Although Sumitra was pampered, she was not spoiled. None of her tantrums were tolerated. She was made to feel special, but was also made to realise that certain responsibilities went with such privileges.

The privilege of being born into a *zamindar* family which was educated and enlightened, the privilege of getting the best education in the best institutions of learning helped mould Sumitra in such a manner as to attain more privileges later and to use this to further her own goals. Born into a family where Saraswati was worshipped, Sumitra was soon to come to a family where Laxmi was the presiding deity.

Two Leading Houses Unite

One summer, the brothers Bharat and Charat stayed as guests of the Raja Jwala Prasad family in Nainital. The brothers came from the illustrious Shriram family of Delhi, which originally hailed from Jhajhar in Rajasthan. The Shriram family had established itself as a reputed industrial house under the overall guidance of Lala Shriram and Lala Shankarlal, sons of Lala Madan Mohan Lal. Lala Shriram, married to Phoolan Devi, had three sons, Murlidhar, Bharat and Charat. Anusuya and Savitri were the two daughters of Lala Shankarlal.

The hills of Nainital provided a backdrop for the blossoming of romance between Charat and Sumitra. The initial attraction gave way to a more serious commitment and by the time Sumitra was sent to Delhi to pursue higher education at the Lady Irwin College, Charat was totally besotted with her. Lala Shriram had been entrusted with the role and responsibility of becoming Sumitra's local guardian in Delhi; it was his youngest son Charat who took the responsibility literally and more than kept an eye on Sumitra. He would intentionally drive past the college several times a day, blare his horn and occasionally request the college hostel gardener to let him have a glimpse while Sumitra tended her little rose patch. In addition to roses, love was blooming too and more than anyone else the gardener knew.

Despite a previous alliance of Sumitra, Charat married her on May 25, 1941. As was customary and expected of a new daughter-in-law, Lala Shriram asked Sumitra to receive the blessings of all the elders in his family, including his close friends, Raj Narain Bahadur and Dr. Kapoor. Raj Narain Bahadur's son, Shivraj Bahadur was to play a significant role in their lives, later. A week after their marriage, the couple left for Calcutta, where Charat was undergoing training at Jay Engineering, a family concern. In Calcutta, initially, they stayed with Charat's sister, Savitri, who was married to Pratap Singh, son of founder of the Modern School in Delhi, Lala Raghuvir Singh.

The patriarch of the family, Sir Shriram with son Charat Ram. ▶

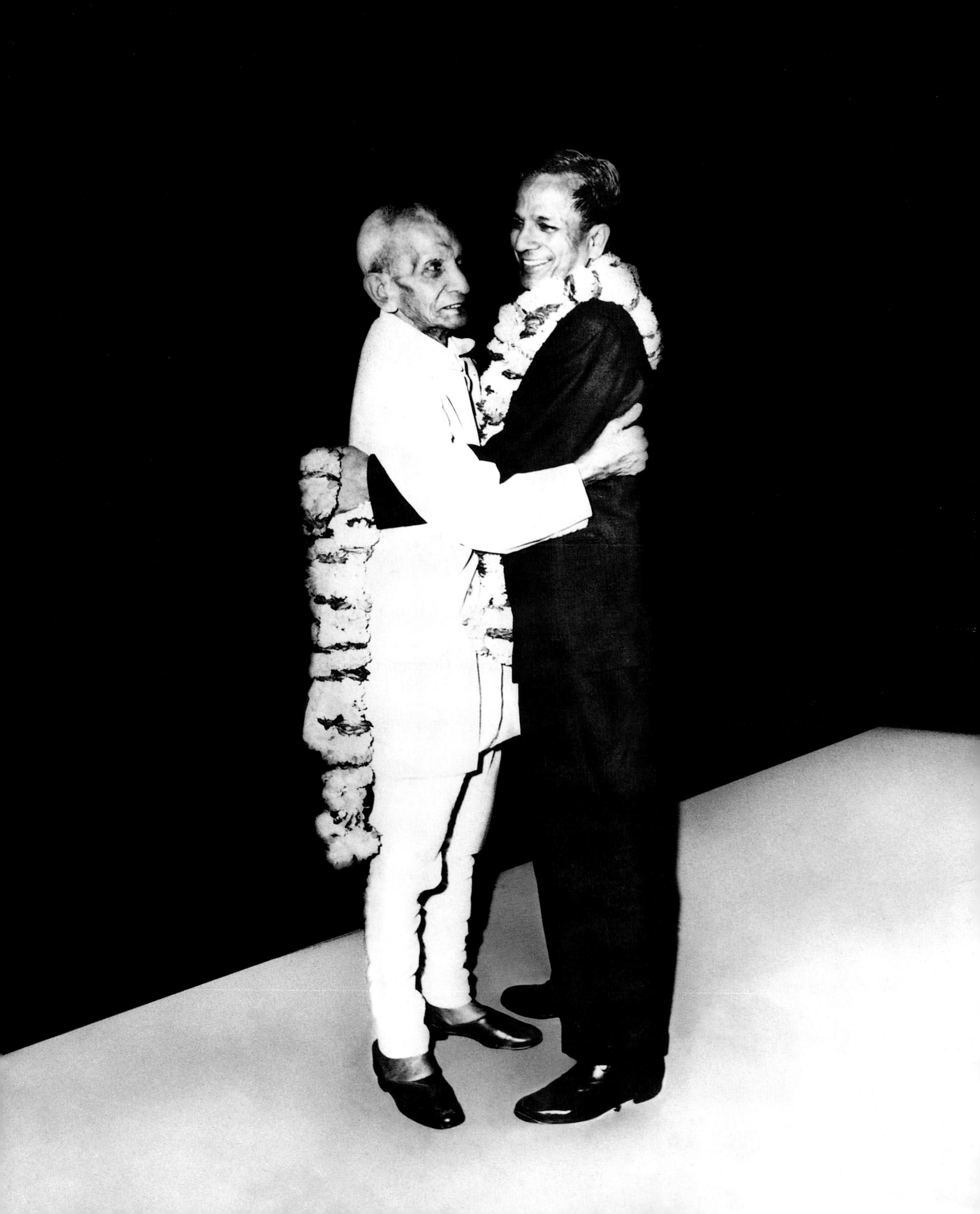

The scare of war had left Calcutta in a miserable shape. It was plagued with electricity cuts and other shortages and threats. It was not considered a safe place and after having barely spent a few months there, Lala Shriram asked them to return to Delhi.

It was in the early twenties that the Shriram family left their Kucha Mai Dass residence, next to Begum Samru's palace, in the Bazar Sita Ram area of Old Delhi, and moved to 20 Rajpur Road, a posh area of those days. It was in the early forties that the British authorities persuaded some of these prominent families to move to the new city Lutyens had built, called New Delhi, out of novelty or want of a better name. The authorities desired that some old and well-known residents be invited to settle in this part of the city in order to make it habitable and activated. Lala Shriram's shift from Old Delhi which Shahjehan built to the new city which the British were busy building, spoke of changing times and values.

The Shriram family moved to 20 and 22 Curzon Road. The two Kothis, the *Baddi* and the *Chhoti,* or the big and the small, had no separating wall and the families lived like one, although individually they maintained privacy. There was nothing small about the Chhoti *Kothi* for it had a billiard table and the adjacent house had a swimming pool and a dining seater for 64!

Lala Shriram was fond of simple living and he occupied the adjacent *Chhoti Kothi.* Collectively called the Shankar Niwas, after Lala Shriram's younger brother Shankarlal, this place was soon to become a historical landmark in the annals of Delhi's art and cultural life. Visitors were in plenty. One room in the *Baddi Kothi* was reserved for Sarojini Naidu. Sir Purushottamdas, Thakurdas, Walchand Hirachand, Uday and Amala Shankar, Ustad Ali Akbar Khan, Pandit Ravi Shankar, S.L. Kirloskar, T. Sadasivam and wife, M.S. Subbulakshmi and Padmaja Naidu were some of the regular guests who stayed at the Shankar Niwas. Partly it was the hospitality of the Shrirams, and partly, the fact that very few hotels were in existence. Today, *The Hindustan Times* building stands on the site.

Cultural Efflorescence

The Shriram family had two members who were particularly fond of *mushaira: Sir* Shankarlal and Lala Murlidhar. In fact, Sir Shankarlal was renowned as a *shair,* a poet and connoisseur. Lala Shriram on the whole encouraged his daughters-in-law to learn the arts or be associated with them in some way. Bharat Ram's wife, Shiela, had learnt the sitar from the renowned Ravi Shankar and Manipuri from Guru Amobi Singh. Thus, it was easy for Sumitra, when she became a part of this family, to pursue her artistic leanings, supported and encouraged by both her father-in-law, Lala Shriram, and her sister-in-law, Shiela Bharat Ram. Shiela had also been part of Dada Uday Shankar's experiment, at Almora, where she spent the summer learning the various arts.

It was in Almora that the legendary dancer, Uday Shankar, had set up his studio to train and teach artists. In this formidable task, he was helped by several people—the Elmhirsts, the Boshi Sens and Dharam Vira, Sumitra's brother, who was posted there as the Commissioner, having earlier joined the Indian Civil Service. It was to Almora that several artists came and later went on to become world famous names: Zohra Segal and Uzra, Simkie, Kameshwar, Sachin Shankar, Prabhat Ganguli and Narendra Sharma were all products of the Uday Shankar School. It was in Almora, again that Ustad Allauddin Khan came to teach and it was here that his daughter, Annapurna married Ravi Shankar.

It was while visiting her brother in Almora in late 1939, that Sumitra got the opportunity to closely watch the process of the creation of this school by Dada Uday Shankar. She would often visit the area and spend the day in observing how classes were conducted, what teaching technique meant and how a master created his masterpieces. 'The Almora experience really left a lasting impression on me. I had never seen any organised art activity. I had never seen artists, legendary names, at such close quarters. It excited me to think that so much could be done under such humble and modest circumstances. It was a real education,' recalls Sumitra of her visits to the Uday Shankar India Culture Centre.

Elsewhere too in India, a spirit of national resurgence had taken hold of people and the formation of the Indian People's Theatre Association (IPTA) led to the creation of a committed core of creative people who through their art took the message of resurgence and revival of India to the masses. Almost every artist of every genre had some connection with IPTA in its heyday. The IPTA endeavour took the form of a mass movement which involved many across the length and breadth of the country.

Internationally, Indian arts and artists were getting acclaim and attention. The legendary classical dancer, Ram Gopal mesmerised international audiences with his god-like form and dances. His offerings invited and excited thousands and wherever he went he won critical acclaim. With dancers like Mrinalini Sarabhai and M.K. Saroja, both trained by Vidwan Muthukumara Pillai, and later with dancers like Tara Choudhury and Kumudini Lakhia, Ram Gopal recreated the magic and mystery of Indian music and dance.

In south India, lawyer-turned-critic-turned-dancer, E. Krishna Iyer, espoused the cause of the *devadasis* who were facing threats of extinction, owing partly to the tirade of Muthulakshmi Reddy who fought for legally abolishing the custom and practice of *devadasis*. A young Brahmin girl, Rukmini Devi, married a theosophist, Dr. Arundale, and set the river Adyar on fire by dancing the dance of the *devadasis*. Sadir, as Bharata Natyam was then called, overnight became associated with a respectable class, which appropriated for itself some culture.

The poet, Vallathol Narayanan Menon of Kerala, dedicated himself to

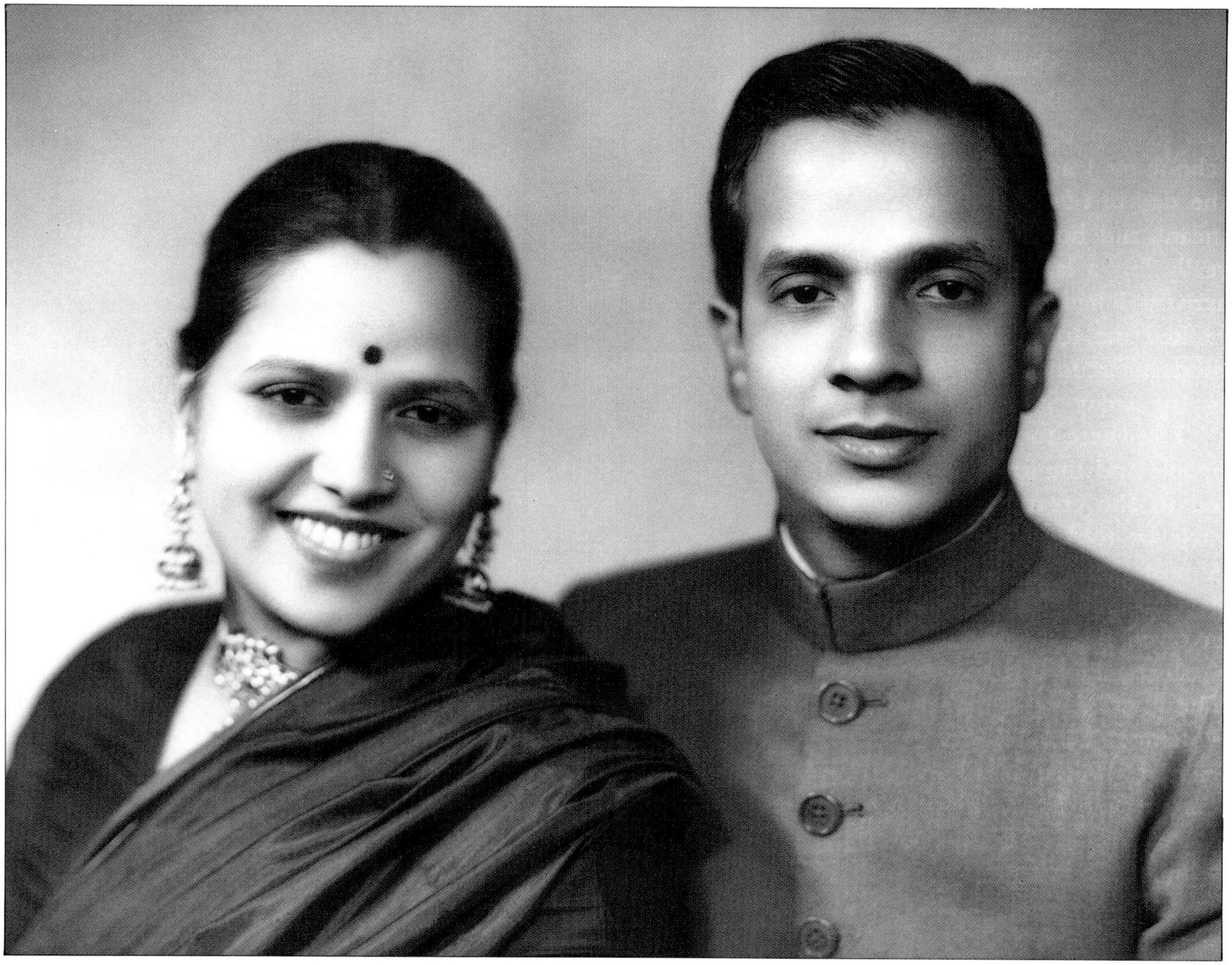

The newly weds—Charat and Sumitra.

H.T. 8-9-80

Love is not taking life partner for granted

Hindustan Times Correspondent

NEW DELHI, Sept 7—"Life consists of sorrow and joy. It is wrong to think that sorrow does not leave am indelible mark on one's personality — something dies inside, the hurt remains."

With these words the author of a beautiful new novel in Hindi — "Pratham Purush" (First man) explains its underlying theme. This is Mrs Sumitra Charat Ram's first publication, to be followed by many more, she hopes. She has always been interested in the philosophy of life, in the toll events extract from a person and the link between intensity of feelings and reactions. Through her writings she hopes to illustrate what love is all about, embedded in the traditional upbringing and culture of our country.

The message of "Pratham Purush" is that love cannot be taken for granted by man or woman. Marriage, too, must be subjected continously to repairs and readjustments. If love is taken lightly, it can destroy a human being and break a home. There must be full confidence and communication between husband and wife, muses the author, while taking note of the fact that women when they love remain consant though men sometimes look out for a change.

Mrs Sumitra Charat Ram, a noted connoisseur of music and art and well-known for establishing the Bharatiya Kala Kendra in Delhi, is a wife, mother and grandmother besides having varied involvements in the cultural field. She has always been found of writing and this novel was at first just an expression of her own pent-up feelings on the subject till she was persuaded to have it published. It all took her around six months.

"Pratham Purush" is the story of Shivani, beatiful young and intelligent girl of a Zamindar family who falls in love with a wealthy though yet unsettled boy named Kameshwar. Their union is not possible because of the fathers' attitudes and she is married off to Manoj, a boy of her father's choice. She tells him before the wedding that she loves another and can be his wife in name only — terms he accepts, hoping to wim her love by and by. But Shivani remains constant to her true love.

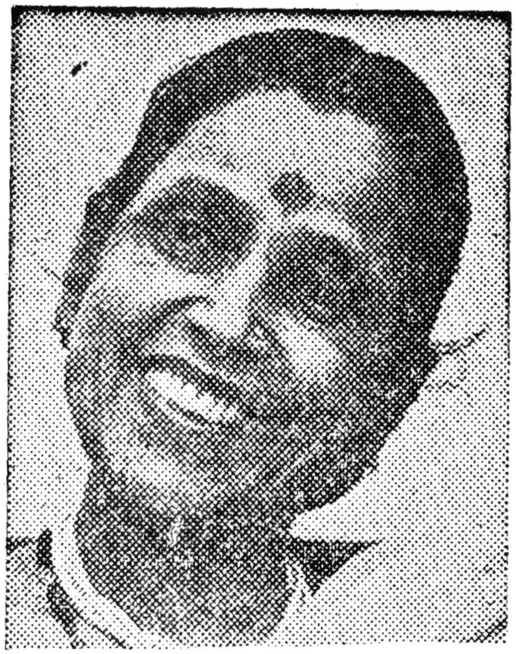

A keen student of literature, Sumitra Charatram authored Pratham Purush---*a love story.*

the task of reviving the arts of Kerala and thus was born the Kerala Kalamandalam which trained students in the art of Kathakali. Later, as the institute developed and progressed, other art forms were added to its curriculum such as Ottan Thullal, Mohini Attam and Nangiar Koothu. It was thanks to such efforts in different parts of the country that several art forms of India, which had been submerged if not altogether lost under the five hundred years of colonial rule, were revived and got a fresh lease of life and identity.

In Bengal, Gurudev Rabindranath Tagore established Santiniketan, a meeting point for different cultural streams of India. In addition to literature, poetry, drama, dance and music, philosophy and higher learning was encouraged. Most leaders of the community, both artistic and even political

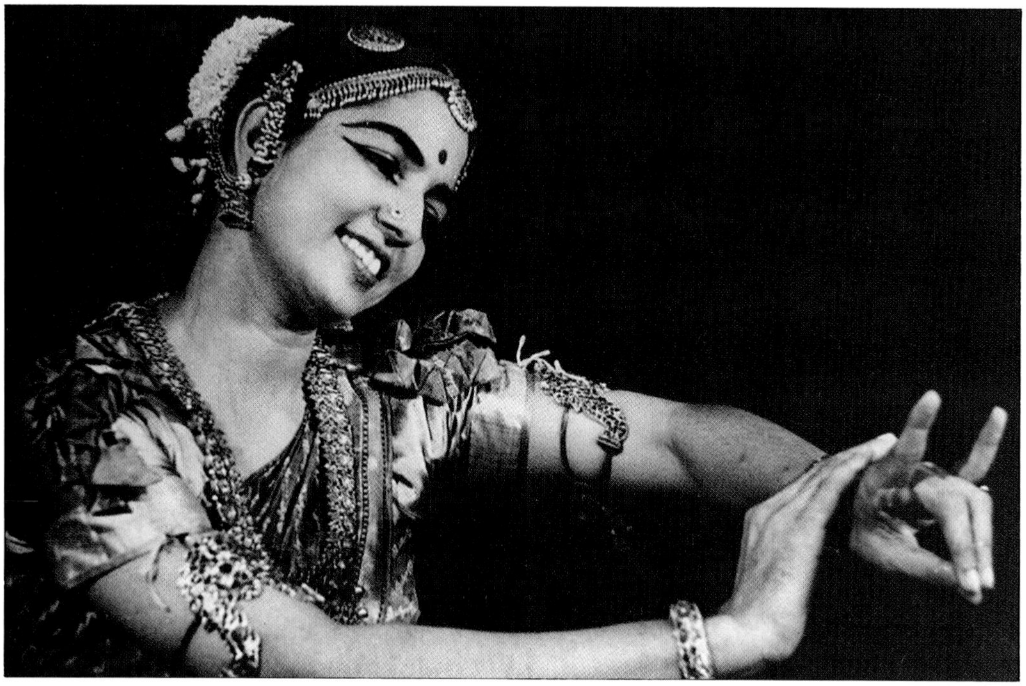

Rukmini Devi Arundale ushered in a renaissance of Bharata Natyam.

emerged out of such institutions. If Santiniketan helped create a Mrinalini Sarabhai, it also provided exposure to things Indian to Indira Gandhi. Kamla Chowdhry, the noted environmentalist of India today, whose roommate at Santiniketan was Indira Gandhi, recalls that 'although I had little interest in dance or drama, the ambience of Santiniketan helped develop my aesthetic taste, especially my fondness for music'. These centres, in different parts of the country, contributed immensely to the enrichment of Indian culture and its people.

Delhi had been under the influence of the Mughal court for long. The Kothas of Delhi were not merely for providing entertainment but education in *tehzeeb* and *tameez* (etiquette and courtesies). Children of prosperous families, especially the male offsprings, were sent to such Kothas in order to imbibe some of this 'culture'. Later, Delhi was subjected to Victorian etiquette as bequeathed by the colonial rule. The city, old and new, remained impervious to the undercurrents prevailing elsewhere in the country for several reasons: it was directly under the aegis of the colonial administration and Victorian customs prevailed; it had a distinct court culture of its own, partaking of the *mujra-mehfil;* and its populace was of mixed cultural moorings, almost migrant-like which had left its own home-settings and had adopted Delhi. Old Delhi retained its distinct identity and cultural contexts; it was New Delhi which was caught between the two worlds of trying to ape the Western masters and trying to forge an independent Indian identity. Thus for every *mujra* and *mehfil* there were ballroom dances and

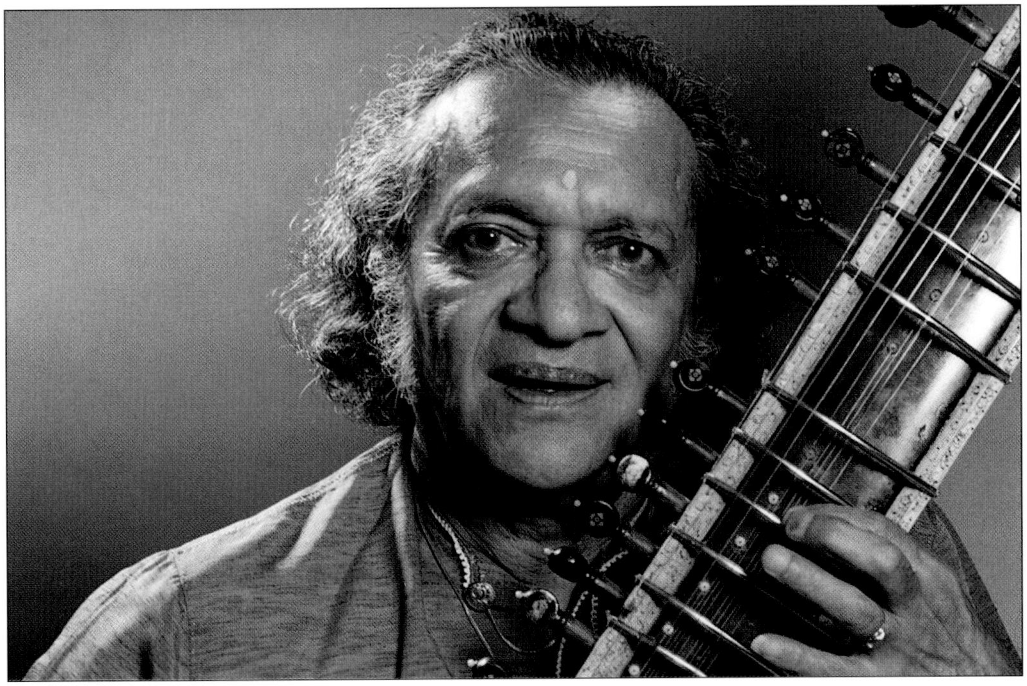

Ravi Shankar—the star of sitar.

Western bands. In hotels like the Imperial, then called the Tavern, Western music bands played popular tunes while couples danced and became acquainted. It was here, reminisces sugar baron, Narinder Lal, that the Western ambience almost defied Indian culture. Lala Narinder Lal's wife Kamala Lal was to become one of Sumitra's dear friends and together they gave the initial boost to the arts by staging many productions in which Kamala Lal took an active part. 'I can never forget how valuable her inputs were and how alert she was to the demands of stagecraft and aesthetics.

Uday Shankar, the father of contemporary Indian dance, was a major force on the dance scene and helped contribute to its enrichment. ▶

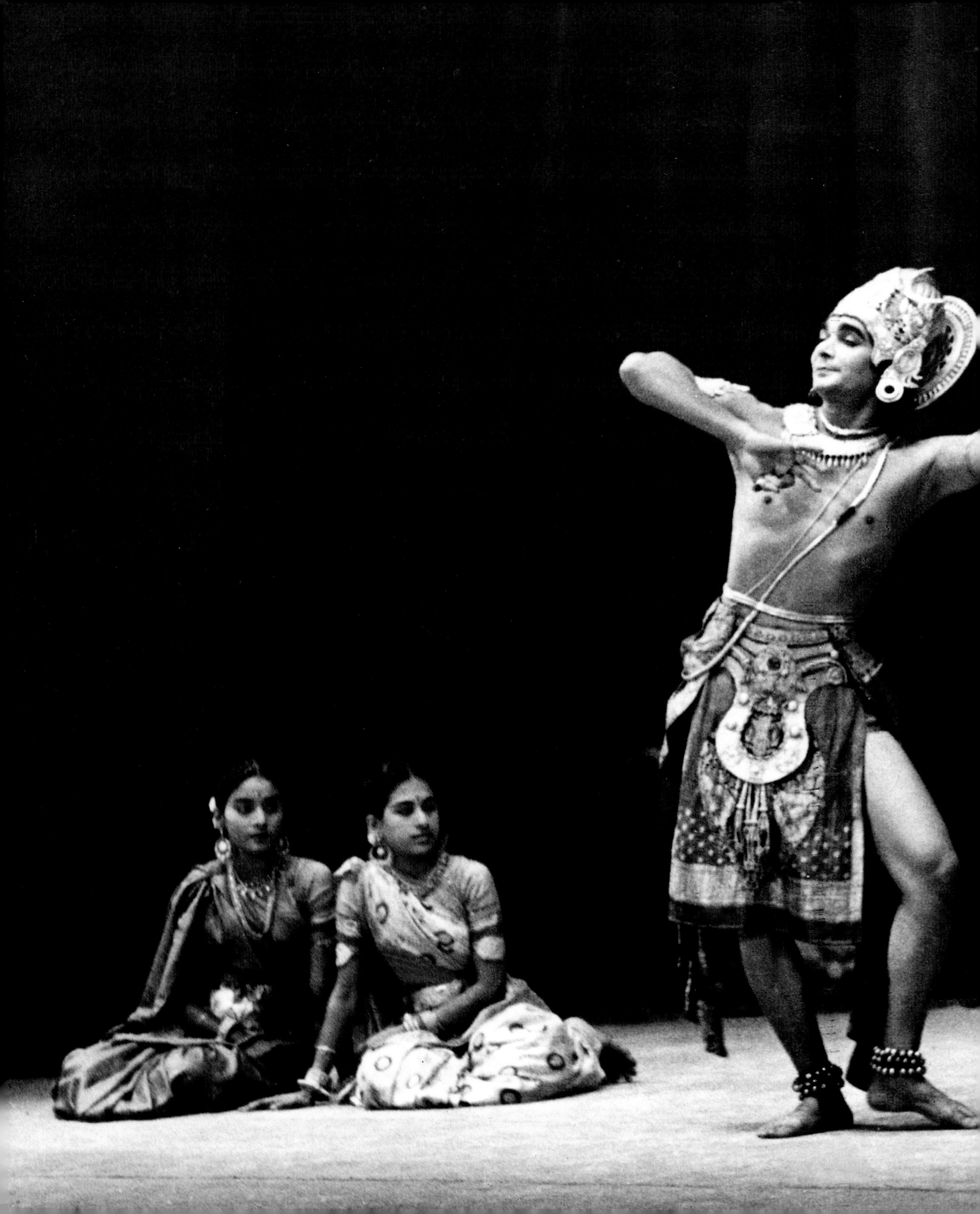

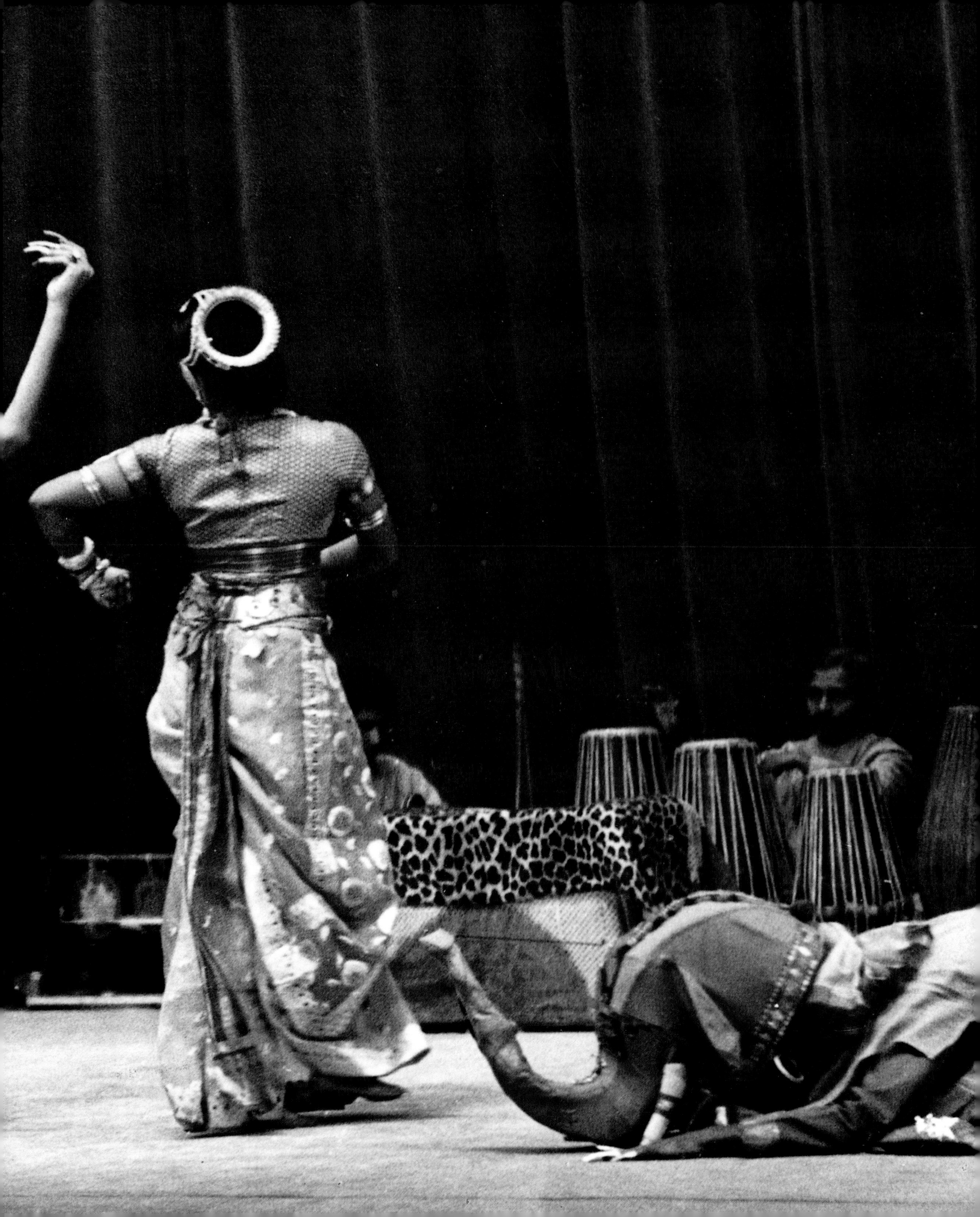

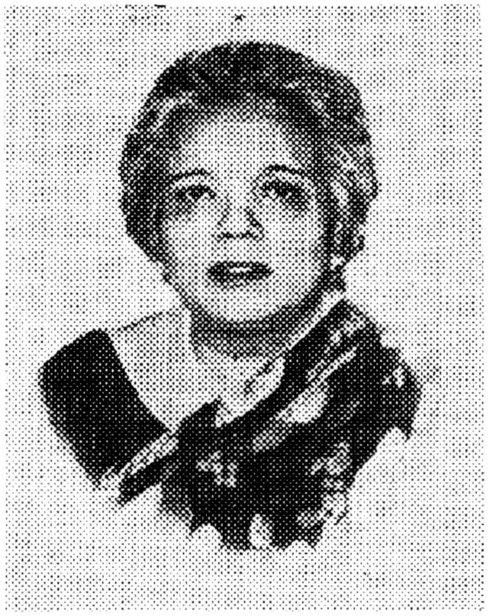

Mrs. Uma Daulat Singh

It has been my pleasure to be associated with Shriram Bharatiya Kala Kendra particularly the Ramlila Ballet for many many years.

During my husband's posting in Jullunder, as Corps Commander in 1958-59 I was responsible for organising a Ramlila Ballet Troupe and arranged for this 'Troupe' to tour Punjab and J & K. Our jawans who get very little opportunity to witness cultural shows of such excellence, watched these performances with great enthusiasm.

In 1960-61, while my husband was serving as Army Commander, Western Command in Simla, the Governing Council of Bharatiya Kala Kendra invited me to accompany the Ramlila Ballet to Nepal. I was overjoyed to see the enthusiasm and pleasure of the King of Nepal and the common people, who repeatedly came to see the shows.

After the sudden demise of my husband, I bacame fully involved in the welfare of the Ramlila artistes and organised a dispensary, a mess and a creche for their children. This was a very rewarding experience and they gave me a lot of love and affection.

I am very happy to learn that the Shriram Bharatiya Kala Kendra is celebrating its Ramlila Jubilee year this September. I send all my good wishes for this occasion and hope that the Ramlila Ballet carries on to give as much joy to future generations.

She was involved, devoted and conscious of artistic quality and her contribution lay in vesting all productions with finesse. Without her friendship, support and guidance, I don't think I would have attempted all that we undertook. Kamala Lal, along with Uma Daulat Singh and Brinda Lal, remain my most significant collaborators, friends and guides who inspired me to aspire to higher artistic achievements', recalls Sumitra Charat Ram.

It was in such a setting, that at midnight on August 15, 1947, India attained freedom from foreign rule. 'It was such a memorable occasion. I

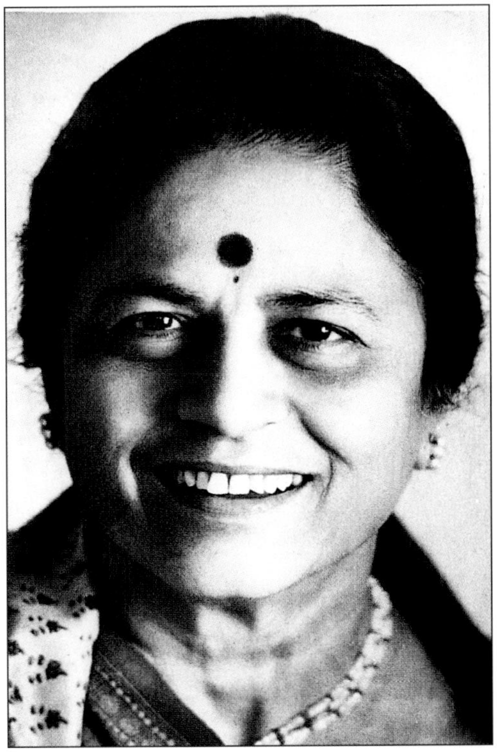

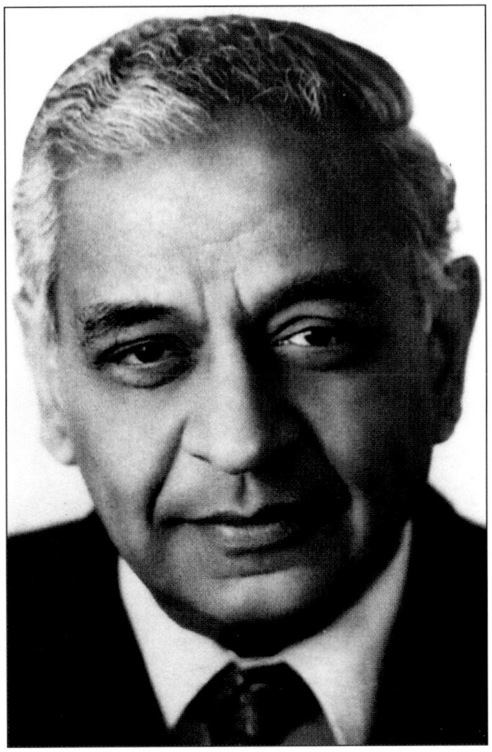

Kamala and Narinder Lal remained major forces in the setting up of the Kendra.

happened to get to go to hear the speech by Pandit Nehru where he said, at the stroke of the midnight hour when the world sleeps, India will awake to freedom ... That night was very special when we attended this ceremony and even today, when I recall being a part of it, a part of history being made, I feel shaken and fulfilled at the same time. It was such a momentous occasion,' remembers Sumitra Charat Ram.

◀ *Reflections of Uma Daulat Singh, a principal supporter of the Kendra.*

Four veterans who provided impetus to the growth and development of the Kendra.

Left: *Ustad Ghulam Sabir Khan*
Right: *Ustad Nisar Hussain Khan*

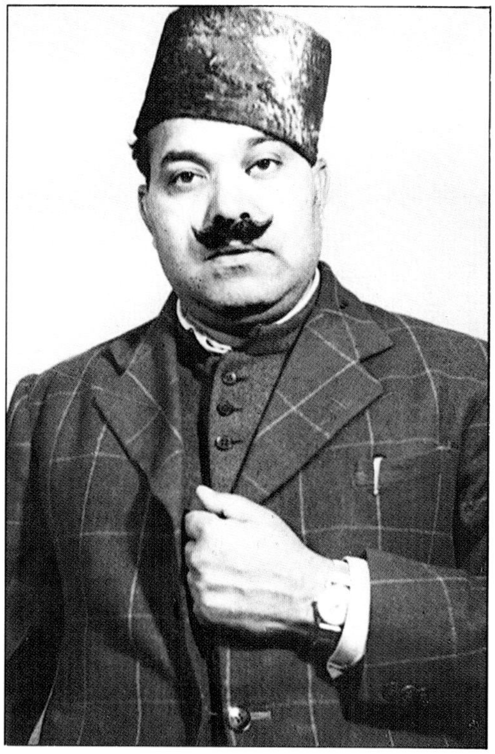

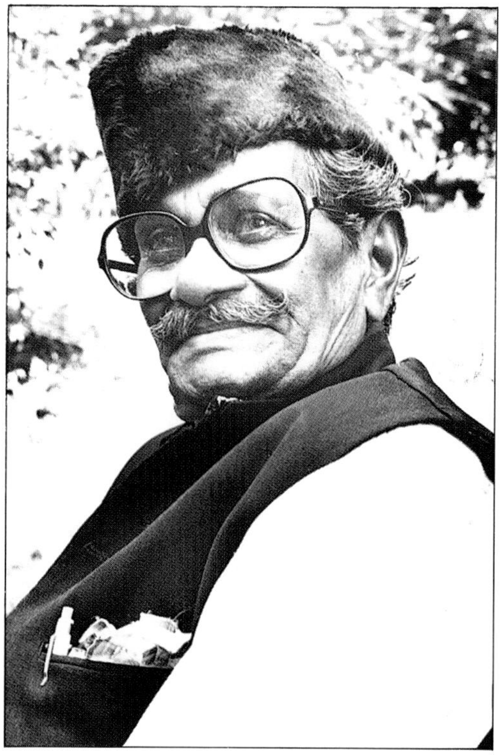

Left: *Ustad Mushtaq Hussain Khan*
Right: *Ustad Allauddin Khan*

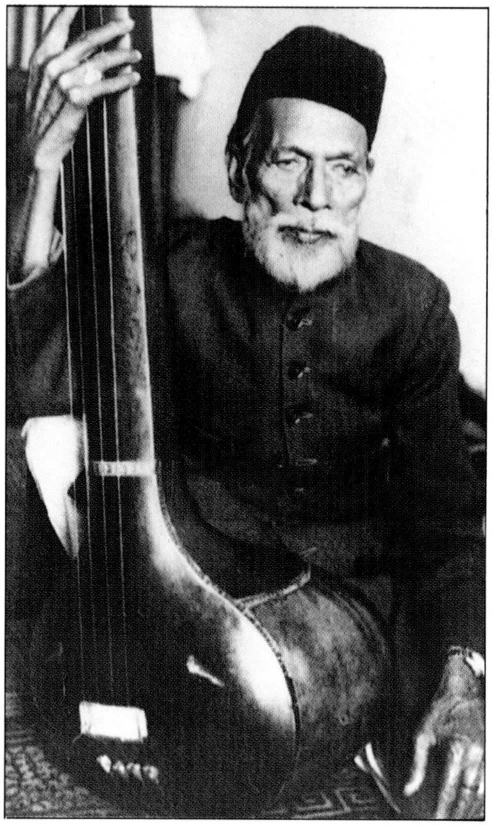

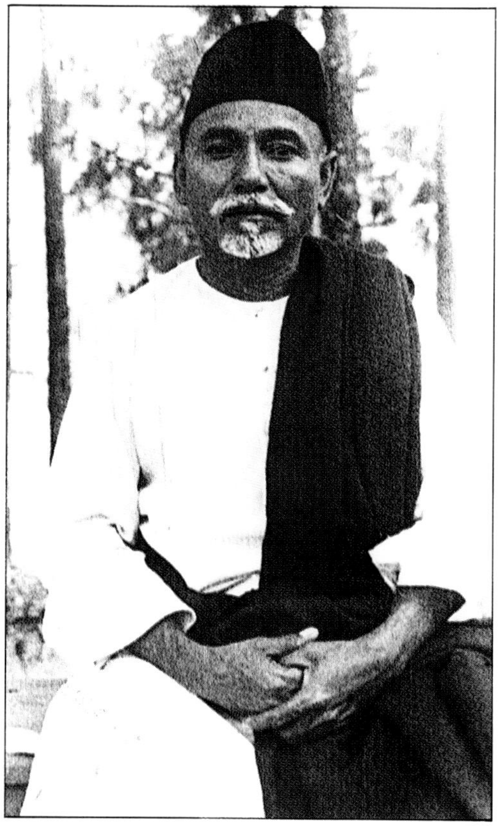

Midnight Mehfil

To celebrate the occasion—India's attaining Independence—it was decided to host an evening of music. The idea came from Ravi Shankar himself who was in Delhi at that time. This idea was endorsed by all. 'Easier said than done! I had no money (of my own) and more importantly, we needed *Bhaiji's* (Lala Shriram, as he was fondly called) permission, for he was the head of the household. We also needed the formal permission of *Chacha* Shankarlal, as he too lived in the *Baddi Kothi*, where we planned to host the event.'

'Both *Bhaiji* and *Chachaji* were supportive and generous in granting the resources and the permission to host the function. The big day finally arrived and what an event it turned out to be. Thanks to Robuda's (Ravi Shankar) initiative, nearly all the leading artists participated: Ustad Allauddin Khan, Ustad Hafiz Ali Khan, Robuda himself, Ustad Vilayat Khan, Vidwan Raja Ali Khan, Ustad Mushtaq Hussain Khan, Pandit Samta Prasad, Pandit Pannalal Ghosh, Ustad Faiyaz Khan and several others mesmerised the audience until the early hours of the morning. In those days it was not frightfully expensive to host artists and they did not charge very much. We were guided by Robuda who suggested that token payments be paid to participating artists, who in any case liked the idea of celebrating this occasion of our independence. We did not print any formal invitation cards but by mere word of mouth almost a thousand guests turned up and stayed all night, listening to the notes of the sitar, sarod and tabla. Perhaps, never before had an evening of such dimension and participation been organised. In fact, in the cultural milieu prevalent in those days the Indian arts were rather looked down upon and it was perhaps the first time that so many distinguished denizens of Delhi had assembled to partake of this Indian offering.'

By all accounts, it was a grand success. The next morning Lala Shriram heard that the event had continued through the night till the early hours of the morning. He smiled and suggested that if she was so truly fond of presenting the arts and artists, perhaps she should pursue it seriously. He repeated this suggestion several times later too and when he saw no serious action forthcoming, he even chided her implying that she was not taking note of his suggestions.

The Jhankar Music Circle

It was thus in 1947, after the grand success of this music soirée that the Jhankar Music Circle was formed with Shivraj Bahadur, Pandit Haksar,

Nawab of Pataudi, Dr. Sen, Shiela Bharat Ram, Ravi Shankar, Nirmala Joshi, Brinda Lal, Kamala Narinderlal and Sumitra Charat Ram as members.

The Jhankar Music Circle organised monthly music concerts and an annual Music Conference, which nowadays are called festivals. These Music Conferences were rather interactive in nature, with both the participating audiences and the artists enjoying an exchange. It was through this interactive process of sharing and learning that gradually an interest in the traditional Indian arts was revived and over a period of time the audiences for such activities grew.

'The presentations of the Jhankar Music Circle were held at the Constitution Club, the only venue available those days, which seated about 250. When there was a larger audience, *durries* or mattresses were put out on the lawns. People would bring their own baskets of snacks and have a

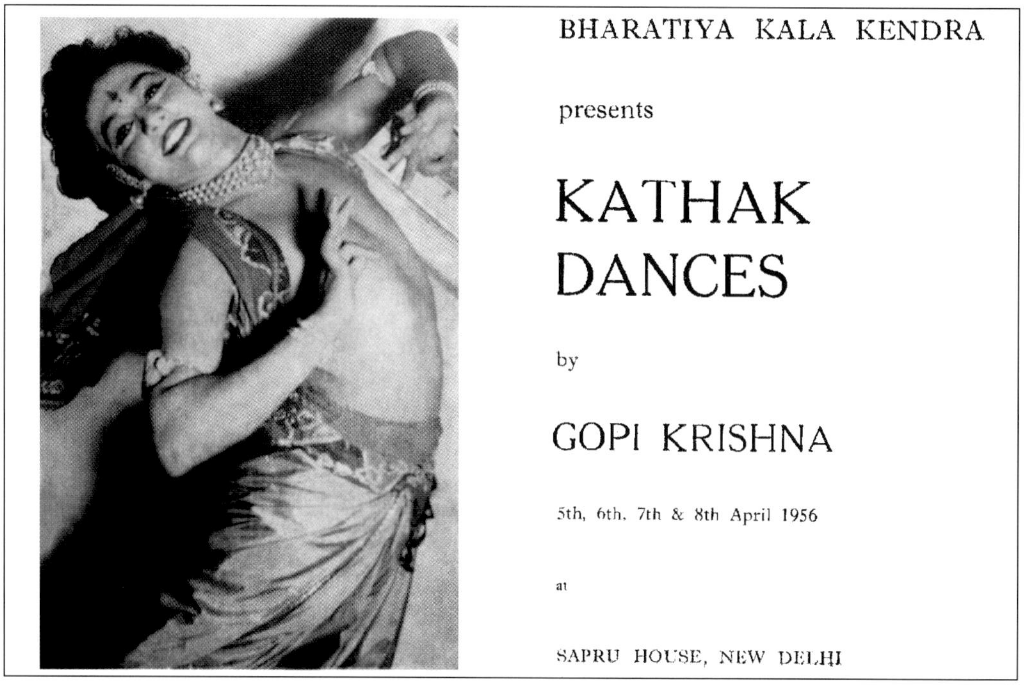

The fourteen-year old debutante, Gopi Krishan, went on to become a dance legend.

picnic of sorts while listening to the music. The Begum of Bhopal (cricketer Pataudi's mother) brought her own *paandaan* and with great delicacy of wrist movements, made *paans* for all of us. Pandit Haksar brought home-made Kashmiri delicacies and all in all it became more a treat than work for us. Though both were the Vice-presidents of the organisation, they behaved without affectation or airs of any sort. In the etiquette and culture of those days, courtesy, gentility and a lack of vulgar display of wealth were the signs of a truly civilised person. Money was not flashed about, but values, recalls Sumitra Charat Ram.

Jhankar presented unusual music events such as the Ravi Shankar-Annapurna duo and the trio featuring Ustad Ali Akbar Khan, Vilayat Khan and Ravi Shankar. It also premiered Santi Bardhan's *Panchatantra* and presented Gopi Krishna who was then a lad of fourteen. He was accompanied by his grandfather, the legendary Sukhdev Maharaj. Dr. Kailash Nath Katju, the first President of Jhankar, took a keen and active interest in the activities of the society, whose guiding force was Nirmala Joshi.

Daughter of a well-known medical practitioner, Nirmala Joshi was charged with energy and enthusiasm to do something for the arts. She was a motivator, an organiser and an activist. She had founded the Delhi School of Hindustani Music and Dance, as early as the mid-thirties. This first cultural institution, which later became the Sangeet Bharati, still stands today at the Mandi House roundabout, close to the Triveni Kala Sangam and the Shriram Centre for Arts and Culture.

It was at the Sangeet Bharati that the renowned Achchan Maharaj came

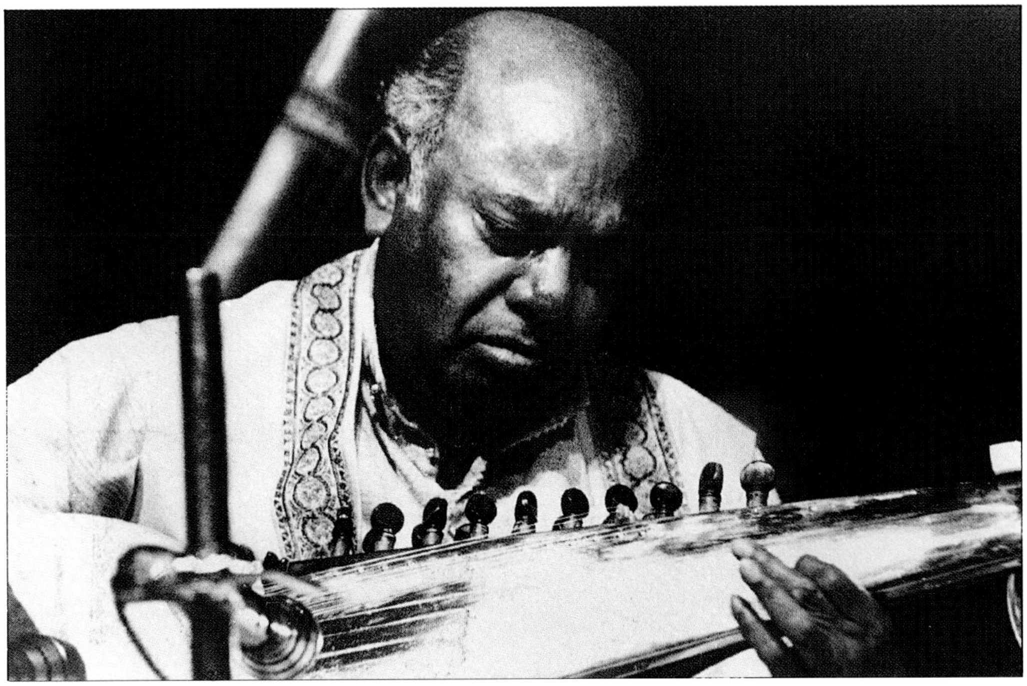

Ustad Ali Akbar Khan regaled audiences at the Jhankar presentation.

to teach Kathak. His original name was Jaganath Prasad but he was so noble and good in his demeanour that he came to be known as *achcha* or Achchan Maharaj. When quite young, he had been appointed dancer at the Court of the Nawab of Rampur. Many years later, when Kathak had fallen on days of disrepute, owing to its association with prostitutes, Achchan Maharaj was brought to Delhi by Kapila Malik (Vatsyayan) whose parents were active in the field of culture and social work. He started teaching and with his ten-year-old son, Birju, he delighted Delhites with his art. Several students were attracted to him, chief among whom were Kapila Malik and Nirmala Joshi herself.

Nirmala Joshi became Sumitra Charat Ram's adviser, guide, friend and

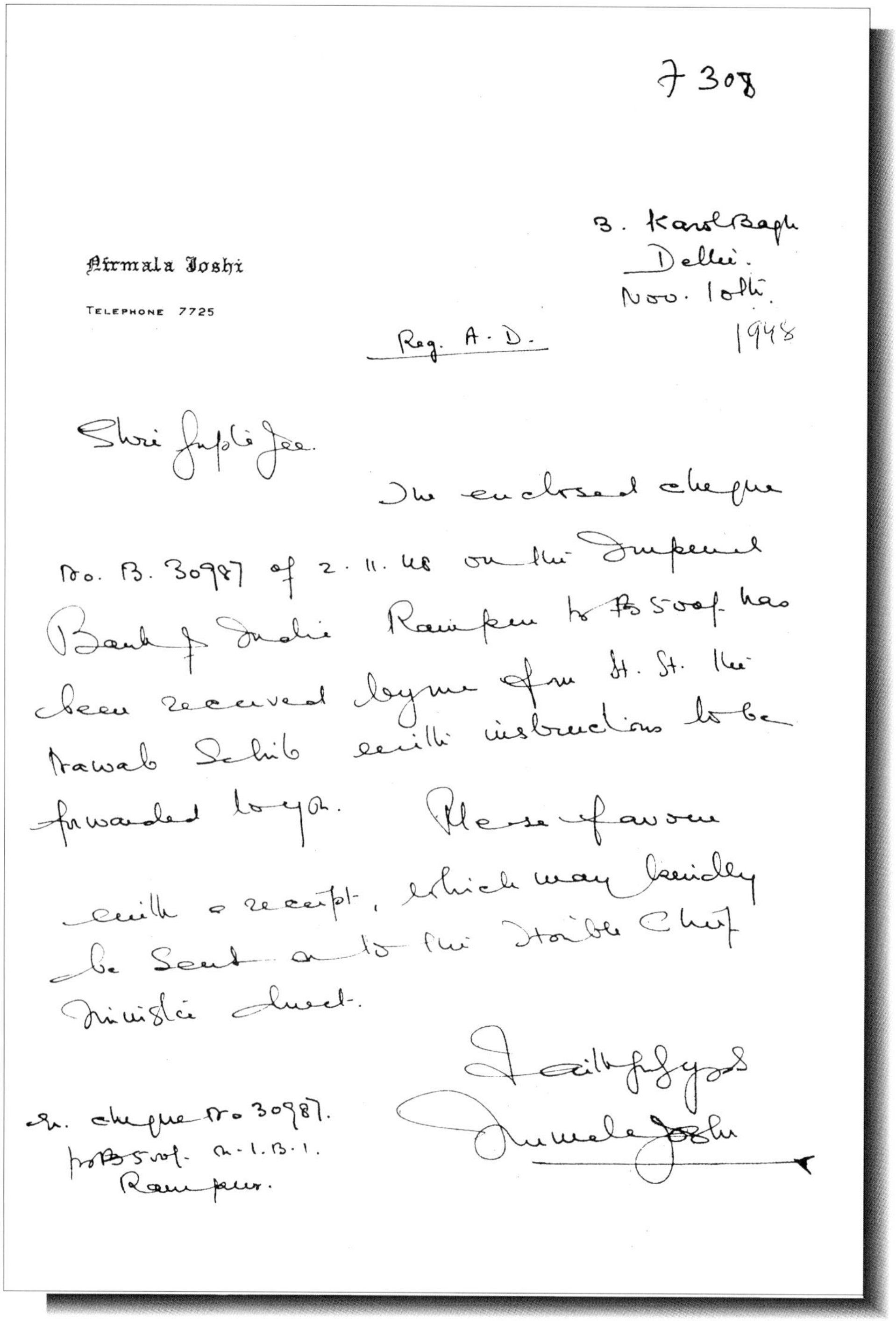

7 308

Nirmala Joshi

TELEPHONE 7725

3, Karol Bagh
Delhi.
Nov. 10th.
1948

Reg. A. D.

Shri Gupta Jee.

The enclosed cheque No. B. 30987 of 2.11.48 on the Imperial Bank of India Rampur for Rs 500/- has been received by me from H. H. the Nawab Sahib with instructions to be forwarded to you. Please favour with a receipt, which may kindly be sent on to the Hon'ble Chief Minister direct.

Faithfully yours
Nirmala Joshi

Encl. cheque No. 30987.
for Rs 500/- on I.B.I.
Rampur.

Nirmala Joshi, the founder member of the Kendra, dedicated her life to the cultural progress of young India and headed the National Academy--the Sangeet Natak--as its first Secretary. Her trusting nature was taken advantage of by certain unscrupulous characters, who made her sign huge amounts of government money and later embroiled her in unsavoury embezzlement cases. This handwriting specimen reflects her generosity of personality, misused and abused by those she trusted.

supporter. It was thanks to her efforts that the Jhankar Music Circle actively undertook the task of presenting artists. Judging by the success of these music conferences, Nirmala Joshi suggested that Sumitra form a proper society for the promotion, teaching and training of artists.

The Sangeet Bharati had become a popular centre for art activity and a few elements within the organisation took advantage of Nirmala Joshi's trusting nature and wrested control of the organisation from her by manipulation. A motivated organiser, she formed another society, the Bharatiya Kala Kendra in 1952. When the National Academy for Dance and Music, the Sangeet Natak Akademi, was set up in 1953 by an Act of Parliament, Nirmala Joshi was appointed its Secretary. It was then that Nirmala Joshi, not having enough time to devote to the affairs of the

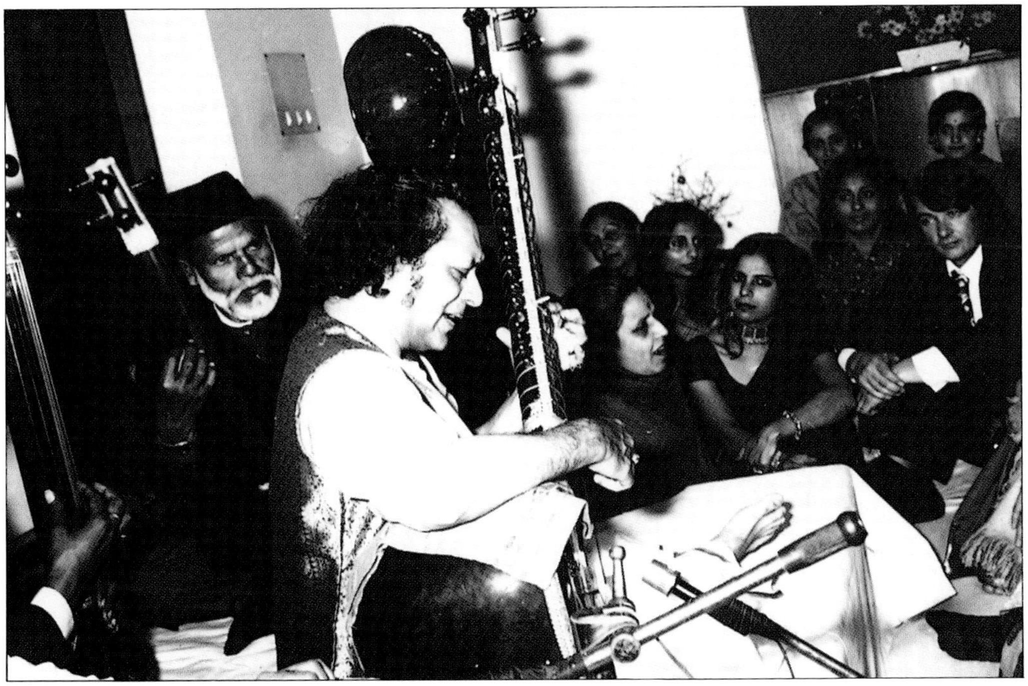

Pandit Ravi Shanker, a chief motivator of the Kendra, often performed at special occasions at home—for he treated the Kendra family as a part of his home.

Bharatiya Kala Kendra, suggested to Sumitra that she take over the responsibility of running the Bharatiya Kala Kendra which was at that time also receiving a modest government grant of Rs. 20,000 to teach music and dance.

Thus, in addition to her own four children—Deepak, Shobha, Siddharth and Gauri, Sumitra Charat Ram was blessed with a fifth child—the Bharatiya Kala Kendra. And 1947, which saw the germination of the idea and activities of the Jhankar Music Circle, can be taken as a starting point for the activities of the Shriram Bharatiya Kala Kendra. That midnight concert in 1947 led to the formation of the Jhankar, which became a precursor for the Jhankar Music Circle starting its activities and also for the activities of the Bharatiya Kala Kendra. Through it all, Sumitra Charat Ram was the connecting link.

Projection of National Arts

Nirmala Joshi, fond and devoted as she was to the arts had come into close contact with Pandit Nehru and his official hostess, Indira Gandhi who took a keen interest in the arts and became the first Chairperson of the Bharatiya Kala Kendra in 1956.

In the early years of Independence in order to celebrate India's variety of folk arts, it was decided to launch a folk festival. Recalls Usha Bhagat, a close adviser-associate of the Nehru family who also functioned as their Social Secretary: 'In many travels abroad, especially to the Soviet Union, it was seen that they had organised their arts for projection worldwide. It was felt that given the richness of our country and its artistic traditions, it would

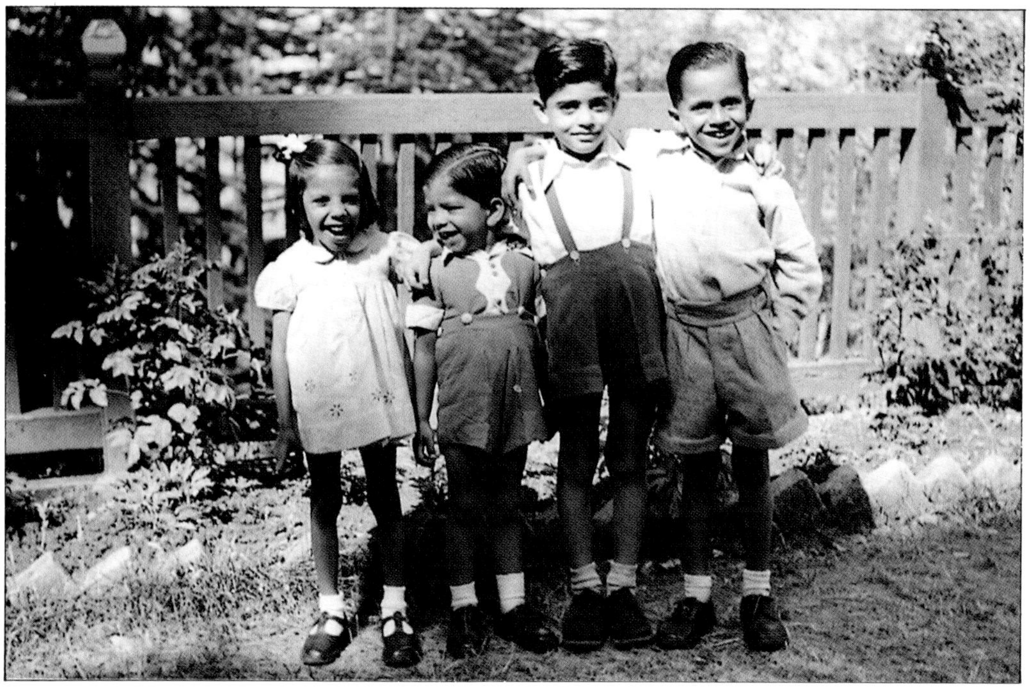

In addition to her four children Deepak, Shobha, Siddharth and Gauri, Sumitra Charat Ram was blessed with a fifth child—the Bharatiya Kala Kendra.

be meaningful to organise groups of folk artists for presentation on special occasions. Pandit Nehru supported the idea and instructed district officials to help identify folk artists.' Nirmala Joshi, in her capacity as the Secretary of the Sangeet Natak Akademi too felt that folk artists should be presented to urban audiences and requested the Bharatiya Kala Kendra to prepare a folk festival. 'When we presented the paper to Pandit Nehru, he felt that the idea was ripe for implementation, since on his own he had been thinking of such a folk festival. So we were all invited to become part of the Committee which was to select and organise the folk festival,' observes Sumitra Charat Ram.

Soon, this was to become a regular feature of the Republic Day parade, with prizes instituted for the best group. Colonel Gupte, helped with practical arrangements and often rehearsals would continue late into the night. 'It was a learning experience. We wanted to show the authenticity of folk cultures to urban audiences and when these villagers came to perform in Delhi, they came in their best, modern clothes. We had a trying time telling them to come in their original, normal costumes! During the rehearsals, we had to obtain permission from the requisite authority to get even a cup of coffee. The distance from one part of the National Stadium to the other was so vast that by the time we got the slip of permission signed and coffee delivered from afar, it was cold ! From the following day, I started filling a big flask of coffee in order to make the cold evenings more tolerable. Today, with all the facilities and inputs, I find the charm of those days more acceptable and refreshing when simplicity ruled the roost. The folk festival has become a major feature of the

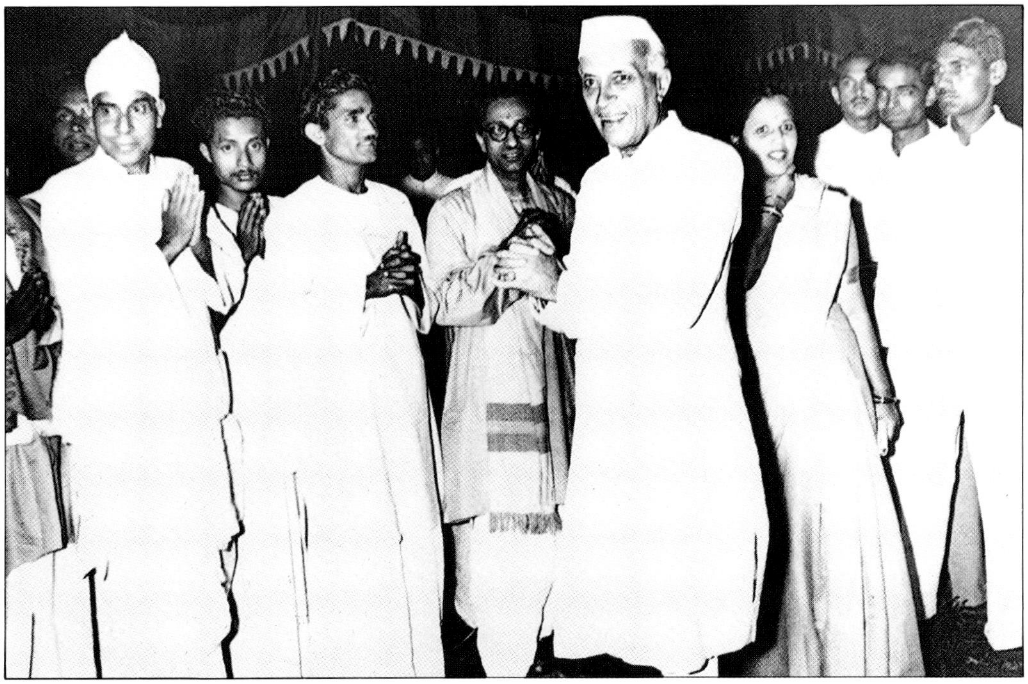

Pandit Jawahar Lal Nehru made it a point to meet artists when he came to a performance.

Republic Day parade today and it is heartening to see that from a humble beginning it has grown to such big dimensions.'

The November 1955 National Dance Festival too proved to be a milestone when the Kendra actively participated helping the Sangeet Natak Akademi. We felt honoured to be given the task of presenting this important occasion,' maintains Sumitra Charat Ram.

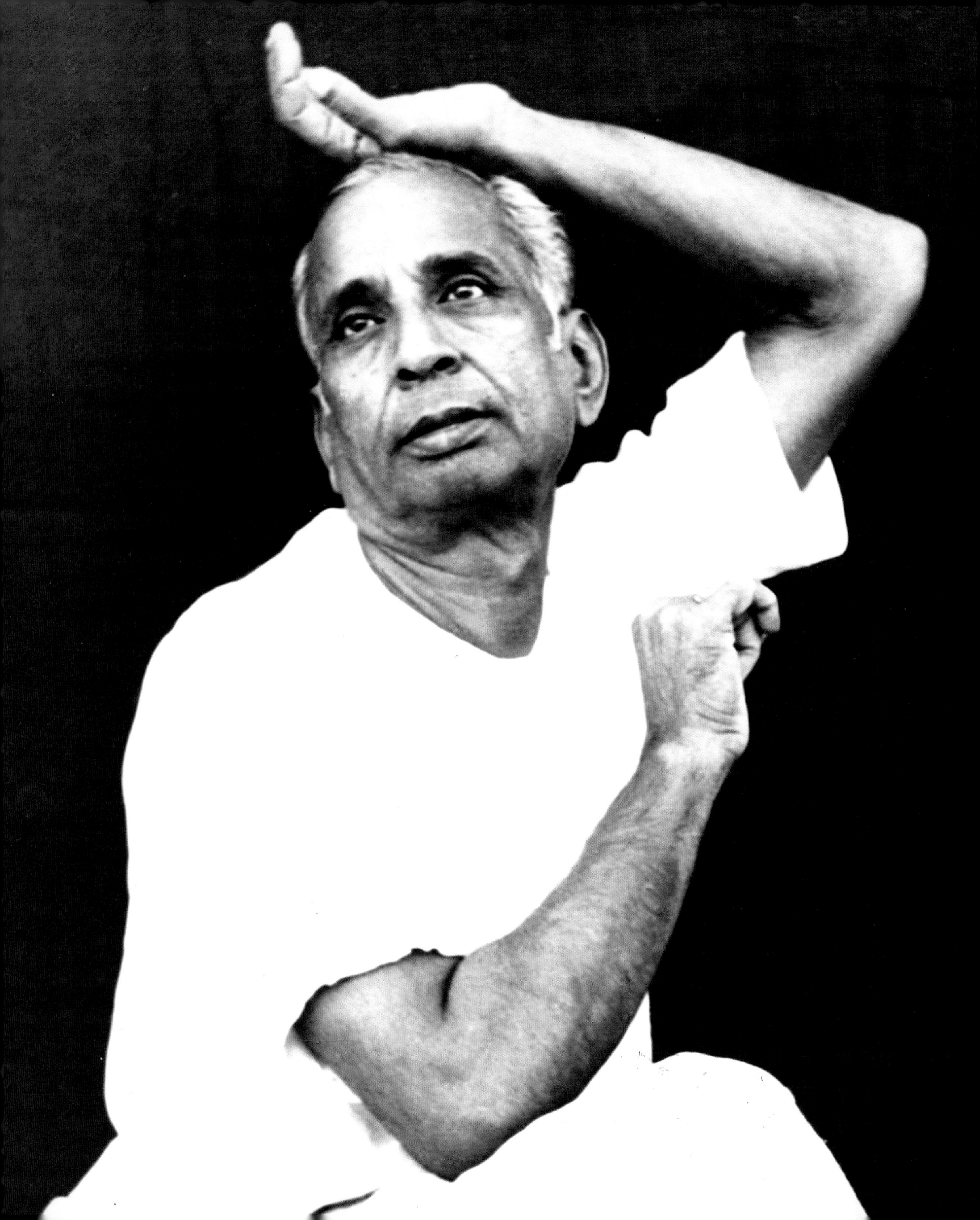

The Bharatiya Kala Kendra

The Bharatiya Kala Kendra physically started in the Shankarlal Niwas, located at 20 Curzon Road. The first concrete activity was the initiation of the Kathak class under Shambhu Maharaj with his first student, Maya Rao. The year, 1955.

Son of Kalka Prasad, younger brother of Bindadin and older than Bhairon Prasad, Shambhu Maharaj was the youngest of three brothers, the elders being Achchan and Lachchu. Hailing from a legendary family of musicians and dancers, Shambhu Maharaj was instrumental in giving Kathak a larger profile by being based at the Kendra.

Of the early teaching days at the Curzon Road Kothi, Maya Rao distinctly remembers, 'that there was no provision for tabla accompaniment and the guru beat at a small table to keep rhythm, having beaten his thighs black and blue maintaining rhythm'. Shambhu Maharaj was a colourful personality, often prone to a democratic use of abuses while teaching. He was one of a kind, extremely talented and highly individual.

Tara Ramaswamy, a disciple since 1947, recalls that 'Shambhu Maharaj was not only a dance guru but someone who could be consulted on any personal problem—love, marriage, property, business... He shared his food and drink with everyone present. He just could not be selfish. When he drank his Scotch, he would first offer it to Kali and then consume it as *prasad.*'

It was in the same year (1955) that he was blessed with his first son, Krishan Mohan, on the day of Nagapanchami and 'he came running through the gate, waving the pink telegram, ecstatic with joy at the news', recalls Maya Rao. Maya also remembers that 'for my first performance, Sumitra Charat Ram offered me the use of her real jewellery!' The initial years of the Kendra were family-like with Sumitra Charat Ram as the mother-figure, providing care and nourishment and treating both the *guru* and *shishya*, the teacher and the taught, as her own family. In the first year itself this family grew and outgrew the confines of the Curzon Road *kothi*, so a new house, located at 5-B, Pusa Road, was hired in 1956 for the Bharatiya Kala Kendra's College of Music and Dance.

The house on Pusa Road became a hub of art activity and in no small measure this was due to the appointment of Naina Devi as its Resident Director. A trained singer, Naina Devi had suffered personal misfortune and

◀ *Shambhu Maharaj, the Samrat of Kathak and* abhinaya.

wanted some support. It was Sharada Rao, wife of C.B. Rao, a literary figure, who had been on the Jhankar Committee and who had christened All India Radio as the Akashvani, who introduced Naina Devi to Sumitra Charat Ram, when she arrived in Delhi and was looking for some meaningful involvement. In Sumitra Charat Ram, Naina Devi found a benefactor and in Naina Devi, Sumitra Charat Ram found an able artistic director, whose own background in the arts helped her run the place effectively.

Naina Devi came from an illustrious and artistic family of Bengal and her great grandfather, Keshub Chandra Sen was an established educationist. Her older sister, Sadhona Bose was an acclaimed dancer. Naina Devi was initiated into music by Sangeetacharya Girija Shankar Chakravarty. It was, however, her tutelage under Ustad Mushtaq Hussain Khan and Rasoolan Bai, and also her affiliation with Ghulam Sabir Khan of Ambala, Badi Moti Bai and Siddheshwari Devi that helped her evolve her art.

Sumitra Charat Ram feels deeply indebted to these two women, Nirmala Joshi and Naina Devi, who helped her create and develop this institution. 'We were like a threesome: Nirmala Joshi gave the idea, Naina Devi helped in its implementation and I helped financially. Often Naina Devi would call me up saying a certain artist was passing through Delhi and suggesting that we host him or her. I readily agreed. Thus, the Kendra took the shape of not only a teaching institution, but also one where artists could meet and interact. On one such occasion, I got a call around lunchtime that the legendary Balaswaraswati desired to see Shambhu Maharaj's *abhinaya*. Despite the late hour, quite a gathering had collected and their exchange continued into the late evening. It was such a momentous occasion when both danced impromptu. After a point, the technique did not matter; both wove an imagery of exquisite beauty through their expressive dance. That experience stayed with me for long time.'

At 5-B Pusa Road, Naina Devi stayed in one portion of the house, the drawing room of which duplicated as a classroom and in the annexe of the house stayed Ustad Hafiz Ali Khan with his two sons, Rahmat Ali Khan and Amjad Ali Khan. A gardener was employed to tend to the small patch and *chchapar* was used to cover the roof for additional space. 'What we achieved in artistic terms in this small house in those years, we did not achieve in bigger buildings', reminisces Sumitra Charat Ram who is convinced after the experiment that 'man works harder and delivers better under pressure and poverty than under ideal and comfortable conditions'. Publications like the *Kitab-i-Navras* or *Naurasnama* began, followed by *Man Kauthuhal*. The *Naurasnama* was personally supervised by Nirmala Joshi and Naina Devi.

The second batch of Kathak students consisted of Bela Arnab and Keshav Kothari. 'Keshav was a devoted youngster but he was not particularly cut out for dance. However, he imbibed the nuances of Kathak and later this was to go a long way in helping him in his career in arts administration', says Sumitra Charat Ram, who saw him grow, was party to his marriage with Rita Ganguly and today, in his retirement has brought him back to serve her Kendra as an adviser.

The college soon attracted the best teachers in the country: the senior Dagar brothers, Ustad Nasir Moinuddin and Nasir Aminuddin Khan Sahibs, Guru Shambhu Maharaj, Ustad Vilayat Hussain Khan of Agra, Ustad Mushtaq Hussain Khan, Ustad Wahid Hussain Khan, Guru Sundar Prasad, Guru Purushottam Das, Ustad Inam Ali Khan, Prof. Dilip Chandra Vedi, Vidushi Siddheshwari Devi, Ustad Ishtiaq Hussain Khan and Pandit Birju Maharaj.

A number of students enrolled over the years, among whom were Kumudini Lakhia, Uma Sharma, Rani Karna, Prabha Marathe, Pratap Pawar,

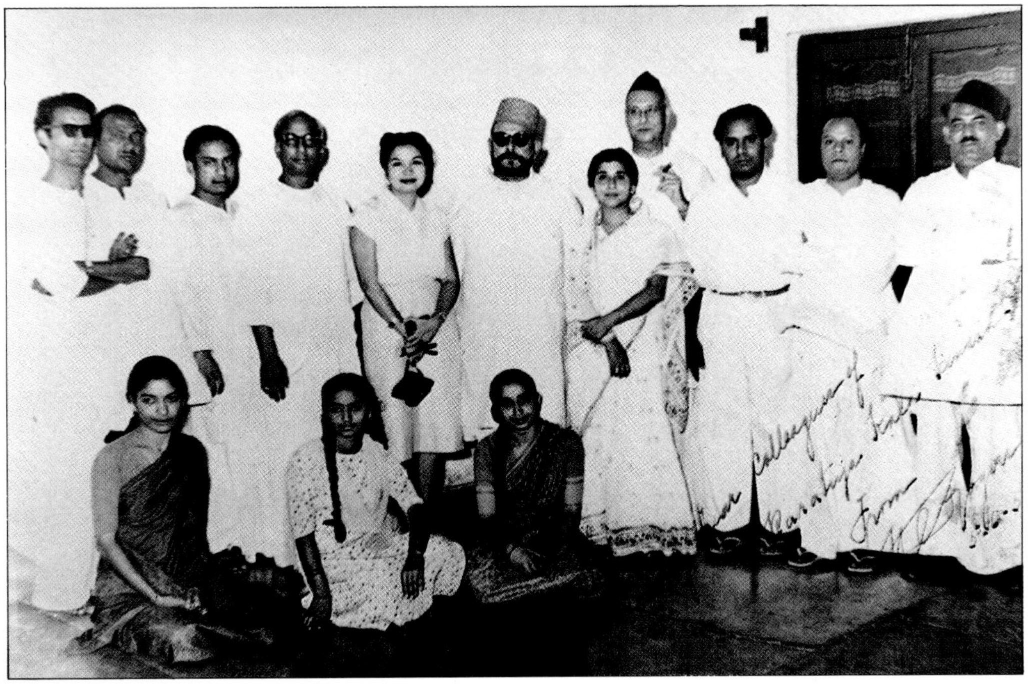

The Kendra became home for many—Ustad Hafiz Ali Khan, Naina Devi, Maya Rao, Birju Maharaj among others—who were also part of its teaching faculty.

Tirath Ajmani, Bharati Gupta, Durga Lal, Rashmi Jain (Vajpeyi) and Shovana Narayan. The Kendra became a grooming ground for the best known names in the field.

Ramlila: An Evergreen Production

Over the years, the Kendra grew from a teaching institution to a performing institution and this happened most coincidentally, when the idea of doing the 'Ramlila' came up. Since her childhood days, Sumitra had been fed on a diet of daily bed-time reading of the *Ramayana* at her father's bidding. She had also been exposed to the 'Ramlila' at Benaras.

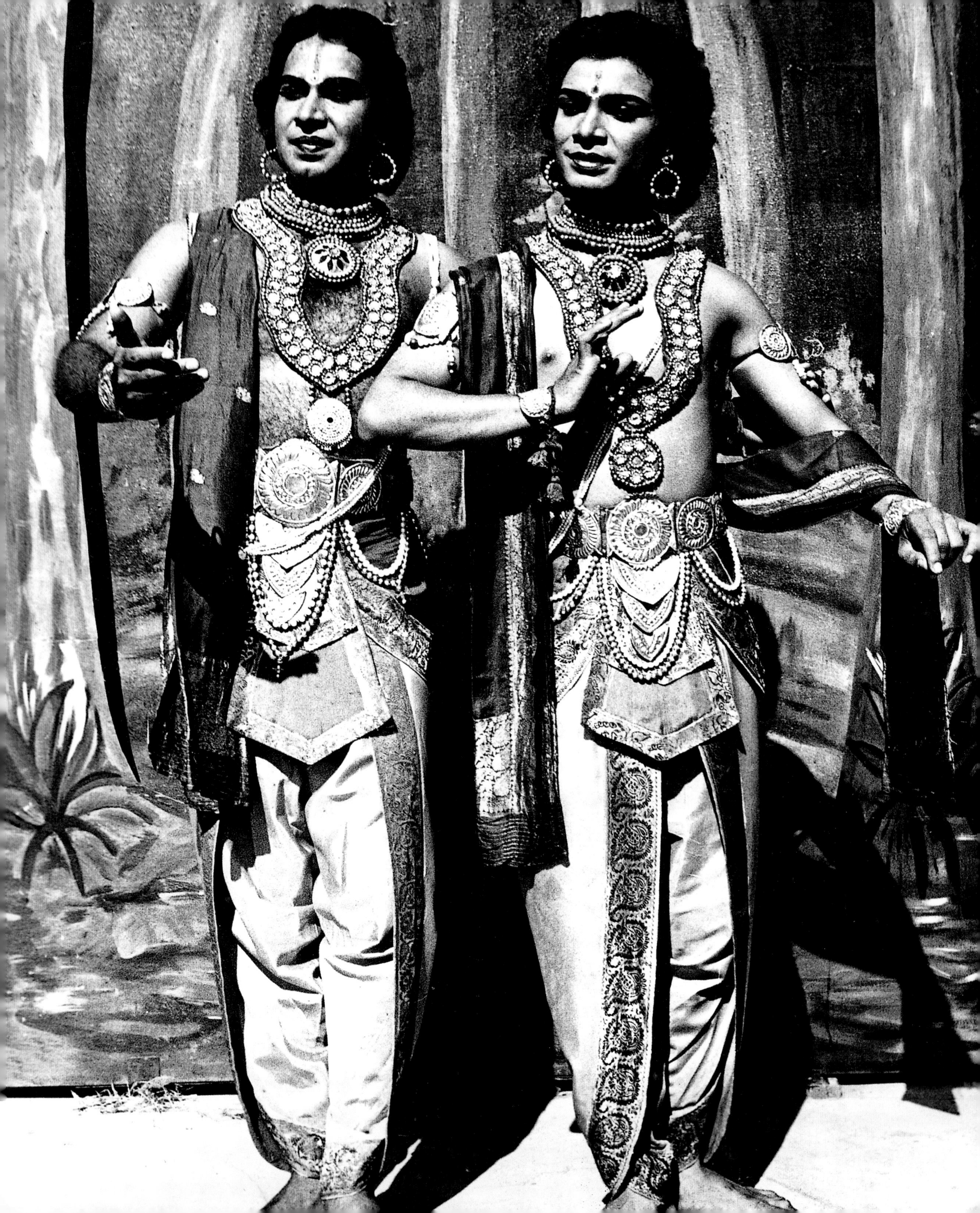

Some fifteen years into her marriage, chance provided her the opportunity to undertake a phenomenal task, the staging of a full-scale 'Ramlila'. The idea of doing a 'Ramlila' was mooted by Pandit Nehru and he requested the Chief Commissioner of Delhi, A.D. Pandit, to organise a presentation of this epic tale for the citizens of Delhi and a large number of diplomats posted here.

A.D. Pandit, who was Sumitra's guardian in her Benaras Hindu University days, called meeting after meeting to discuss the staging of the 'Ramlila'. Nothing happened at these meetings because no one agreed. Exasperated with one such meeting, Sumitra wrote him a note saying: 'Pandit *bhai*, I do not know what will come of these meetings but now I have decided to do our own Ramlila!'

Easier said than done. In order to mount a production of such an epic the first basic requirement was a script. The well-known poet, Ramdhari Singh 'Dinkar' was known to the family. Sumitra requested his assistance. Aghast at the proposition that a poet of his stature and eminence was reduced to this task, he nevertheless, out of sheer affection for her, agreed to do it.

He did, however, suggest that she find someone who could help link the various passages (*chaupies*) of the *Ramayana*. This was found in the person of Rahi. Actually a puppeteer, he was a talented writer and he connected the couplets beautifully. In fact, he brought in his own special touch and infused great feeling into the plot. The result of this endeavour was shown to Dinkar for his approval and he was delighted.

That attended to, someone was needed to artistically direct the production. Narendra Sharma, a teacher at the Modern School, who had learnt at Almora under Uday Shankar and had worked in the Bombay film industry and at IPTA (the Indian People's Theatre Association) was found to be a suitable candidate for undertaking this task. The artistic foundation he laid helped other talented choreographers build upon it, among whom most notably were Bhagwandas Verma; Guru Gopinath, the legendary Kathakali dancer; Debendra Shankar, brother of Ravi Shankar; and Yog Sunder, the prince-turned-dancer.

Narendra Sharma was instrumental in bringing artists like Bhagwandas Verma, who played the role of Rama. Narendra Sharma's wife, Jayanti, was the first Sita, with Sharma himself adorning the role of Ravana. Inder Razdan helped design the stage and Sushil Dasgupta and Jyotirindra Moitra, fondly called Batukda, composed the music.

The basement of the Curzon Road house was used for preparations. The entire production required a budget of Rs. 60,000, which in 1957 was a princely sum. M.O. Mathai, Secretary to Pandit Nehru, the then Prime

◀ *Raghvan Nair as Ram and Harish Rawat as Laxman, immortalised themselves in the Kendra's 'Ramlila'.*

In the same production, Narendra Sharma, Rekha Shanker and Uma Sharma in the roles of Ravana, Mandodari and Sita, respectively. ▶

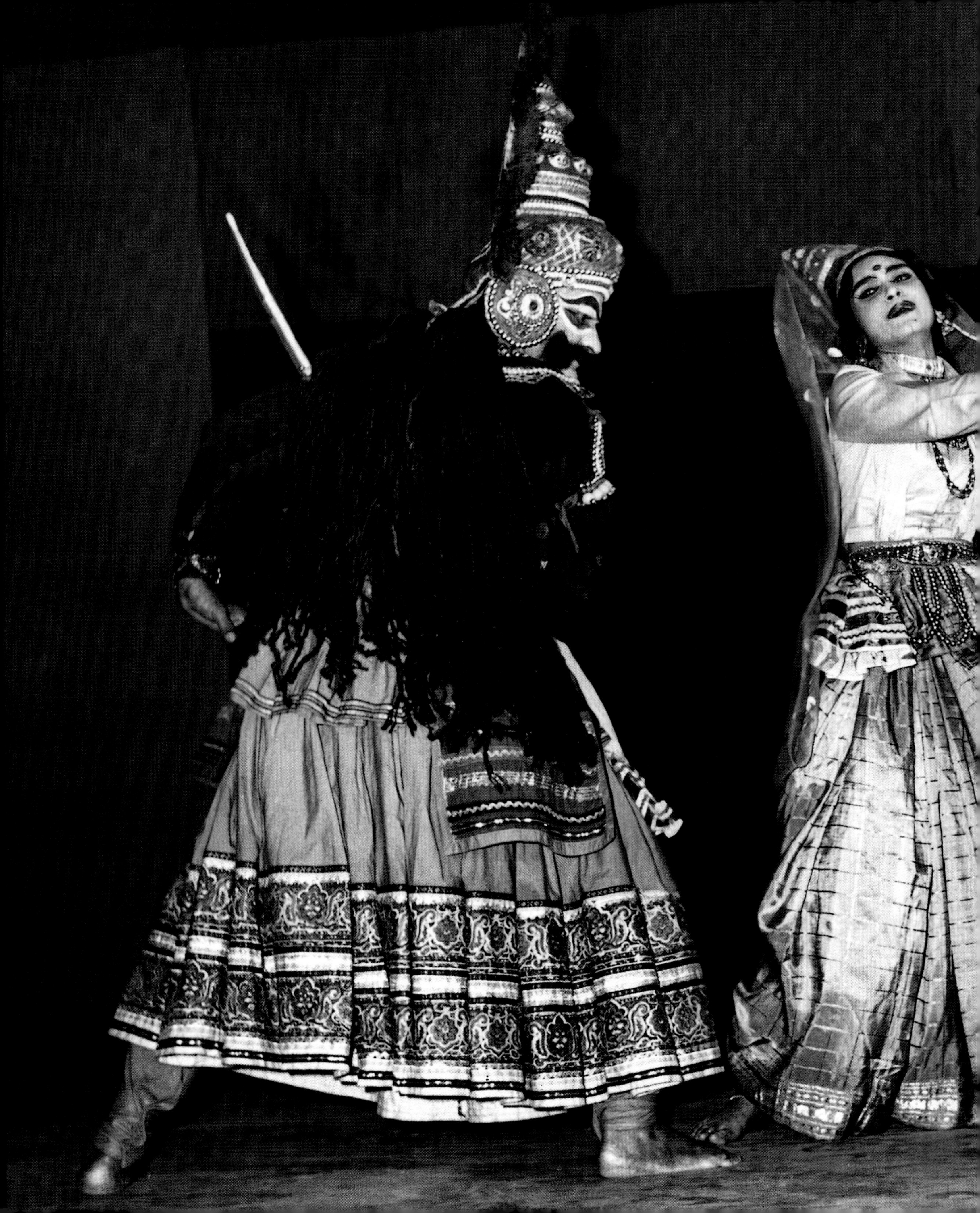

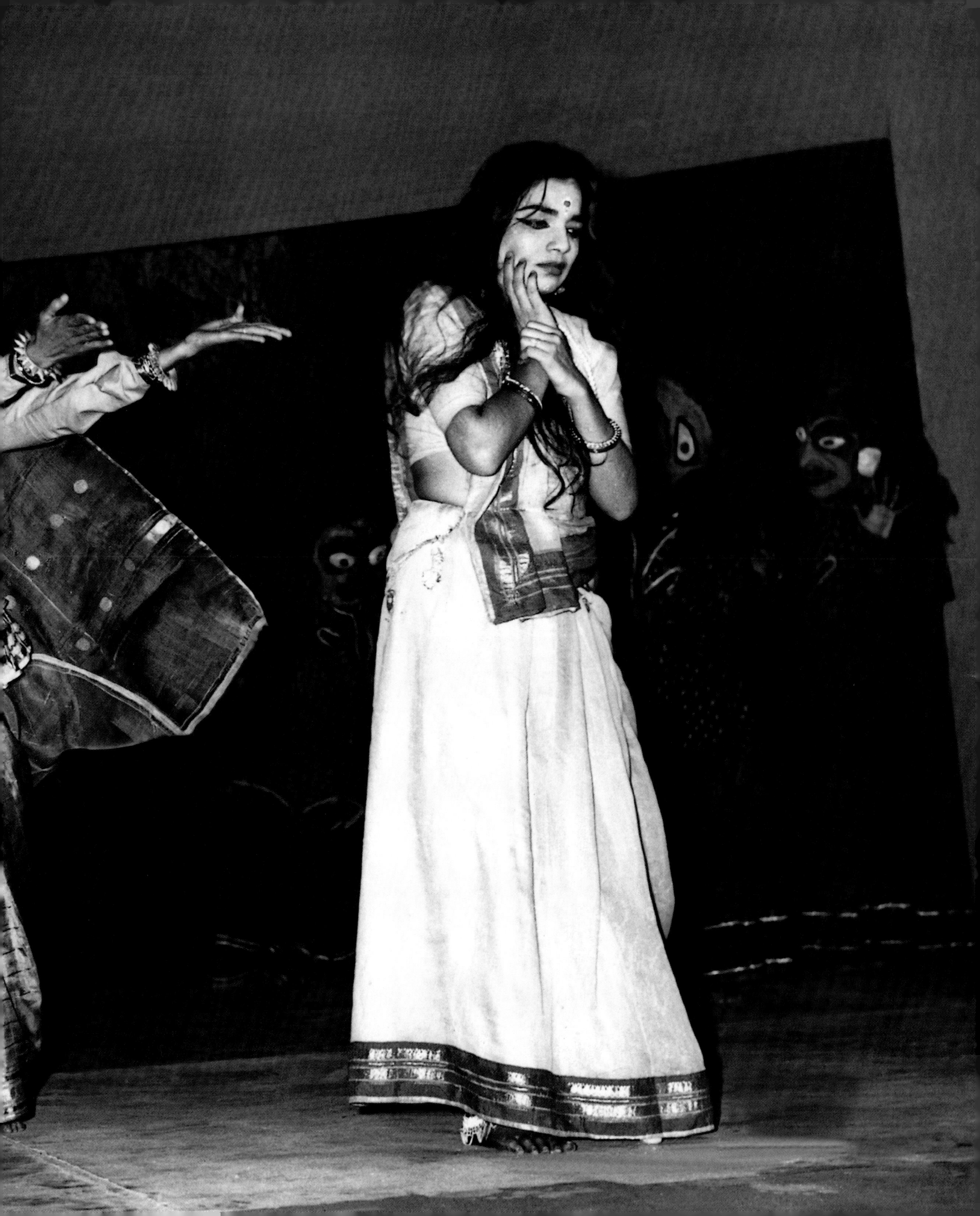

EDUCATIVE FORUM FOR DANCERS

By BALASARASWATHY

IT was a pleasure and a privilege to be invited to participate in the National Dance Festival, and I am grateful to the Sangeet Natak Akadami and the Bharatiya Kala Kendra for having given me an opportunity to contribute my mite towards this worthy effort of presenting our traditional dance-art form at the Festival.

Such festivals will most certainly serve to further the cause of dance by helping to encourage the various artistes, by arousing the interest of the people and by giving an impetus to a study of the technique among the younger people who are learning the art.

To my mind, the Festival is a forum where eminent artistes of different schools of dance participate with the earnest hope of revealing the significance of their traditional dances, and paving the way for the younger generation to follow in their mission of popularizing classical dance.

Expressions of Art

On this occasion, the participants look at other styles of dances not from a point of comparison but as expressions of the beauty of life and art. We have never had the opportunity of appearing on a common platform before, because each of us dances to an audience which appreciates a particular form only.

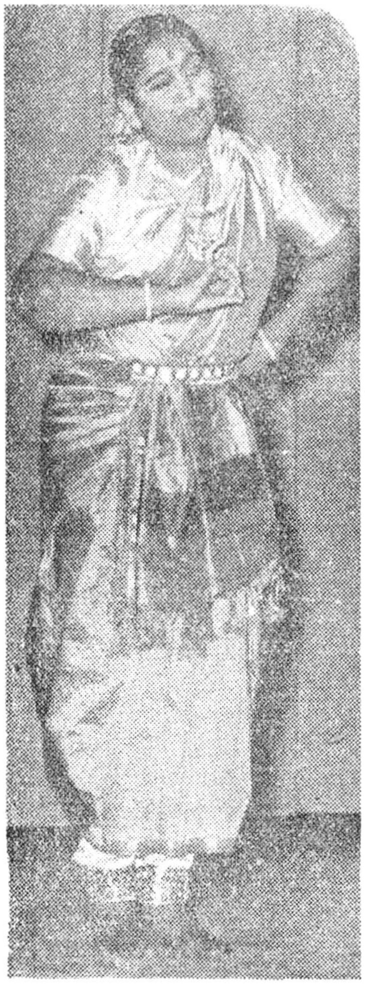

Balasaraswathy

Two Purposes

But this National Festival serves a dual purpose—of educating both the dancer and the onlooker so that dance does not become static and stagnant appreciated only by a devoted coterie. Each dancer strives in all sincerity to present an art mastered to the best of his or her ability, inspired by the devotion to the subject. Naturally, secondary embellishments like stage personality, showmanship and stage decor are not considered as the criterion by us to put forth our ideals. I only hope we could find an audience equally responsive, sympathetic and appreciative.

The Festival, indeed, has been a wonderful experience to me as it has brought me closer to the public, to the other artistes participating in the Festival and, above all, to the two classical dance forms of North India—Kathak and Manipuri.

I will speak more of Kathak because I had the opportunity to study its intricacies and subtleties more this time. In spite of the hideous distortions and misinterpretations of Kathak I have seen in Madras, I have always felt that this dance form has a unique beauty of its own. Achan Maharaj confirmed my opinion regarding this years ago at a music conference, by displaying a variety of permutations and combinations of time-measure not to mention the intricate footwork. I had glimpses of the finer elements of the dance when I saw Shambhu Maharaj at the Akadami Award function which left a deep longing in my heart to see more of Kathak.

A Feast

As I was feeling very sad at having missed the inaugural dance, Shambhu Maharaj gave me a special performance at a private gathering. Brij Mohan, the great Achan Maharaj's son, illustrated a few 'bols,' and 'parans' with graceful movements, along with a thrilling variety of 'tatkar' (foot-work). After treating us to a feast of pure dance, Shambhu Maharaj took the floor with his inimitable abhinaya. Seated on the carpet he started singing a thumri, the plaint of a gopi: "Shyam Ghunghat pat khole jora jori" (Shyam forcefully attempts to pull off my veil).

He seemed to tell a thousand tales out of a single musical phrase, drawing upon a rich and amazing imagination. The alternating expressions of joy, desire, frustrated hope, despair, coquettish invitation, etc., of the gopi were rendered in facial expressions and delicate gestures with irresistible charm that I could not hold my joy, I felt like sitting next to him and learning the abhinaya. If his captivating

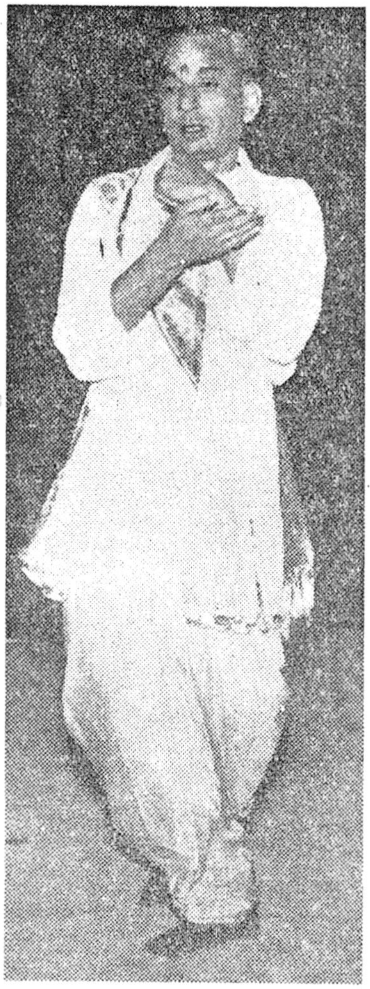

Shambhu Maharaj.

rendering of song in gestures and portrayal of emotions is not abhinaya, then what is it?

Without going too deep into the history of the arts, it is evident that both Kathak and Bharatanatyam are varying manifestations of the same form or twin sisters from the same parent stock. Whatever the merits of the question regarding the decadence of Kathak in its association with the Moghul Court, I feel that it affords an excellent scope for an accomplished artiste to express himself both in nritya as well as in abhinaya.

The art of Shambhu Maharaj in abhinaya and the adept handling of 'layakari' by Brij Mohan is a clear indication of the working of the forces of tradition in the families dedicated to art. I feel that owing to deep-rooted prejudices sufficient encouragement has not been given to Kathak.

Each dance style has its own beauty in technique as well as in interpretation, hence it is only the lack of understanding on the part of the onlooker to draw comparisons between two or three styles. Artistes and art critics ought to be fully conscious of the background and evolution of each technique.

Minister, helped with a grant of Rs. 25,000. The first 'Ramlila' took place in 1957 and Sumitra Charat Ram took her fourteen-year-old daughter, Shobha to it. 'I clearly remember the day, for I had seen all this activity happening right in our basement and I was very curious as to its outcome. I went with my mother in one of my best dresses and it was a memorable occasion', recalls Shobha Deepak Singh.

The show was a huge success by all accounts. This can best be measured by the fact that ever since, it has been performed every year, come what may. 'There were occasions, when it was nearly impossible to continue. Once, I was very unwell and had to leave for the United States for immediate medical attention. I thought we had to defer the show but no, our administrator, Thakur Harnarain Singh, and the choreographer, K. Shekharan Panikar said: "*Didi*, you go, we will handle it." And they did,' Sumitra recalls.

Several leading artists immortalised themselves and the production with their participation. If Bhagwandas Verma grew to become a leading choreographer after donning the role of Rama in the first 'Ramlila', Narendra Sharma, the first director, formed his own outfit Bhoomika, catering to 'contemporary dance' and children's theatre. The dignified Raghavan Nair who was the longest serving Rama is now India's cultural ambassador in Australia. Uma Sharma and Aloka Panikar, both Sita at different points in time, grew to become leading classical dancers of Kathak and Orissi, respectively. Surinder Kaur and Bhushan Lakhandri went to the Bombay film industry and newer and younger dancers have got a secure platform. Nand Kishore and Kamala Kiritikar today serve the Indian arts in Mauritius. For long Pratap and Priya Pawar served the art form in London and today both continue to do it separately.

There had been other stage adaptations of this epic tale, most notably Uday Shankar's shadow—*Ramayana* and the puppet-*Ramayana* by the Little Ballet troupe of Gwalior but the Kendra's 'Ramlila' set the tone for several others to follow (and copy). The 'Ramlila' also contributed its bit to the growing interest of the *Ramayana* as a stage production which reached its national peak through Ramanand Sagar's celebrated TV serial. The Kendra's 'Ramlila' is one dance-drama production, on the modern proscenium stage which has run for forty years. And it is perhaps the only stage production in India to have run for so long.

◀ *The legendary Bharata Natyam dancer Balasaraswathy expressed interest in witnessing Vidwan Shambhu Maharaj's* abhinaya, *an occasion which became material for this piece.*

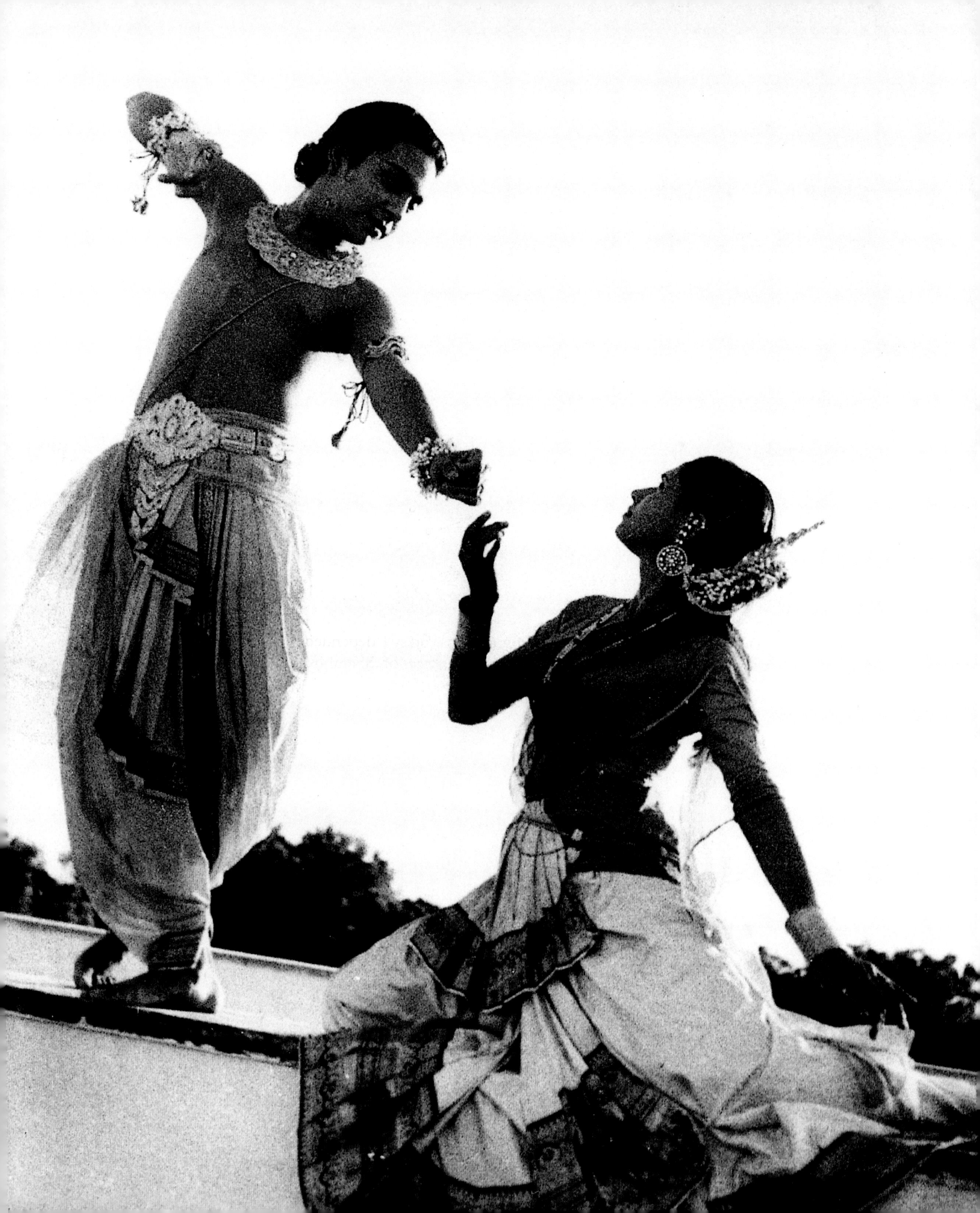

Of Kathak and Kathakars

If the 'Ramlila' proved enduring, the Kendra's efforts in the field of Kathak proved everlasting. By platforming Kathak as a dance form and by mounting productions and supporting various gurus of the form, the Kendra played a crucial role, viewed in retrospect.

Kathak as a dance style had been rather neglected and subjected to step-motherly treatment by those purists who associated it with what the British masters had dubbed it: Nautch. The *kothas* of Lucknow had degenerated and the artists had little support. This also coincided with the decline of royalty as a patron. Although some retained their interest and continued to be *rasikas*, very few could sustain the artists with the former grandeur.

The country was young and the government agencies woefully inadequate to handle promotion and projection. It was in keeping with this milieu that the work of institutions like the Kendra became pioneering even without realising it. Sumitra Charat Ram came from Uttar Pradesh. 'Since my childhood days, particularly in Lucknow, Allahabad and Benaras, I had seen the true beauty of the form and was a witness to the greatness of the Maharaj family in the art. As I was emotionally close to this dance form, when I came to Delhi and slowly started mounting artistic works, I depended more and more on Kathak as a form. Largely the presence of Shambhu Maharaj helped us in this direction and today looking back, I think without him perhaps our efforts would not have got such a boost'.

Thus was born 'Kathak Ki Kahani', the first dance-drama production after the 'Ramlila', in Kathak style. 'The occasion was the UNESCO meeting in 1958. Shambhu Maharaj was raring to create some lasting work and with a batch of students he had helped train, he mounted this production. With the modest success of this production, we felt emboldened and decided to produce 'Malati Madhav'. The script was devised by Nirmala Joshi. Pandit Lachchu Maharaj, brother of Pandit Achchan and Shambhu Maharaj, was called from Bombay to direct it. He selected the heroine of the production too, a winsome girl who was proving to be a dancing sensation in Bombay, Kumudini Lakhia. The hero was Krishna Kumar. Birju Maharaj played the role of Makarand. The Dagar brothers, Moinuddin and Aminuddin, created the music. The production was well received.

Birju Maharaj recollects his participation thus: 'I was new to Delhi, a mere youngster, but I had the desire to be seen as a hero on the stage. Thus, when

◀ *Birju Maharaj teams with Kumidini Lakhia in the Kendra's 'Malati Madhav'.*

the role of Makarand was offered to me, I was not very elated. Upon realising later that this role had more dance portions, I felt finally I could prove myself and in the bargain, possibly impress the audience. In those days, I wanted to prove myself and the support Sumitraji gave to us, personally and professionally, can never be forgotten. She was the eternal sister and confidant. We could always depend on her and despite her wealth and trappings, she was rather modest and easily accessible. Patrons like her are few and she never dictated her wishes or terms. She proved, in her own low key way, that teamwork be gets the best results. In those days, I did not mind participating in her puppet productions, often singing and playing the *dholak.* None of us felt that it was beneath our dignity or stature to participate in whatever manner the production demanded. We felt motivated and to a large extent it was Sumitraji's spirit which made us do whatever she requested us.'

The Puppet Section mounted many productions, such as 'Dhola Maru', 'Jhansi Ki Rani', the most significant, however, being 'Prithviraj-Samjukta' which won the first prize in the Udaipur Puppet Festival. Shambhu Maharaj was impressed with Keshav Kothari, who took a keen interest in these productions and on one occasion called him 'Kathputli Ka Badhshah!' 'In those days we did rehearsals on the roof top of the Pusa Road house, with only an asbestos sheet to protect us in the harsh summer months. Yet, some of the best productions came out of those days. Today, when I look back on those days of limitations and paucity of resources, I feel that what we achieved then is much more than what we can attain today, when we have every resource in hand. For anyone, especially an artist, suffering and pressure can lead to heightened creativity and comfort and luxury often prove counter-productive to artistic excellence', philosophises Sumitra Charat Ram.

The success of 'Malati Madhav' led to the creation of 'Kumar Sambhav' which won the first prize in the Ujjain Kalidas Samaroh. 'The team of Kumudini-Birju was a great hit with their "Rati-Kamadeva" piece in great demand. The Soviets saw this production at the Trade Expo and invited us to tour the Soviet Union. It was to be our first tour abroad!

'Kumudini Lakhia (then Jayakar) came to stay with us at Curzon Road and whenever she desired to leave, my children would start crying, so fond had they become of her. She had endeared herself not only to me but also to the children to whom she would tell stories from mythologies and the Indian tradition.'

Kumudini Lakhia recalls her long association with the Bharatiya Kala Kendra with fondness: 'I was thrust into an entirely new environment and had it not been for Sumitraji, I would have left Delhi long before I actually did. First, it was the strangeness of this capital city which was such a change from my Bombay culture. Although my dance was well-received and appreciated, I found it difficult to adapt myself to a new situation. It was by chance that one day Sumitraji happened to see where I was living as a paying guest. She immediately asked me to pack my bags and took me home. It was such a spontaneous act that I felt for the first time I had someone of my own in this big city. I stayed for three long years in her house. I saw her at very close quarters. Her dedication to both her family and her profession was equal; she neglected neither at the cost of the other. She stood by the side of her husband and children as a dutiful wife and mother and she was around her artists and institution when needed. She gave Kathak a new lease of life; there is little doubt about that. But for her and Nirmala Joshi, Kathak may not have had the stature it has today. By giving it institutional support, platform and projection, she helped the art become established. If in those, post-Independence years, all the languishing gurus and dancers had not been employed or encouraged, who knows where their art may have gone. By creating the Kendra and by focussing primarily

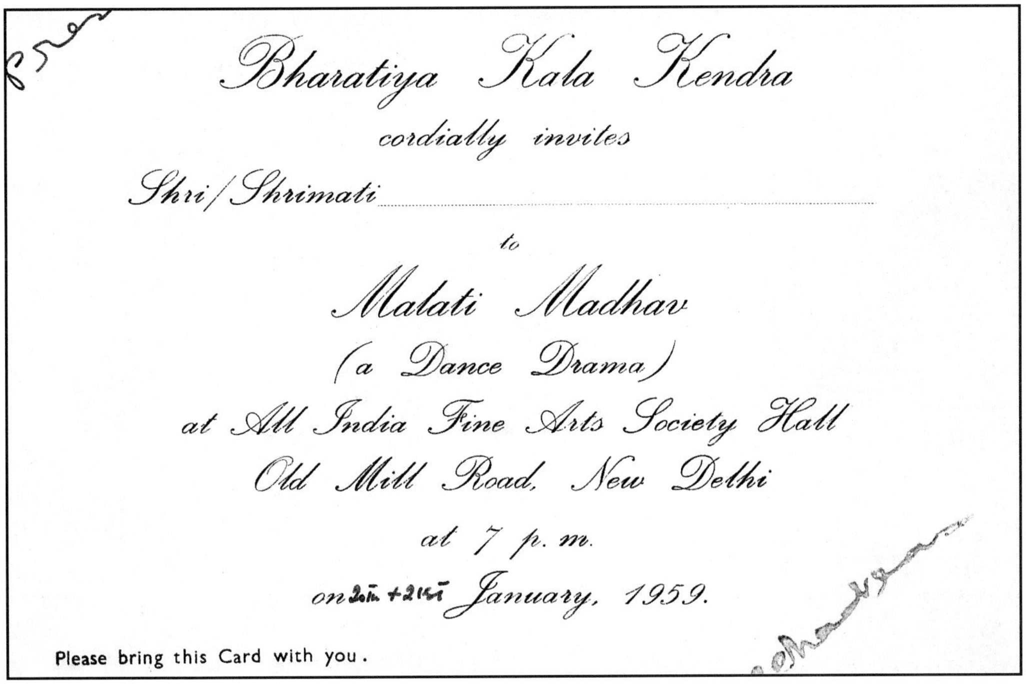

Bharatiya Kala Kendra

cordially invites

Shri/Shrimati ....

to

Malati Madhav

(a Dance Drama)

at All India Fine Arts Society Hall

Old Mill Road, New Delhi

at 7 p.m.

on 20th + 21st January, 1959.

Please bring this Card with you.

A stamp-signed invitation to the 1959 show of the Kendra classic: 'Malati Madhav'.

on Kathak as a form, in those years, partly thanks to the financial support of the Sangeet Natak Akademi, Sumitraji helped further the art form. Once the seed was sown, it grew into a tree and on its branches several gurus, teachers and dancers blossomed.'

A New Site

Slowly, the activities of the fledgling institution grew and the need to enlarge the work space was acutely felt. In 1958, the Kendra sought institutional land for building an institution. 'I wanted a site near the Income Tax Office (ITO), between Old and New Delhi but I was offered land on Lytton Road, near Mandi House, now Copernicus Marg. I remember both Pandit Vinay

Chandra Maudgalya and myself standing in front of the Land Commissioner, who asked Maudgalyaji, 'How will you build an institution when you have no resources?' To which the learned man replied: 'I have Saraswati, Laxmi I will try to collect!' We both got land allotment in the same year, although I had desired land positioned between the Old Delhi, from where my family hailed and New Delhi, where we now lived. But it was not to be. Gandharva Mahavidyalaya by virtue of having started much earlier, in 1939 itself, got the ITO site and we were told to take what we were getting before that too slipped away. We thus came to our plot which was occupied by huts and we spent some time in the Ferozeshah Road hutments creating art!'

'The land was ours on paper only because there were hutments on it those days. I approached Gopala Reddy, the then Housing Minister and complained in jest that we neither had the land nor interest on the money we had paid for the land. In those days Ministers (or politicians) were so responsive that he immediately asked me to drive with him to Mata Sundari Road, where he showed me six houses which could be given to us for use until our encroached land could be cleared. We built a temporary hostel there and a tea shop run by a man called Tony was set up for the artists and visitors to refresh themselves. Here, in these tenements, our humble institution grew,' recalls Sumitra Charat Ram.

By then the Kendra was officially conducting classes in the two principal *gharanas* or schools of Kathak, the Lucknow under Shambhu Maharaj and the Jaipur under Guru Sundar Prasad. 'There were no *gharana*-related fights, ever,' says Shovana Narayan, who went there to learn. 'There were often light-hearted jokes but never disagreements or duels. There was little ill-will, much less heartburn. We were like one big family and to a large extent the motherly attitude of Sumitraji and Naina Devi had an overall impact on us. No one had pretensions of being a big star. There was much give and take and a spirit of camaraderie. It was not a relationship where the owner of the institution stood on one side and its employees on the other. It was a big family; all lived in that spirit. It was such an honour to see and learn from the best gurus of India, in different fields. They were all giants yet they taught us with affection. I think the single most important contribution of the Shriram Bharatiya Kala Kendra is to have got all the great gurus together under one roof and to have utilised their art and expertise in training us youngsters, who could carry their work forward, in our own modest ways,' feels Uma Sharma.

In 1961, the well-known scholar and authority on Delhi, Maheshwar Dayal, became the Secretary of the Kendra. A learned man and a connoisseur, he had acquired first hand knowledge of the workings of Delhi's art and culture, even of the *kothas* and *kothewalis*, the courtesans. His writings on the history of Delhi as a city of culture and learning were inspiring and through him much of Delhi's ambience could be captured for posterity. A close friend of Charat Ram, he hailed from a prominent Mathur family of

Delhi, to which the sarodist Sharan Rani Backliwal and dancer Charu Sija Mathur also belong. Himself a *shair* of repute, Maheshwar Dayal's association with the Kendra, further helped guide the institution. By then Naina Devi had become somewhat busy with her own organisation, the Raag Rang. Indira Gandhi had entered active politics and she opted out of the Presidentship of the Kendra, suggesting that S.K. Patil take charge. He, too, took an immense interest in the affairs and activities of the Kendra.

Honours Pour In

In 1963, Sumitra Charat Ram was honoured with the Padma Shri. 'Much against my wishes, it was during the Presidency of S. Radhakrishnan that

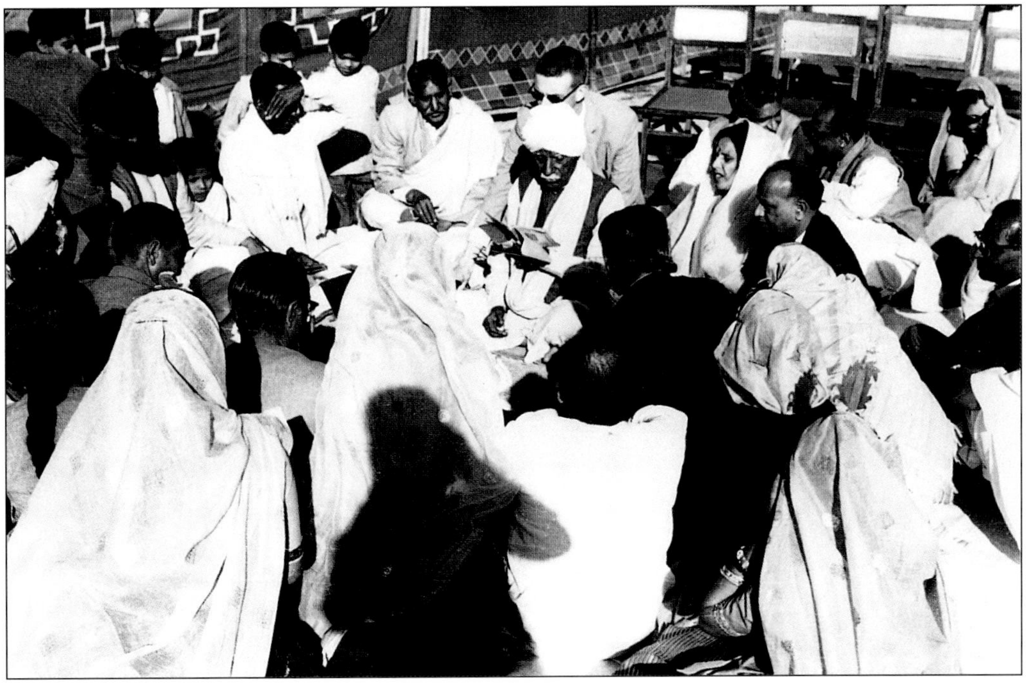

At the bhumi-pujan *ceremony of the plot on which the Kendra is built.*

my name was proposed. I was not keen to be singled out and when I was informed of the award, I was actually disappointed that artists like Shambhu Maharaj had not been honoured and yet I was being decorated. When I heard that the Prime Minister Lal Bahadur Shastri had proposed my name and the President had accepted it, I felt I had no choice but to accept it. But not before I wrote a polite letter thanking the Prime Minister requesting that artists like Shambhu Maharaj be honoured. I am elated today when artists get this honour on a regular basis.'

'These awards meant little to me because my reward is my work with the artist community. They gave me so much affection, love, attention and

Architectural plans of the Kendra. ▶

ARCHITECTURAL PLANS OF THE BHARATIYA KALA KENDRA

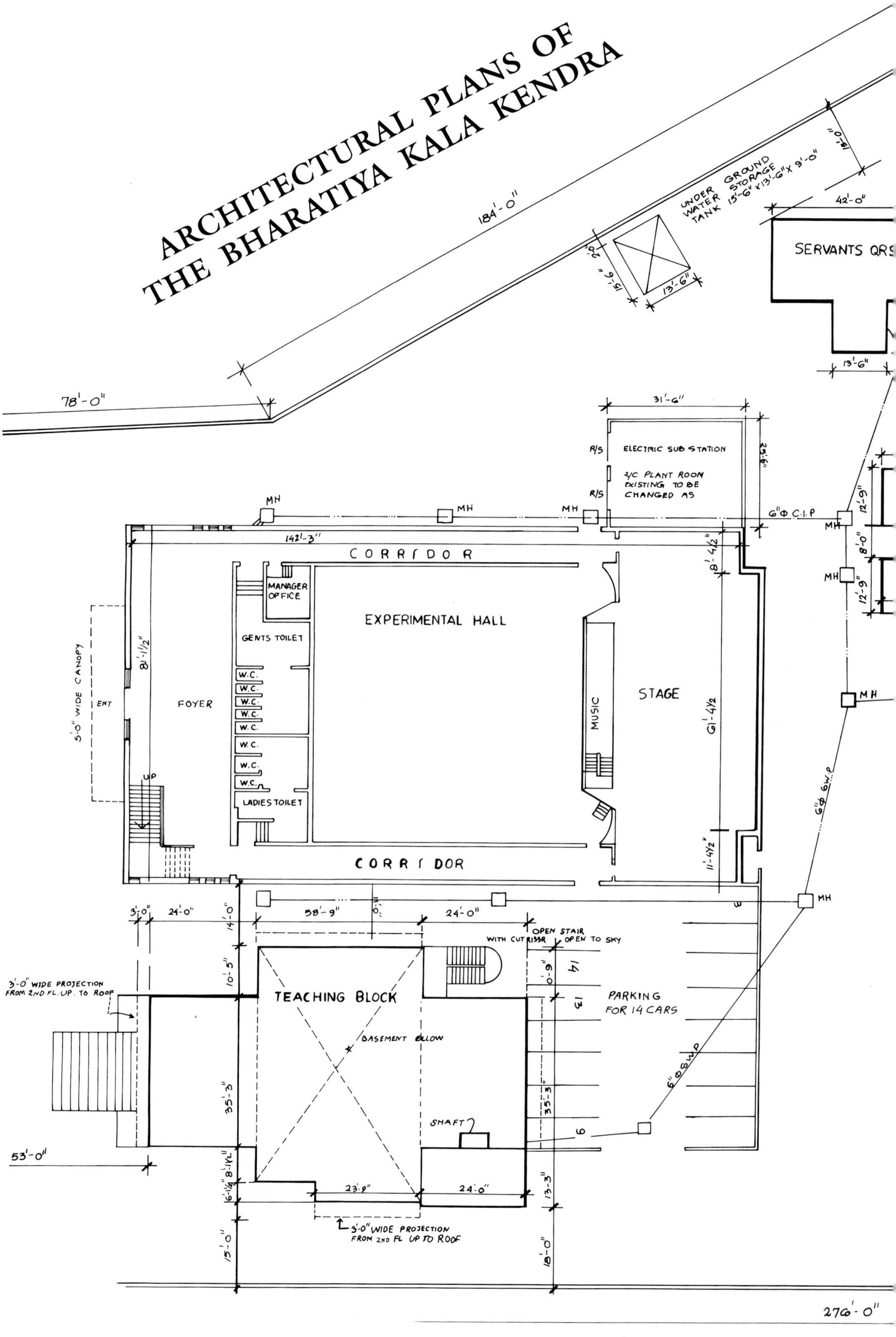

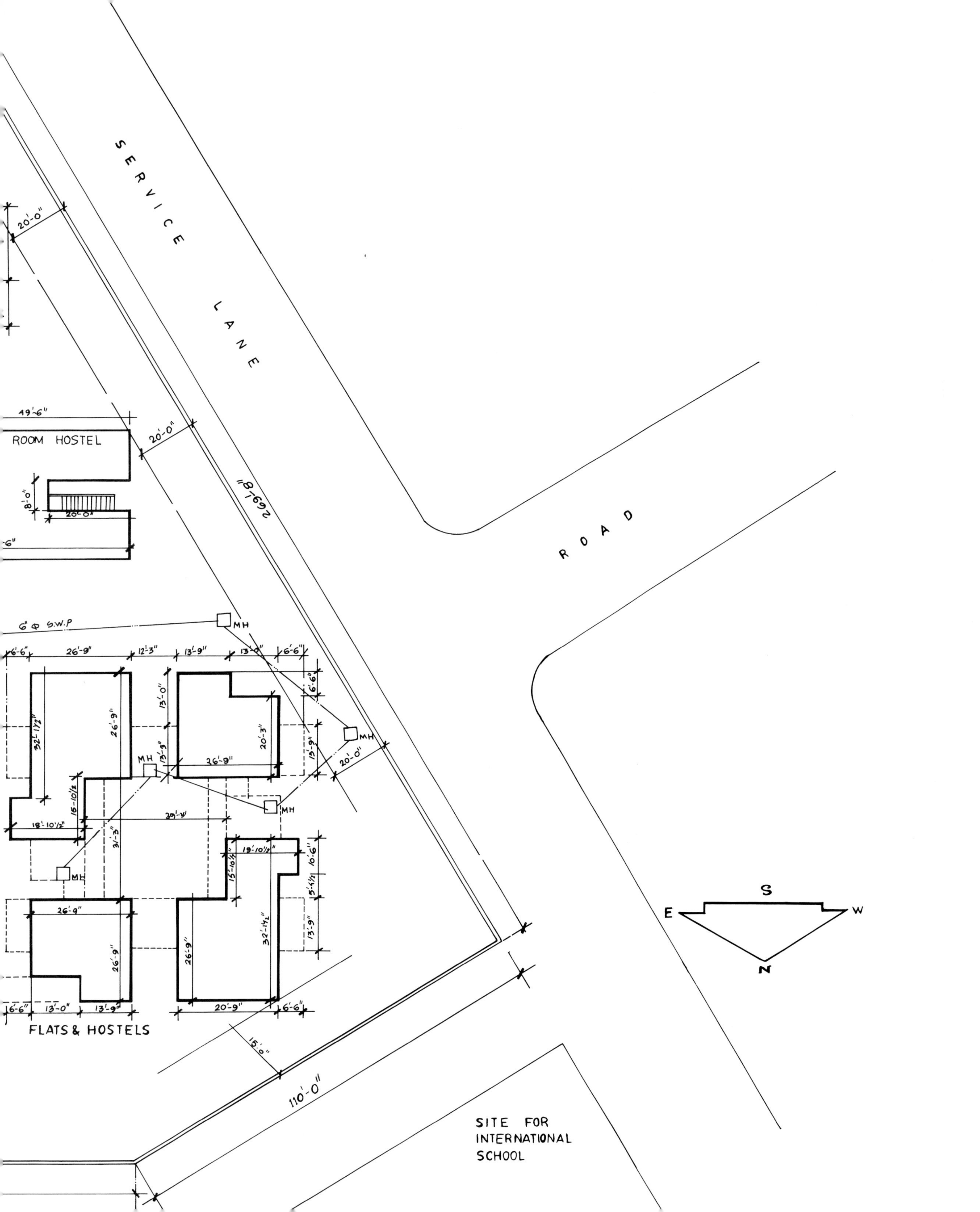
SERVICE LANE
ROAD
ROOM HOSTEL
FLATS & HOSTELS
SITE FOR INTERNATIONAL SCHOOL
MH
6" Φ S.W.P
S
E
W
N
269'-8"
110'-0"
20'-0"
49'-6"
26'-9"
15'-0"

respect that any other award was not worth its weight in gold. Today, after more than fifty years of work in the field, I feel fulfilled not because of honours or awards but because of how close artists feel to me and I to them,' reiterates Sumitra Charat Ram. A feeling which is shared by the artists themselves. Amjad Ali Khan, who came as an adolescent boy to the Kendra's Pusa Road house, observes: 'In Sumitraji, we found not merely a promoter or a patroness, but a mother figure. My initial professional moulding too came from her and today I may be an established artist, but I cannot forget her selfless devotion, in helping artists grow and arrive nationally on the professional scene.'

Mohan Upreti, the reputed artist, music-composer and expert of operatic traditions of the Kumaon region, came into contact with Sumitra Charat Ram in the Mata Sundari days. His Marxist leanings and heavy involvement with the Communist Party of India had landed him in jail in 1963 and he was barred from moving about in the eight hill districts of Uttar Pradesh. He recalled the day when he was called for an interview. Sumitra Charat Ram had been briefed about his background by Keshav Kothari and Nirmala Joshi, who had introduced him. Upreti remembers her first question: 'I hope you will not do any *gadbad* here!' He responded with equal openness: 'If I wanted to do *gadbad*, I would have gone to a factory not come to an art institution!'

This was the beginning of a relationship that lasted over two decades, from 1964 to the mid-eighties. Although he came for administrative work, his interest lay in the creative aspect of the institution. He held the Kendra to be one of the most significant art institutions in India since the days he had seen their 'Ramlila'. The Shankarlal Music Festival started in the early sixties, had gained great momentum and had a committed audience. New productions like 'Krishnayan', 'Geet Govind', 'Meghdoot', 'Urvashi', 'Bahubali', 'Keno-Upanishad', 'Surdas', 'Konark' and 'Khajuraho' were produced. The Holi Mela and Varsha Utsav had also gained popularity.

Tours abounded. Mohan Upreti remembered one tour particularly, the tour of the Soviet Union. 'Sumitraji would joke about it and say we have come to Upreti's Fatherland (since I was known to be a committed Marxist). One day, in Armenia, we were provided with bad food which was beyond our level of tolerance. Sumitraji just flared up and ordered all of us out of the hotel's dining room saying, "I will take you to a restaurant at my own expense!" It was not the food but her concern which touched the artists most. This is a quality about her—she was always personally involved with the welfare of artists.'

The Governing Council of the Kendra shows Indira Gandhi as the Chairman and many eminent persons on board. ▶

Pages 70-71: *An authority on the history and heritage of Delhi, Maheshwar Dayal brought depth and vision to the activities of the Kendra.*

BHARATIYA KALA KENDRA

President

Dr. K. N. KATJU

Vice-Presidents

BEGUM PATAUDI ... SHRI R. N. HAKSAR

Governing Council and Executive Committee

Smt. Indira Gandhi	.. *Chairman*
Smt. Sumitra Charatram	.. *Secretary*
Smt. Kamla Narendralal	.. *Joint Secretary*
Shri B. P. Shungloo	.. *Joint Secretary*
Shri M.L. Sodhani	.. *Treasurer*
Smt. Vimla Lal	.. *Assistant Treasurer*

Members

Shri Hansraj Gupta
Smt. Sharda Rao
Shri Ramdhari Singh 'Dinkar'
Lala Shri Ram
Shri S.P. Jain
Shri R. Sahai
Dr. S.K. Sen
Rajmata Kamalendumati Shah of Tehri
Smt. Rukminidevi Arundale
Smt. Rama Jain
Shri Ram Gopal Gupta
Lala Jagannath
Shri Shivraj Bahadur
Dr. N.B. Bhatt
Begum Qudsia Zaidi
Dr. Sumati Mutatkar
Shri Jiwanlal Muttoo
Shri N. Jain
Smt. Sushila Rastogi
Smt. Krishna Satish Chandra
Shri Rajeshwar Dayal
Shri Maheshwar Dayal

THE Dilliwala, like Delhi, has an infinite capacity to live in a world all his own. He is immune to change, for better or for worse, a quality characteristic of the region. Invader after invader succumbed to its cultural ethos. The only way not to become a Dilliwala was to escape from the city fast and quick, but who, having stayed here for a while, could tear himself away from the magical streets of Delhi as Zauq put it?

The Dilliwala's capacity to absorb external influences, retreat into an inner haven, and yet be tolerant has given him a unique power to resist other value systems. There is nothing belligerent about this attitude of his. There is everything snobbish in it. It is a sense of inferiority which makes him resist. It is sheer confidence which makes him live and let live.

There is a famous anecdote which illustrates this attitude. During one of his periodic visits from Agra to see how the work on the construction of the Red Fort in Delhi was progressing, Emperor Shahjahan once saw a little bird returning to its nest in a tree only to find a huge bird already lodged there. It was a dramatic encounter. The little bird pecked furiously at the large intruder. Its assaults made no impression on the big bird but it persisted so vehemently that the latter finally lumbered out of the nest, only to remain perched on the same bough. Having got him out of the nest, the little bird lost its rancour and rested companionably along with the big one on the bough.

The Emperor was amazed. "What's that bird?" he asked a local man. "Sire", replied the man, "I do not know its real name, but we could certainly call it the Delhi bird. It is like the Dilliwala who hates the intruder at first, begins to forget his hostility after a while, and then just accepts the newcomer."

Tolerance

There have been many eminent persons who came from outside Delhi but loved the place so much that they not only settled here, but came to love it. One such was Amir Khusrau, undoubtedly one of the greatest and most fascinating figures of his time. Khusrau was a patriot who praised the country in glowing terms. But more than that was his love for Delhi as embodied in the following couplet:

Delhi, the refuge of faith and equity,
In the garden of paradise; may

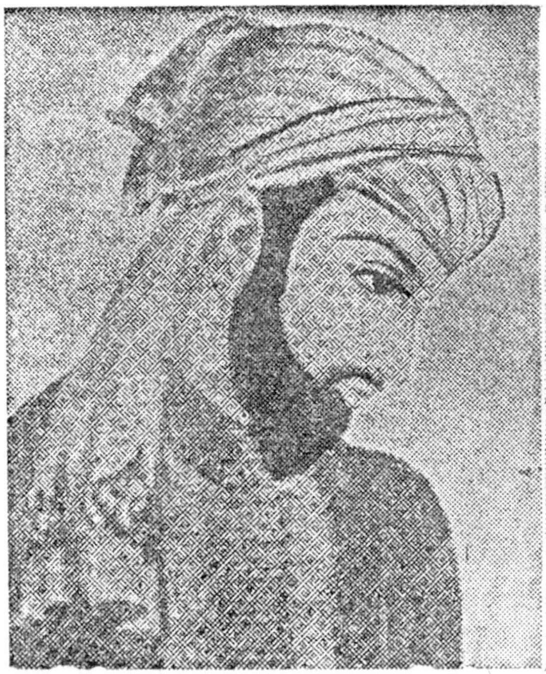

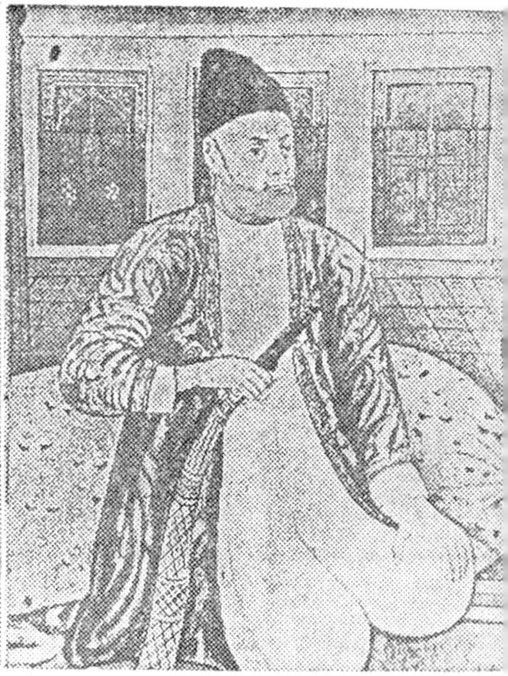

Spellbound by Delhi: Amir Khusrau (left) of Patiyali, district Etah, and Mirza Gha[lib] of Samarkand and Agra.

LIFE IN DELHI—

him. Looking at his odd attire, one of the audience asked where he had come from. He retorted: "What shall I say about that place and the implied ridicule in your question? I come from a city which was the glory and envy of the world not so long ago, inhabited by many eminent and distinguished persons, which has now declined into almost a desert. I belong to that same deserted city (Delhi)."

Ghalib, the Urdu poet whose ancestors came from Samarkand and whose childhood was spent in Agra, fell a victim to Delhi's insidious charm in the same way. He came to live in Delhi only after he had married Umrao Begum, the daughter of Illahi Baksh "Maroof". He identified

---

Ghalib, the Urdu poet whose ancestors came from Samarkand and whose childhood was spent in Agra, fell a

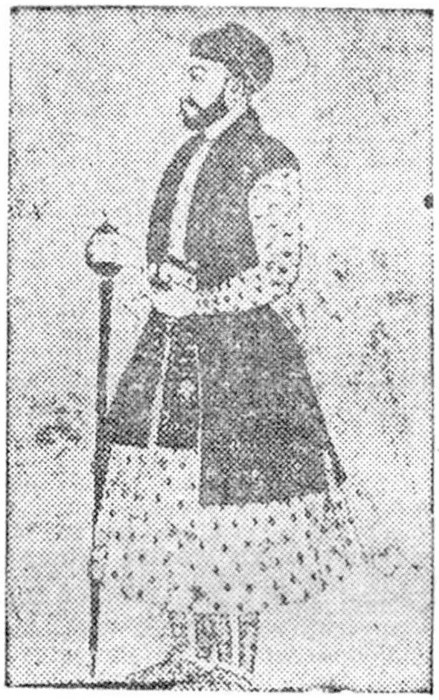

Ali Mardan Khan, administrator and engineer in Shahjahan's court who built the famous canal that once flowed through Chandni Chowk

added. "are ghamarah (un-

the Mughals who came to but stayed on to become Indi Delhi would not have had show its military power. It only to open its cultural w wide enough for the newco to revel in its shade. Ghal ghamarah, the boorish intru ultimately became a pucca D wala. This phenomenon rep itself time and again.

Adventurers

In 1911, when the Bri shifted the Capital of India f Calcutta to Delhi, a large in of masons and contractors c from Punjab to build New De They were hard working ad turers who translated the p of Lutyans and Baker into reality we now know as the r nificent complex of Rashtra Bhawan, flanked by the Secretariats, the long ave down to India Gate, and whole circular design that f its epitome in Connaught Cir New Delhi's shopping area.

While these newcomers w ed hard and made their mo Delhi's own contractors refu to avail of the opportunity *ntil urbanisation disturbed its even tenor, life in Delhi as not the stress and strain it is today. It centred around e joint family, the events of day-to-day life providing members with all the excitement they could hope for their sheltered existence. The Dilliwala was a snob oud of his culture. He was hostile towards those who truded into his city, yet tolerant enough to accept them.*

limpses of social life in this memorable era are rovided in a series of articles, beginning today, by AHESHWAR DAYAL, whose family has lived in Delhi r over 300 years. He is the author of two books, "Re-scovering Delhi: The Story of Shahjahanabad", and Dilli Meri Dilli", three Urdu plays and a number of ticles on the hoary past of Delhi, its traditions, customs nd rituals.

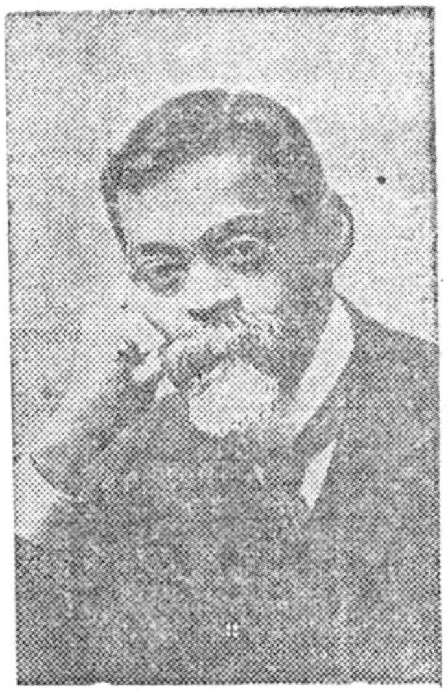

Sushil Kumar Rudra, the first Indian principal of St. Stephen's college.

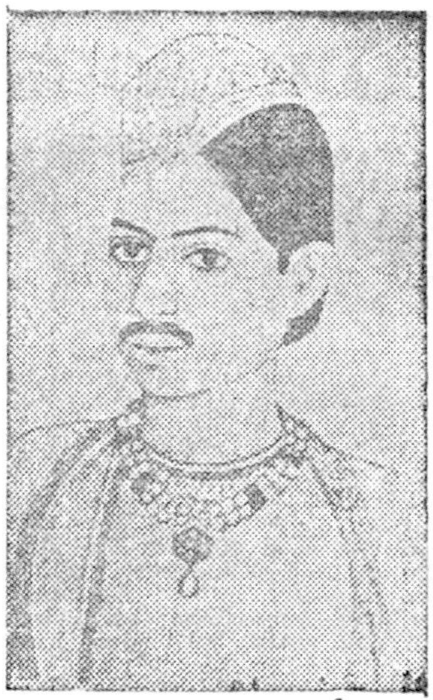

Ramji Das Gurwala, a millionnaire who helped the last Mughal King and was executed by the British.

HAT WAS

What the Dilliwala regards as ticularly crude are incorrect onunciation, grammatical er- and the use of hard or usive language. There have to refinements even in abuse as alib once pointed out when a end told him how someone d abused the poet behind his ck by a vulgar reference to his ther. Ghalib was then old. He nmented caustically, "He is viously not a man of taste or cernment. He does not know it even abusing is an art. If u want to insult an old man, u should refer to his relations th his daughter, not his other"

The early Mughals had built empire renowned in the orld for its abounding wealth, arvellous industry, and architural monuments unparelleled beauty. learning, poetry and usic. They wisely sought suprt for their polity in the goodll of their subjects and rerded both Hindus and Muslims pillars of their authority. hey were enlightened patrons Indian art and letters and ught ways to reconcile religis differences. They observed e Hindu festivals along with lamic ones.

rulers did give rise to party politics with different groups like the Iranis, Turanis, Afghans and Hindustanis (both Hindu and Muslims of Indian origin) trying to further their own interests. But these rivalries did not have a communal character.

The famous shoe-sellers' riot was a typical example of non-communal party politics in which a Hindu jeweller, responsible for the murder of a Muslim shoe-seller, was given shelter by Sher Afghan Panipati in his home.

With the arrival from Deccan of 'Vali', the poet, Urdu became the common language of both Hindus and Muslims and both the communities produced men

The Punjabi contractors who were mainly from the Sikh community calmly settled down in Delhi with all the flourish of the nou-

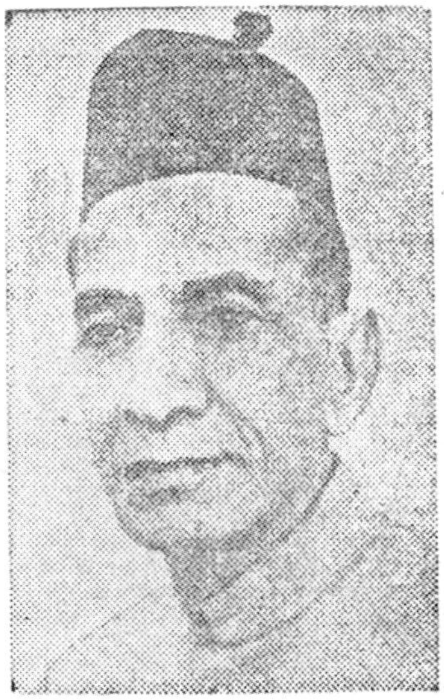

Lala Shri Ram, industrialist, city father and philanthropist.

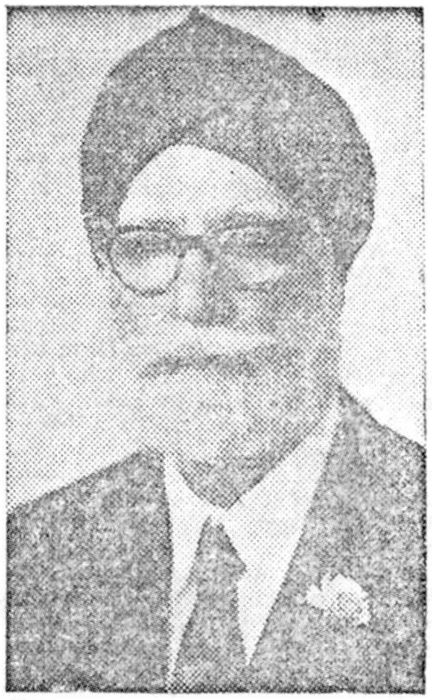

Sir Sobha Singh, builder of New Delhi.

he noticed a rare volume lying among the books scattered haphazardly on the floor on a white sheet. He picked it up and asked its price. The book-seller, also a typical Dilliwala, looked at his customer from top to toe, took the book from his hands and put it back on a desk. The man was surprised but again asked the price of the book. This made the book-seller furious. "You may be well dressed but you have no regard for masterpieces of literature. Do they have a price? Can they be

his plate, the kababi would hit his hand with a hot iron tong. They were surprised and a little angry for the boy was not a beggar and had money to pay for his kababs. "What's the matter with you, why are you hitting him like this?" asked a customer furiously. "Ah, sir," replied the kabab seller. "You don't know this boy. He is a thief. He gives me stolen money for my kababs. I do not want it. *Is kamai mein koi barkat nahin hai.*" (This kind of money does not bring prosperity)."

Talented people like Mohan Upreti helped her to build the institution. Another such talent was Tapas Sen, who became instrumental in helping to create the best auditorium Delhi was to see, the Kamani Auditorium.

New Institutions Bloom

New institutions connected with the arts had been taking shape in Delhi since the 1930s. The first and foremost was the Delhi School of Hindustani Music and Dancing formed by Nirmala Joshi in the generation before Sumitra Charat Ram. Later, the Sangeet Bharati emerged as a new version of Nirmala Joshi's previous organisation. In 1939, the Delhi branch of Gandharva Mahavidyalaya followed. The Jhankar Music Circle was formed in 1949. This was the seed for the Bharatiya Kala Kendra. The Triveni Kala Sangam was started in 1960 thanks to the Shridharanis. In fact, Sundari Bhavnani met her husband-to-be Shridharani, in Sumitra Charat Ram's *Kothi* on Curzon Road and soon there were wedding bells in the air.

All these fledgling institutions were initially housed in the Connaught Place area above coffee houses or in the by lanes of imposing buildings. The Regal Theatre used to be the prime venue for both visiting troupes and for cinema. Several leading luminaries of the art world —Ram Gopal, Uday Shankar and Prithviraj Kapoor —performed here. On one occasion, when IPTA's 'Discovery of India' was performed, Pandit Nehru got on the stage and stated that the production was better than his book! He also went to meet the artists backstage creating in the process, much commotion.

In the fifties and early sixties, Delhi had very few auditoriums, even Sapru House had not been constructed. The Regal Theatre was a prime venue for all visiting groups. The AIFACS (All India Fine Arts and Crafts Society) auditorium was among the first to come up after the Wavell Theatre and the NDMC Hall near Jantar Mantar had gone out of use. The Talkatora Gardens was another important venue where theatrical presentations took place. The emergence of new theatres like the AIFACS and the Sapru House also heralded the advent of professional lighting and stagecraft.

In this field, the shadow of lightsman Tapas Sen loomed large. He started as a switchboard attendant with the Delhi Electrical Supply Undertaking (DESU) and then moved on to study professional lighting in the Bombay film industry, before joining the Calcutta theatre world. This lighting maestro was often called to Delhi and he was instrumental in creating an ambience of light for the 'Ramlila' productions. He worked closely with Inder Razdan,

The tour to Soviet Union led to a long artistic association with the various cultures of the world.

Pages 74-75: *Artists under one roof: stalwarts Guru Gopinath (seated garlanded in the centre) Mohan Upreti, Uma Sharma, Aloka Panikar, Pratap Pawar, K. Shekheran Panikar, Thakur Harnarain Singh among others.* ▶

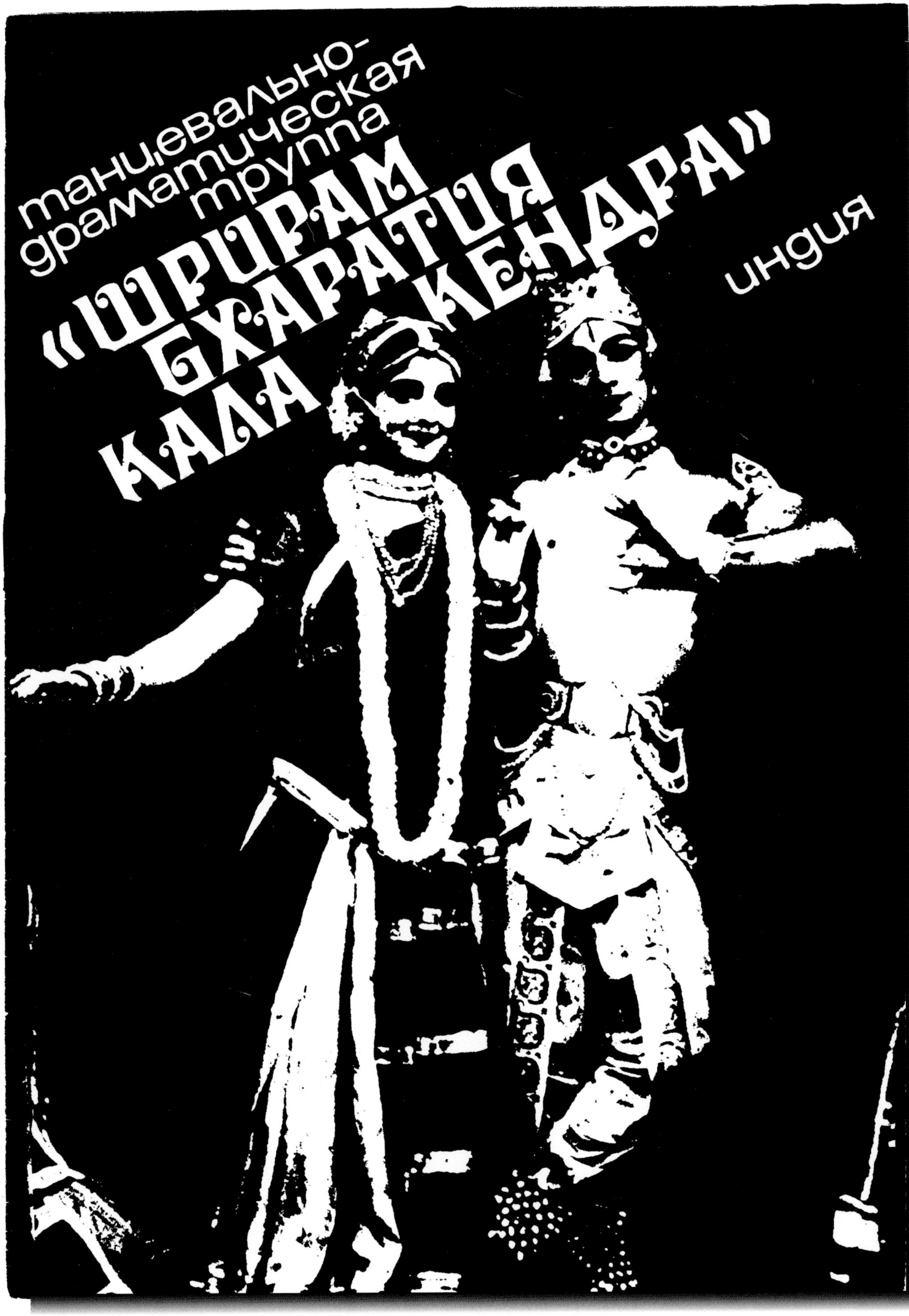
танцевально-
драматическая
труппа
«Шрирам
Бхаратия
Кала Кендра»
индия

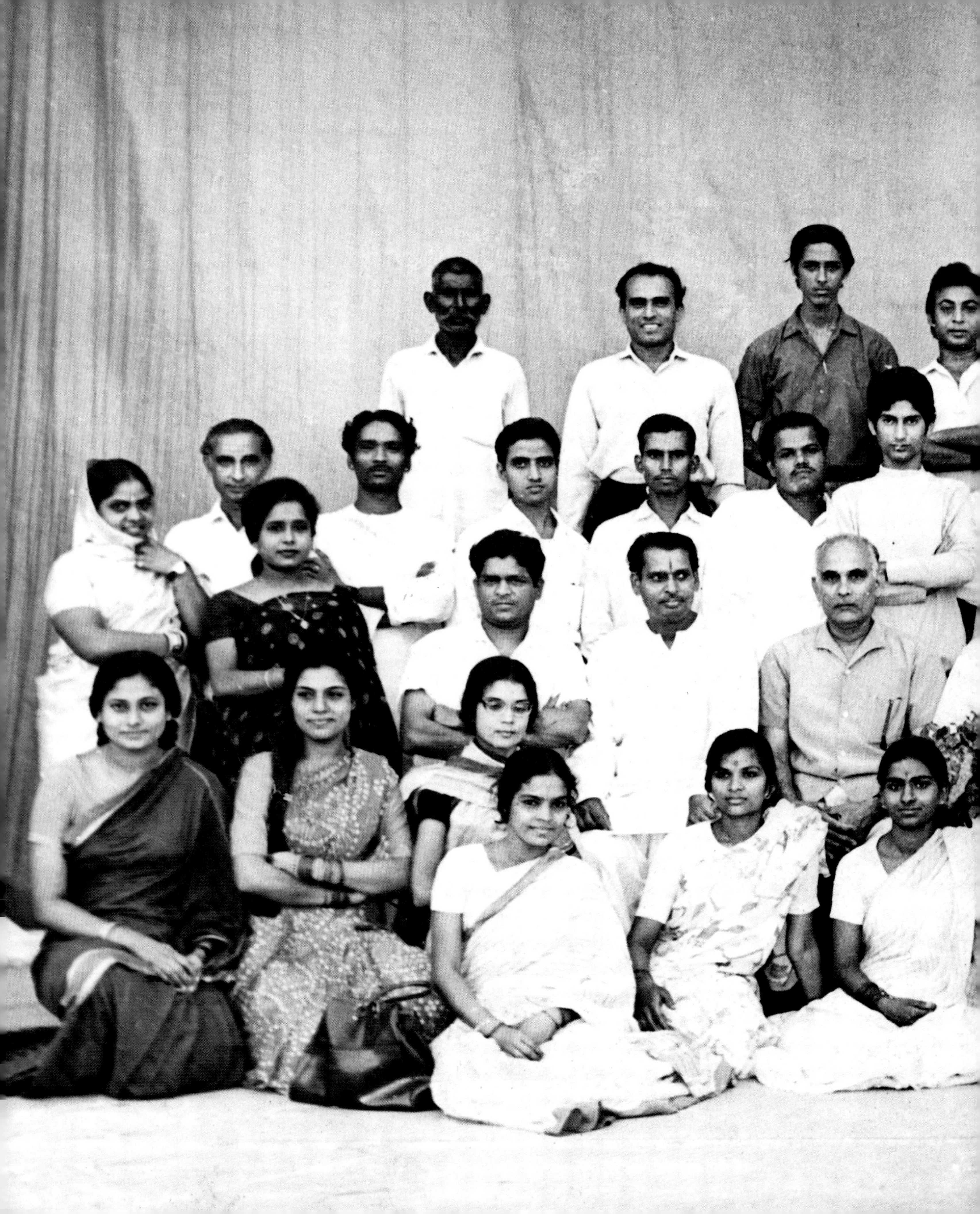

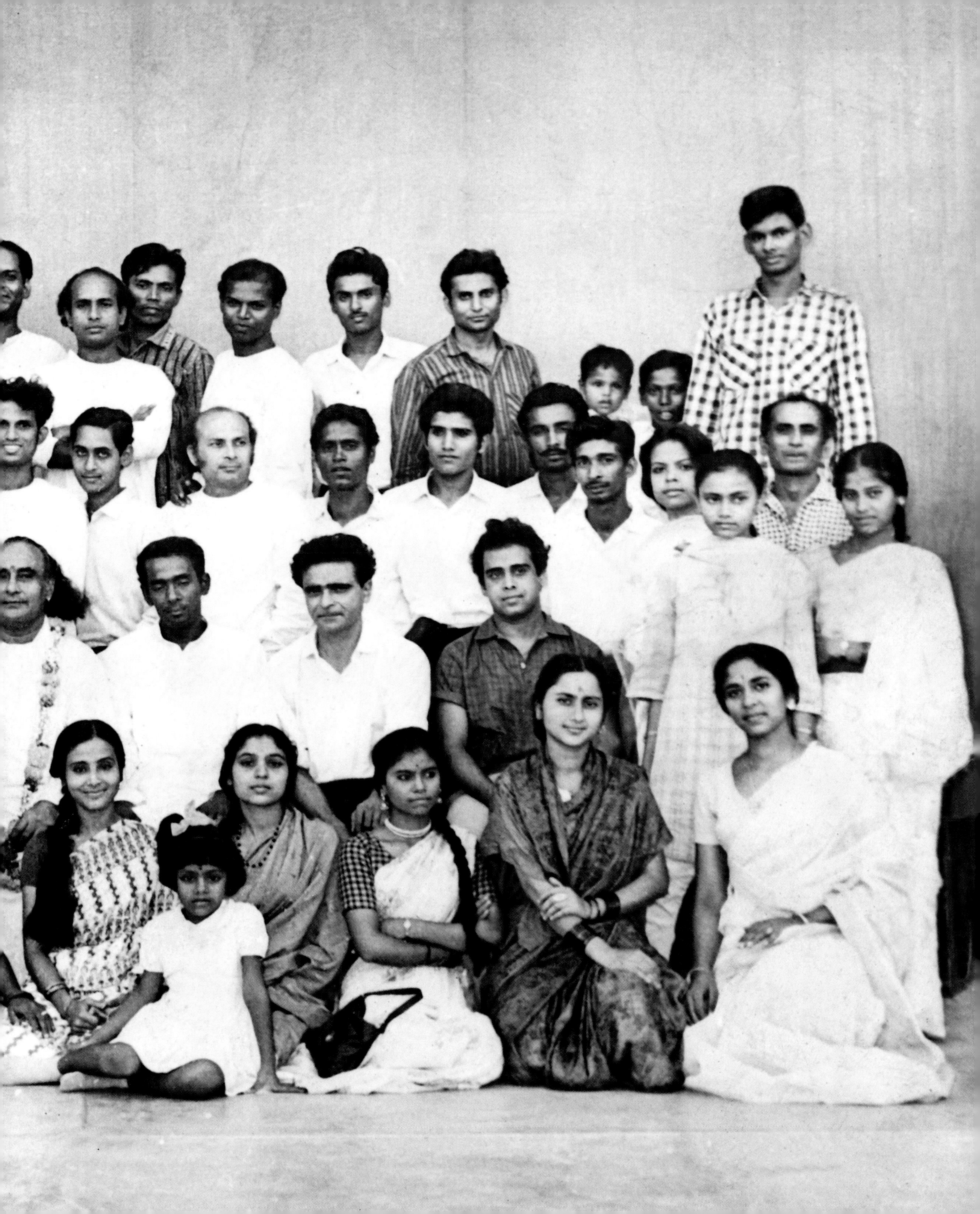

Under the patronage of the
Prime Minister, Pt. JAWAHARLAL NEHRU

BHARATIYA KALA KENDRA

Presents

RAM LILA

(A Ballet based on Tulsidas's Ramcharit Manas)

with all its glory and splendour
Produced Jointly By

National Ballet Centre & Bharatiya Kala Kendra

From September 15th to 18th (Daily at 7 p.m.)

at FOOTBALL STADIUM, Delhi Gate, Delhi

Rates of Tickets Rs 5|- 2|- and 1|-

Tickets Available At: Pt Brothers, Chandni Chowk,
Pt. Brothers, Connaught Place.
Daurala Shop 16, Lodi Market
Triplex, 5W|1, West Patel Nagar
New Delhi and at the Gate

The organisation regrets that due to heavy rains shows for the 12th, 13th & 14th September have had to be cancelled. Tickets and invitations for these days are valid for the 15th

H.S.T. 15.9.57

who designed wonderful stage sets. It was Razdan who devised the split-level stage and revolving ones for the 'Ramlila', which helped in changing scenes quickly: thus the Court of Dashratha, with a quick spin, became the Panchvati; the splendours of Ravana's Court in Lanka became a burning city in a swift transition.

The 'Ramlila' itself had attracted the best talents in every field: for choreography, after Narendra Sharma's initial foray, the foundations for solid productions along classical dance lines were laid by the Kathakali maestro, Guru Gopinath, who himself played the role of Hanuman. After him, the practice of inviting guest choreographers such as Debendra Shankar and Yog Sunder was established. Soon thereafter, the ballet artists themselves started helping in choreography and graduated from being artists to becoming choreographers. Krishnan Namboodri continued and later K. Shekharan Panikar had a long innings. After him, the production was so established and set that no choreographer was really needed and principal participants, like Bhushan Lakhandri, themselves undertook the dual roles of acting and directing.

Against this scene, the stage was literally set. Thus entered a long line of dancers associated with the 'Ramlila' production: Bhagwandas Verma as Rama, later enacted by Hirendranath Kundu, Pratap Pawar, Raghavan Nair and Bhushan Lakhandri. Sita was portrayed by many: Jayanti Sharma, followed by Saroj Sen, Uma Sharma, Rani Karna, Aloka Panikar, Surinder Kaur, Vishnupriya Pawar, Chandra Makkar, Rekha Shankar. Ravana was initially performed by Narendra Sharma himself and later by Chandrakant, Keshavan Namboodri, Shambhu Bhattacharya, Krishnan Namboodri, K. Shekharan Panikar and Tinkoo.

Many artists remember their 'Ramlila' days fondly. Says Aloka Panikar, now a senior Orissi dancer: 'I had merely gone to learn dance and the fact that I one day became Sita was only because Sumitraji prevailed and insisted that I be made Sita! I was thin and petite, demure and small, and Sumitraji felt this brought out the helplessness of Sita appropriately. Over the years, she encouraged me tremendously and many years down the road, my daughter, Ambikaa, became Sita in her turn. It was quite funny because when I was Sita, my husband Shekhar Panikar enacted Ravana. Most people who knew this were amused and wondered how he could abduct his own wife! And when my daughter, Ambikaa played Sita, many joked that she was safe with him (he still performed the role of Ravana) for he was her father! Sumitraji helped me become a solo artist and even today, despite changes in time and circumstances, whenever I leave India for my travels abroad, I seek her blessings. I know, she is genuinely sincere at heart.'

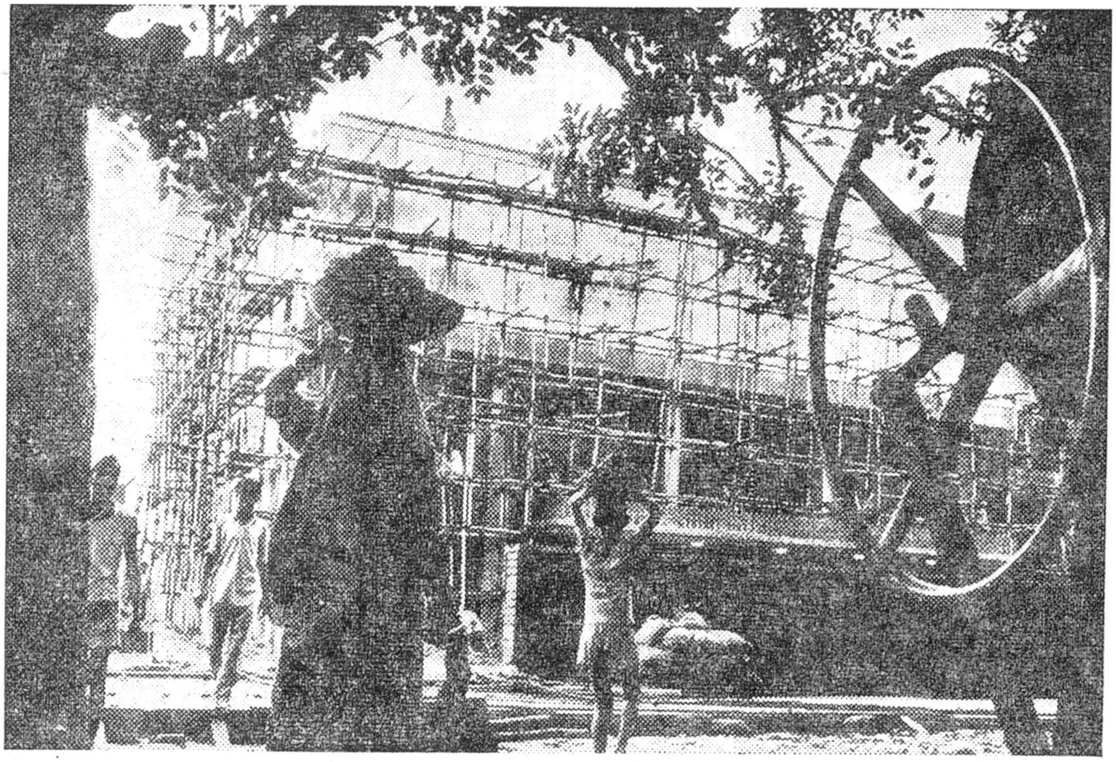

The Bharatiya Kala Kendra auditorium in New Delhi being given finishing touches.—Statesman.

KALA KENDRA'S GYPSY DAYS ARE OVER

BY A STAFF REPORTER

THE Bharatiya Kala Kendra has never had a convocation. Not for lack of students, but because there was no auditorium where a convocation could be held. Neither did this college of music and drama, founded in 1952, have a place to call its own. Makeshift arrangements had to suffice. And until recently, its members were literally performers in search of an auditorium.

The gypsy days of wandering are now over. On August 22 Mr Giri will inaugurate the Bharatiya Kala Kendra's new auditorium and the next day the belated laurels and diplomas will be given.

Kamani auditorium, as it has been named, is getting the finishing touches and workers are racing against time to get it ready for the inauguration. The auditorium, with a seating capacity of 650, is an impressive structure which has cost Rs 16 lakhs. It forms a prominent part of the complex forming the Bharatiya Kala Kendra. Sprawling over a two-acre plot on Lytton Lane—in the heart of the city's cultural arena —the Kendra has, in addition to the auditorium, a teaching block and a hostel for students and the staff.

The outstanding feature of the auditorium is its stage. Large by any standards with its 48-foot opening, it will do justice to all enactments of epics depicting armies in full strength and with arrangements to project sound effects through two 280-watt speakers directly above the stage. The best in sound is ensured by the fact that there is no exposed concrete surface that might cause sound reverberations. The walls are covered with plywood or plaster of Paris to provide the best in acoustics.

Another special feature of the auditorium is its "flying system" for manipulation of curtains and sets. There are 21 pipes connected by pulleys and counterweights, spanning the 40-foot-depth of the stage, and can operate 21 curtains and scene sets simultaneously. The number of pipes is just 11 short of that in the Vienna State Opera, believed to be the world's largest stage.

An innovation in the auditorium is the control room above the balcony which affords a frontal view of the stage. A mobile intercom system enables the stage manager to communicate with technical personnel and the performers from any point in the hall. Behind the wings, in the hall or the control room, he has a direct line with the performers on stage or in the rehearsal hall or the greenrooms in the basement.

For the spectators in the hall, chairs slope considerably towards the stage making sure that heads do not get in the way. And the show, does not have to be "live"—there is a permanent place for a 35 mm film projector.

The Stage is Set

'It was our President, S.K. Patil, who knew industrialist Ramjibhai Hansraj Kamani, who was keen to donate some money to an arts complex. Ideally, he desired to create his own institution but he had no land. We had land but no money to build! I had known Kamani *bhai* but did not know he had this secret desire. When Patil Sahib informed me, I felt it would be a worthy collaboration. Soon after, a sum of seven and a half lakh rupees was given to us for the construction of an auditorium, the only condition being that it should bear his name. Ultimately, the Kamani Auditorium cost us over twenty lakh rupees and in the meantime, there were hints or suggestions from within our family that the money taken from the Kamanis be returned, even with interest, if necessary. I would not accept any of that, firstly because Kamani *bhai* had come forward in the time of need and more importantly, because he was no more. I wanted his memory to stay.'

During the travels of industrialist Charat Ram abroad, occasionally his wife Sumitra joined him. Such a tour to America provided the impetus to her understanding of stage design and crafts which she utilised while setting up the Kamani Auditorium. 'It was at the Lincoln Centre in New York, where I was most inspired because it was such a community effort. Dr Young, the Director, informed us that each chair in their main auditorium was donated by a corporate house; the giant chandelier was a gift from Austria; silk from China; mosaics from Egypt and lights from the Netherlands. I was also very impressed with the Carnegie Hall. Since my Almora days, I had seen the Uday Shankar Studio come up and I was very interested in creating an excellent art facility. So when the plans for Kamani were drawn up, I had certain ideas which in view of our realities in India had to be toned down but Kamani nevertheless stood as one of the best halls, with a separate orchestra pit (the first in Delhi then), plentiful green-room space and a stage which could open up from behind to let in a truck or an elephant! Just before the opening, I fell ill and was plagued by the thought of how it would get completed on time. My husband, Charat, took full responsibility and it stood completed on time for the President to inaugurate.' Kamani was inaugurated on August 22, 1971 by the then President of India, Shri V.V. Giri. For the occasion, M.S. Subbulakshmi rendered her soulful music.

◀ *A home for the artists, finally! With the acquisition and construction of the Kendra building on Copernicus Marg, the institution came to life.*

After two decades of being homeless like wandering minstrels, the Kendra finally had a complex of its own which could be called home. It had moved from place to place: from the Curzon Road *kothi* to Pusa Road house, Ferozeshah hutments, Mata Sundari Road flats, Jawaharlal Nehru Road and finally to Lytton Road, now named Copernicus Marg. Although the construction on the 1.7 acres of land commenced in 1966 with the Teaching and Residential Blocks, the Kendra officers, college and staff moved into the new premises on January 1, 1970. And within another twenty months, the new addition, the Kamani Auditorium, stood inaugurated.

Kamani ushered in a phase of professional theatre going. The hall itself denoted excellence in acoustics, logistics, lights, curtains and wings. In itself, the Kamani set the tone for how halls were to be constructed thereafter and others followed suit. The Shriram Centre for Arts and Culture catering to puppets and drama, the FICCI (Federation of Indian Chambers of Commerce and Industry) and much later the Siri Fort Auditorium. It is interesting to note that the team which created Kamani, was called upon some ten years later, by the then Prime Minister of India, Rajiv Gandhi, to create the Siri Fort Auditorium, the biggest in Delhi seating 2000 plus. The Kamani Auditorium stood as a testimony and a test of the times.

Kathak Kendra Separates

Since its initial years, the Kendra had platformed Kathak. The Sangeet Natak Akademi supported it with a grant just as it supported several other institutions all over the country. Over the years, the Kathak section of the Kendra had become synonymous with the institution. 'It was thus a shock when in 1972, barely a year after Kamani had opened and we could offer a professional environment for our productions, most of which were in the Kathak mould, that the Sangeet Natak Akademi decided to undertake direct control of the Kathak Kendra and wished it housed separately. The irony was that for over two decades we had nurtured it and at one swift go, the Akademi felt that the setup needed to be independent of us. What was more amusing was that the new location for housing the Kathak Kendra was bang opposite our institution, in the Bhawalpur House. Upset as we were, at this turn of events, I felt the artists would stand to benefit by the security provided by a government job. Ultimately, it was keeping that in view that we let go; although for me personally it was like a limb being cut off from our body.'

'The biggest achievement of the Bharatiya Kala Kendra was its resurrection of Kathak', notes Keshav Kothari, one-time student of the Kendra, later to serve the Sangeet Natak Akademi and the Kathak Kendra in an administrative position.

History is the best judge of circumstance: today, three decades down the road, while the Kendra continues to flower having turned its energies in other directions, the Kathak Kendra has been gradually reduced to a hotbed of controversy and poor management It is now like just any other government-run institution and whatever little creative output and excellence it showed was due largely to the presence of Pandit Birju Maharaj.

'In India, everyone, nearly everyone, desires to build an institution. While the thought is laudable, it is not so easy to build one. More difficult than building is its maintenance and continuance. And institutions are not mere buildings; it is made up of artists, a committed group of people who spend

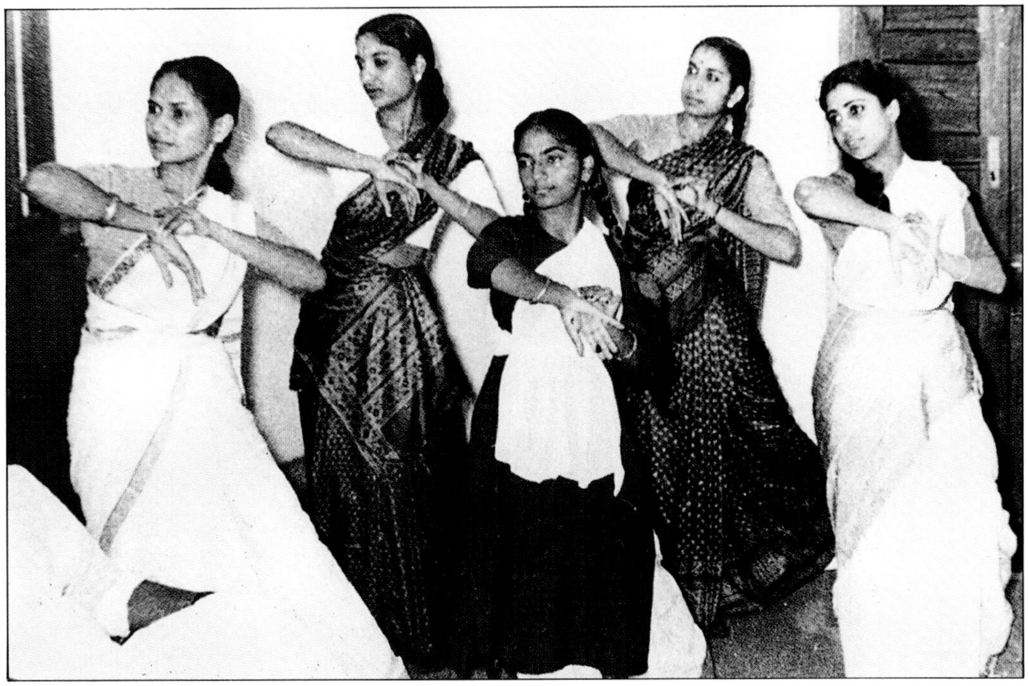

Left to right: A Kathak class featuring Kumudini Lakhia, Maya Rao, Bharti Gupta among others.

a lifetime nurturing and supporting it. But for them, an institution will remain a mere physical space. In our case, I am deeply satisfied to see how this institution grew. People, artists, *rasiks* came from all nooks and corners of the world to help contribute to this institution,' acknowledges Sumitra Charat Ram gratefully.

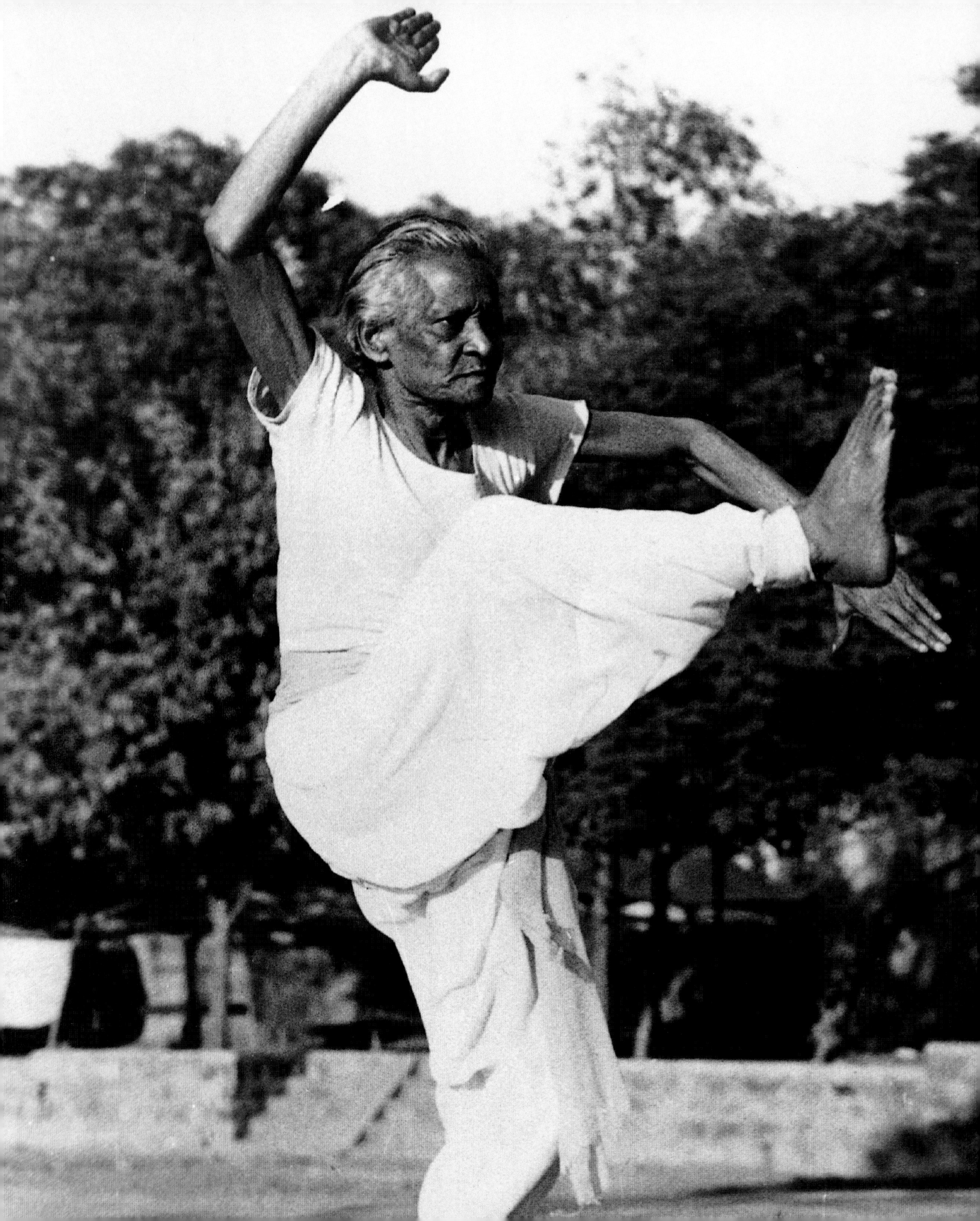

Efflorescence

The new directions the Kendra undertook largely coincided with the emergence of a new generation. Shobha, the fourteen year-old-girl who accompanied her mother to the first show of 'Ramlila' in 1957, had grown to assume responsibility. Having tried her hand in the corporate world, she felt her interest lay in artistic pursuits. It was thus that Sumitra Charat Ram felt that Shobha could initially help her and then assume charge, if she showed potential and aptitude. 'Had Shobha not shown an interest, I had already thought of dedicating the institution to the nation. By which I mean that I did not desire to control or continue forever and certainly had no interest in projecting or promoting any of my offspring, unless, they measured up to the task. Since childhood, Shobha had shown an artistic inclination: she learnt dance, stayed with artists and generally was well disposed to art activity.'

In the seventies, Shobha started by designing costumes for the productions of the Kendra. 'It was a learning experience to see Shekharji and others at work and to see how with simple means and material one could transform things into great beauty. Personally, I wanted to use new materials like velcrom for binding jewellery or for costumes. This was necessary because most artists undertook different roles in a production, calling for quick change in costume, without also spoiling the make-up. So, backstage there was no time for taking off an entire costume slowly and for retouching make-up. It sounds simple but it is a reality: in a scene in 'Ramlila', Sita is all decked up one minute, befitting her queenly status and in the next, she is banished to the forest. There are less than two minutes for her to change. I studied the problems backstage and tried to make suitable provisions.'

For long the Kendra had concentrated on mythological themes. At that point in time when India was a young nation, and its heritage and history needed platforming, it was important to do that. In the late seventies and early eighties however, the country had established itself as a leading power in the region, the largest democracy in the world and an important world player, internationally. It was time to chart new courses and it was thus with this spirit in mind that under Shobha, the Kendra undertook new themes like 'Masks' and 'Karn'. Soon other productions on different themes followed.

◀ *Chhau guru Krishan Chand Nayak whose presence at the Kendra helped further the art form.*

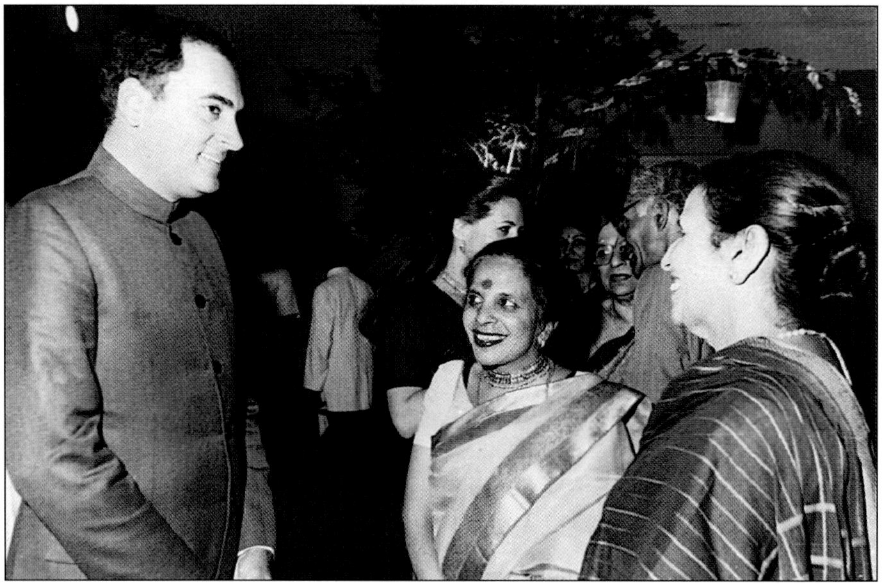

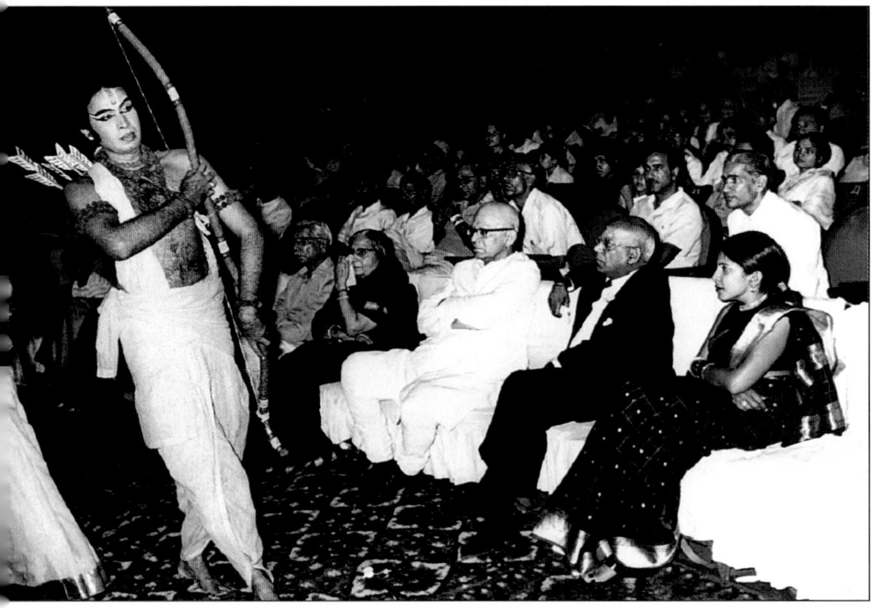

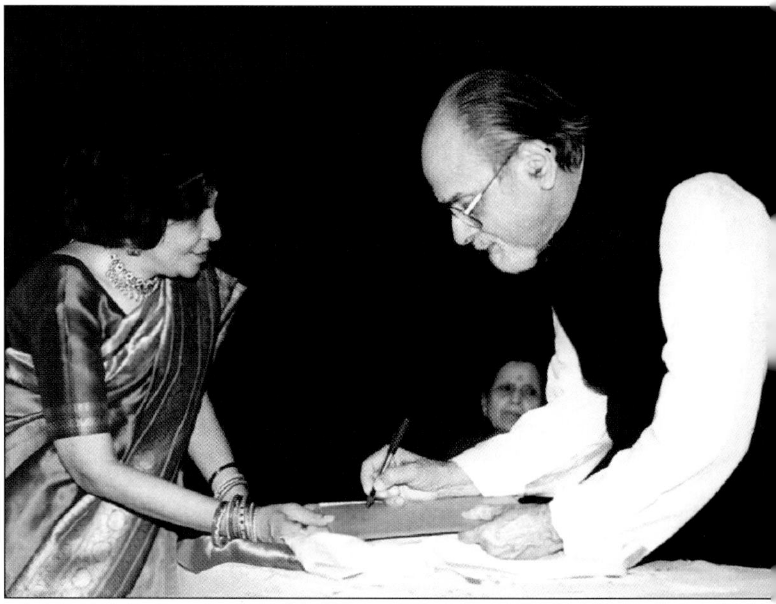

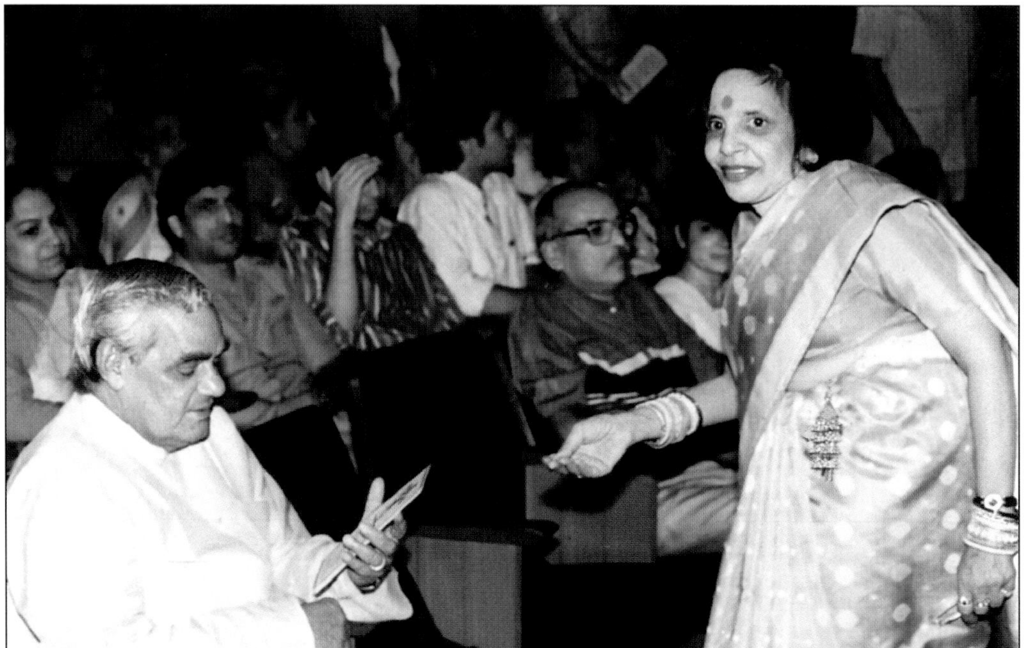

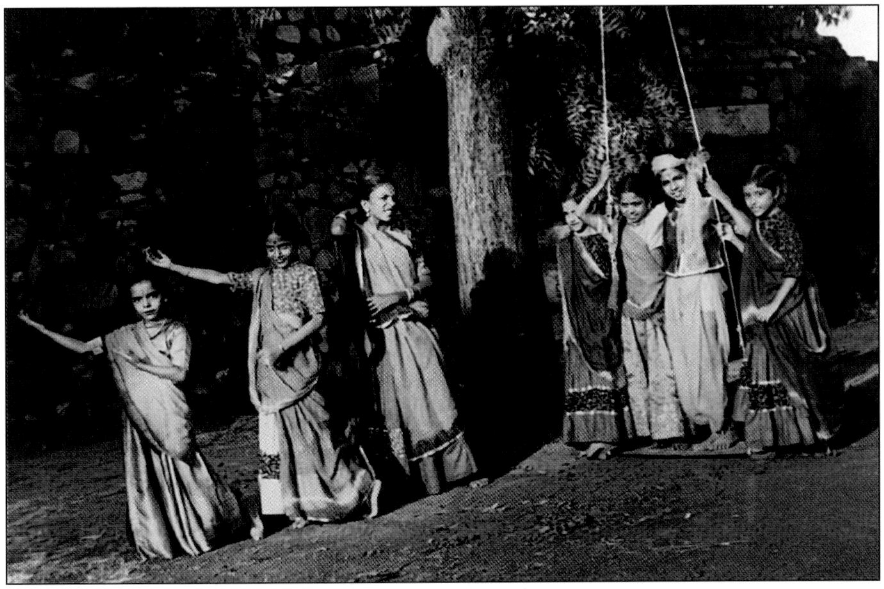

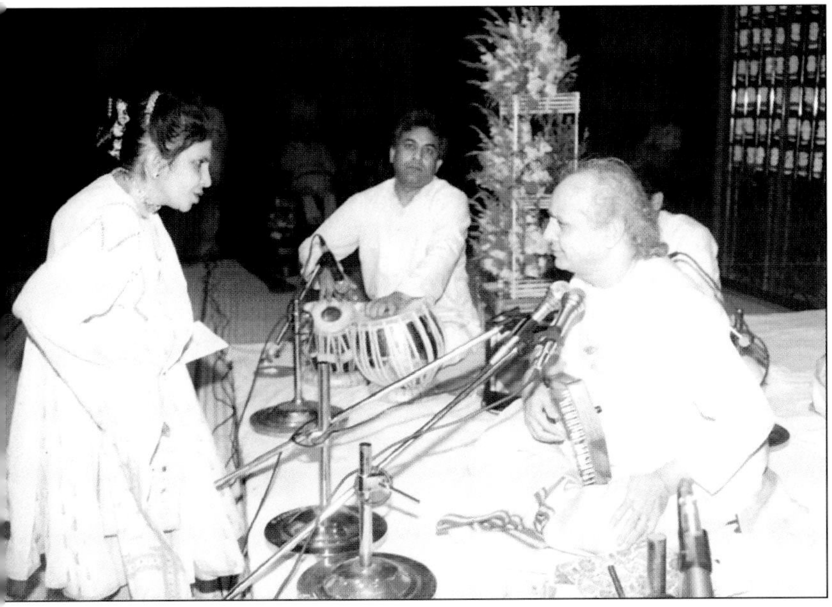

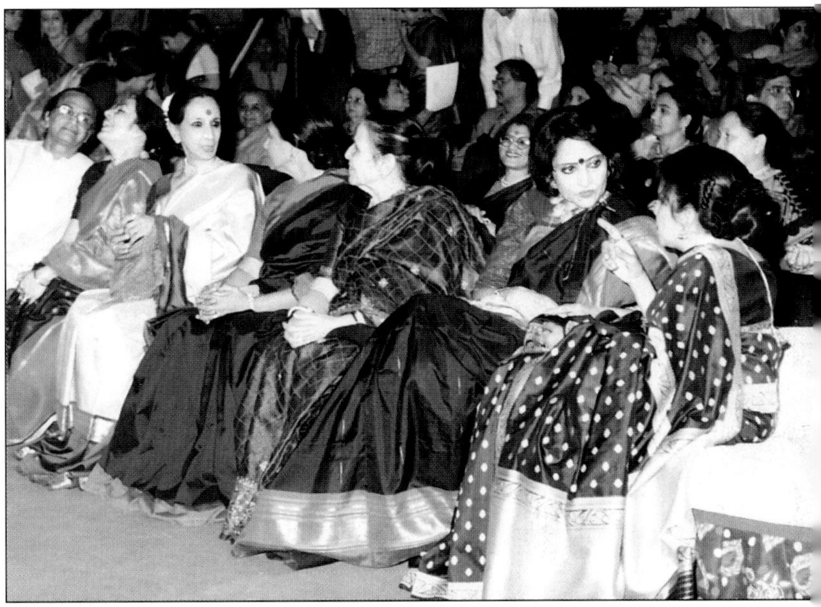

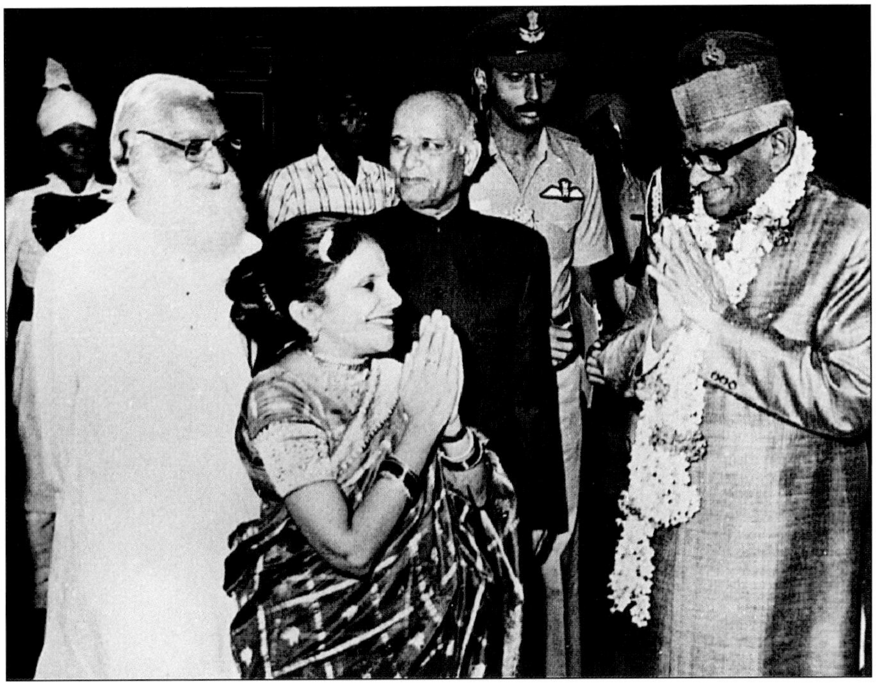

SHOBHA DEEPAK SINGH, THE FOURTEEN-YEAR OLD WHO ACCOMPANIED HER MOTHER TO THE FIRST 'RAMLILA' SHOW IN 1957, TODAY STRIDES TOWARDS NEARLY THIRTY YEARS OF ASSOCIATION WITH AND SERVICE TO THE KENDRA.

Changes came about in the directions the Kendra set for itself. Having supported Kathak, it felt the need to support other forms. Under a scheme initiated by the Sangeet Natak Akademi then under Mohan Khokar, senior gurus of lesser known forms were identified and attached to different institutions for 2-3 years.

Guru Krishna Chandra Nayak of Mayurbhanj had served at the Little Theatre Group, Gwalior, and after his term was finished, the Akademi approached several institutions like Mrinalini Sarabhai's Darpana. Only the Kendra agreed to avail itself of the scheme. It was thus that Mayurbhanj Chhau as a form was to get much larger notice, especially when the Kendra used it to create new productions like 'Jagdeo' (1977), 'Konark' (1978), 'Kalinga Vijaya' (1979) and 'Khajuraho' (1980) among others.

Guru Krishan Chand Nayak helped train a number of students such as Daksha Sheth, Ranjana Gauhar, Shashidharan Nair , Bhushan Lakhandri and Bharat Sharma, who furthered the form and, more importantly, progressed in their own art. Today, if they are established names in the field of choreography and dance-direction, it is in no small measure to the credit of the Kendra in general and the late Guru Krishnan Chand Nayak, in particular.

Likewise, efforts at platforming Orissi as early as the sixties caught the imagination of several enthusiasts who undertook a career in Orissi, then in its infancy. It was thanks to the efforts of Guru Deba Prasad Das and his prize pupil, Indrani Rehman that Orissi could be seen outside Orissa. Although Orissi was being formalised by the four leading lights—Guru Pankaj Charan Das, Guru Kelucharan Mahapatra, Guru Deba Prasad Das and Guru Mayadhar Raut—it was still limited to Orissa. In fact, a few of its main proponents like Sanjukta Panigrahi and Mayadhar Raut had gone to Kalakshetra in Madras to learn Bharata Natyam. Orissi as a mainstream classical dance was not established and as early as in the mid-fifties, the Sangeet Natak Akademi's National Seminar on Dance did not take cognizance of Orissi as one of the principal classical dance styles of India.

It was thanks to the efforts of critic Charles Fabri and dance historian Mohan Khokar, whose visits to Orissa and subsequent platforming through writings, helped establish the form. In Delhi, Guru Deba Prasad Das taught at the Bharatiya Kala Kendra. 'It was in fact, in the Mata Sundari Road tenements that few of us had an interest in taking private classes in Orissi from Harekrishna Behera', recalls Aloka Panikar, who went on to become a reputed Orissi exponent.

After Guru Deba Prasad Das, Guru Mayadhar Raut proved to be the fulcrum of the form at the Kendra and he prepared such excellent students as Aloka Panikar, Kiran Segal and Ranjana Gaur among others. Of these, Aloka Panikar taught at the Kendra and later Mayadhar Raut's brother-in-law, Dibankar Khuntia, continued the work. After a hiatus of ten years, Aloka Panikar returned to the institution, recently. The Kendra thus focussed its attention on Orissi and helped make it accessible and popular.

The Bharata Natyam classes started much later largely because 'there were too many institutions and dancers teaching this form already'. It was only when a sparkling specimen of the form, Leela Samson, agreed to teach in the mid-seventies that the form came to stay. Her disciple, Justin McCarthy, now continues teaching at the Kendra.

An interesting experiment undertaken in the mid-seventies was the opening of the Jhankar Chamber Theatre where every evening some artists could be presented. 'This happened owing to the growing demand from tourist companies and agencies, who felt there ought to be one institution where every evening some Indian dance and music can be witnessed. Delhi

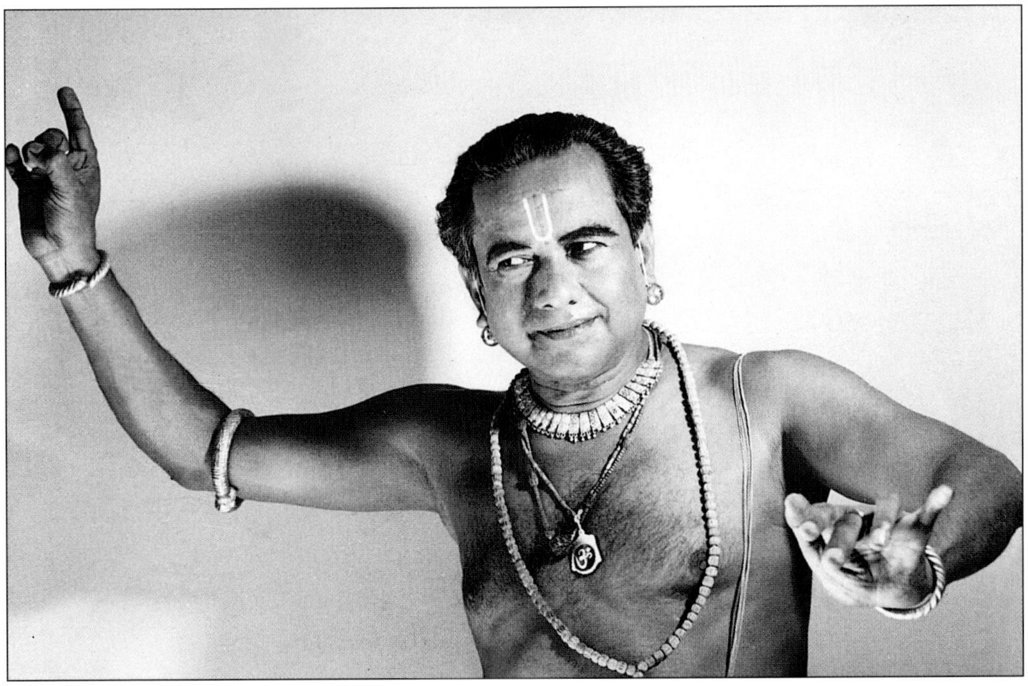

A founding father of Orissi dance as seen today, Guru Mayadhar Raut's art contains lyricism and beauty.

had so many institutions at that point but none were doing this service, except the Triveni occasionally. The tourist trade needed continuous inputs, not seasonal. So we decided to platform upcoming and senior artists and in this task, Kumudini Lakhia's stay with us helped,' reminisces Sumitra Charat Ram. After a few years of functioning the theatre had to be demolished because it seems the municipality did not give permission for this additional construction!

An intimate music session with maestros like Pt. Mallikarjun Mansoor involves all— (clockwise) S. Kalidas, Arts Editor of the Pioneer, Sharbari Mukharjee, Secretary of the Sangeet Natak Akademi, Biswajeet Roy Chaudhry, sarodist and Shobha Deepak Singh. ▶

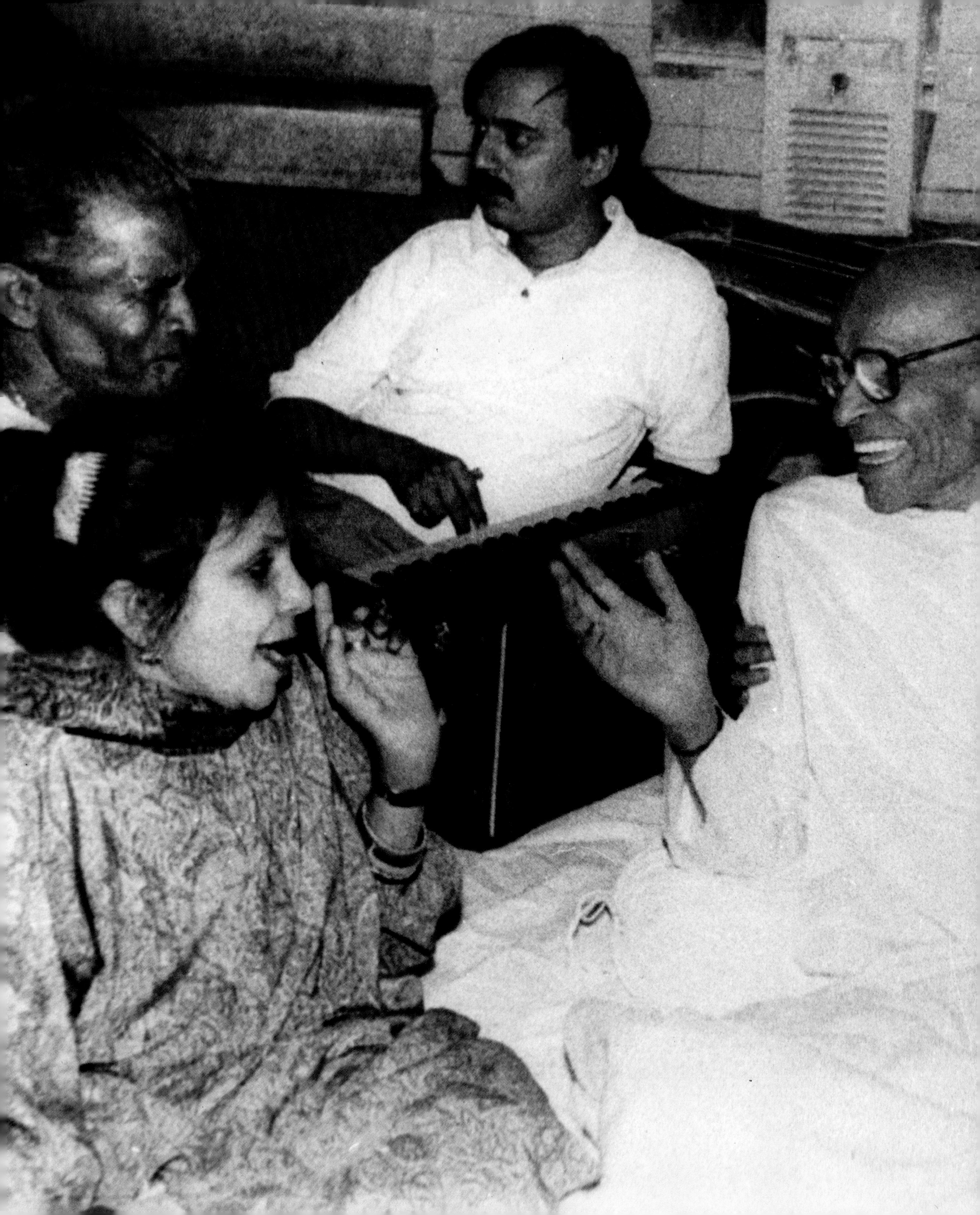

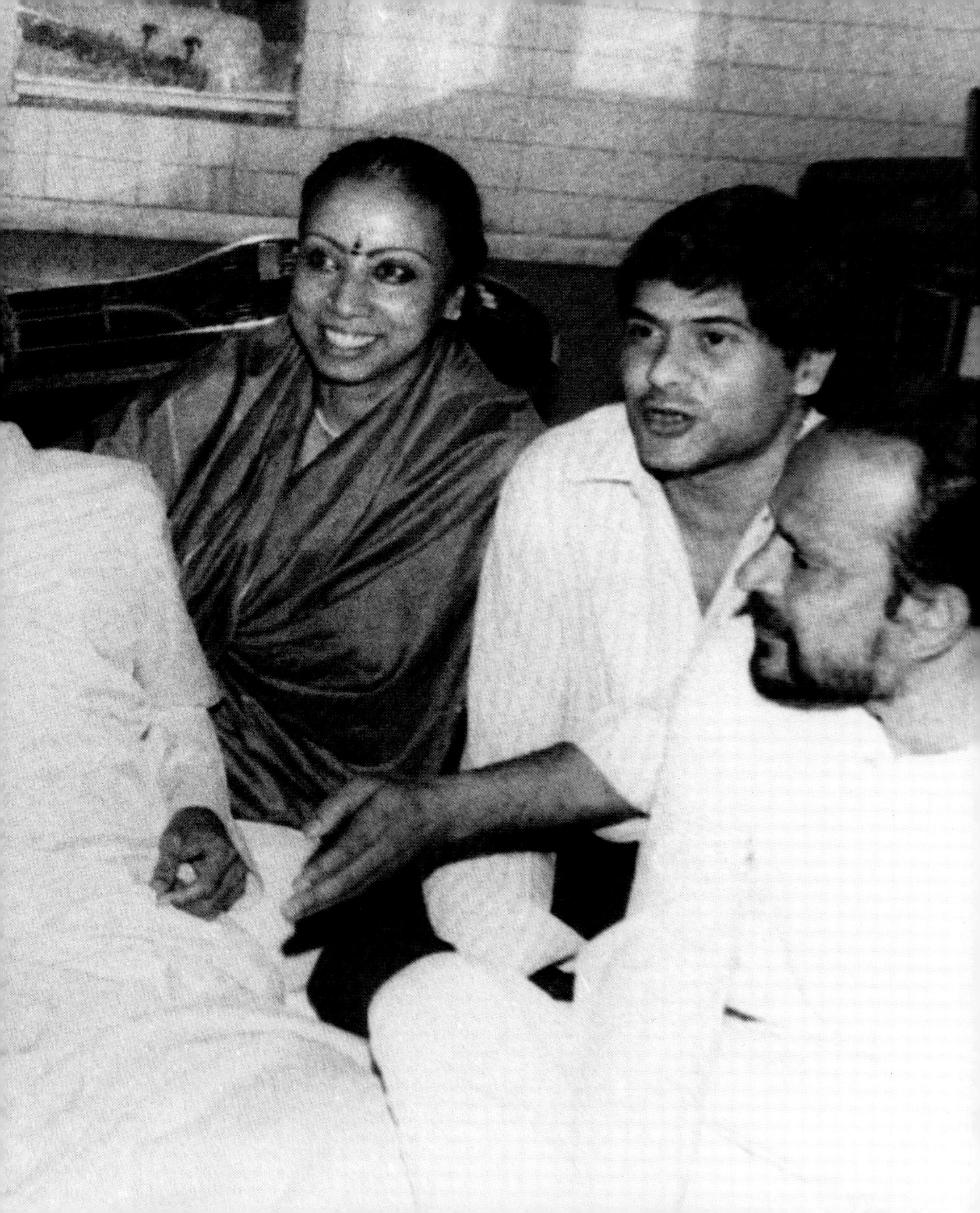

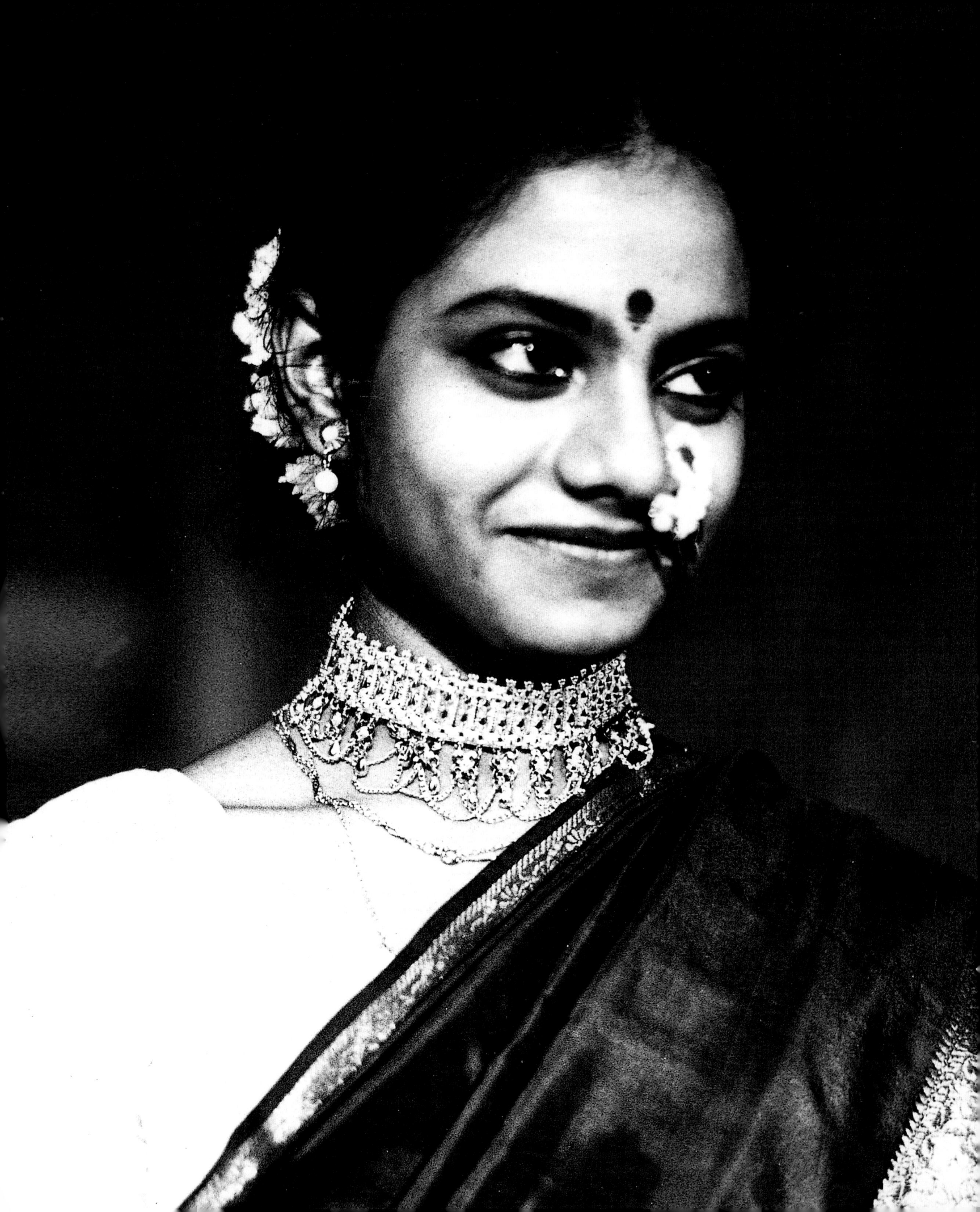

Reminiscenses

Artists are very often emotional people. They can easily come under the influence of others, as was the case with the two strikes at the Kala Kendra. The first strike, towards the end of the sixties had a motivator in Ashok Bajpayi of Doordarshan. Artists such as Pratap Pawar, Sushil Sharma and Rahiji would sit in a *pandaal* outside the building and shout slogans. My husband provided total support and security, so I actually had nothing to fear. One day, as I was entering the building, they asked me to come inside their tent, to cross the *Lakshman-rekha*. I went in and sat with them. I told them there was no *Lakshman-rekha* in Tulsidas's *Ramacharitmanas,* which they were reading. I also asked them to read a *prasang* from the Dharma Chakra, a passage in which Rama voices the need for support in fighting Ravana. The following day, the strike was over.

The second strike was many years later in 1984; I was not allowed to handle it by some family members who said they were familiar with unions and that they would settle it. If I had been allowed to intercede, I'm sure the strike would have been settled as amicably as the first one. At the end of this one everyone lost, however. We, in terms of a disrupted 'Ramlila' and other shows. The artists got their dues in the end, but at tremendous cost. It is my greatest regret that I was not allowed to talk to the striking artists, who were led by Subhash Dutta, Shekharan Panikaar, Barun Gupta and others.

In the running of an institution, sometimes harsh decisions have to be taken in the larger interest of all concerned. An artist can arrive drunk or misbehave with girls. This needs to be corrected. My task has been to be a mother figure. In this respect my hands have been tied, which I consider a shortcoming in my running of the Kendra. I have always been personally involved with the welfare of artists. Their births, deaths, weddings and children. There are countless occasions when artists would seek my help. Sometimes I wonder if God created me only for attending funerals and births. Like the time when Shambhu Maharaj died after a long illness. I went to the hospital and asked that his body be brought to the Kendra where everyone could pay their respects. I saw to it that the various ceremonies connected with his death were attended to. If I could help anyone, I did. For Mohan Upreti, I had to match-make, asking his future

◀ *Orissi artist Ambikaa Panikar who danced the role of Sita, in a theatre production: 'Ghasiram Kotwal'.*

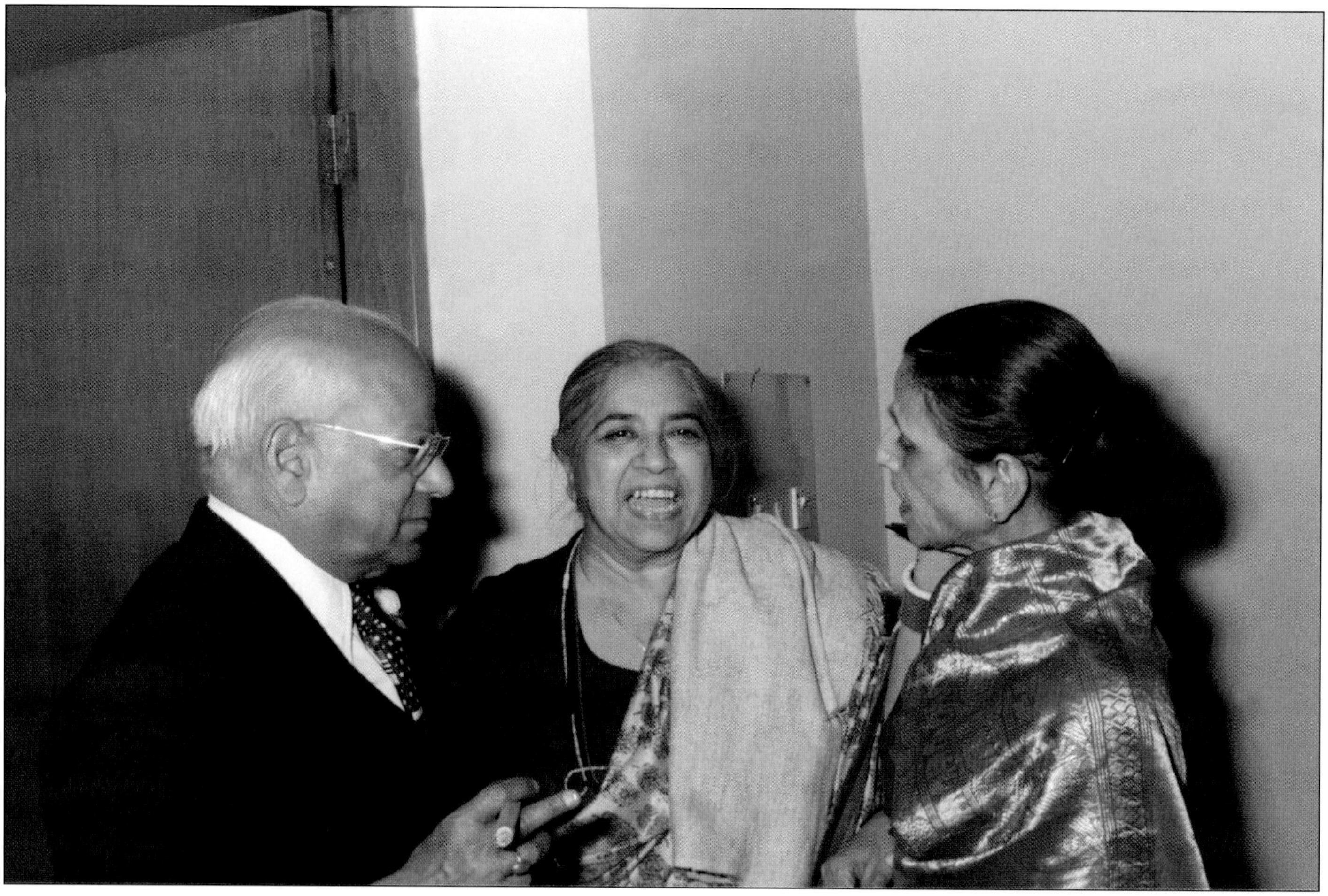

Dharam Vira, late Pupul Jayakar and Sumitra Charat Ram exchange notes.

mother-in-law for her daughter, Naima's hand. Being a Muslim, the mother was against it. Rita Kothari was already married and was learning music at our institution when she fell for Keshav Kothari and subsequently married him.

It is not my ego: I simply feel if God has given me this possibility to help, why not? My father taught me that no one should leave your doorstep empty-handed. My brother Dharam Vira is the very personification of this magnanimity or munificence. His name comes from Dharam Nagari. This title was given to a group of villages, like Meer near Mandawar, acquired by my father whose charitable and philanthropic deeds was the reason for the area being called Dharam Nagari. Thus when my *bhabhi*, Dharam Vira's wife, complained of his selfless help to one and all, I told her it was my father's blessings to Dharam *bhai* that were being manifested.

When Siddheswari Devi had to be admitted to hospital, the then Secretary of the Sangeet Natak Akademi, Mohan Khokar, rang me up past midnight to say she was ill and in urgent need of help. His hands were tied administratively and at that hour he could not do anything officially. I stepped in and she was admitted and attended to. It may sound like self-praise but people realised that I was genuinely interested in the welfare of artists and the arts, not my own glory.

I also wanted to see Shekhar Panikar when he was ill and Aloka Panikar after she had a nasty accident, but I could only go when he had died. Even then, I went to offer *Shradhanjali,* largely because he had served the Kendra and served so well. How can I forget his years of work and contribution to its enrichment?

So it came to pass that over all these years, my fifth child blossomed and bloomed and occasionally fell ill. But through it all, the Kendra had become a home for arts and artists. When people praised its work, when people respected my artists, I felt a sense of pride. I had not planned it at all, but by God's grace it indeed became a centre for the arts, a true 'Kala Kendra'.

The seeds then sown have grown into a mighty oak. Today, in the nineties, Guru Krishna Chandra Nayak's ace disciple Shashidharan Nair has graduated from student to star-chorographer, under the direction of Shobha Deepak Singh. They have created productions like 'Cakravyuhu' and 'Parikrama'. Shobha's talent in photography has helped her document the Kendra productions, as also win critical acclaim from none other than the grand old man of theatre, Ebrahim Alkazi, under whom she also studied theatre administration.

Today, any number of stars in the field of music, dance or choreography are either the products of the Kendra or have had some professional link with the institution. That the Kendra has helped further the arts and artists is best evident from the scores of artists and art-activity it has 'produced' (see Appendix).

In the nineties, the Kendra focussed, with renewed energy, on the revitalising and revival of its core activities, like the celebration of its Founder's Day on Basant Panchami (coinciding with that of Sumitra Charat Ram's Alma Mater, the Benaras Hindu University), celebration of Holi through a Mela and by new presentations of its age-old epic productions, the 'Ramlila' and 'Krishnalila'.

Shobha is supported by her husband Deepak Singh in the running of the Kendra and she has called on the talents of different disciplines to help her continue and expand the activities of the Kendra. I often tell my daughter not to emulate my shortcomings like bad temper and impatience, but to inculcate my one good quality which is believing in and giving credit to teamwork. More importantly, there is no need to pursue name or fame; your work should speak for itself. If it is deserving, it will win you attention and awards. To be with artists and people who love and live the arts, is reward enough for me.

Senior choreographer K. Shekharan Panikar. ▶

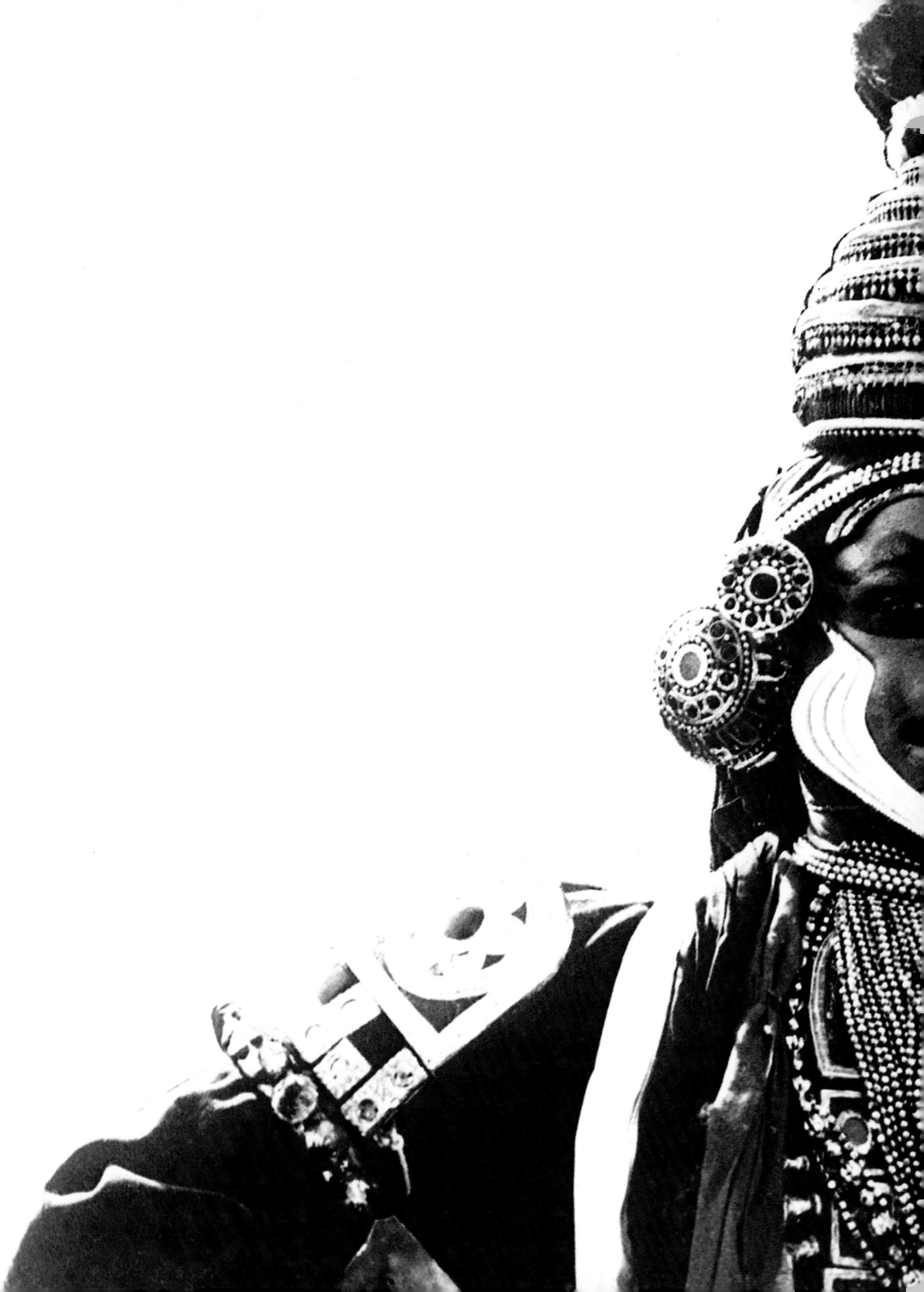

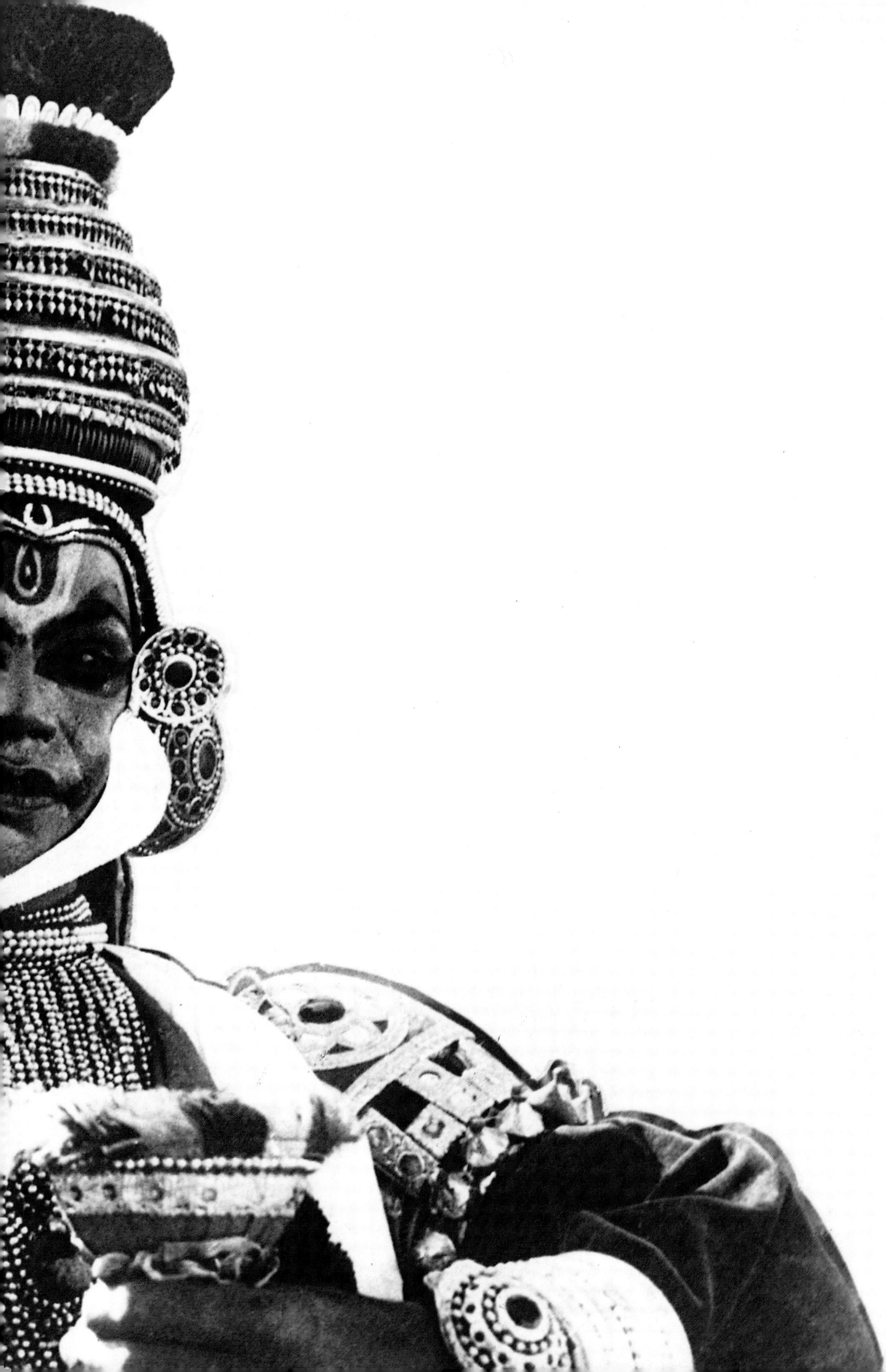

MAESTRO SHAMBHU MAHARAJ'S ILLNESS BECAME A CAUSE-CELEBRE AND AN ISSUE OF NATIONAL CONCERN.

AIIMS Hospital Out Patients Ticket

Name: Pt. Shambhu Maharaj

Age: 62

Sex: Male

Date 12 Aug. 1970: 8.30 a.m.

Pandit Shambhu Maharaj is suffering from acute left ventricular failure and needs immediate hospitalization. Delay in admission may endanger his life.

Because of his international fame he should be admitted in a private ward.

Prof. Sujoy B. Roy
Prof. & Head: Cardiology

P.M.'s aid for Kathak king's treatment

By A Staff Reporter

NEW DELHI August 17.

THE "King of Kathak", 63-year old Guru Shambhu Maharaj, has been admitted to a private ward in the All-India Institute of Medical Sciences.

The Guru had been refusing admission to hospital although gravely ill because he feared he might lose his month's pay and his family might remain unprovided for.

But the interest taken by the Prime Minister, Mrs. Indira Gandhi, who is Chairman of the Sangeet Natak Akademi, and Mr. Mohan Khokar, its acting Secretary, has given him assurance that his family would be looked after during his stay in the hospital.

The Prime Minister promptly sent a cheque for Rs. 1,000 for his immediate needs when she was informed about his condition.

Mr. Mohan Khokar took the Guru personally to the All-India Institute of Medical Sciences and got him admitted in a private ward.

Mr. Khokar also said that the Sangeet Natak Akademi, where the Guru is employed as a teacher in the Kathak Centre, was not indifferent to Shambhu Maharaj's plight.

He pointed out that two years ago when the Guru had a heart attack and had to be admitted to hospital the Akademi lost no time in making Rs. 1,000 available to him from its discretionary fund.

The Akademi was doing all that was possible to help the Guru.

The kind gesture of the Prime Minister and his colleagues at the Sangeet Natak Akademi, has reassured the Kathak King, that in his old age and his present grave condition there were those who thought of him with pride and affection.

Mainz Mayor calls on V. K. Malhotra

By A Staff Reporter

DELHI, August 17: Mr. Jockel Fuchs, Mayor of Mainz, West Germany, today called on Mr. V. K. Malhotra, Chief Executive Councillor. They exchanged ideas about the problems faced by the two cities, Mainz and Delhi, and their respective efforts to solve them.

babuji. T.O.I. 18.8.70

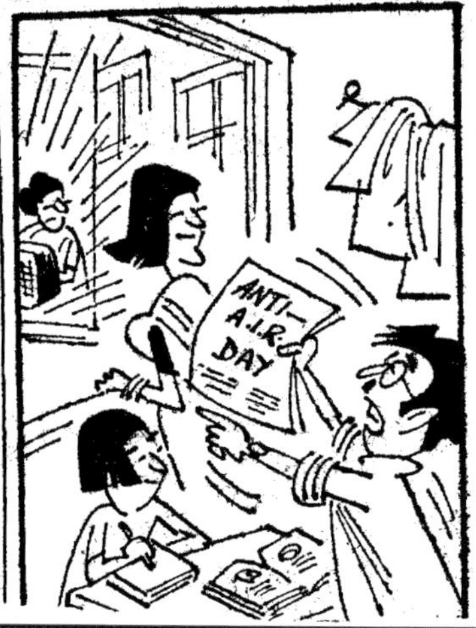

super... The... to the... in) pr... high-... police... Kh... worki... years, the h... ourers arrest... track, He police to pa... illegal howev... was a track... Kha... carryin... to anc... force t... was nc... way at... A t... labour... the ... Railwa... Nanda... tation... grieva... But i... police of the... report... mental... Mea... remai... for ov... return... ence...

Cultural institutions are not merely institutions for dance and music but culture itself. That needs to be understood and approached in a suitable manner. It is attitudes that are called cultured, not merely manifestations of artistic elements in a society at any given point in time.

The Story Continued

In the early years of this century court patronage for the arts was on the decline. This shift created immense problems for artists who were until then rather protected and provided for. Often, a patron in the form of a ruler or even a landowner took under his wing an Ustad or his family, bearing their entire responsibility. In return, these artists were attached to the courts and their benefactors. If a patron so desired, his children were trained in the art form, otherwise the artist's talents were for his own pleasure. Thus, this feudal set up in a way encouraged *gharana* artists to continue furthering and nurturing their art forms.

Once the country attained Independence and the feudal patrons slowly decreased, patronage shifted to the State and a means was evolved to support the arts and artists without the State directly interfering. India deliberately did not plan a cultural policy because the diversities inherent in India are immense. With the variety of people and languages, beliefs and religions, it was felt that culture and philosophy could not be promoted by an official policy. This was prudent on the part of the political leaders of the country, especially Pandit Nehru and Mrs. Gandhi, who left culture outside state control.

The country was young as an independent nation and the Government was setting up new institutions. By an Act of Parliament in 1953 the three national Akademis, the Sahitya Akademi for literature, the Lalit Kala Akademi for the fine arts and the Sangeet Natak Akademi for the performing arts were set up. Shortly thereafter, the Indian Council for Cultural Relations, under the vision of Maulana Azad, was created to deal with cultural exchange worldwide. Additional institutions of training like the National School of Drama, the new Kathak Kendra and the Jawaharlal Academy in Manipur came into being. By the sixties, Delhi began to be dotted with small art institutions specialising in different forms like the International Centre for Kathakali, the Odissi Kendra, and several Bharata Natyam training centres like the Bharata Natyam Academy run by Swarna Saraswathy. The Delhi administration set up its state academy the Sahitya Kala Parishad in 1969. In the seventies, the Ashok Hotel's cultural wing under Jaspal Singh did a lot to platform top artists and the pace was accelerated by the coming of age of several artists who taught their own styles or art forms. In the eighties this was carried further when several artists received land from the Government to build their own institutions. Thus, Yamini Krishnamurthy,

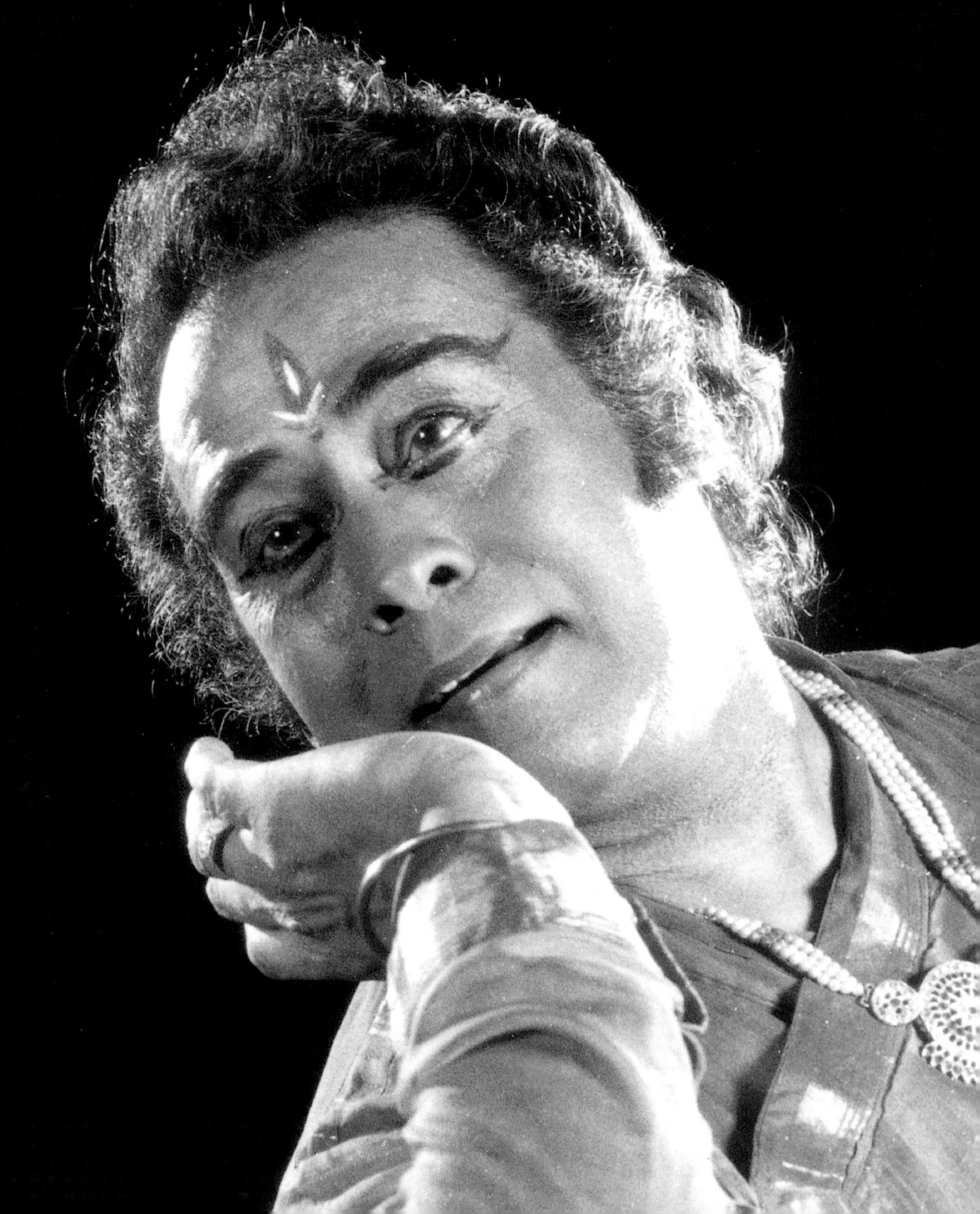

Birju Maharaj, Sonal Mansingh and ten others started to build their own institutions.

At the time of Independence the corporate sector was not organised and had no tradition of supporting the arts. More importantly, there was and still are very few incentives in the form of tax reliefs to the corporate sector. This left only individuals who could spearhead a revival of the arts, and the history of art institutions in post-Independence India abounds with examples of individuals who built and maintained institutions. Earlier, Tagore had built Santiniketan, Vallathol his Kerala Kalamandalam, and Rukmini Devi Arundale her Kalakshetra. Uday Shankar created the India Culture Centre and elsewhere many others worked unobtrusively and with dedication to build areas of excellence. 'It is for history to judge how far we succeeded,' affirms Sumitra Charat Ram modestly.

'Neither my husband Charat nor I felt the need that the Kala Kendra be regarded as ours. In the first place, I had no intention of building an institution, much less of trying to become one. I was merely there, active and interested. I was fortunate on many counts too. First, I had a family which indulged me, then I married Charat who supported my endeavours. My father-in-law's contribution cannot be underestimated, for he was a pillar of strength and encouragement. Nothing can be done alone in life, and my family and my extended family, the Kendra, taught me that.'

Some like Sharada Rao, a close friend of several decades and a former official of the Department of Culture, feels upset that due credit and recognition has not been given. 'Somebody like Sumitra should have been celebrated. More importantly, the work of the Kendra has not received sufficient recognition. The Kendra productions were never sent abroad to the several Festivals of India. A person like Sumitraji ought to have been nominated to the Council of the Sangeet Natak Akademi and other agencies dealing with culture. What is appalling is that the very Kathak Kendra she nurtured has accorded her no place of honour.' Pandit Birju Maharaj also agrees with this. The Kendra's greatest achievement lies in having trained scores of soloists, gurus, choreographers and professional artists. This is no mean achievement, for in India, the arts and artists are by definition very independent and individualistic. For an institution to have created over a hundred top national artists is a major feat. A list appears later in the book of some of the names in the fields of music, dance and dance-drama, that the Kendra helped create.

◀ *The first ganda-bandh shishya of Birju Maharaj, Pratap Pawar served Kathak and the Kendra, both at home and abroad.*

'Sov. Land' — 5-10-58

DANCING AND MUSIC—"MUST" FOR YOUNG LADY

By SUNDARI SHRIDHARANI

Sundari Shridharani, an exponent of classical dances of India, had her training at Tagore's Shantiniketan and Uday Shankar's Cultural Centre. Later she studied the modern stage technique in England. She was invited to dance in Prague in 1947 for the Youth Festival when she travelled through France and Switzerland successfully completing her European trip. She runs at New Delhi a cultural organization called the Triveni Kala Sangam.

LOOKING AT THE history of the world, one comes to the conclusion that woman has contributed as much to the cultural enrichment of mankind as man. In fact, if I may be permitted to forget my feminist inclinations for a moment, I must confess that perhaps man has contributed more towards the cultural development in the world than woman.

With the advent of modernism all over the world, especially in India, this disparity between man's contribution to culture and that of woman has started to disappear. Man is devoted more to politics and money-making. In the graces of life, therefore, woman has to play a predominant role, and she is playing it.

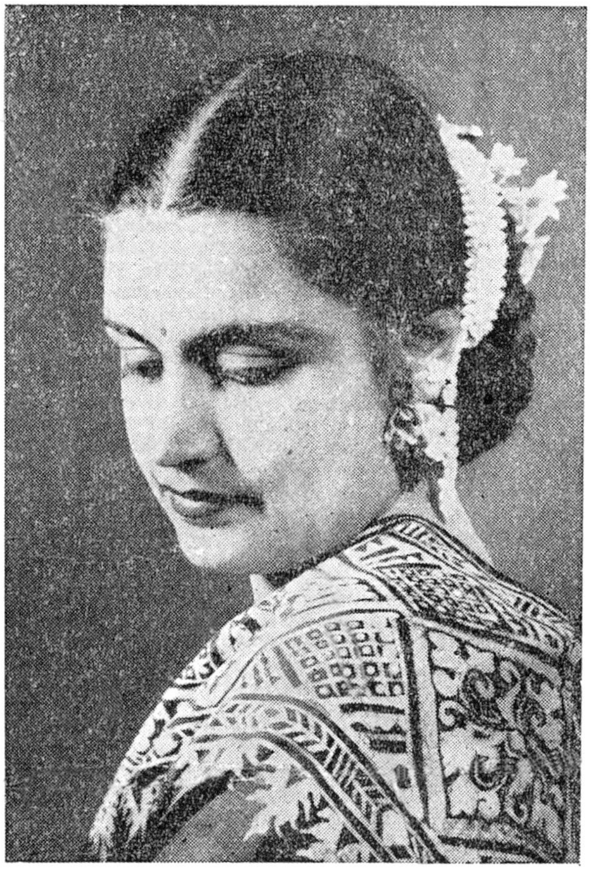

Sundari Shridharani

I would give you one incontestable example. It is Indian women who have been in the forefront in the revival of classical dances of India. Starting from Rukmini Devi and Bala Saraswati, one can think of such oustanding names as Shanta Rao and others. Of course, here too, the contribution of man cannot be ignored, and I would naturally think of Uday Shankar who has been the spearhead of renaissance in Indian dance.

In the field of education, women of India have played a distinguished role from the beginning, but of late they have acquired positions of authority and influence. Until very recently Mrs. Hansa Mehta was the Vice-Chancellor of Baroda University. One can think of many other names. Even in the field of painting, Indian women have gradually been coming to the fore. If one can make a list of painting exhibitions held in Delhi in the last three years, one would be convinced that at least 20 per cent of these exhibitions were held by women artists.

Graceful and Dignified

The Indian woman by her upbringing and surrounding is a very graceful and dignified sight. Her walk is especially noteworthy. Although slender and delicate in comparison to Western and Russian women, she does not fail to give an impression of vitality. One of the reasons why she is thus made is that most of our village women carry water pitchers poised on their heads. Poorer women have to carry bundles and parcels over their heads. This may be a routine, but it has its rhythmic implications. When I was in Europe and America, I noticed that in dance schools young girls were made to walk with books on their heads. Such exercises come natural to Indian women. This is perhaps one of the reasons why Indian women have taken easily to dance and they are very graceful in that art.

At the Triveni Kala Sangam in Delhi we are devoting ourselves to the development of the three arts of dancing, music and painting as the name of the institution itself indicates. It was a group of women that was at the core of the Triveni movement. Even today most of the activities are carried on by ladies associated with the Triveni Kala Sangam. Most of our students are girls. There is a tradition in India that such arts as dancing and music (not so much painting) are "Musts" for a young Hindu lady. Unless she is accomplished in such arts it is said that she finds it hard to get a suitable husband. With the advent of freedom, however, the old Indian value of tutoring our young girls in music and dance has been revived. All over the country now there are schools of music and dance mainly attended by young girls. Many of these schools are run by women.

Upbringing of Children

WHEN BOTH THE HUSBAND and wife work, it is right that only the mother should be responsible for the child's upbringing? I believe that under no circumstances should a woman alone bring up a child. The upbringing of a child concerns both the mother and father. If the husband and wife love each other and are devoted to each other, both should take part in bringing up their children. Both should equally share the responsibility for their upbringing until the children are of an age when they can look after themselves. In India there exists the system of joint family. When the husband and wife work, the elders in the family look after the children in their absence. I have seen the same system in the USSR in peasant families in the Tajik and Uzbek Republics. I have also seen in the Soviet Union that when both the mother and father are employed at an industrial establishment, the children are sent to nurseries and kindergartens during working hours, where they are looked after very well.

Ashoka Gupta.

Epilogue

I dislike being the focus of attention, which is one reason why I have not so far written a book about the Kendra or aspects of my life. I am doing so now largely so that artists may know that institutions are not made by money but by the artists themselves. Both my husband and I never desired anything for ourselves from this institution. We were happy and honoured to have Lala Shriram's name added as a prefix. In 1961, the trustees of the Shriram Trust expressed an interest in our work and wanted to provide the institution with financial security.

Although we were receiving an annual grant for ballet productions from the Department of Culture, we needed more support to enhance and expand our activities. And artists need much more than token recognition. They need security, insurance, medical and old-age benefits. They give their best to the country, to its international standing and identity; ought not the State to provide handsomely for them? Freedom fighters and sports people have, it seems, been more privileged than artists. For us, at the Kendra our association does not cease once the person, or our artist, dies. In affection and in memory of the late Guru Krishan Chand Nayak, we still send his family a token sum, which in a village helps meet their expenses. Other artists and their families can vouch for this. Two major instances may be cited: medical support to Siddheshwari Devi and bearing all costs upon Shambhu Maharaj's death. His family continued to be supported by the Kendra. In the case of Guru Sundar Prasad too, we continue to support his wife.

We have striven to serve the arts as best as we can. Often people say that I have not received adequate recognition or awards. Independent India today is fifty years old. We have seen so much and travelled far. But much, of course, still remains to be done. In the field of culture, we need cultural managers who understand the medium. We need more critics who are better equipped with the history of the arts and possess a greater depth of knowledge.

The Government, too, needs to be more discriminating. The Department of Culture has done a lot of useful work and continues to support a wide variety of activities, but it needs a review policy. Does the Department of Culture have a committee which ascertains the extent to which each group utilises the grants it disburses? Some institutions have been getting grants for years, even decades now. Does the Department of Culture know of their

◀ *Sundari met her husband Shridharani at the Kendra and soon there were wedding-bells in the air. In 1958 dance was treated as a 'must' for a young, refined lady.*

PRESIDENT'S INAUGURAL SPEECH ON THE OCCASION OF THE NATIONAL DANCE FESTIVAL, NOVEMBER 2, 1955.

I am very glad to have been asked to inaugurate the first National Dance Festival organized by the Bharatiya Kala Kendra under the auspices of the Sangeet Natak Akadami. It is, indeed, a happy augury that since Independence we have been going ahead not only in the field of economic and material development but also in the sphere of fine arts.

Music and dancing have been an essential part of the life of the people of this country. According to our traditional belief, fine arts sprang up from the same source which gave birth to meditation, spiritual aspirations, philosophy and literature of this country. When the different branches of knowledge took shape in the Vedic age, arts like music and dancing also appeared at that time. That is the real reason that for centuries these arts have played such a prominent part in the religious and spiritual life of the Indian people. In the eyes of ancient seers and thinkers, music and dancing were the means of achieving life's *summum bonum* on this earth. Gradually, as these arts developed and the general people started taking interest in them, they became broad-based and popular.

How the art of dancing developed in course of time, how it took different forms in different regions, how it became a household affair under State patronage and how it came to be looked upon as a source of entertainment and of achieving physical and mental health—of all these things, I am sure, you are already aware. The vicissitudes of time and foreign invasions in the middle ages led the dance away from the generality of people, particularly in the North where a social stigma came to be attached to dancing and respectable classes kept away from its so-called evil influences. How far this attitude was correct or proper is a matter of opinion, which does not interest us here. Our duty in the changed circumstances of today should be to re-establish time-honoured arts of music and dancing to their proper places so that they may be looked upon once again as a means of integral development of human personality Let not

actual work? Has any official ever gone to visit or done a surprise check on whether a group actually exists? These and other matters should be the concerns of the respective Government agencies, for by their own admission the resources for culture are limited, making their proper utilisation of paramount importance. After fifty years, we do not have a directory of artists. There is no adequate compilation of what exists. Documentation does not mean mere photo and video recordings, but a proper coverage of all the great artists the country is privileged to have. The Government agencies could play an important role in developing this as there is so much that needs to be documented.

It is often held that artists are commercial or charge too much. I do not hold this view. An artist spends half his life acquiring and mastering an art form. If an instrumentalist breaks his finger or a singer develops a throat problem, he or she needs resources for survival. By definition, many kinds of artists have a short shelf life, so they need to earn well in those few years. They have no job security, no pension, no provision for the future for their families. Thus, if luck favours them, they must make the best use of their active years.

I tell my sons, Deepak and Siddharth, who are industrialists, that Delhi was once a dull place, with little cultural activity. Over the years so much has changed, partly no doubt with corporate support. But corporate participation is now a must and most welcome. Any work which helps enrich a community and is in the national interest is welcome. Today it is not easy to meet the phenomenal production costs of say the 'Ramlila', by ticket sales alone. We need advertisements and donations. The arts are the bedrock of a society, hence it is our duty to support them in whatever way we can. I am glad my sons share my concerns and support the arts.

In Shobha Deepak Singh we have a committed person to continue the work. She must believe in teamwork and be humble, two qualities which won me more acclaim and affection than anything else. Her husband, Deepak Singh, supports her work totally, like mine did too. Thirty years ago, Shobha detested Hindi: today, she reads scriptures and makes scripts. I had a weakness for mythological themes and we produced several ballets on that aspect of our traditional lore but Shobha wants to try new things and supports younger talents, thus in a way continuing the ideas and ideals, the perceptions and perspectives for which I founded the Kendra. The third generation, represented by Meenakshi is already here to carry forward the task for which the Kendra has become so renowned.

In the late forties, we initiated the Jhankar Music Festival which later took the shape of the Shankarlal Music Festival, in memory of my uncle-in-law, Sir Shankarlal. In 1993 the Shankarlal Foundation felt that it could no

◀ *Excerpts of the speech by the President of India on the occasion of the National Dance Festival, 1955.*

longer continue with the Festival. They asked if we could run it, and suggested that we might change the name of the festival if we did so. Having become a known and an established event in the cultural calendar of Delhi, we decided to assume the responsibility of organising the Festival and added the name of Shriram to it. After all, both Shankarlal and Shriram were brothers. It is only befitting for them to share the occasion. As children, we were taught to share and share equally. Where have those fine feelings gone today when I see brother fighting brother?

In the coming years, I feel the Kendra must expand. When this institution started, I had no plans, it just happened. But today, after seeing fifty years of its functioning, I feel a future fifteen-year perspective is necessary in order to streamline our concerns. People die but institutions must remain and continue to fulfil its obligations to society. It should have and offer recording studios to artists, courses in costume and dress-design, a chamber auditorium

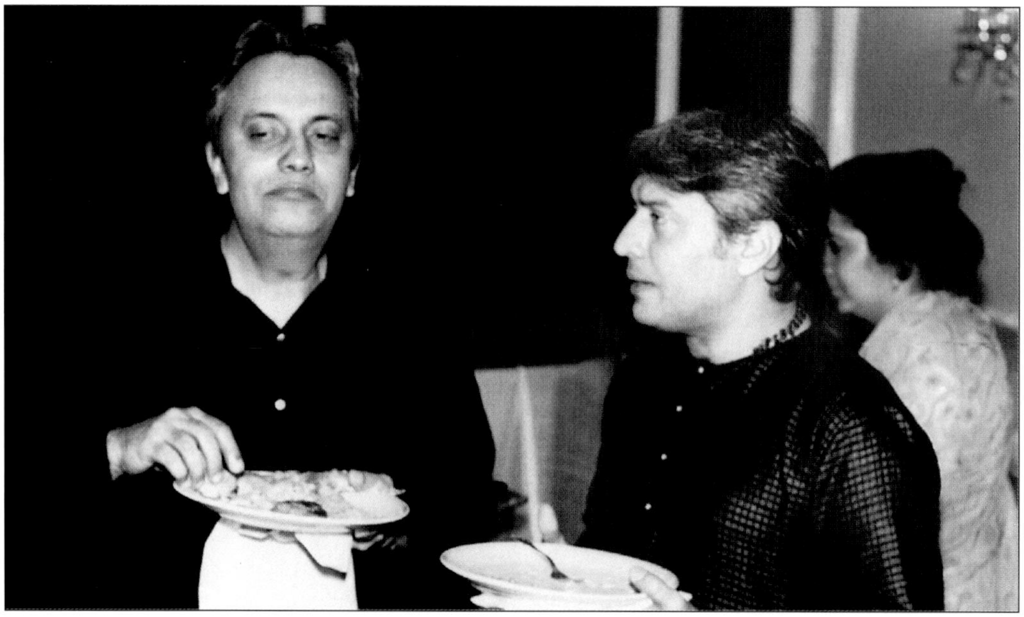

Maestro Amjad Ali Khan exchanges notes with Deepak Singh.

(we did start the Jhankar Chamber but after six years of its functioning one day we were told that the plans were not sanctioned by the concerned authority, so we had to pull it down), a friendly atmosphere for the art fraternity to meet, an art gallery and even specialised studies on the history of the performing arts. We can help organise orientation courses where leading art historians, critics and artists can discuss their experiences. Such a course can also be helpful to a number of foreigners posted in India, who need to learn more about the country and its culture.

We need to train cultural administrators, for only a sensitive person with a trained mind can run an art institution effectively. We would like to support specialised journals dedicated to the arts because it is a good platform for the exchange of ideas and values. Impresarios need to have a closer relationship with artists. Big sponsors have sprouted but do they have an individual, personal contact with artists I am proud to say, we have had excellent relationships with artists, some of whom still keep in touch despite the passage of time. Ultimately, this close rapport is what has resulted in great art.

In future, it will be our endeavour to provide scholarships to deserving students who show the potential of becoming professional artists. Today, training has become very critical in every sphere and my husband, the ever-professional management person, Lala Charat Ram, feels 'the main purpose of an institution like our Kendra is to train, support and prepare future stars of the form. This will be our best service to the heritage and culture of India'. I cannot agree with him more.

We also need to have a responsive audience. All students who come to learn one art form or the other need not necessarily become artists. Perhaps, after learning a form they are better exposed to the arts. This makes them a great audience, a *shrota*, a *rasika*, for as much as an audience love to see artists on stage, an artist needs an audience too and if it is an enlightened audience or a knowledgeable audience, it makes the process of sharing more enjoyable.

Today, there are many awards and incentives for artists but this was common even in our ancient days when Amrapalli stood celebrated or a Kalidas was worshipped. One of the biggest advantages of having had an institution like the Kendra was that staying in the Kendra the artists began to understand us and we, them. Sitting in our houses, we could not reach them, their hearts or they ours. By having a common meeting point which was both a work and a worship place, we helped spread the aura and spirit of artistic genius around. In the process, we were enriched.

At a personal level, I firmly believe that no one from our family should draw a salary in working with the Kendra. It should be a labour of love. My advice is also that no one who wishes to serve the Kendra should do it for the sake of reputation, fame or image-building. If you work sincerely and seriously, fame will follow in all probability. I have left a will through which I do not want my name perpetuated by anything new. I hope I go before my husband. I joke with him that he need not construct a Taj Mahal for me, since a Taj in my name already stands constructed!

Today, India stands poised to play a larger role in the world in every sphere. It is a major Asian economy and internationally is known for its culture. I feel humble and proud, happy and fulfilled to have partaken of some of its greatness. If in the process, I, through the Shriram Bharatiya Kala Kendra, made any contribution or difference, it is for history to decide. My service to the arts and artists has been my reward. God has been extremely kind and generous. And he made me an instrument of His will. I stand fulfilled.

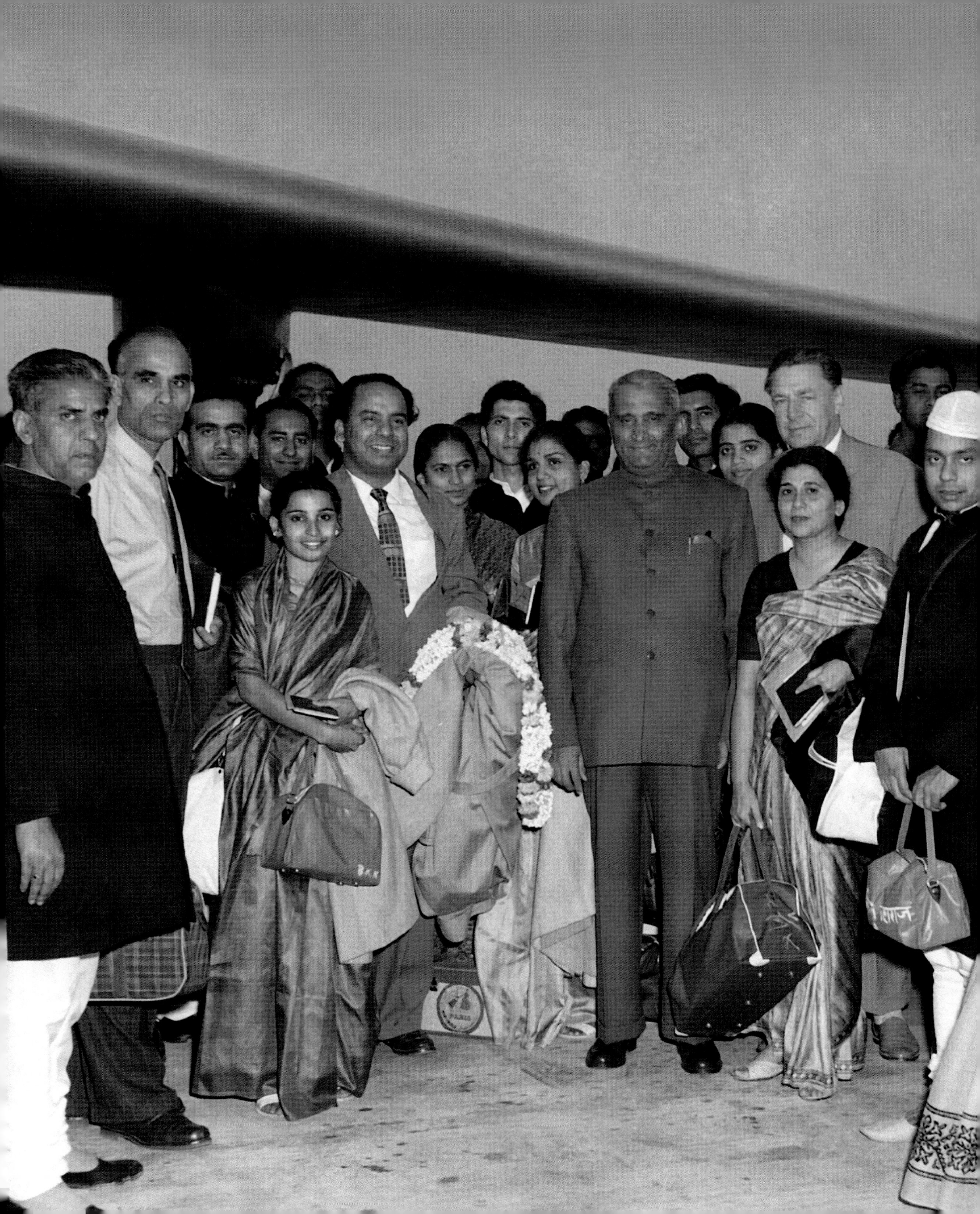

Kendra Faculty over the Last Fifty Years

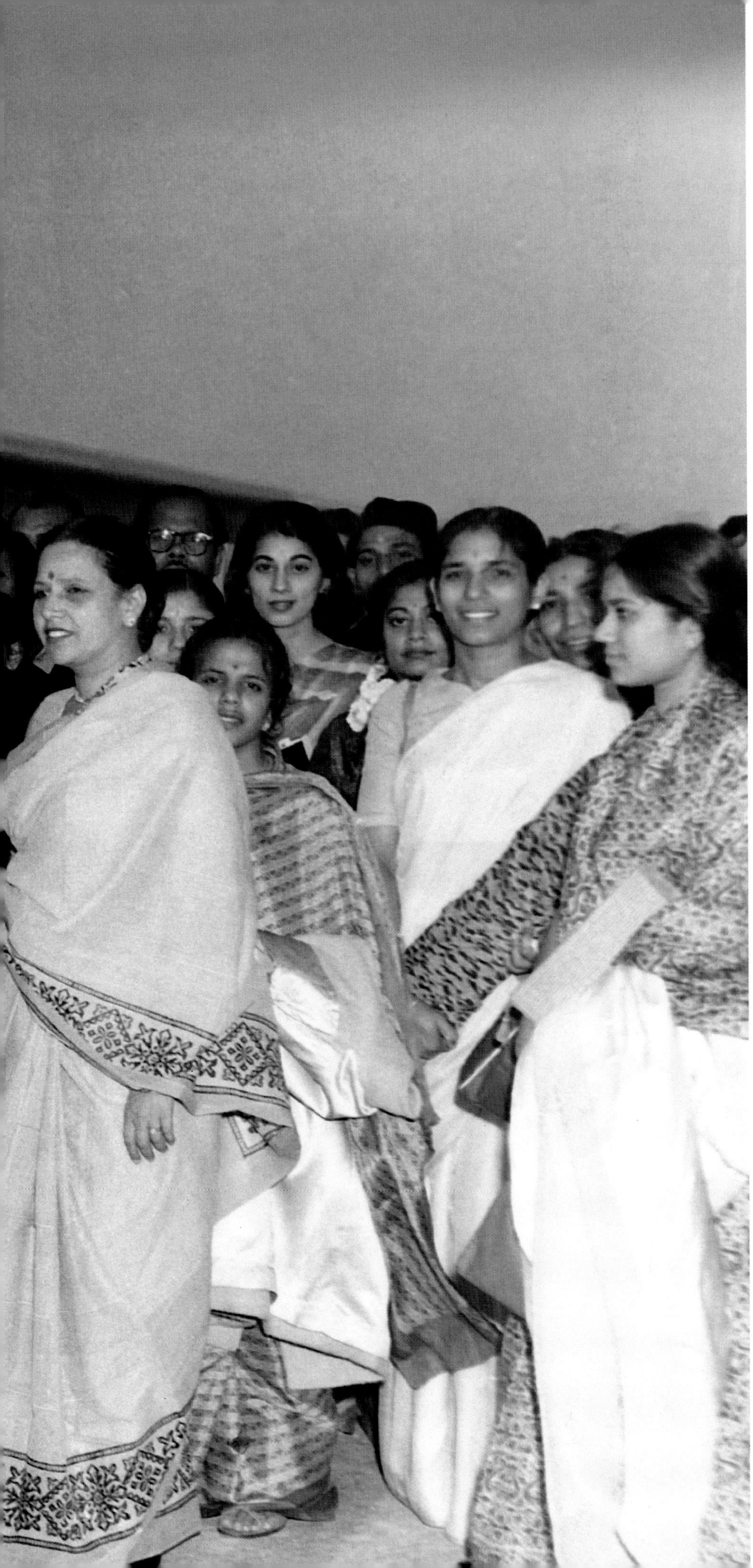

FIRST FACULTY (1950-60S) AT THE KOTHI AND LATER PUSA ROAD

Kathak Samrat Shambhu Maharaj
Ustad Hafiz Ali Khan
Ustad Nasir Moinuddin Khan Dagar
Ustad Nasir Aminuddin Khan Dagar
Ustad Mushtaq Hussain Khan
Ustad Vilayat Hussain Khan of Agra
Prof. Dilip Chandra Vedi
Guru Sundar Prasad
Birju Maharaj
Naina Devi—Director in Residence
Rahi—puppetry

FACULTY AT MATA SUNDARI ROAD (1970S)

All of the above plus
Pandit Purushottam Das
Siddheshwari Devi
Ustad Waheed Khan
Ustad Ghulam Jaffar Khan
Ustad Habibiuddin Khan
Ustad Inam Ali Khan
Manika Prasad
Ustad Asad Ali Khan

FACULTY AT LYTTON ROAD/ PRESENT SITE ON COPERNICUS MARG (1970S ONWARDS TILL DATE)

In addition to most of the above
Guru Harekrishna Behera
Guru Mayadhar Raut
Guru Bansilal
Debu Chaudhury

Kendra artists on tour flanked by (left to right): Thakur Harnarain Singh, Dagar Sahib, Kumodini Lakhia, Naina Devi, Birju Maharaj, Sumitra Charat Ram, Shobha Deepak Singh, Billy Singh.

EMINENT TEACHERS/GURUS/ STUDENTS/CHOREOGRAPHERS OF THE KENDRA

Vocal Music

Ustad Moinuddin Khan Dagar
Ustad Aminuddin Khan Dagar
Ustad Mushtaq Hussain Khan
Ustad Vilayat Hussain Khan (Agra)
Prof. Dilip Chandra Vedi
Smt. Siddheshwari Devi
Ustad Ishtiaq Hussain Khan
Ustad Munnawar Ali Khan
Pandit Amarnath
S.K. Banerjee
Anita Roy
Subhash Dutta
Hem Chand
Shanti Hiranand
Sulochana Brahspati
Shanti Sharma

Sitar

Pandit Ravi Shankar
Ustad Wahid Khan
Ustad Hashmat Ali Khan
Pandit Debu Chaudhury
Pandit Satish Kumar
Shri Jitendra Pratap
Shri Pancharan Sardar
Shri Partho Das

Sarod

Ustad Hafiz Ali Khan
Ustad Amjad Ali Khan
Biswajeet Roy Chowdhury

Veena

Ustad Asad Ali Khan

Tabla

Ustad Hashmat Ali Khan
Ustad Inam Ali Khan
Ustad Munnu Khan

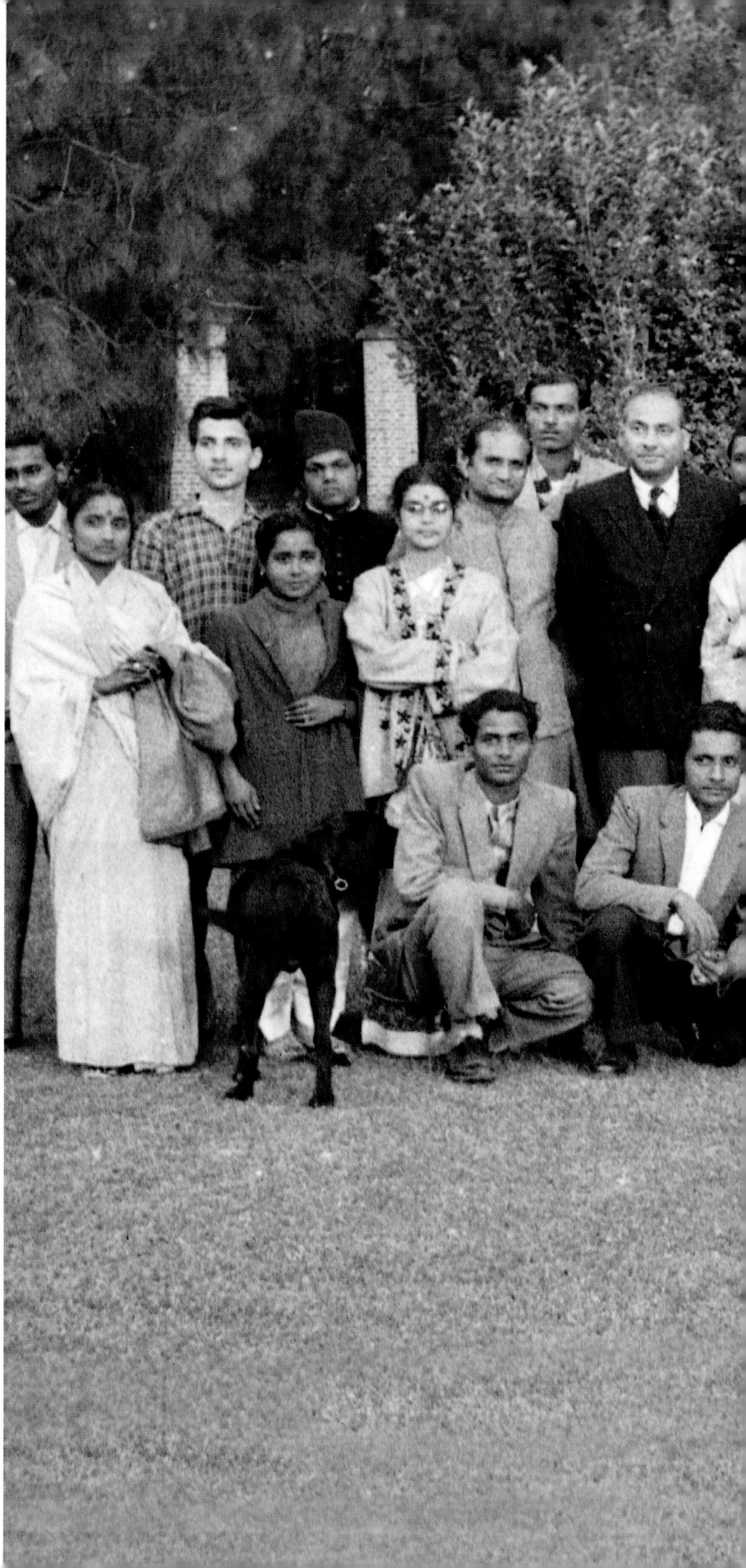

A faculty gathering which include choreographer Narendra Sharma, dancer Rekha Shanker, Jayanti Sharma, Thakur Harnarain Singh among others.

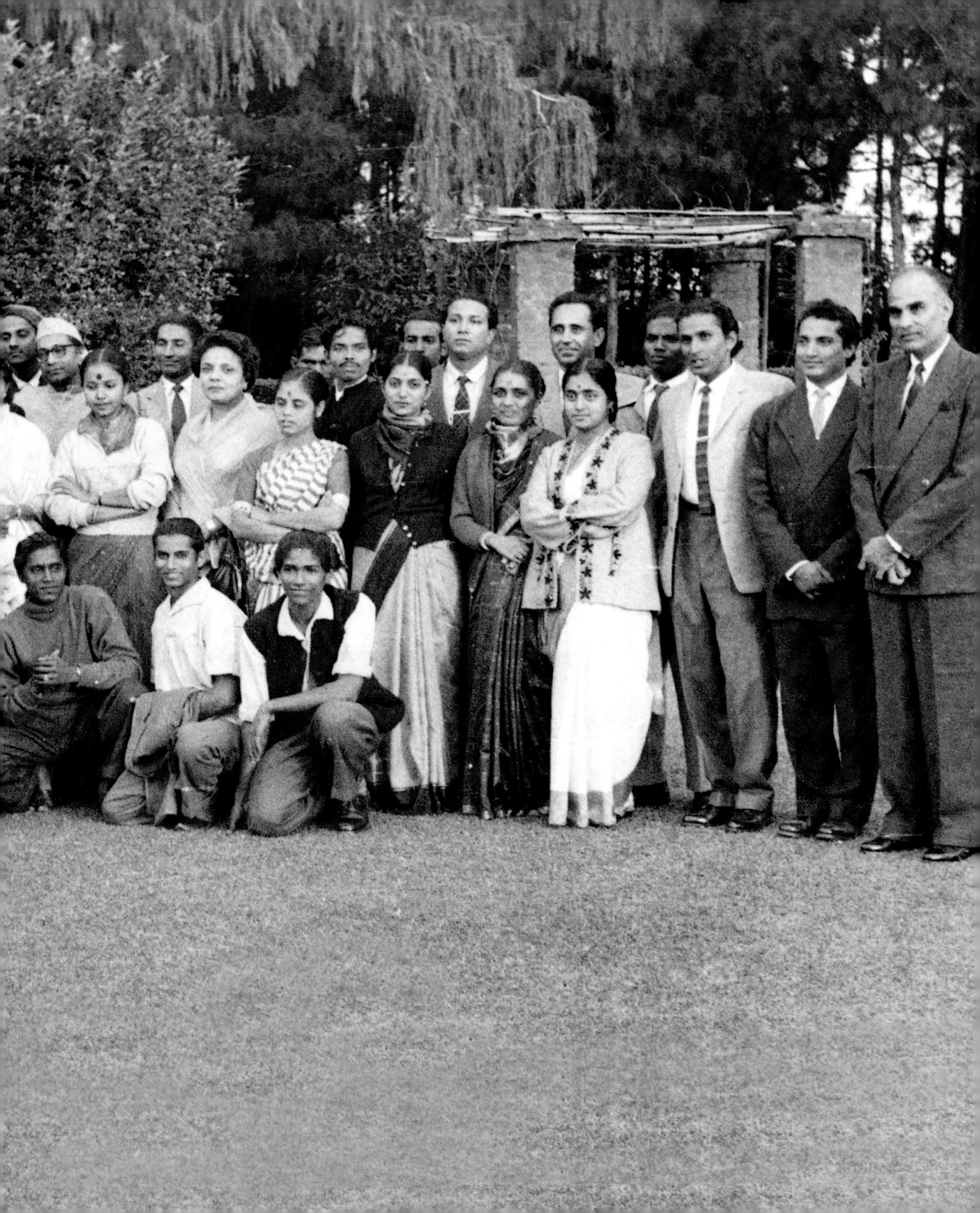

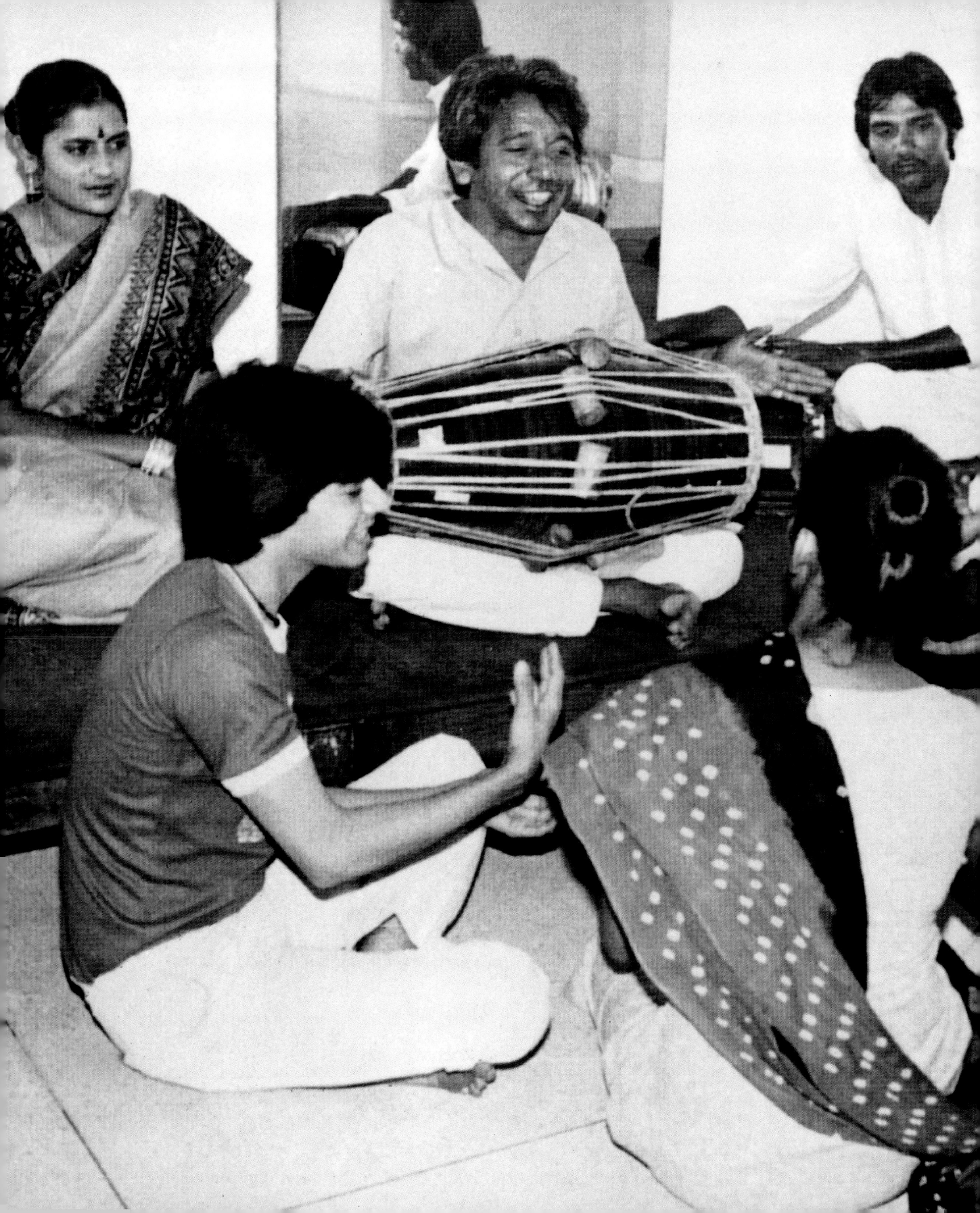

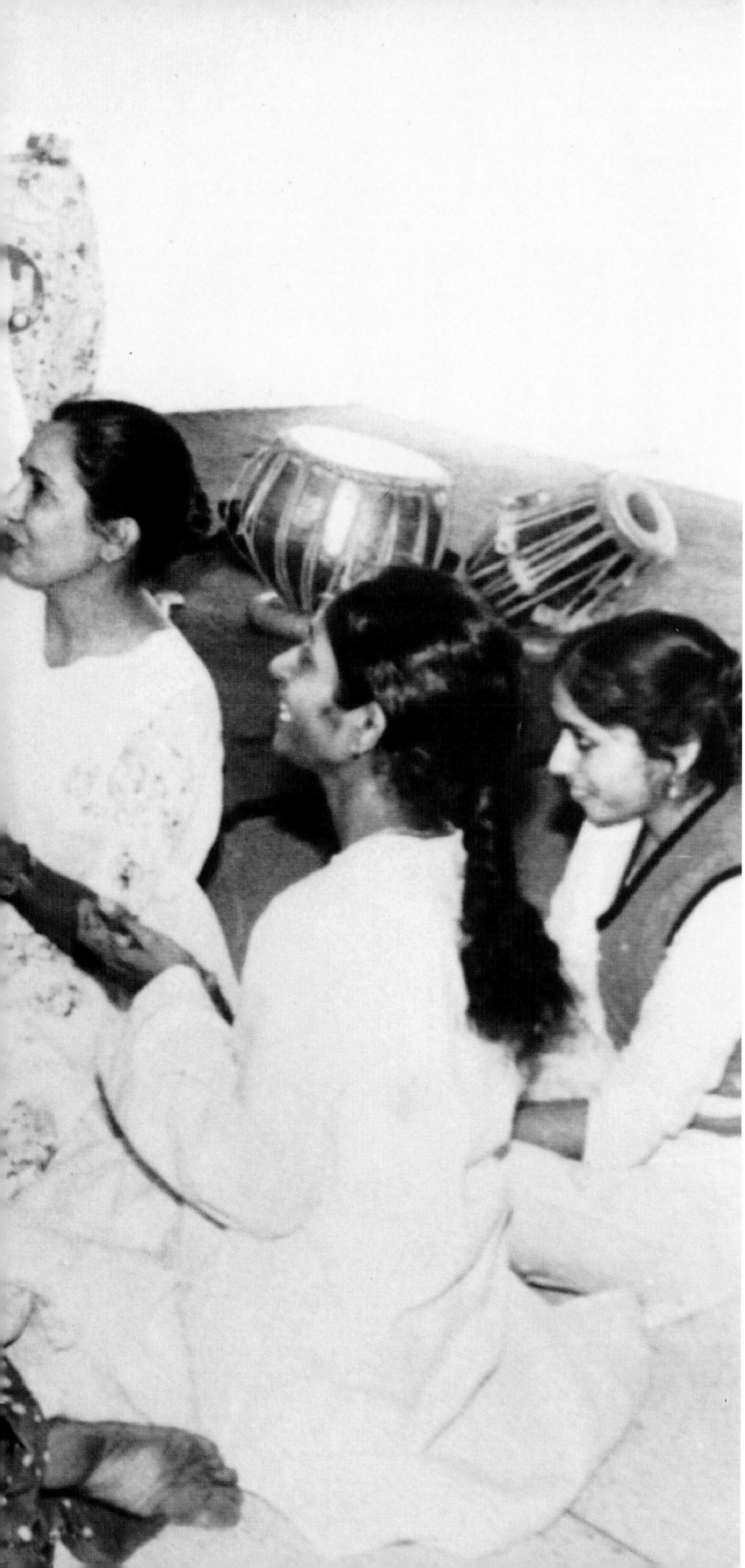

Pakhawaj

Guru Purushottam Das
Shri Bhagwat Upreti

FACULTY OF DANCE

Kathak

Guru Shambhu Maharaj
Guru Sundar Prasad
Pandit Birju Maharaj
Mohan Rao Kalyanpurkar
Pandit Devi Lal
Brojen Mukherjee
Durgalal
Guru Bansilal
Vaswati Mishra
Nandini Singh
Rani Khanum

Orissi

Guru Deba Prasad Das
Guru Harekrishna Behera
Guru Mayadhar Raut
Dibankar Khuntia
Aloka & Ambikaa Panikar

Chhau

Guru Krishna Chandra Nayak
Shashidharan Nair

Bharata Natyam

Leela Samson
Justin McCarthy

CHOREOGRAPHERS

Narendra Sharma
Devendra Shankar
Bhagwandas Verma
Guru Gopinath
Yog Sunder
Krishnan Namboodri

Kathak guru Bansi Lal plays the pakhawaj while conducting a Kathak class.

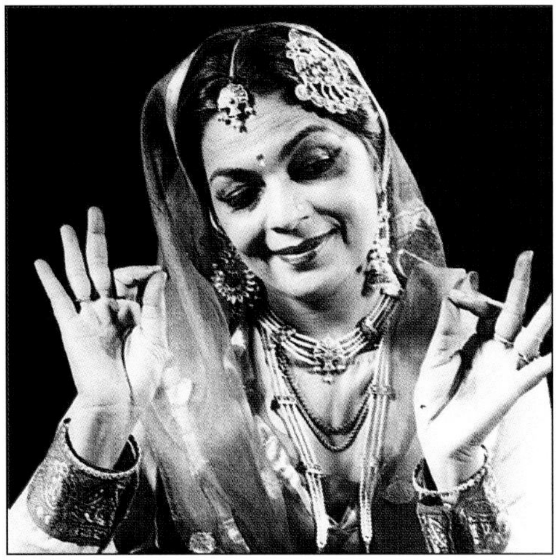

Uma Sharma, senior Kathak exponent.

K. Shekharan Panikar
Bhushan Lakhandari
Shashidharan Nair

COMPOSERS

Dagar brothers
Jyotindra Moitra 'Batukda'
Sushil Dasgupta
Mohan Upreti
Amjad Ali Khan
Barun Gupta
Pandit Shiv Prasad
Shubha Mudgal

LIGHTING/STAGE

Inder Razdan
Tapas Sen
Badal Sawant

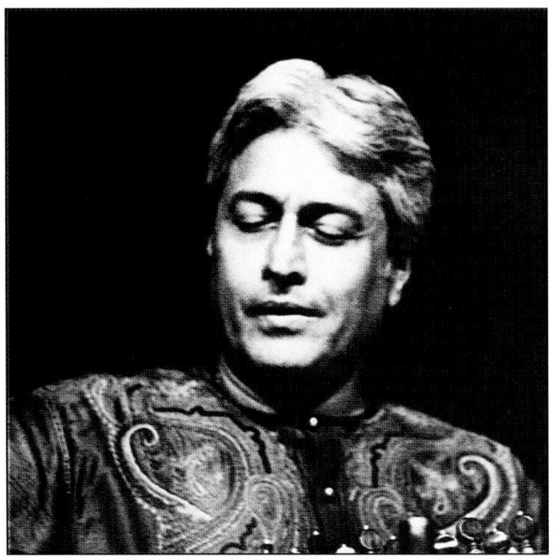

Amjad Ali Khan, sarod exponent.

STAR STUDENTS WHO BECAME SOLOISTS (in alphabetical order)

Aloka Panikar—Orissi
Amjad Ali Khan—sarod
Asad Ali Khan—veena
Birju Maharaj—Kathak
Bhagwandas Verma—ballet
Bharati Gupta—Kathak
Bhushan Lakhandri—ballet
Debu Chaudhury—sitar
Durgalal—Kathak
Justin McCarthy—Bharata Natyam
Keshav Kothari—puppets/administration
K. Shekharan Panikar—choreography
Krishna Mohan—Kathak

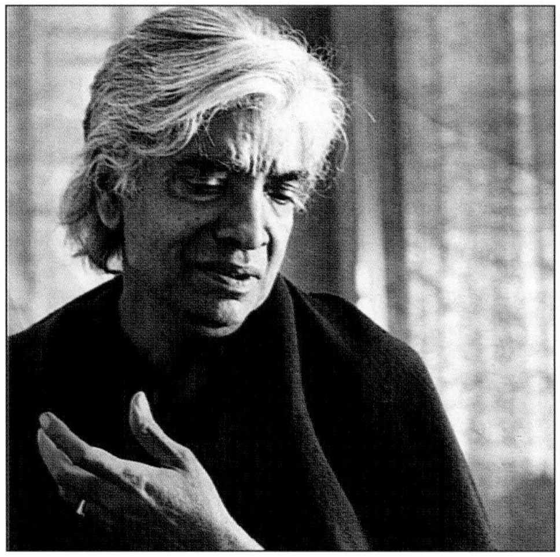

Pt. Amarnath, veteran representative of the Indore gharana.

Maya Rao—Kathak/choreography
Rani Karna—Kathak
Rashmi Vajpeyi—Kathak
Rita Ganguly—vocalist
Shanti Sharma—vocalist
Shashidharan Nair—Chhau/choreographer
Uma Sharma—Kathak
Urmila Nagar—Kathak
Vinod Nagpal—theatre

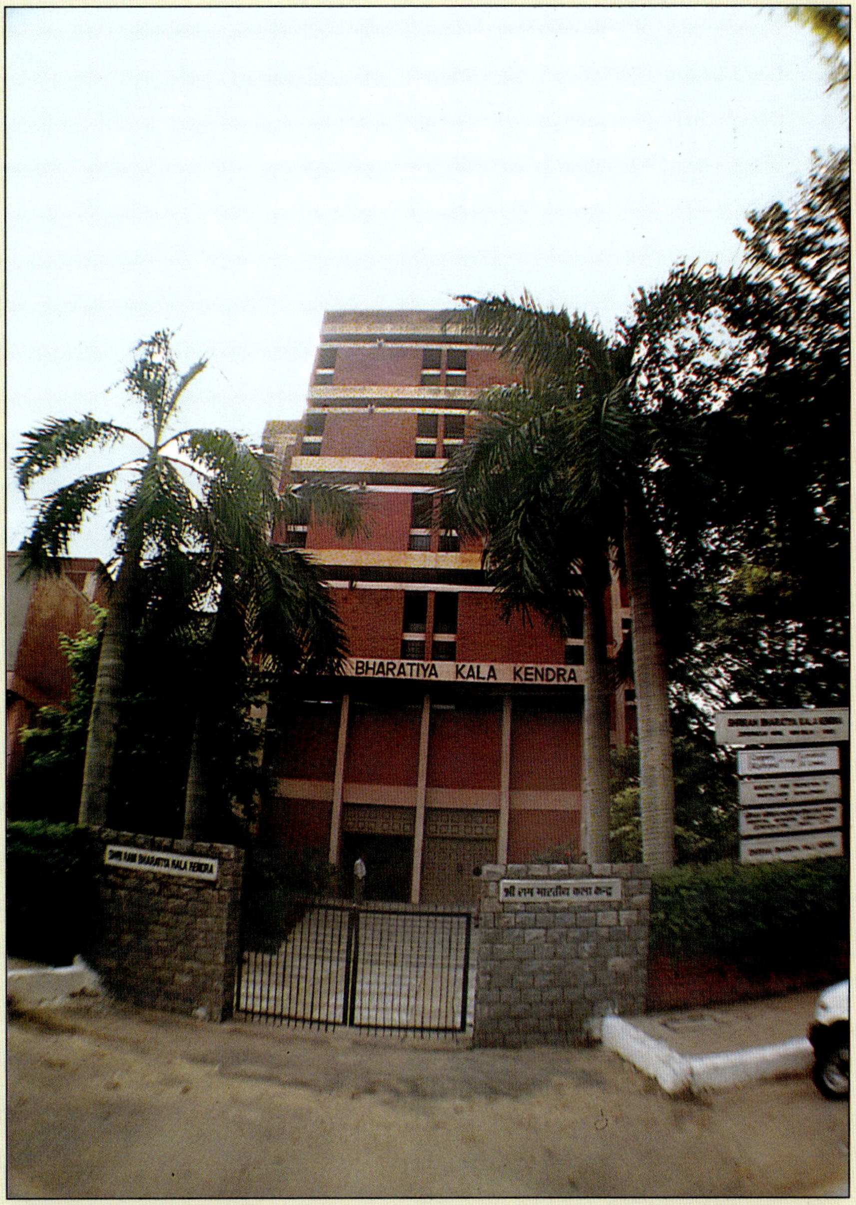

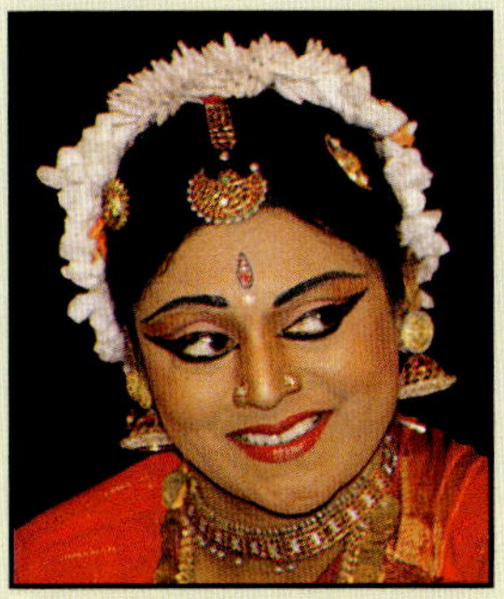
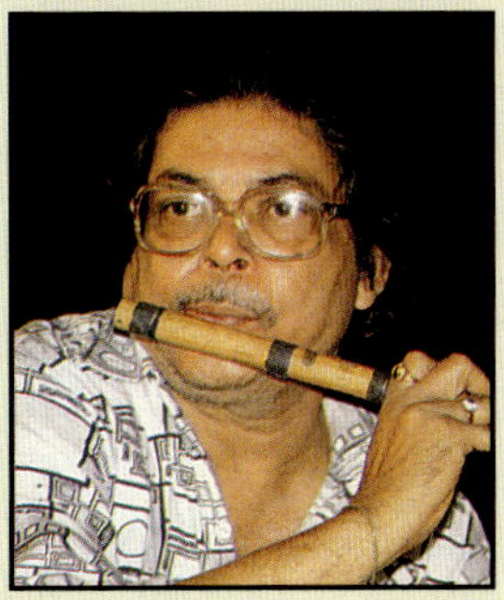
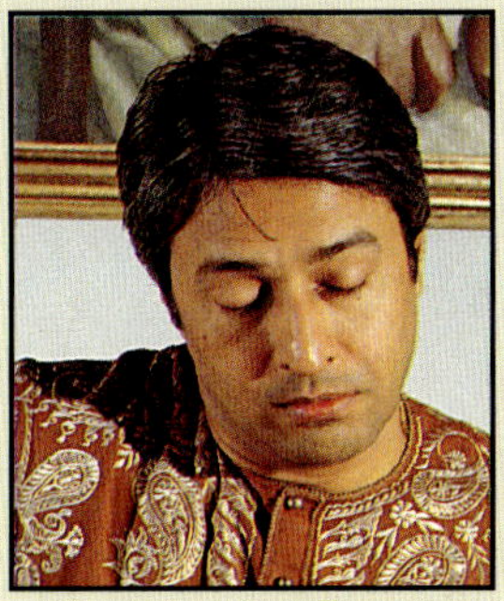
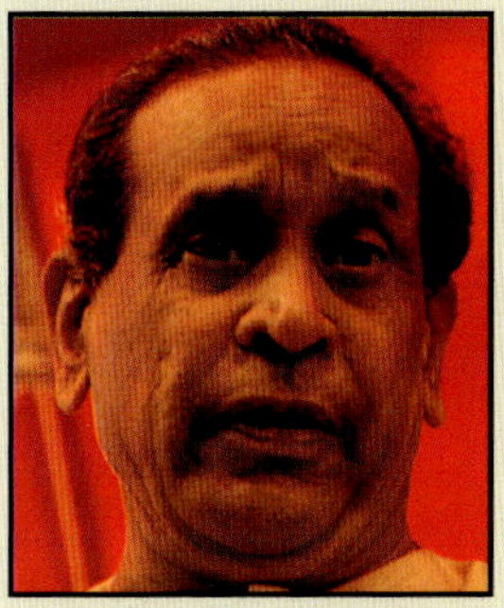
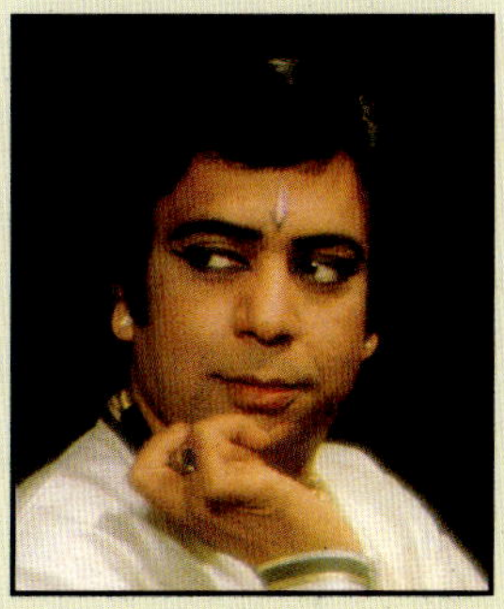

Top: *The Shriram Bharatiya Kala Kendra on Copernicus Marg in the heart of Delhi is famous for excellence in arts.* ***Bottom:*** *From left: Swapna Sundari, Ashok Bhattacharya, Amjad Ali Khan, Bhimsen Joshi, Birju Maharaj.* ***Following pages:*** *Bhushan Lakhandri in and as 'Karna'.*

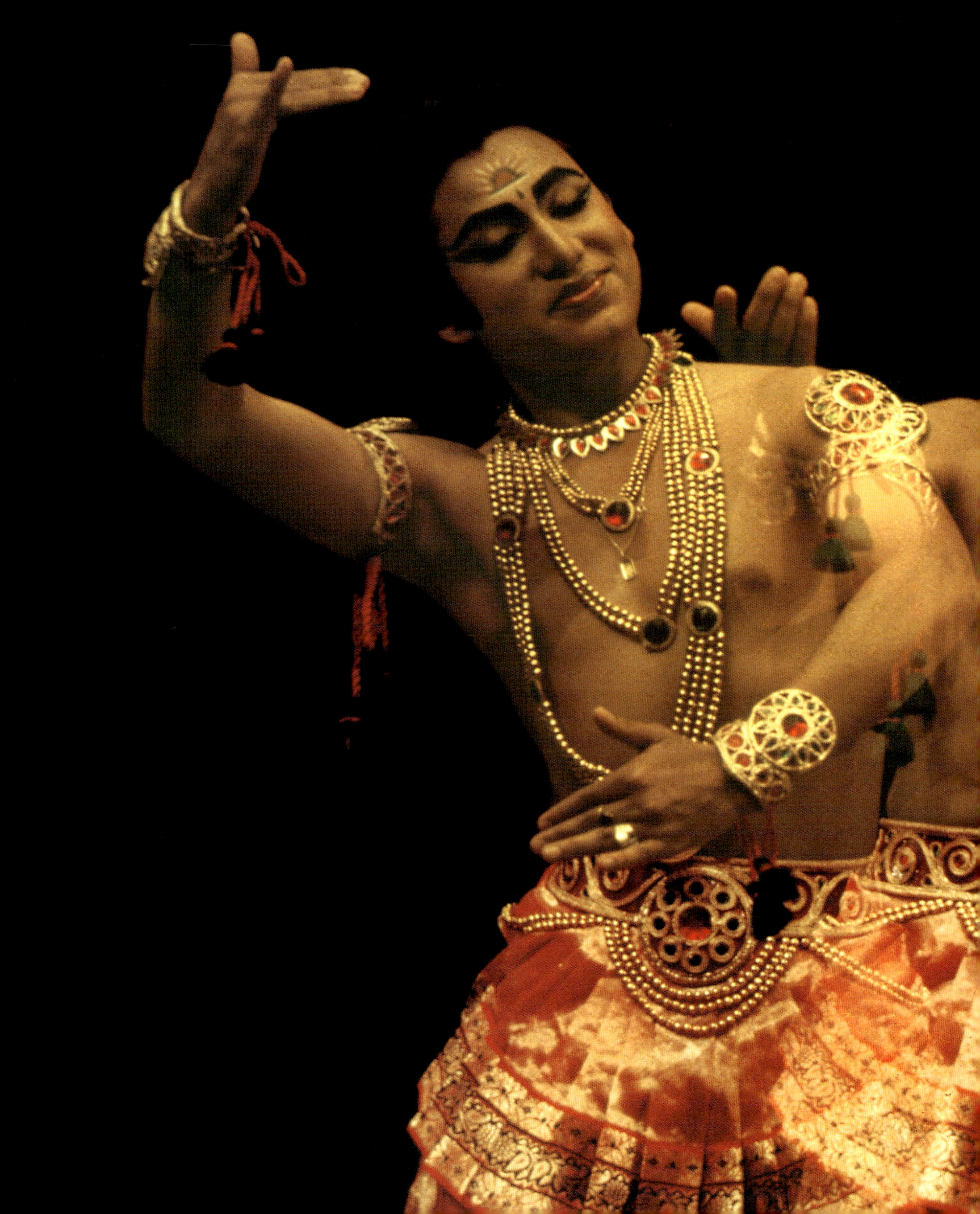

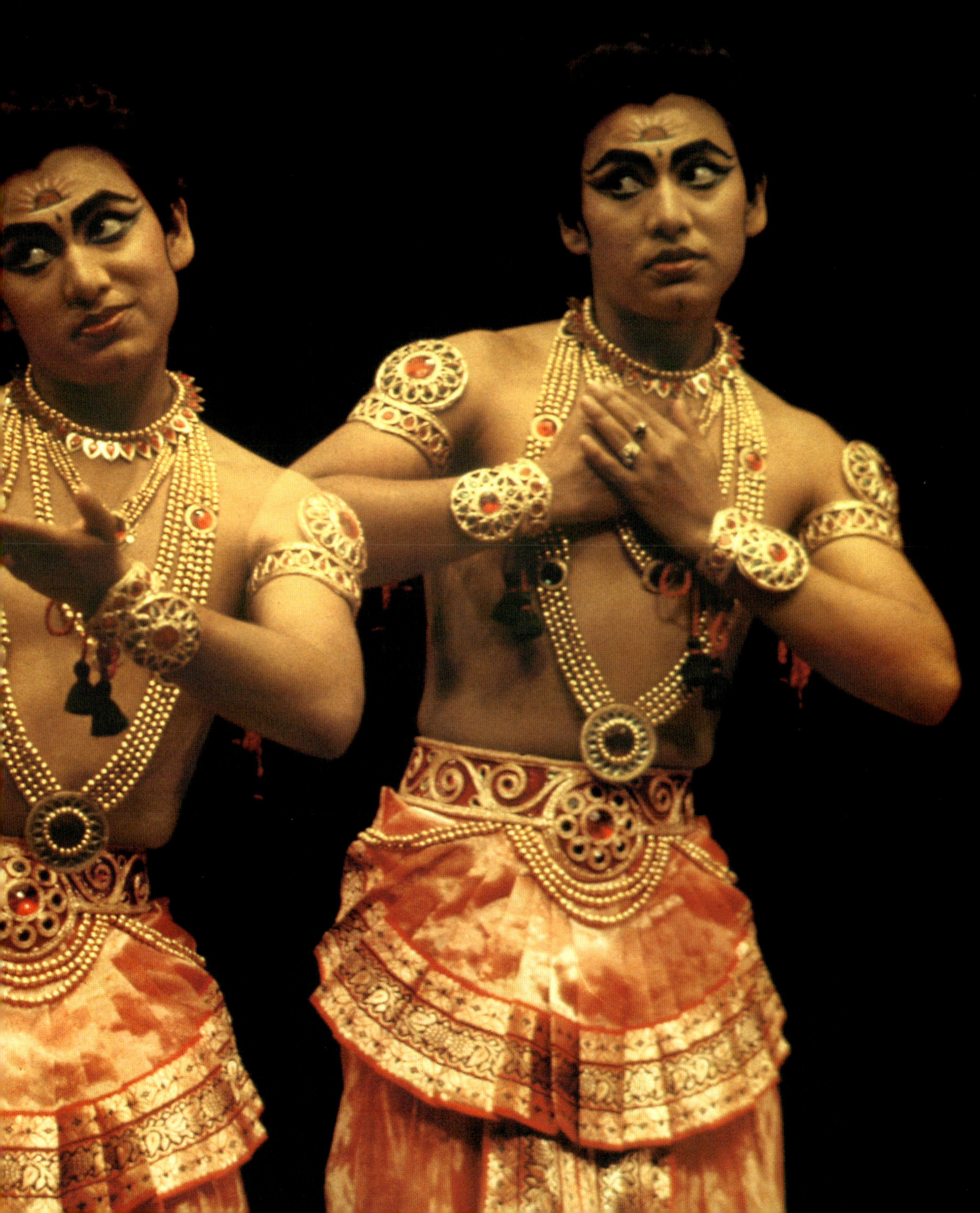

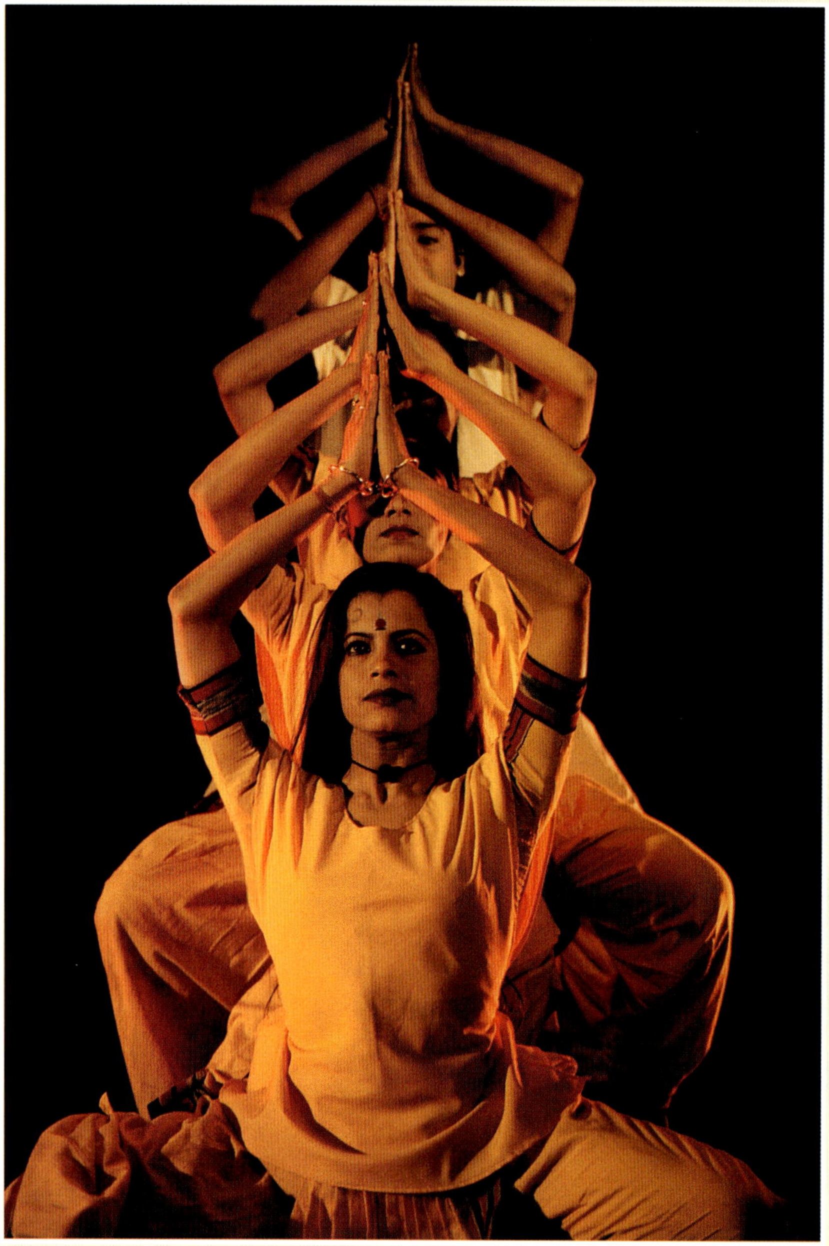

'Parikrama' in Chhau style.
Facing page: *A student of Justin McCarthy, a teacher at the Kendra.* ***Following pages:*** *Neera Batra in 'Shane-e-Mughal' for which the music was set by Ustad Amjad Ali Khan.*

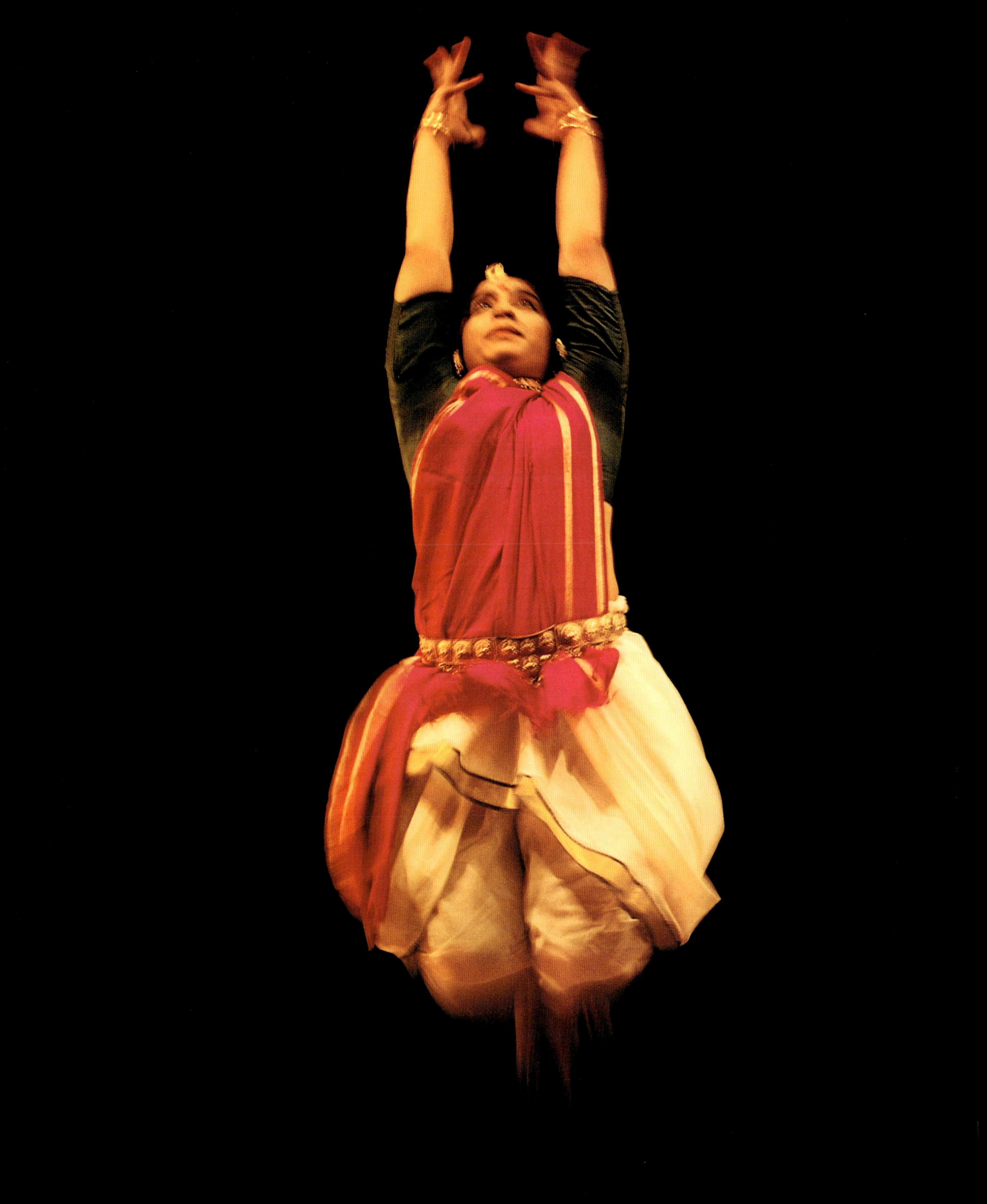

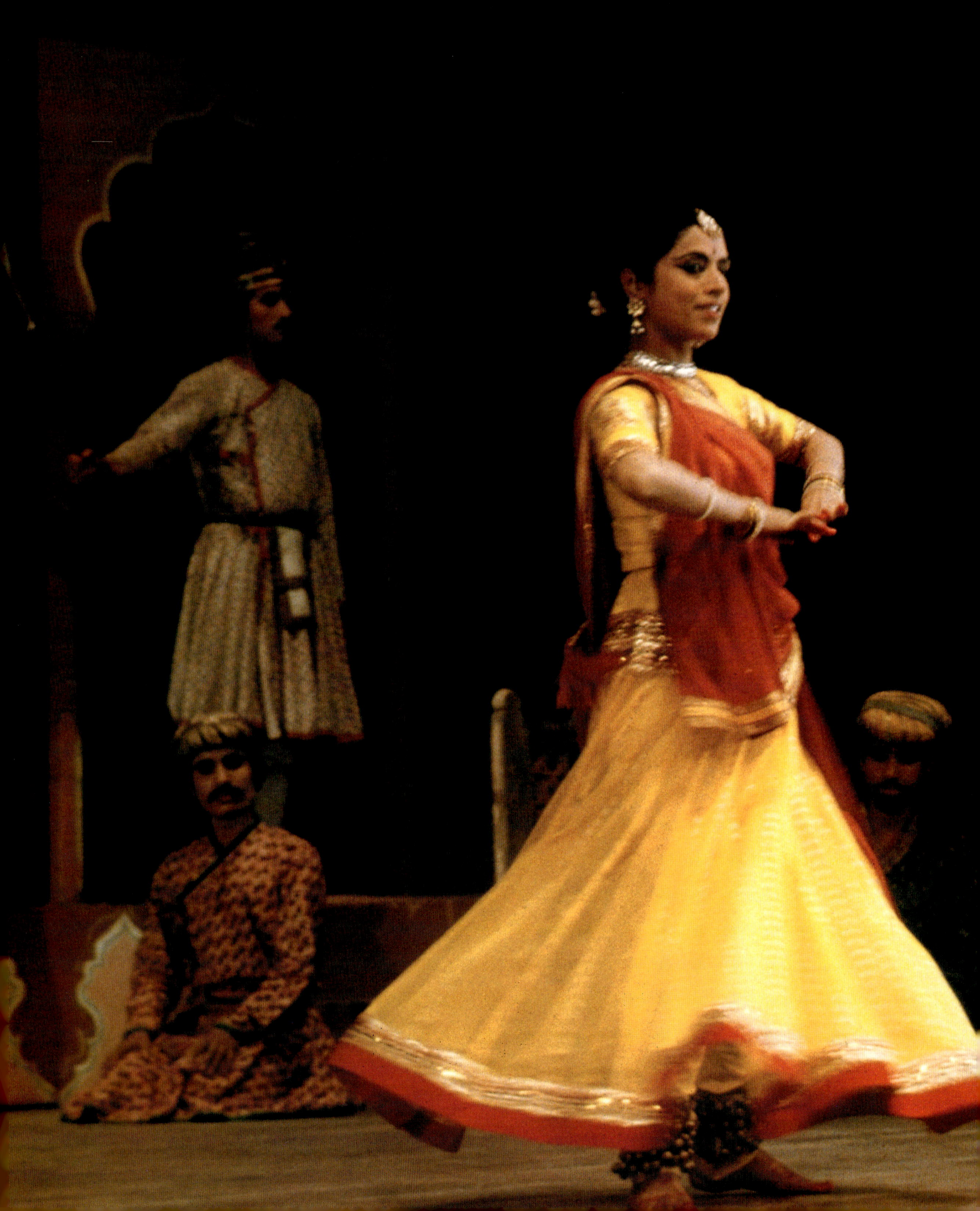

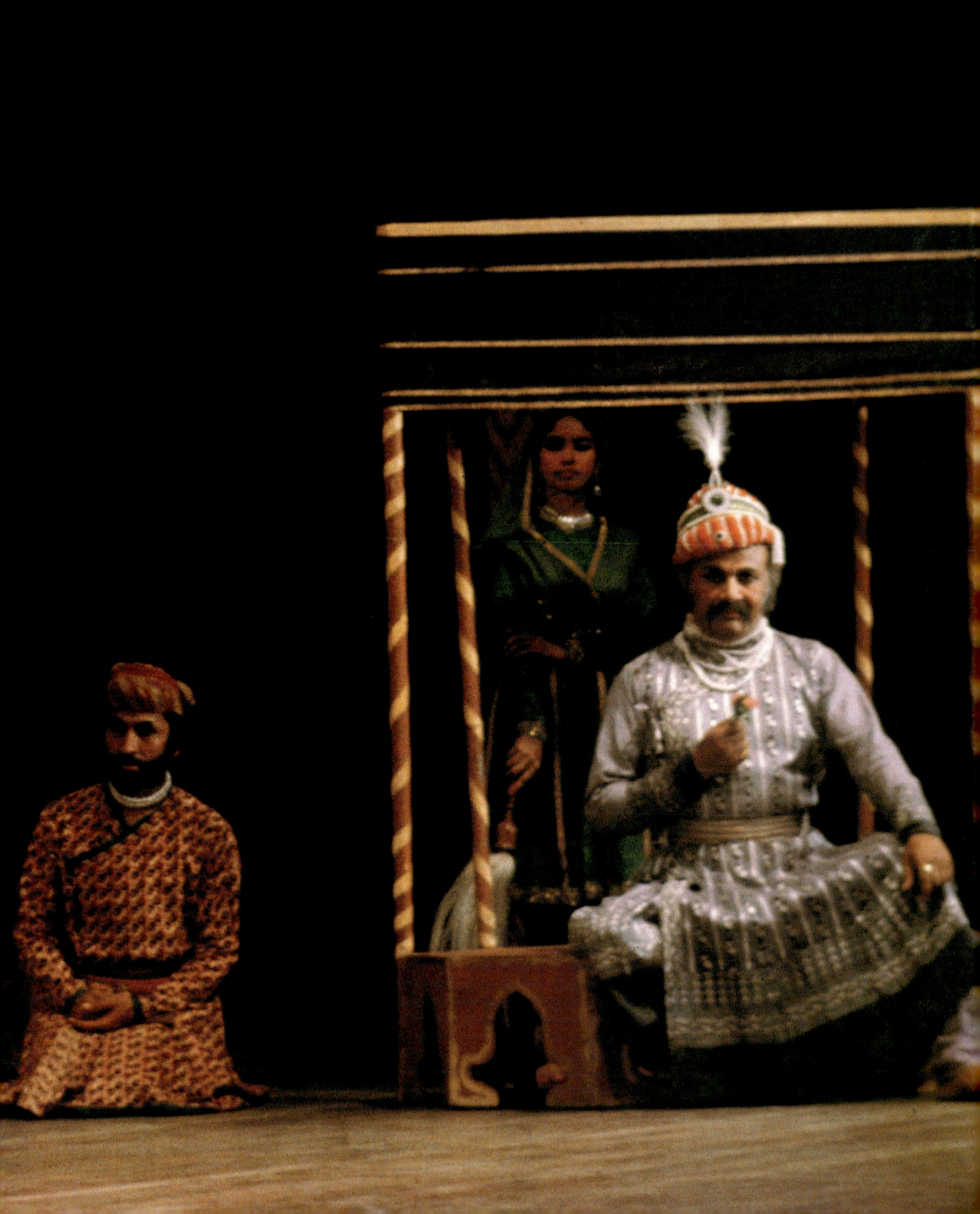

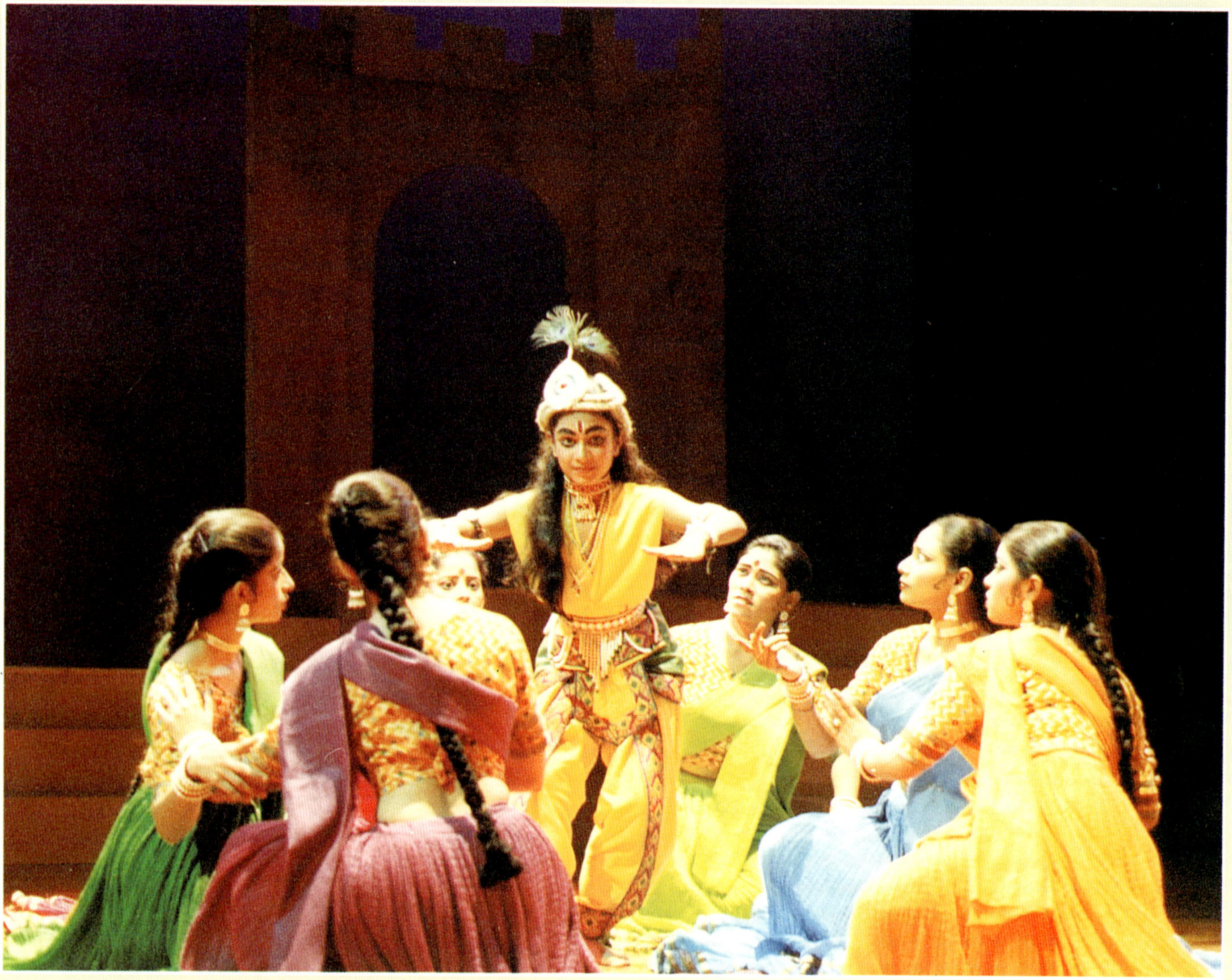

'Krishna-Katha' in the season of Janamashtami regales all. The Kendra students participate in productions gaining professional experience. ***Facing page:*** *Danseuse Uma Sharma in a pensive, poetic mood full of love for Krishna.* ***Following pages:*** *Artists Ravi Chauhan, Narendra and Moulina in 'Chakravyuhu'.*

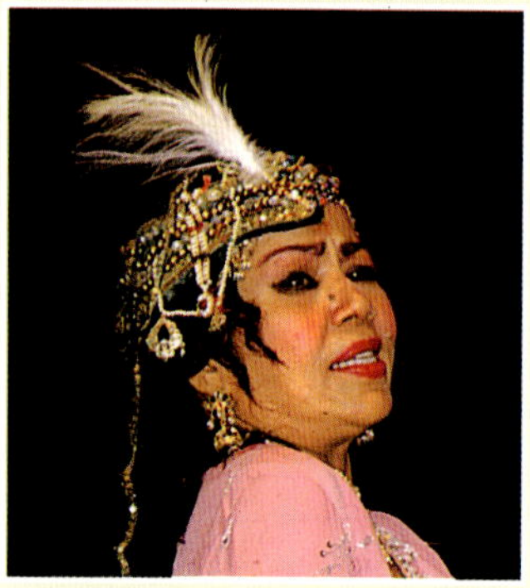

Kathak queen, Sitara Devi.

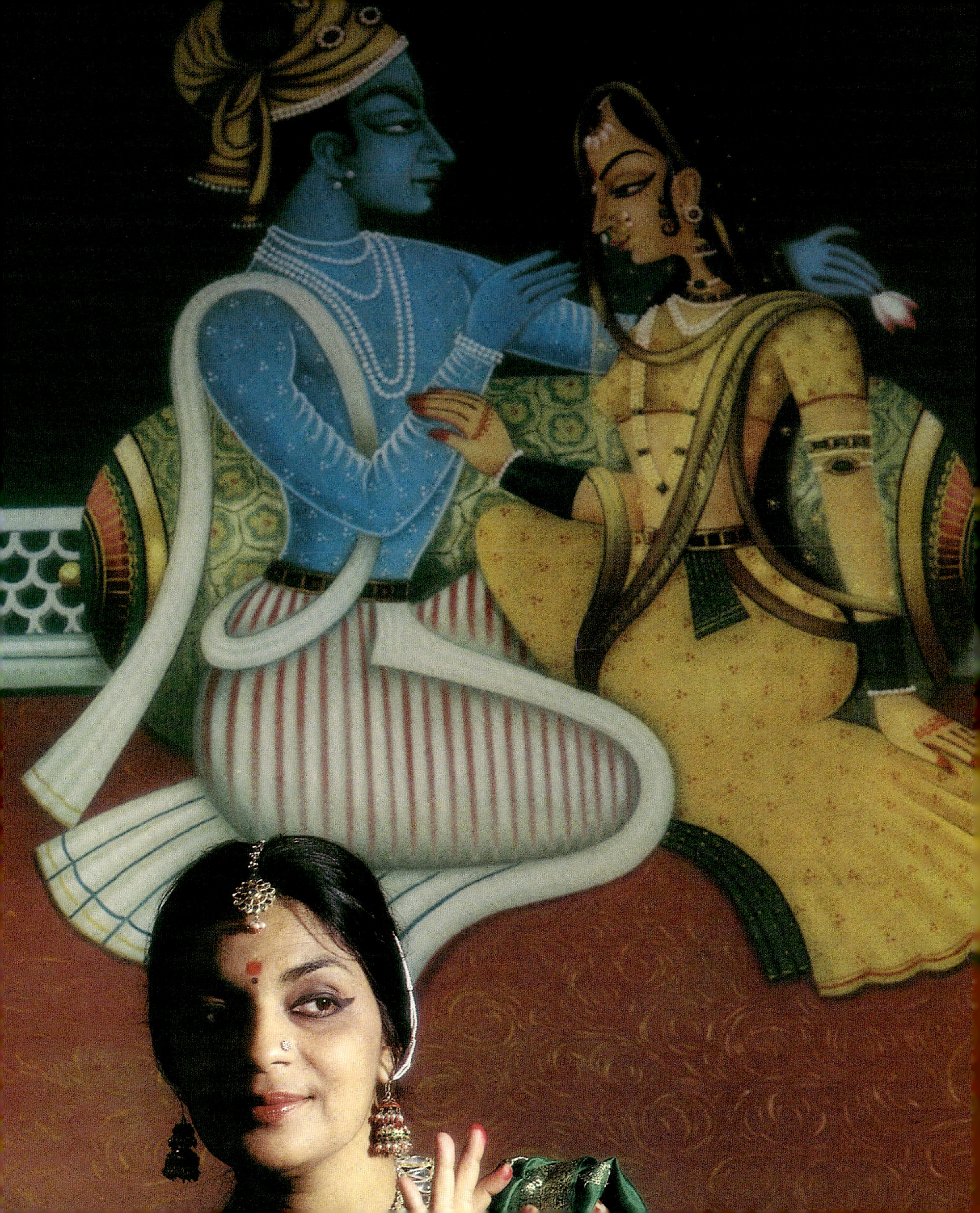

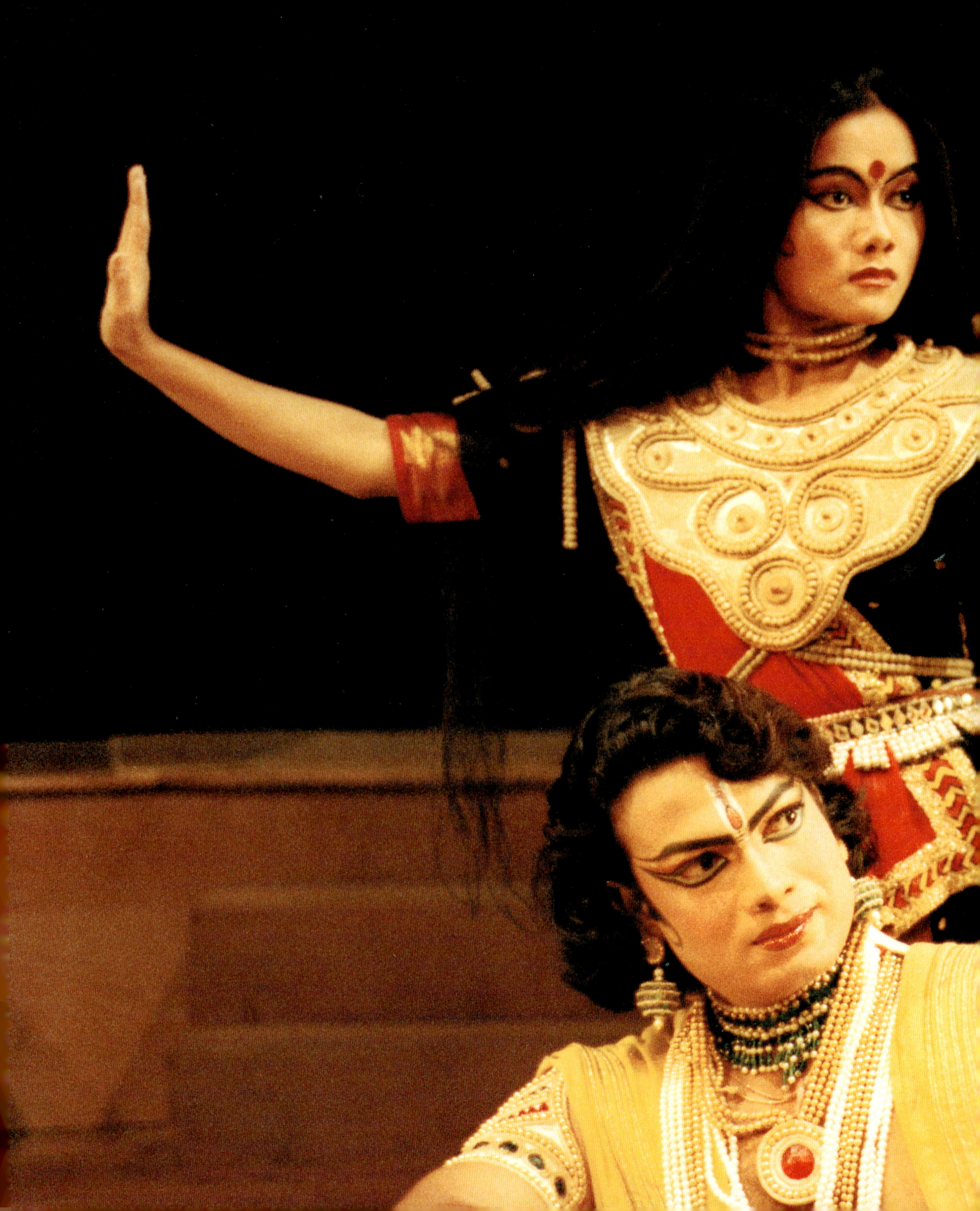

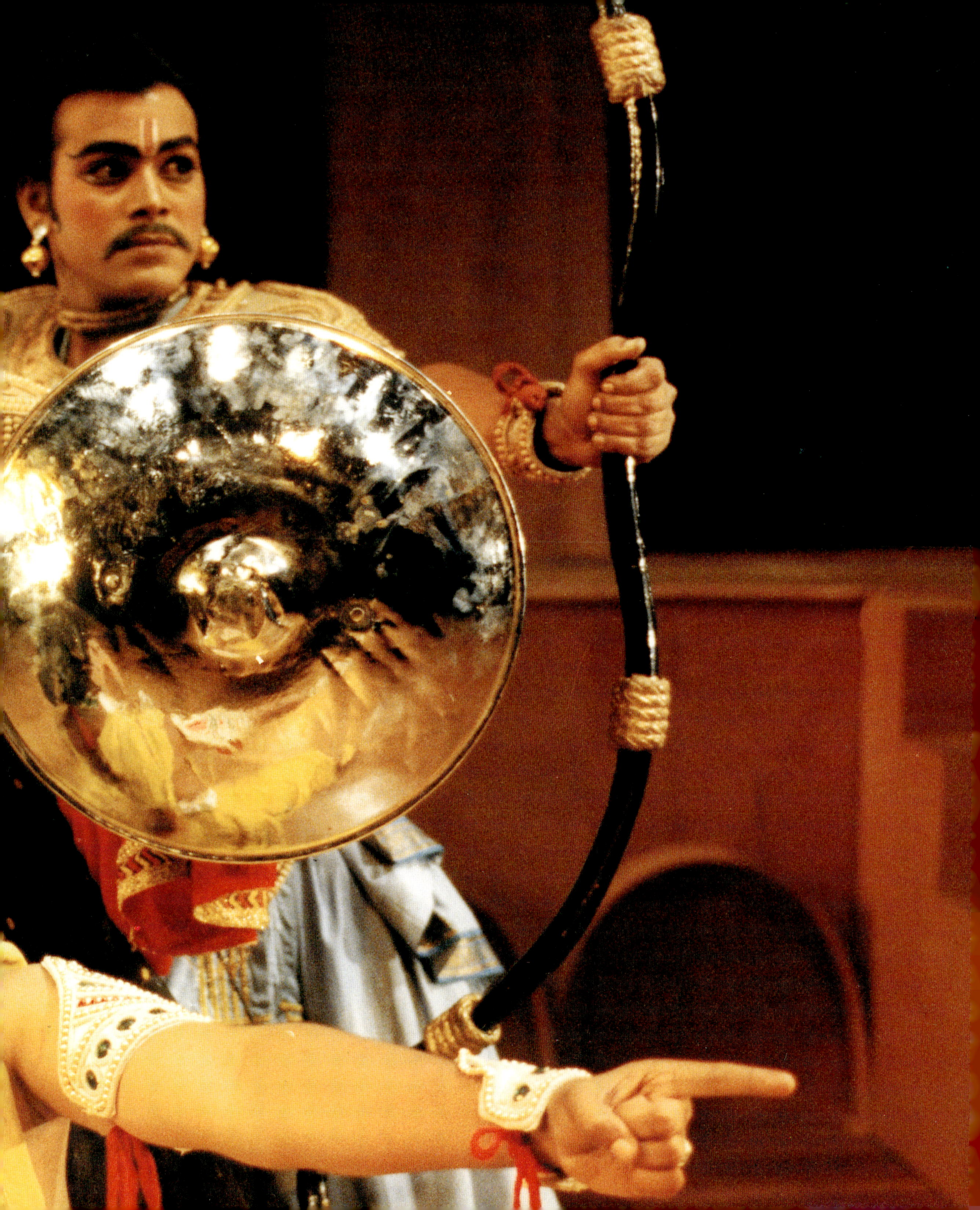

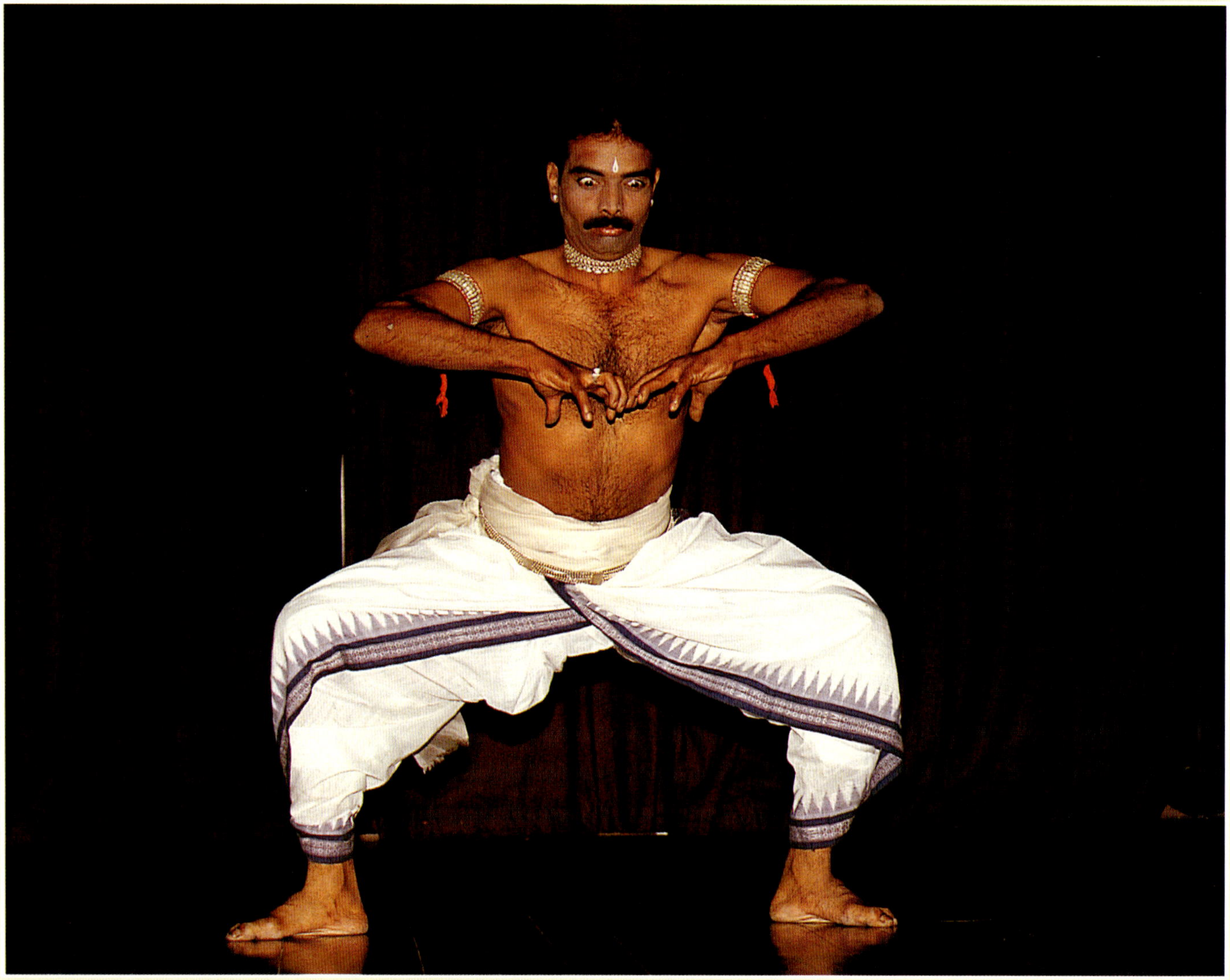

Shashidharan Nair, a trained Chhau artist.
Facing page: *The star of the Jaipur gharana of Kathak, the late Durgalal, left a lasting impact on the dance scene.*
Following pages: *'Chakravyuhu' engulfs Abhimanyu.*

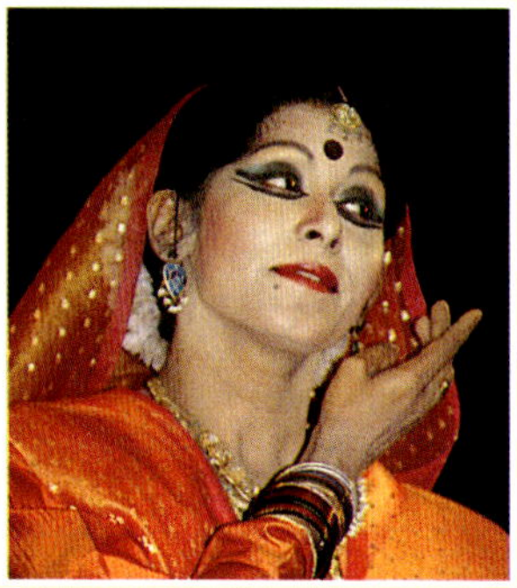

Shovana Narayan in a Kathak 'Bhava' sequence.

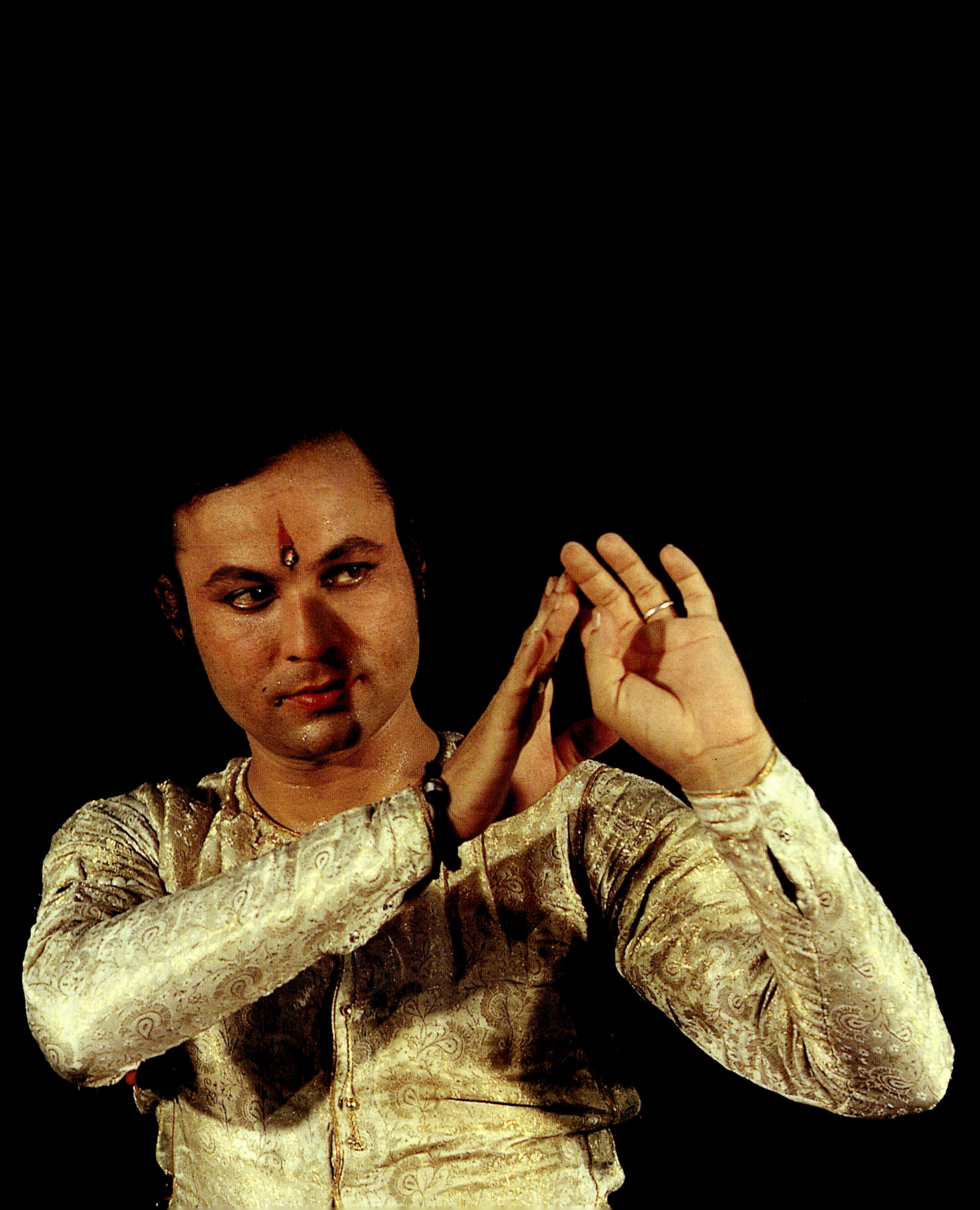

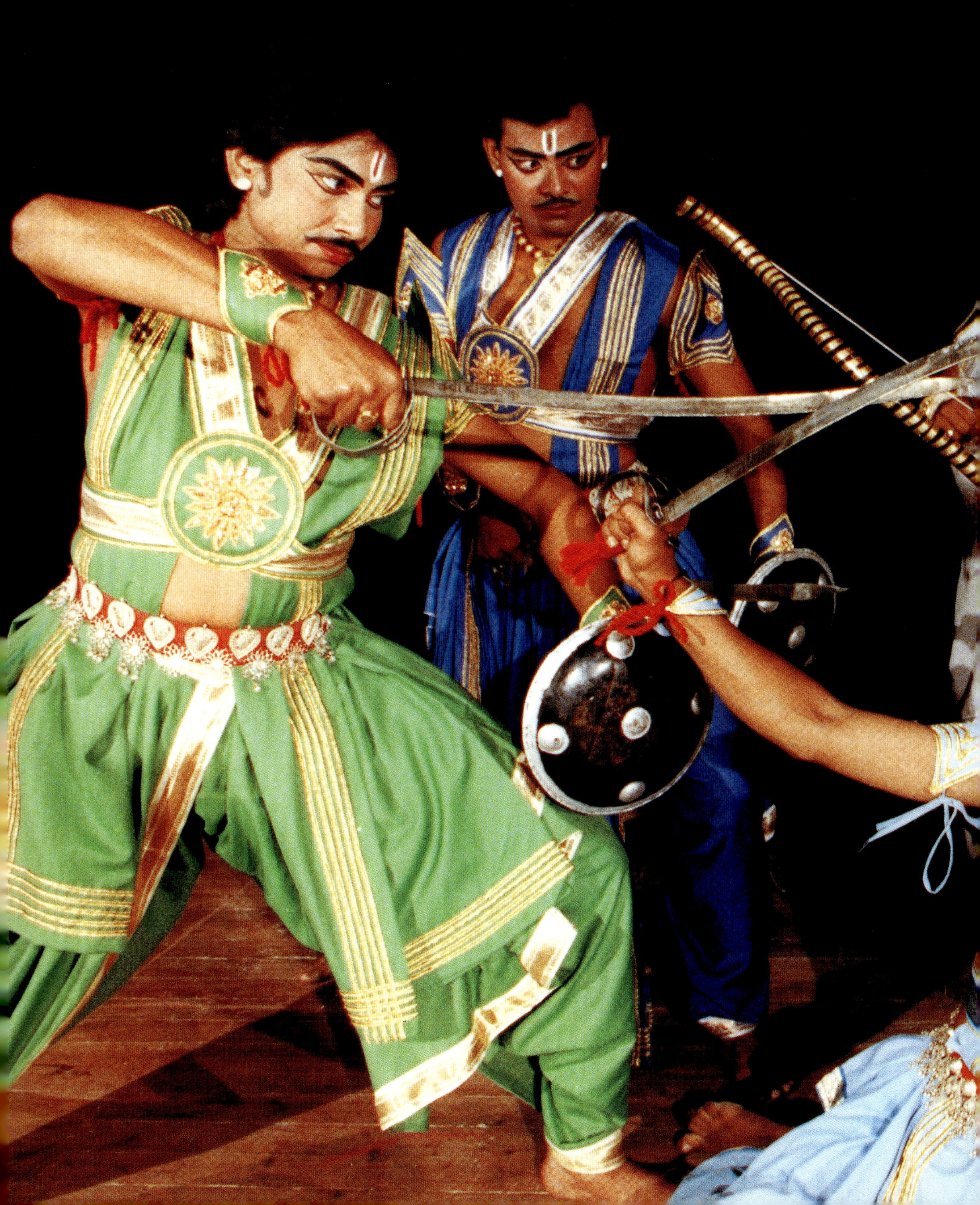

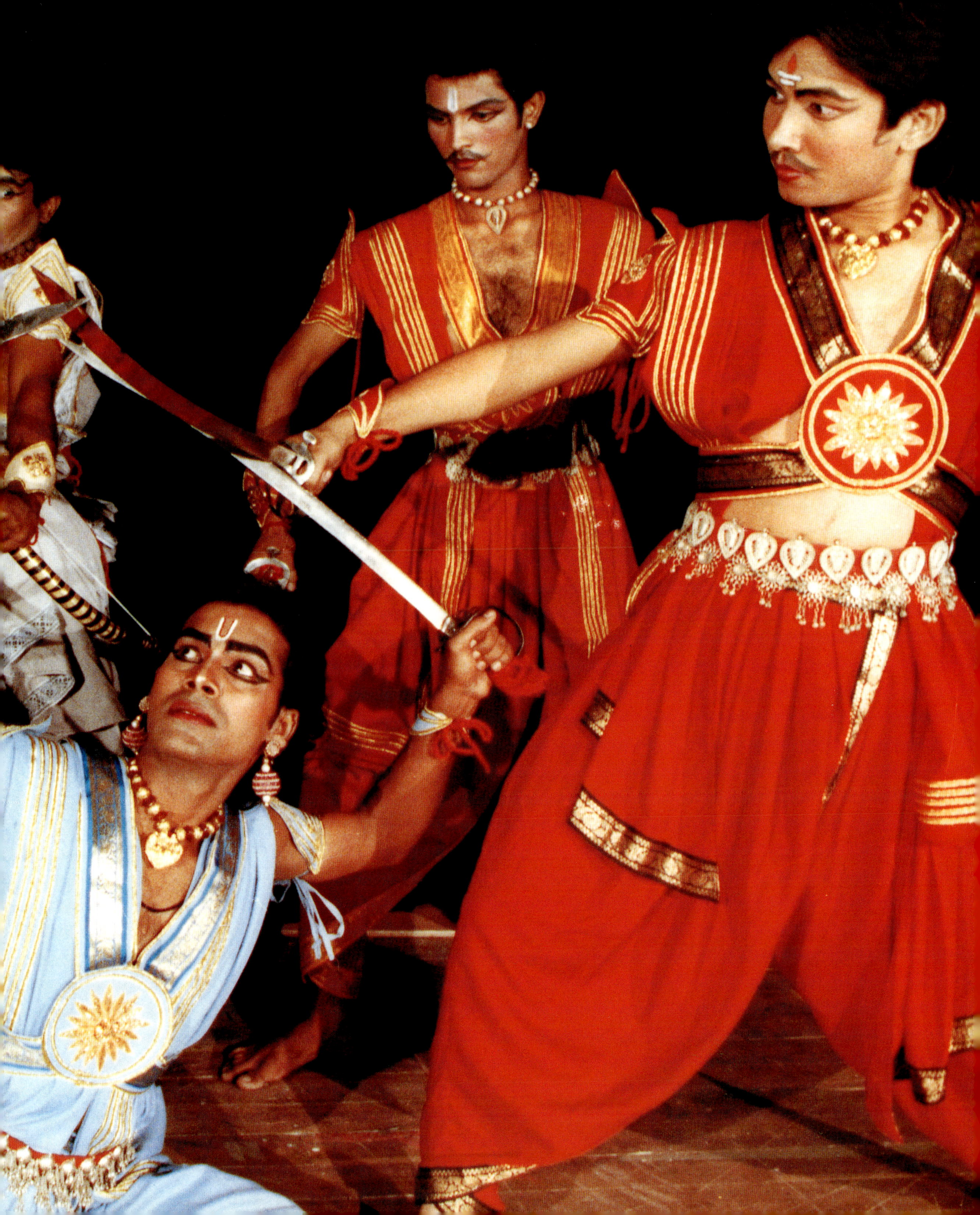

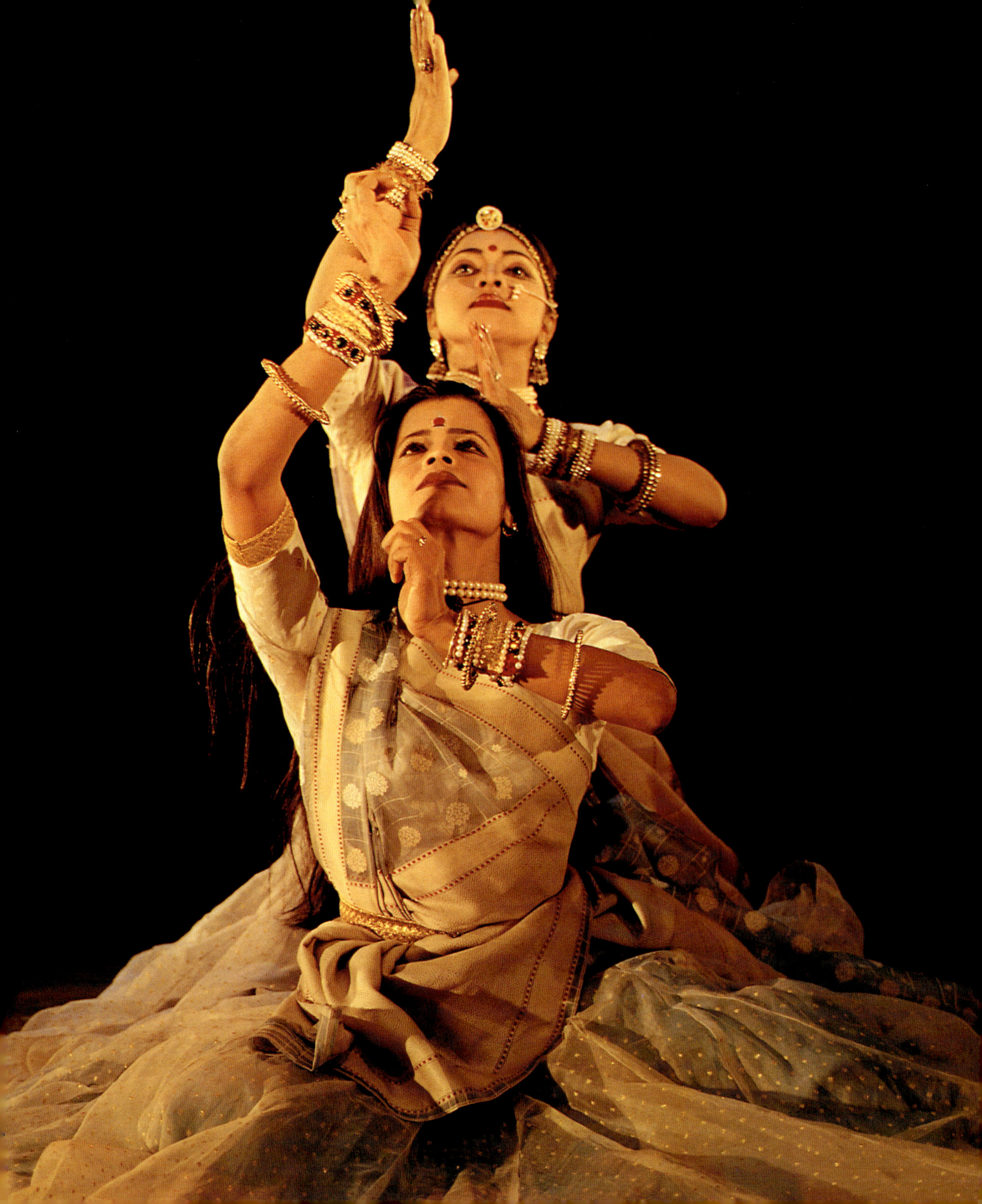

Profiles of Artists associated with the Kendra

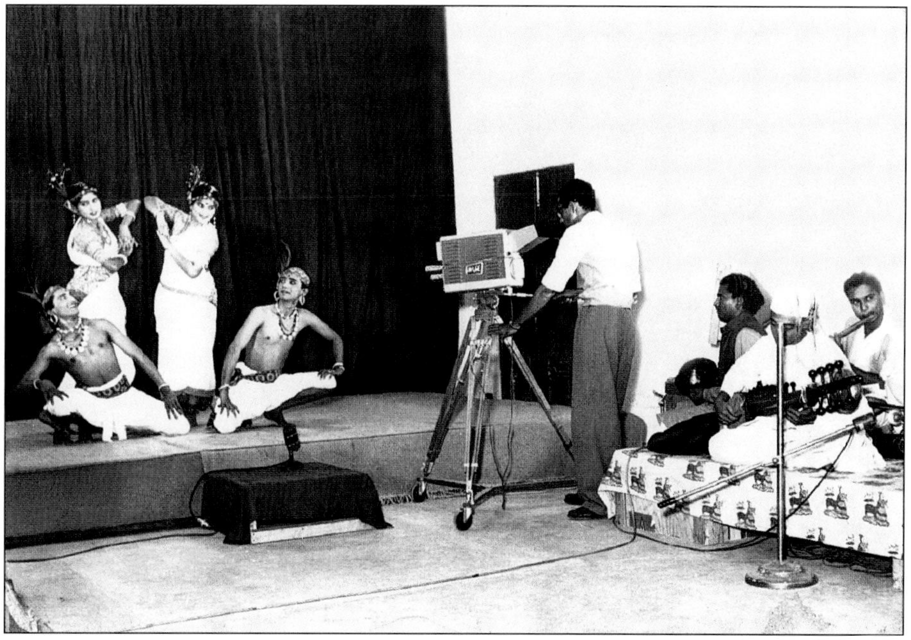

(IN ALPHABETICAL ORDER BY PROFESSIONAL NAMES/FIRST NAME)

◀ *'Meera' gets a contemporary flavour at the hands of Kendra artists.*

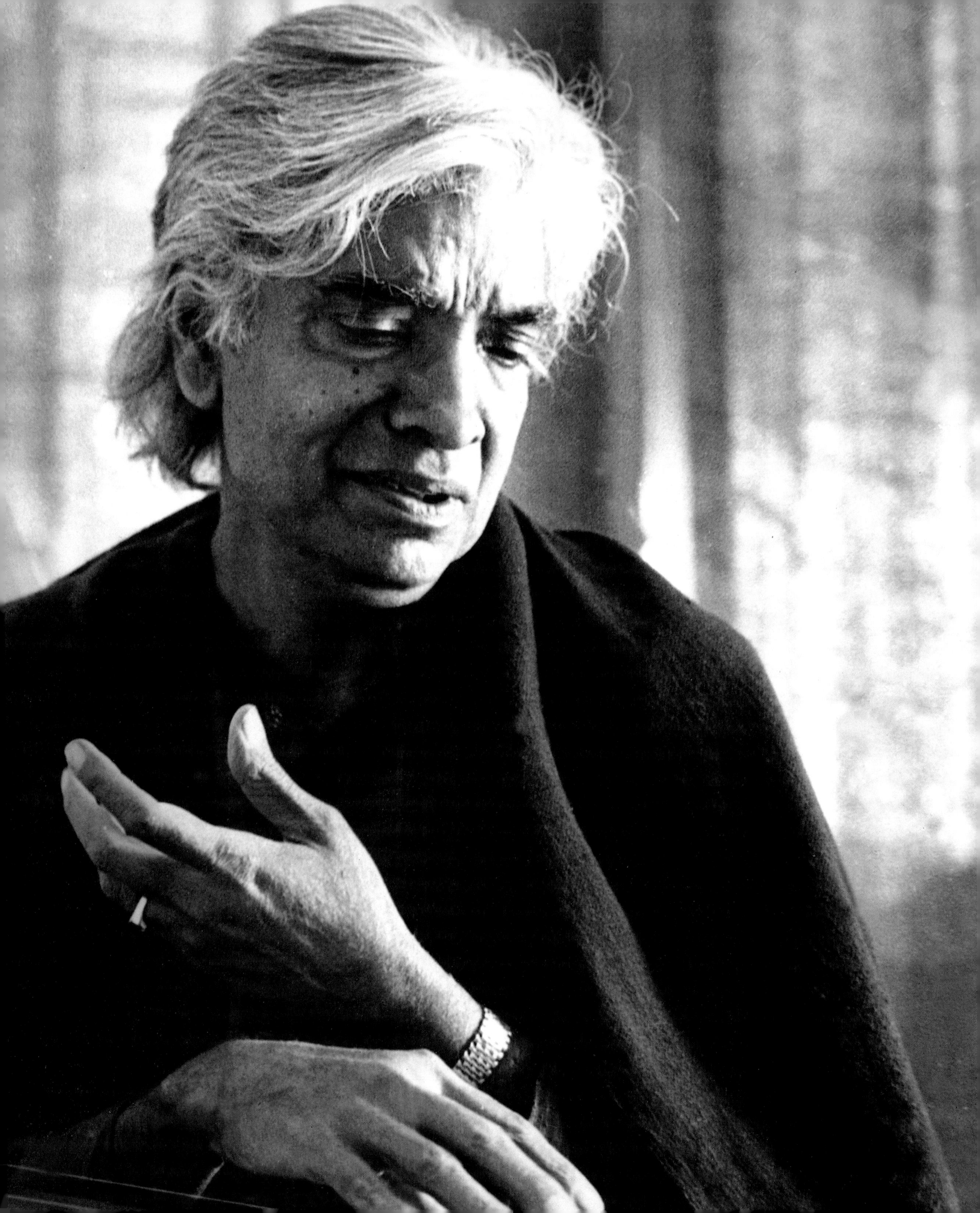

Pandit AMARNATH (1924-1996)

Foremost exponent of the Indore gharana, styled under Ustad Amir Khan.

Born on March 22, 1924, at Jhang in present-day Pakistan, Pandit Amarnath is acknowledged as the foremost exponent of the style of Ustad Amir Khan of the Indore gharana. First trained under the guidance of Prof. B.N. Datta at Lahore, he became a disciple of Ustad Amir Khan in 1948 and was closely associated with him for almost two decades.

He started his professional career in the mid-fifties by teaching as a guru at the Shriram Bharatiya Kala Kendra, after having served as a composer-supervisor at the External Services Division of All India Radio in the forties. Since then, in his fifty years of performing and teaching, he trained several performing artists such as Baldev Raj Verma, Mahendra Sharma and Shanti Vaidyanathan Sharma. As the music composer of Hindustani Theatres in the sixties, he undertook Begum Zaidi's 'Amrapali'; Rajinder Singh Bedi's 'Garam Coat'; M.S. Sathyu's 'Ghalib'; Mohan Rakesh's 'Aashad Ka Ek Din.

In the manner of legendary poet-composers of the Hindustani tradition, Pandit Amarnath has composed over 200 khayals. This achievement put him in a distinguished category of master-musicians: the *vakgeyakars*. He thought out many new ragas and raga compounds, as well as adapted several Carnatic ragas into the Hindustani style, which now form an integral part of the teaching of the Indore gharana. This creative achievement of an entire lifetime has been preserved in archival form at the Indira Gandhi National Centre for the Arts. This project 'Pandit Amarnath and His Gharana', is a compilation in which his original works have been analysed, notated and recorded.

Critically acclaimed as a musician's musician, he performed widely in India and abroad, and was the first Indian musician to have performed at the prestigious Fogg Arts Museum at Harvard, in Cambridge, USA. Over the years, he presented several recitals and concerts for academies and centres like the Sangeet Research Academy, Calcutta; Bharat Bhavan, Bhopal; Kalakshetra, Madras; Sangeet Natak Akademi, Delhi and the National Centre for Performing Arts, Bombay.

A senior artist with the All India Radio for many years, he had over fifty years of broadcasting behind him. On Doordarshan, the national television circuit, he received extensive coverage, in addition to having been featured in their Great Masters Series. He has several discs and cassettes to his credit.

He taught students under the cultural exchange programmes of the Indian Council for Cultural Relations. He authored *Living Idioms of*

Hindustani Music, a dictionary of terms and terminology, published by Vikas Publishers and now in its third edition by Rupa & Co. He had undertaken a biography of his guru, Ustad Amir Khan Sahib, in addition to a seminal work on his music years before he died. For his art, he had been honoured with the Swarmani Award in 1987-88 and the Sahitya Kala Parishad Samman in 1987. He died on March 9, 1996.

ALOKA PANIKAR
(Born 1941)

A senior exponent of Orissi, Aloka represents the best of Guru Mayadhar Raut's style.

Aloka Panikar comes from a family of artists of Bengal. She was born on November 26, 1941 at Chittagong, now in Bangladesh. She came under Guru Gopinath's professional grooming and enacted the role of Sita, in the Shriram Bharatiya Kala Kendra's production of 'Ramlila'. She married artist-choreographer, K. Shekharan Panikar.

As a staff artist of the Kendra, she served in the Ballet Section for several years before branching off to learn Orissi. She first learnt under Guru Hare Krishan Behera and later under Guru Mayadhar Raut. Soon after Aloka Panikar emerged as an Orissi dancer of repute, she was invited to make a performance tour as the State Guest of Orissa. Later, she taught Orissi at the Kendra and continues to do so. She collaborated with the dance scholar Mohan Khokar for a film on Orissi made by the Theatre Department of the University of Rome. She toured and performed extensively in India and abroad. Today, she is a renowned Orissi dancer and considered Guru Mayadhar Raut's principal protege. Her art has taken her on several performance tours and she has been a Visiting Fellow at the Rabindra Bharati University, Calcutta. She regularly conducts classes in Italy at the Teatro Tascible, Bergamo, in addition to having her own school in Delhi where she teaches Orissi. Among her principal disciples are Rajshri Gupta, Ambikaa Panikar, Luigia and Tiziana of Italy, Shagun Butani, Sahana Misra, Yaminey Mubayi, Himani Pandey and Sucharita Majumdar. She participated in *Taal-Mel*, Doordarshan's magnum opus on dance.

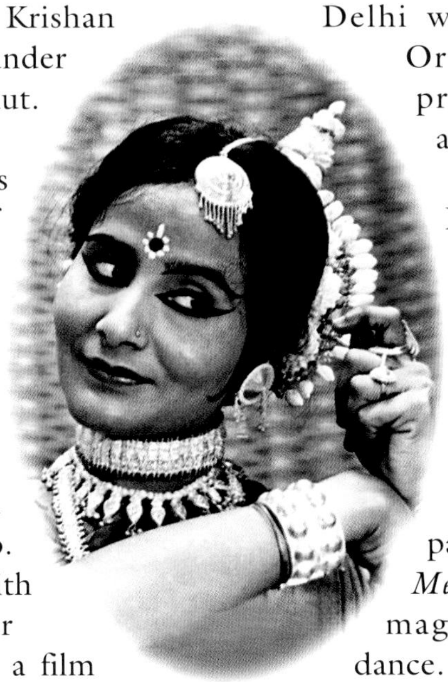

AMBIKAA PANIKAR
(Born 1962)

Represents a continuity of classical Orissi wedded to pristine music.

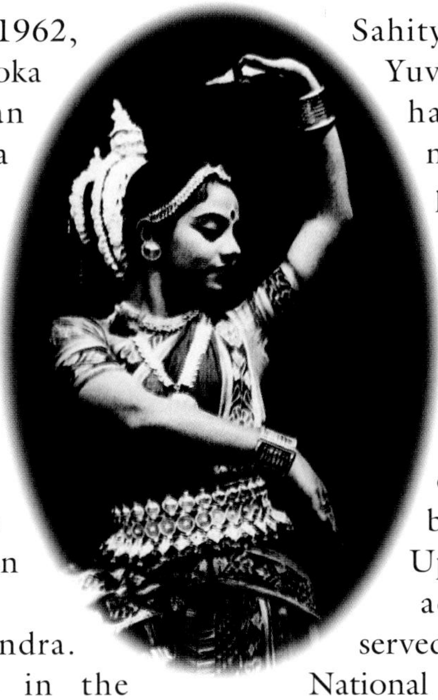

Born on April 20, 1962, to artist parents, Aloka and K. Shekharan Panikar, Ambikaa imbibed the finer nuances of the art of dance at home. She trained in Orissi under her mother, Aloka Panikar, and like her played the role of Sita in the 'Ramlila' production of the Shriram Bharatiya Kala Kendra. She also worked in the Kendra's other productions such as 'Karna' and 'Khajuraho'.

A trained Orissi dancer, she participated in the Sangeet Natak's Young Artists' Festival and the Sahitya Kala Parishad's Yuva Mahotsava. She has performed at major festivals and presented her art of Orissi in Italy, France, Switzerland and Denmark. As a textile designer, she helped design costumes for operas conceived by veteran Mohan Upreti. As a cultural administrator, she served the Indira Gandhi National Centre for the Arts working as a documentationist. She is currently on the Faculty of the Art Kendra as an Orissi teacher and has participated in *Taal-Mel*.

ANITA CHAUDHURY

Anita Chaudhury started dance under the renowned choreographer, Bhagwandas Verma in the sixties. She learnt different styles before taking to the stage professionally. As a staff artist of the Ballet Unit of the Shriram Bharatiya Kala Kendra, she has about two decades of association with the institution and has admirably portrayed different roles, most notably the role of Kaikeyi in the Kendra production of 'Ramlila'.

ARATI SARKAR

Arati Sarkar comes from a family of artists. She took to learning Bharata Natyam at an early age under Guru T.K. Maruthappa Pillai. Later, she learnt Manipuri at Nritya Bharati, Calcutta. She made her professional entry to the stage with Yog Sunder's Indian Revival Group. Her role as Chandalika in the dance-drama by Rabindranath Tagore earned her much praise. She enacted the leading roles in all the ballets produced by the Indian Revival Group and also performed various folk-dances of India.

The next phase of her professional life saw her working

JANUARY 14, 1955: the day I was to commence my training under Guru Shambhu Maharaj, the greatest living exponent of Kathak. I was awaiting his arrival at the Akademi with mixed feelings of delight and anxiety. At 10.00 a.m. sharp a dark, handsome person clad in a *sherwani* and *churidar* outfit walked in, wafting the fragrance of attar. The scent of roses! How very reminiscent of the Moghul courts, I thought, and would have wandered on the wings of fancy to the setting of the romantic Moghul gardens but for the rude jerk I got when he said dryly, "Is this the student from the South who has come to receive training under me? I must say she has disturbed our old family setting and made me travel so far. Women are the same the world over."

Not knowing why he talked in an accusing tone, I stood up meekly, folding my hands in a *namaskar*, for I guessed who he was. That was my first meeting with Shambhu Maharaj. Without waiting for any formal introduction he turned to me and said: "Listen, Maya, I am in my fifties now, and never before have I worked in an institution as an employee. Now I am to work in Bharatiya Kala Kendra. And, what is worse, this letter in a huge envelope from the Government thrusts a great responsibility on my shoulders. It says I have been chosen to impart training to Government of India scholars such as you, who want to specialise in the art of Kathak. The result is I have had to leave my ancestral home in Lucknow and come here to start a new life."

I mustered courage to reply: "Maharaj, I have also come all the way from my home in Bangalore just to study under you. I did not know really that I was disturbing the peace of your retired life..."

Patting me with paternal tenderness, he said: "No, my child, I am not annoyed. I felt sad to leave my people behind, so I had to scold someone. But, now, I see that you are also in the same position and are willing to put up with difficulties for the sake of art. But remember one point always: I do not believe in the professor-student attitude of a college. I would rather you treat me as a guru." I wanted to correct his impression but did not dare to lose the sympathy I had just won.

While we were talking he asked me where I had received my previous training and once again flared up when he heard that I had undergone training in the Jaipur style of Kathak. Born and brought up in the Lucknow *gharana*, Shambhu Maharaj does not acknowledge the greatness of any other style but his own. "So I shall have a tough time teaching you," he remarked, "as I will have to work like a sculptor who remoulds statues, but my implements are so delicate, they are meant for ivory and not iron." Fortunately for me, he revised his opinion when he saw me dancing the next day and even complimented me on my rendering of Kathak. I was thrilled even more when, a few days later, he chose me to partner him in one of his dance items. I was hesitant to dance with him, but he gave me all assurance saying: "Maya, you look at me for guidance while dancing, I shall look at you for inspiration and God will look after both of us!" So it was, and the recital was a success. Since then I have danced many times with him, a distinction which I shall always cherish.

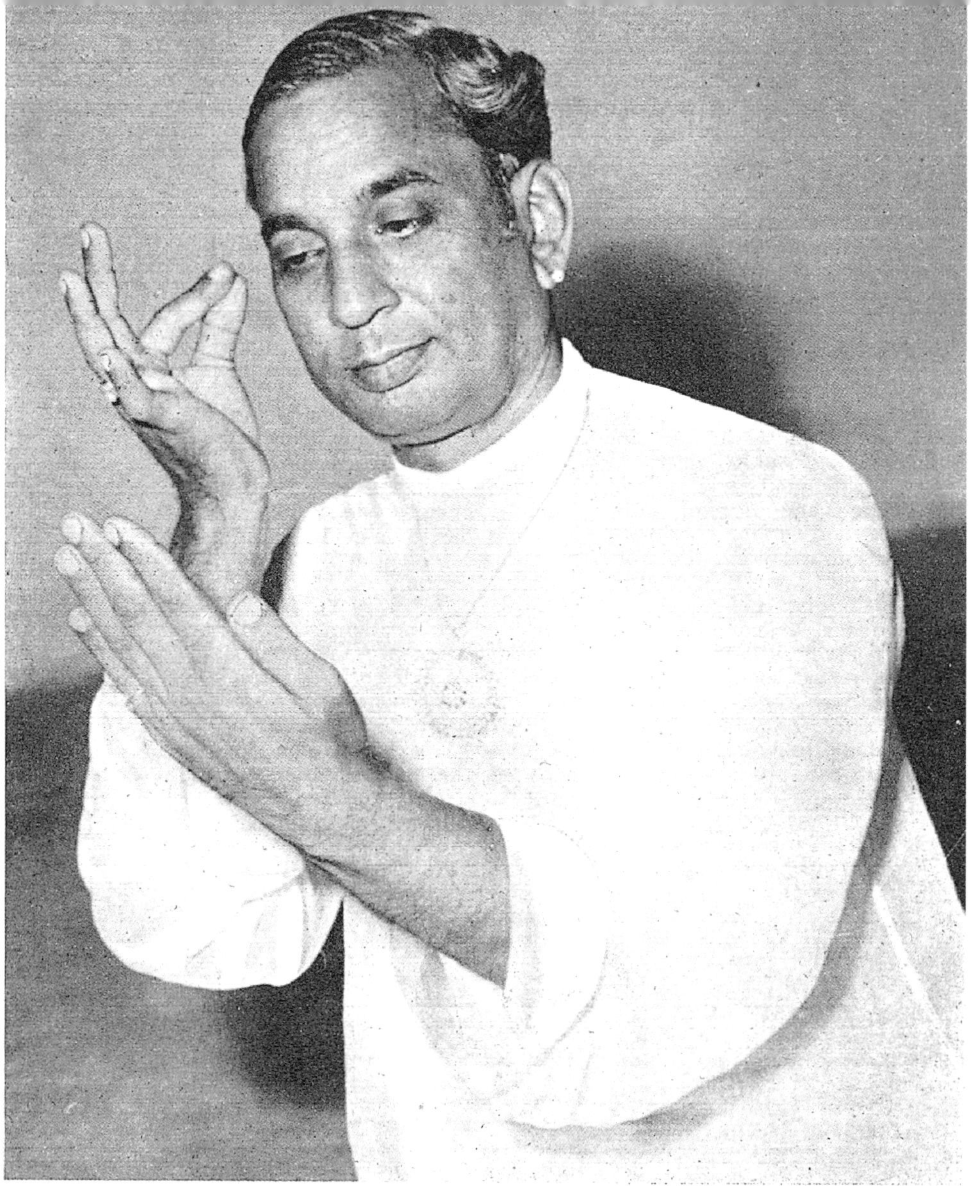

THE RADHA-KRISHNA THEME. The famed exponent of Kathak, Guru Shambhu Maharaj, is seen here in the act of detailing a gopi's make-up. Left: Interpreting a line of music in the language of dance.

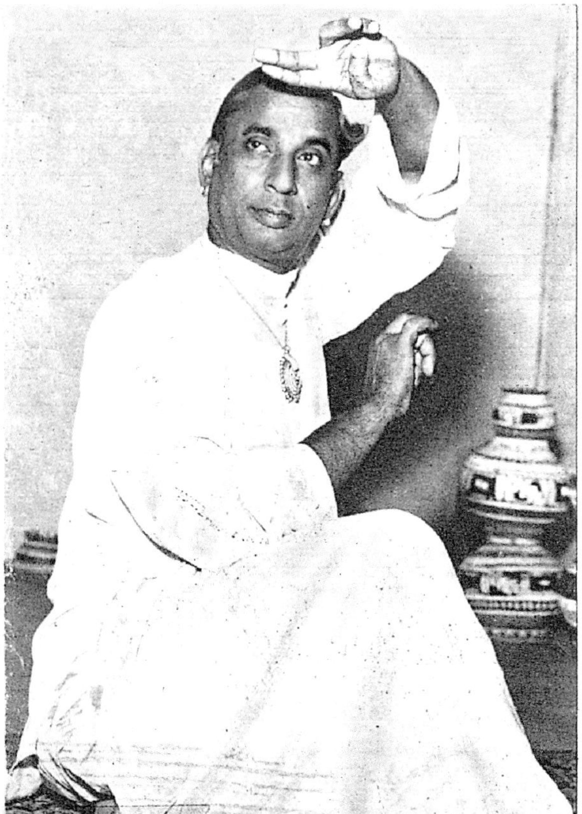

Guru Shambhu Maharaj

by MAYA RAO

Thus I met Shambhu Maharaj and spent several years with him, learning and working with him. Yet, I still marvel at his many-sided personality. Though, in the beginning I had many misgivings about studying under him, I have never found another teacher more sensitive and indulgent almost to the point of pampering his students.

Shambhu Maharaj is today the distinguished holder of the country's most coveted honours—the Sangeet Natak Akademi award and the President's award. Still he is unaffected by success and is never tired of repeating that he owes his position to his brother Guru Achan Maharaj.

At the Akademi Awards function Maharaj was seen in one of his glorious outfits—*kinkhab achkan* and *churidar* pyjama—highlighted by diamond earrings and extra rings on his usually bejewelled fingers! But he was not his usual jovial self. He was silent with a melancholic face, till he went up to the dais and received his *sanad* and other honours. Then he retired to a corner of the dressing-room, opened the scroll, after touching his ears in reverence. And then, suddenly he burst out laughing to the astonishment of his admirers around: "The predictions of my brother and my uncle have come true. I wish they were here to share the honour."

Saying this he recalled his early period of training. Youngest of the reputed trio of Lucknow *gharana*—comprising besides himself, Achan Maharaj and Lachu Maharaj—Shambhu was initiated into the art when he was 8 years old by his uncle, the celebrated Bindadin. After imparting training to Shambhu for 6 months, Bindadin passed away entrusting him to Achan Maharaj's care, saying, "This boy has great promise. Impart your full knowledge to him and he will bring credit to our *gharana*..."

Accordingly Shambhu Maharaj was trained for a few years by Achan. "I know, as far as th[illegible] of dance was concerned, I was progressing very well under the inspired guidance of my brother," Shambhu Maharaj continued, "but I could not say the same of my studies . . ." He was not good in English for which he was being given special lessons at home. "I must have exasperated the teacher beyond measure," he said, "for even after a month's intensive coaching I was not sure whether I should say the bird laid a nest in the tree or the bird laid a tree in the nest!" He added: "Both I believe are far from correct! Naturally he was punished mercilessly by the teacher, till Achan Maharaj intervened and rescued him. "Don't maim my brother's arm," he told the tutor. "He may not know English but he will definitely bring honour to our family."

Shambhu Maharaj was happy to pay tribute to his brother's understanding. "The *sanad* in my hands now is thus really an honour to my uncle and my brother, but little do I know what it says . . ."

On his request one of us explained to Maharaj the contents of the citation which named him as "the foremost exponent of Kathak".

Hearing the praise for his technique in executing intricate *parans* and *bols*, Maharaj once again touched his ears and recounted another incident. In the midst of his early training there was a time of financial crisis which threatened a near disintegration of the family.

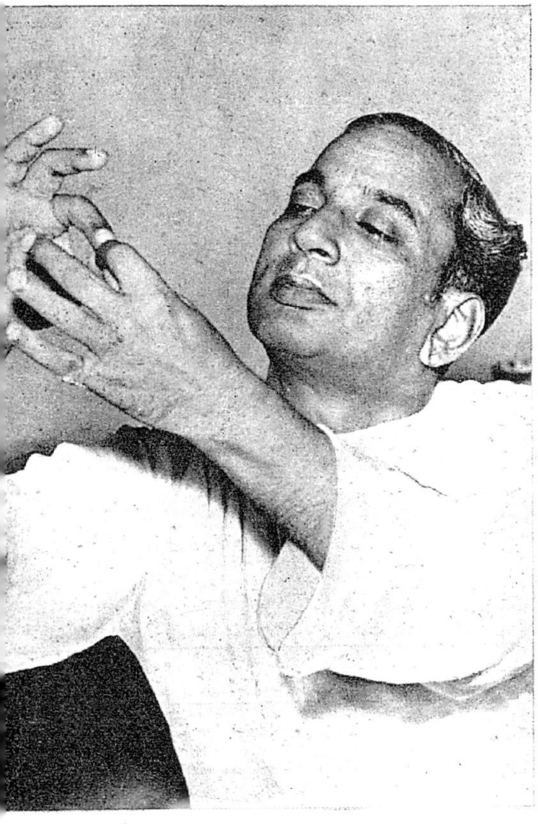

A MASTER of abhinaya, *Maharaj has a very expressive face to suit varying moods.*

Achan Maharaj had to accept a job as a court dancer in Rampur. So he went away leaving Shambhu and their mother to look after the house in Lucknow. Having no one to supervise his practice Maharaj's interests strayed. He was very keen on studying music, so he started learning *thumri* and *khayal* from Ustad Rahimuddin, a reputed musician of the time. As Maharaj had a passion for music he attained proficiency in the art in such a short period that his Ustad advised him to give up dancing and devote all his time to music. This advice alarmed Maharaj's mother who was very conscientious about maintaining the tradition of the *gharana*. She promptly took Shambhu to Rampur and placed him again under Achan's care, saying: "Your brother wants to become a musician. Have you heard of a worse sacrilege to our tradition? Begin his dance training today." So Shambhu started learning again, but his heart was in the *thumris* much to the displeasure of his mother and brother.

Finally, they arranged a dance recital before a select audience, at Achan's house, in which all his disciples were presented and Shambhu was to be the star-dancer.

The programme started well, the students gave a brilliant exposition of the *parans* and *bols* and were highly applauded. But Shambhu was sulky; he was thoroughly at a loss as to what he should dance. All his store of *tukras* and *parans* was exhausted by the students and when his turn came Shambhu could hardly dance one or two items which were novel and not performed earlier. How could he dance more when he had not learnt much in spite of the zeal with which his brother had taught him? Realising his folly he ran away from the stage to crave the pardon of his mother and brother and vowed that he would practise for six to eight hours a day and never again cause them anxiety. With tears in his eyes Maharaj confessed: "It was during that period of rigorous training that I resolved to perfect each *tukra* and *paran* to the complete satisfaction of my Guru, Achan Maharaj. I can remember even now his smile of appreciation at my efforts."

Finishing this story, Maharaj went up to the stage to give one of the most inspiring performances I have seen. Watching the clarity of his style and liquid movements one could see how many years of practice he should have put in ever since he was launched on his dancing career by Achan Maharaj.

Shambhu Maharaj has given over a thousand performances to date. Long ago, in 1936, he was honoured with the title of *Nritya Samrat* at a conference held in Dehra Dun. To Maharaj the most memorable performances of his career are those when he danced with Achan Maharaj. Achan and Shambhu have been acclaimed as "a pair yet unmatched in delineating the intricacies of *nritta* and *nritya* aspects of Kathak".

MASTER OF ABHINAYA

Speaking of *abhinaya* in which Shambhu Maharaj is yet unrivalled, he says that he had watched Bindadin and his disciples performing *abhinaya* standing. While Shambhu was intrigued with the subtle variations in *bhav* (expression), he felt that the variations in music were not developed fully. So, when he learnt music he paid special attention to the melodious patterns one can create in singing a certain line of a *thumri* and then render them in *bhav*. Hence he chose to sit and perform *abhinaya* as he could get more clarity in expressive movements and develop them with unhurried ease. Thus, in course of time, Shambhu Maharaj developed a style of his own in *abhinaya*.

Before starting on *abhinaya* Maharaj sits on the dais and sings the *thumri* for a few minutes and then chooses one line from it for interpretation. He is then free to explore the beauty so as to employ his unlimited imagination to interpret each word of the song. One of Maharaj's favourite *thumris* is *Shyam ghunghat pat khole* (Shyam forcefully lifts my veil). I have seen him perform this over twenty times, but as yet Maharaj has not exhausted his vocabulary in portraying the idea of the first line itself. Every time he seems to tell different tales out of a single musical phrase. He stresses each word and gives a poetic interpretation to it with amazing vividness.

For instance, Shyam is described as Krishna the dark-hued God whose amorous sport is recreated in Brindavan. Again Shyam is associated with the dark blue clouds which play hide and seek with the moon. Shyam is compared to the *surma* (collyrium) which beautifies a gopi's eyes just as Krishna lends charm to her life. As a gopi applies *surma* to her eyes, they smart and the lids cover them instantly. Yet there is a thrill which makes her open her eyes. The thrill of the smarting *surma* is compared with the thrill a gopi enjoys when Krishna pulls her veil.

Thus Maharaj delves deep into poetry with his facial expressions, in which his eyes especially become eloquent. Expressions of joy, desire, annoyance, coquettish invitation and the like are rendered in such quick succession that one cannot help marvelling at his superb command in this field. No wonder he was honoured as *Abhinaya Chakravarti* at the Experts

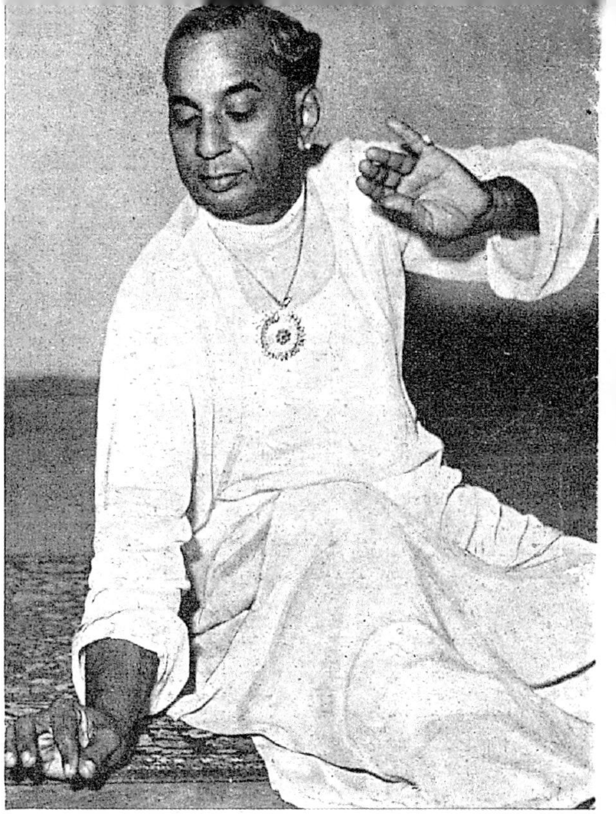

AS KRISHNA in the episode in which the Lord was scolded by Yashoda for consuming a handful of earth and she beheld the cosmic form in his wide open mouth. (Photographs by Govind Vidyarthi.)

Committee Session held by the Music Academy in Madras, 1958, immediately after an exquisite performance by him.

While talking of Maharaj's contribution to *abhinaya*, Balasaraswati, another great exponent, remarked: "The alternating expressions of happiness, longing, despair and hope of a gopi are rendered by Maharaj in such delicate gestures and spontaneous facial expressions that I feel like sitting next to him to learn afresh."

Shambhu Maharaj is not only a renowned dancer but a reputed guru also. He can be easily identified with the ideal dancer and dance teacher immortalised by Kalidasa in his *Malavikagnimitra*. Most of the leading Kathak dancers of the younger generation are the disciples of Maharaj. He works very hard with his students endeavouring to leave the stamp of his style on them. He aims at perfection in every step and movement. He is forever creating new dance sequences emphasising the lyrical aspect. He never lets his student leave the class, until he is assured that he or she is able to perform a new lesson with confidence.

Maharaj is a great favourite with his students and friends. Being a man of varied moods and endowed with a fine sense of humour, his visit each day to the college has a novelty of its own. On a warm day it is refreshing to see him in a gay mood flaunting his new Lucknow *kurta*, saying, with a twinkle in his eye, "It is a gift from one of my admirers!" Another day he would walk in, singing one of his favourite *thumris*, eager to perform it the moment he enters the class. A connoisseur of beauty, he has a *ghazal* or couplet ready when he sees any of his girl students looking charming in a colourful sari.

Yet, there are times too when the students hide from him. That is when Maharaj is in a temper. At that time even a slight mistake is enough to annoy him and make him shout a volley of abuses. When news goes round that Maharaj is in one of those dark moods, one of the students comes prepared with a pathetic tale about an uncle's illness or grandfather's fractured leg. Such tales of human suffering melt Maharaj's heart. He will not only disperse the class for a few minutes but join in the grief of the student.

Personally, I would always like to see Maharaj in one of his hilarious moods, when he sails into the class with the breeze wafting the fragrance of attar, and the spontaneous smile on his lips promises a *ghazal* of sweet melody.

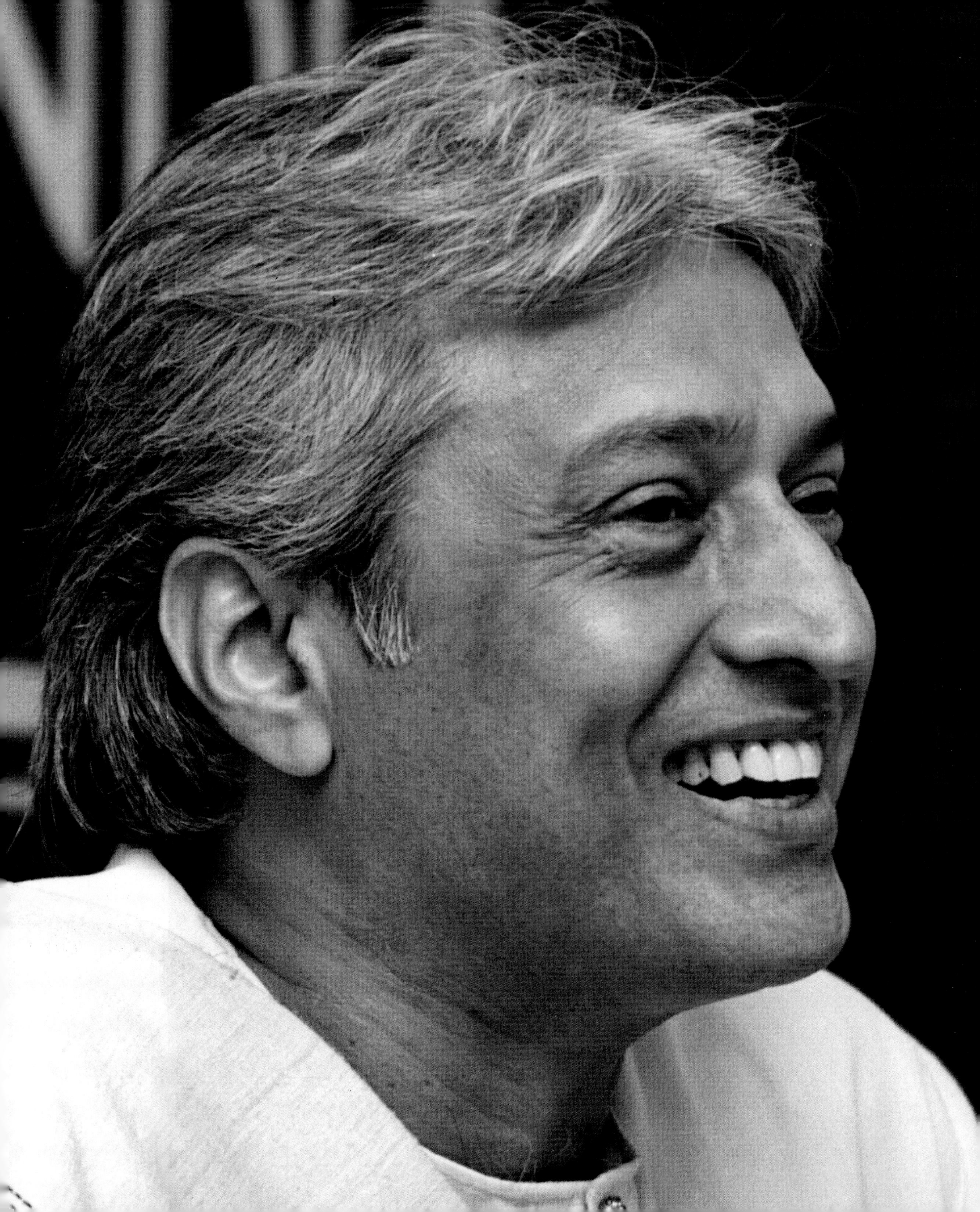

for the famous Uday Shankar in his production 'Shankar Scope'. Arati has been a permanent staff artist of the Shriram Bharatiya Kala Kendra since 1970. Over the years, she played several roles in the evergreen production of the Kendra, the 'Ramlila'. As an artist, she has toured and travelled extensively.

Ustad AMJAD ALI KHAN
(Born 1945)

Son and successor of sarod maestro Ustad Hafiz Ali Khan.

Son and successor of the art of sarod maestro, Ustad Hafiz Ali Khan Sahib, Amjad Ali Khan was born in Gwalior on October 9, 1945. He continues the traditions of the Senia gharana. His deep involvement with the medium has given him the capacity to create anew and he has used this to innovate in classical music and create orchestral scores for children.

After his father, Ustad Hafiz Ali Khan Sahib, he was on the music faculty of the Shriram Bharatiya Kala Kendra and taught several disciples such as Gurudev Singh, Abhik Sarkar, Sharafat Khan, Mukesh Sharma, Debjyoti Bose and Biswajeet. He also composed music for Kendra productions. In 1970 he received the UNESCO Award and the Padma Shri in 1975. The Sangeet Natak Akademi Award was bestowed upon him in 1989.

Ustad Amjad Ali Khan holds a unique position in the world of Indian music today. He has evolved a style that is conventional in technique but highly individual in spirit. He ranks foremost as a sarod maestro today. In memory of his father, he has instituted the Ustad Hafiz Ali Khan Memorial Society, which annually rewards exceptional work in the field of the arts and culture.

Guru BANSI LAL
(1949-1996)

A beacon of the Jaipur gharana of Kathak.

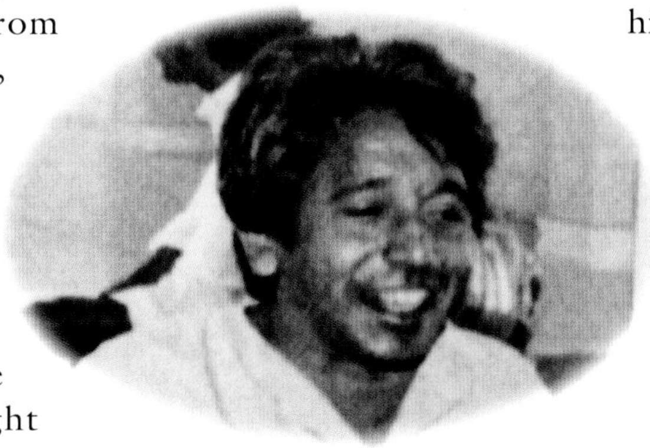

A leading light of the Kathak world, Guru Bansi Lal learnt from Pandit Jailal, the elder brother of Guru Sunder Prasad of the Jaipur gharana. He mastered light classical singing and tabla under the guidance of his father, Shri Bhairav Prasad and under Shri Sohan Lal. Equipped with the best of tradition, he performed all over India and composed ballets such as 'Udhav Sandesh', 'Mohini Bhasmasur', 'Shakuntala' and 'Bhansingh Padawali'. As a staff artist and guru at the Shriram Bharatiya Kala Kendra, he taught several students of whom Panna and Vijay, Prachee Anand, Shambhu Sen, Lalita Hardas, Anita, Sushma Verma and Renu have made a professional mark.

BHAGWANDAS VERMA
(Born 1939)

A ballet artist and choreographer of repute.

A seasoned artist and a leading choreographer of the country, Bhagwandas Verma was trained by Nandlal Bose and Uday Shankar in the thirties. He worked with the Uday Shankar troupe before branching out on his own and coming to Delhi, where in 1957, he enacted the role of Rama in the 'Ramlila' production of the Shriram Bharatiya Kala Kendra in its first year of presentation.

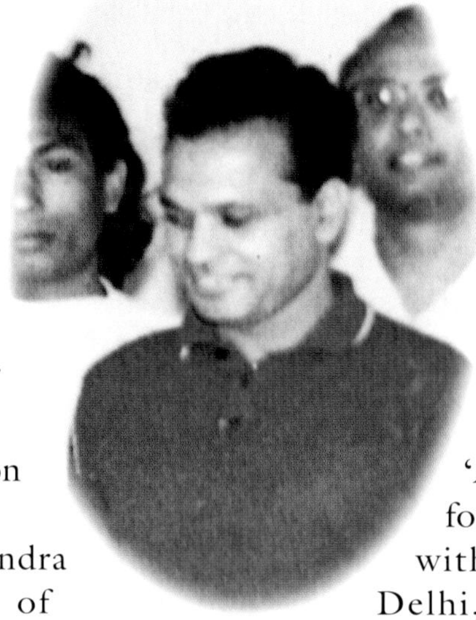

After leaving the Ballet Unit of the Kendra, he joined as the Director of Kamala Narendar Lal's Natya Ballet Centre and undertook productions such as 'Surdas' and 'Krishnalila'. His long association with both institutions resulted in over fifteen ballets. Independently, he worked on productions like 'Amir Khusro'. After four decades of work with the medium in Delhi, he migrated to Australia where he continues to be productive.

BARUN GUPTA

Initiated into the art of Israj playing at an early age, Barun Gupta, fondly called Mintoo, was trained under the expert coaching of his maternal uncle, Abhani Das Gupta. Born in Siliguri, West Bengal, he later migrated to Bombay and came into contact with Pandit Ravi Shankar, the maestro of sitar. He played in orchestral performances composed by the maestro and also worked as a musician in some Bengali films under Jyotirindra Moitra.

In Delhi, he served the Shriram Bharatiya Kala Kendra as Assistant Music Director for ten years before becoming the Music Director of the Ballet Unit. His first assignment, the score of 'Sitayan' won him acclaim. He has since composed music for 'Azadi-Ki-Or'; 'Mahaiv'; 'Surdas';

'Krishnavtaar'; 'Jagdeo'; 'Konark'; 'Kalinga Vijaya'; 'Bahubali' and 'Khajuraho'. For a number of years, he conducted the music of 'Ramlila'. He has also been on the panel of approved Music Directors of the Films Division of the Government of India.

BELA ARNAB

Hailing from a family of musicians in Bengal, Bela Arnab received training in the Kathak dance form in the fifties from Pandit Jailal of the Jaipur gharana and Pandit Shambhu Maharaj of the Lucknow gharana for which she received a Government of India scholarship.

She gave several solo performances before participating in the productions of the Shriram Bharatiya Kala Kendra. After a long stint in Delhi, she moved to Calcutta, where she taught as a lecturer at the Rabindra Bharati University.

BHARATI GUPTA
(Born 1940)

Principal disciple of Birju Maharaj and a star ballet artist.

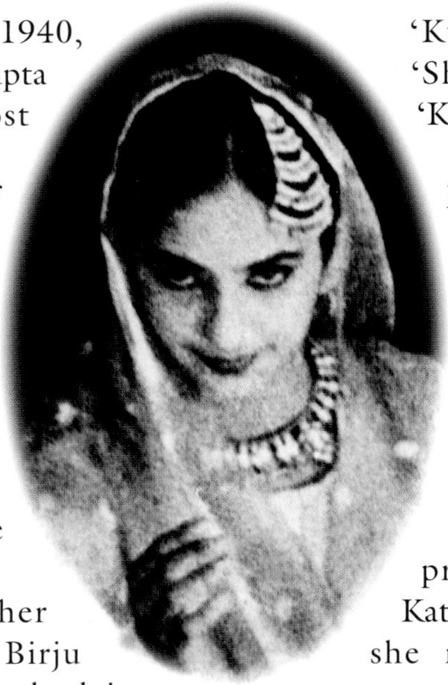

Born on May 28, 1940, in Agra, Bharati Gupta is among the most accomplished Kathak soloists of the sixties and the seventies: Bharati Gupta's name and reputation as an artist is impeccable, as was her training in the art form under the giant Shambhu Maharaj. It was her partnership with Birju Maharaj which resulted in memorable dance-dramas like 'Kumar Sambhav', 'Shan-e-Oudh' and 'Krishnayan'.

She has had a long association with the Shriram Bharatiya Kala Kendra, first as a student and later as a professional dancer. She has participated in nearly all of the productions of the Kathak Kendra, where she now teaches and grooms young Kathak aspirants.

BHAGWAT CHANDRA UPRETI

Born on February 4, 1942, he undertook his Masters from Agra University while pursuing the art of tabla under Ustad Inam Ali Khan of the Delhi gharana at the Shriram Bharatiya Kala Kendra in the sixties. Later he took to the pakhawaj under the legendary Guru Purushottam Das, also teaching at the Kendra.

Bhagwat brings to his music the flavour of Kumaon culture and has accompanied several artists, in addition to playing solo. He has published *Mridang Vadan* and has toured Afghanistan, Iran, Russia, Bangladesh and Greece. As an active member of his renowned brother Mohan Upreti's Parvatiya Kala Kendra, he has been the musical pillar of the group.

BHUSHAN LAKHANDRI
(Born 1960)

A star of Kendra productions.

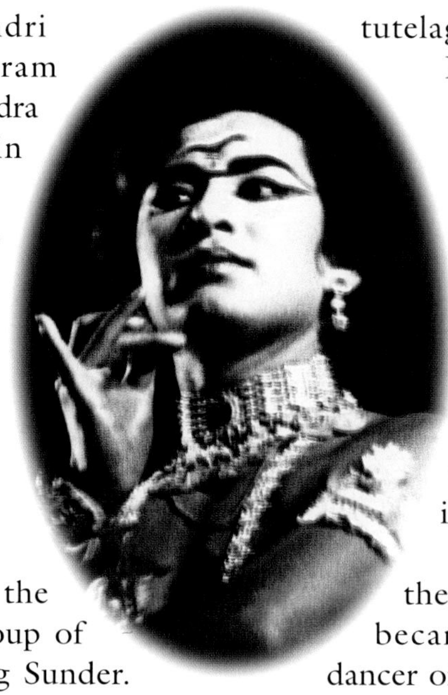

Bhushan Lakhandri joined the Shriram Bharatiya Kala Kendra as a staff artist in 1976 and soon rose in the ranks, enacting principal roles. He has played the role of Jatayu, Bharat and Rama, over the years. As a competent folk dancer, he had earlier worked in the Indian Revival Group of choreographer, Yog Sunder.

In addition to carving a place for himself in the Kendra productions, he came under the tutelage of Chhau Guru Krishan Chandra Nayak. This association led to productions in Chhau such as 'Konark'; 'Khajuraho'; 'Yayati' and 'Karna'. He tried his hand at creative dance with 'Masks' in 1983.

He travelled with the Kendra tours and became an established dancer of its Ballet Unit. He left the Kendra to work with film actress Hema Malini in her dance-dramas in Bombay.

Guru BIRJU MAHARAJ
(Born 1937)

The king of Kathak today, an heir to the Kalka Bindadin gharana of the Lucknow School of Kathak.

Born on February 4, 1937, at Lucknow, Brij Mohan Mishra, popularly known as Birju Maharaj, is the son of the legendary Kathak Vidwan, Pandit Achchan Maharaj. He began his formal training at the age of seven under his father and additionally acquired the finer nuances of the art form from his illustrious uncles, Shri Shambhu Maharaj and Shri Lachchu Maharaj.

The youngest performer ever, he received the Sangeet Natak Akademi award in 1964. His distinguished career has brought out his several capacities and talents in the fields of instrument playing, composing, writing and choreographing. A seasoned dancer, he performed extensively during his career spanning over four decades and was staff teacher at the Shriram Bharatiya Kala Kendra. He took principal

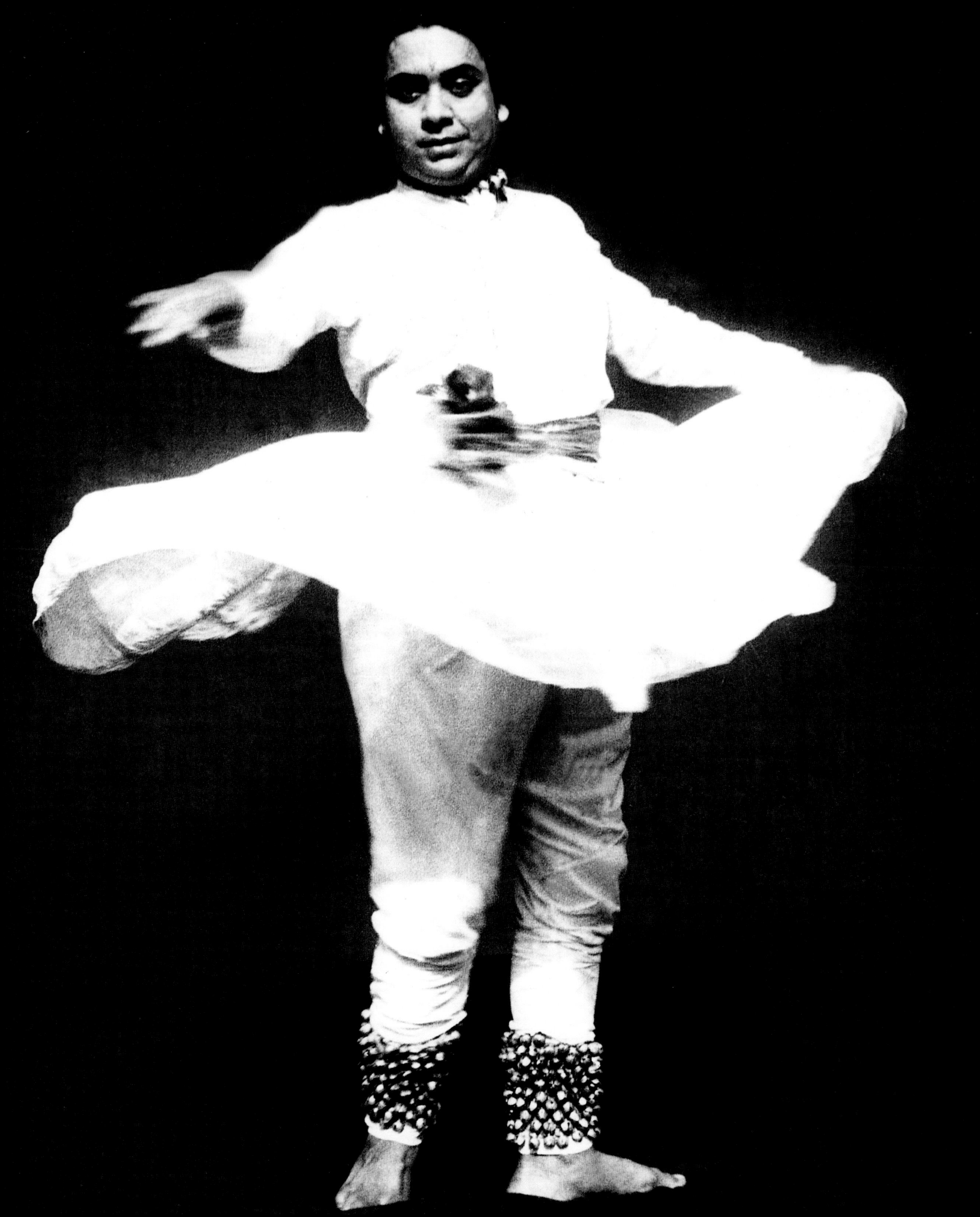

roles in several of the Kendra's early productions such as 'Malati Madhav'; 'Kumar Sambhav' and 'Kathak Ki Kahani.'

He taught and initiated several leading dancers of today, like Pratap Pawar, Tirath Ajmani, Bharati Gupta, Prabha Marathe, Rashmi Jain-Vajpeyi, Shovana Narayan, and later countless numbers of students at the Kathak Kendra, of whom are Brojen Mukherjee, Saswati Sen and Veronique Azan.

He has choreographed several Kathak dance-dramas and has made this essentially solo art form group-oriented. For Satyajit Ray's film 'Shatranj Ke Khilari', he montaged two dance sequences. Having travelled widely, Birju Maharaj has propagated the art of Lucknow Kathak far and wide. Countless titles and awards have followed, including the Sangeet Natak Akademi Award in 1964. In 1996, he participated in *Taal-Mel.*

B.K. SAWANT

'Badal' B.K. Sawant is an accomplished stage craftsman, who has served the Shriram Bharatiya Kala Kendra since 1957. His expertise in using a variety of Indian crafts and techniques in creating stage props, sets and ornaments have long embellished the Kendra's various productions and presentations. For a few years, he also acted as Stage Manager of the Kendra. He has a unique combination of talent and technique, which few have been able to duplicate or improve. He has performed several roles in the Kendra's productions and has travelled with the troupe.

BROJEN MUKHERJEE

Son of Ananda Gopal Mukherjee and a disciple of Pandit Birju Maharaj, Guru Sundar Prasad, Ramgopal Mishra and Manjushri Banerjee, Brojen served the Kendra with distinction. A gentle personality, he left Delhi for Asansol where he runs a centre for dance, teaching Kathak and regaling audiences with his Natwari Kathak.

CHANDRA JAYNAGARKAR

Trained in Kathakali by Keshavan Namboodri and in Orissi by Guru Hare Krishna Behera in the sixties, Chandra served the Shriram Bharatiya Kala Kendra from 1959 to 1975 as a staff artist. She received the Nritya Kala Ratna Award from Swami Shivanand in 1960. For several years now she has run her own dance school.

THE STATESMAN, MARCH 31, 1983 3

SHRIRAM BHARATIYA KALA KENDRA presents

SHAKUNTALA

Choreography : K Shekharan Music : Barun Gupta
Lighting : Tapas Sen

On March 31st, April 1st & 2nd, 7 p.m.
at Kamani Hall, Copernicus Marg, New Delhi.

Tkts: Rs. 25/-, 15/-, 10/-, 5/-
at Cottage Emporium & site.
ENQUIRIES: 386428, 386429

SBKK-3182

SHRIRAM BHARATIYA KALA KENDRA
presents
an evening of dance & music
(dedicated to the memory of the late Guru Devi Lal)
featuring
BIRJU MAHARAJ, DURGA LAL, ALOKA PANIKAR, BISWAJIT ROY CHOWDHURY KIRAN SEHGAL, LATIF AHMED, TULSI NARAIN & OTHERS
On 13th March, 1980—7 p.m.
KAMANI AUDITORIUM
Tickets : Rs 15, Rs. 10, Rs 5, Rs 3
Available from : Cottage Industries, Shriram Bharatiya Kala Kendra & at the gate.
SBKK
Enquiries :
386428—386429

Bharatiya Kala Kendra
92nd Street "Y"
April 1, 1963

Rhythm and director (dancer-drummer Brijamohan Maharaj) were the stars of these Kathak dances from North India. The emphasis was on decorative movements, intricate rhythms, rapid whirls, sudden halts, and the still pose. The approach differed from the more interpretive, emotional Bharata Natyam, just as the royal court differs from the temple. Costumes of tight-fitting pyjamas and knee-length tunics, worn by men and women both, or the men's baggy trousers, bright turbans and sashes, the women's sparkling jewels, were other regional notes.

Brijmohan Maharaj's controlled footwork in rhythmic patterns so subtle his ankle bells shaded into mere breaths of sound was striking evidence of India's cultural expansion into the caves of southern Spain. Uma Sharma's dance of femininity was delicate yet precise. Excerpts from story dances, such as a love duet between the god Madan and his consort Rati: Krishna playing ball with his friends or slaying the serpent Kaliya; a friendly contest between the gods of fire and water, were exuberantly performed by the youthful company. As contrast to the more familiar Bharata Natyam and Kathakali styles, or as an evening of dance on its own, the Kathak presentation was decidedly welcome. *M. M.*

DANCE MAGAZINE May 1963

Sir Shankar Lal Music Festival

By Our Music Critic

The seventh Sir Shankar Lal Music Festival was inaugurated by the Mayor, Mr. Hans Raj Gupta, in New Delhi on Thursday. Highlighted by a recital by Ustad Amir Khan, the opening day's programme also featured Abdul Halim Jaffar Khan and Nirmala Arun.

Nirmala, who has specialised in ghazal, began with a khayal in Puriya Dhanasri. The score provided enough frivolity and fun as Nirmala fluttered about with the agility of a light-winged bird. Her fragile temperament and voice, [illegible] embellished utterance could scarcely measure up to the demands of the [illegible] and dignified khayal. Tying an elephant with a slender string, this is how it looked. Looseness of design and treatment with inadvertent flashes of kalyan spoiled her khayal.

Her thumri in Pahadi, though erratic and unsteady, struck a happier note. But it was Nirmala's ghazal which one liked the most. Here her expression was free, uninhibited and inspired.

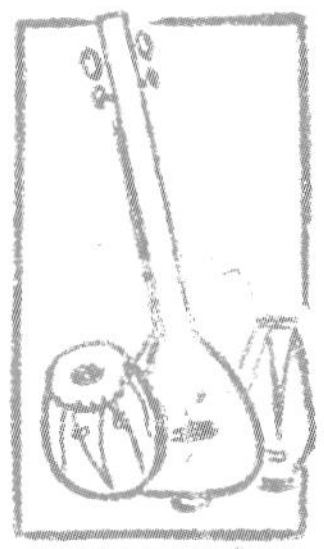

Abdul Halim Jaffar Khan a versatile and polished sitar-player rendered the lyrical and tender Jai Jai Vanti. The initial alap fulfilled the technical demands of the raga. He displayed a fine feel of the notes. One was particularly intrigued by the soft descending movement in which the melody gently touched off Komal Gandhar.

To be precise and unerring in this raga, an artiste has constantly to focus attention on a set of phrases. And this Jaffar did steadfastly even at the risk of being repetitive. Scintillating swift passages tickled the ear with their euphonious charm. Fascinating flourishes kept flashing forth every now and then to enliven the music. However, his imagination seemed to be tied down by the exacting demands of the raga. In spite of its outward ebbulience and robustness, the recital did not stir any shords of deep feeling or exhalted and impassioned creation. The bass notes did not have the sustained and lingering tonal charm associated with them. The galaxy of lovely trailing string tones emanating from a single pluck was as [illegible] as it was [illegible] of the [illegible] technical acumen.

[illegible]

National Dance Festival

Inauguration By President In Nov.

[BY OUR SPECIAL CORRESPONDENT]

NEW DELHI, Thursday.—A five-week National Dance Festival sponsored by the Sangeet Natak Akademi will open here on November 2, at the Arts Theatre in the Indian Industries Fair. The Festival will be inaugurated by Dr Rajendra Prasad.

The dances to be staged during the Festival will include Bharatnatyam, Kathakali, Kathak, Manipuri and traditional dances like Chhau, Tripura, Assamese and Odissi, as well as ballets.

The Executive Board of the Akademi has decided to entrust its organization to the Bharatiya Kala Kendra, Delhi. The troupes, which will participate in the Festival, will be nominated by State Governments.

BHARATIYA KALA KENDRA
PRESENTS
HOLI FESTIVAL
FEATURING COLOURFUL CLASSICAL AND FOLK DANCES
ON 5TH, 6TH & 7TH MARCH
Daily 6-30 p.m.
AT
BHARATIYA KALA KENDRA GROUNDS & 'NRITYA RANGOLI' AT KAMANI HALL, LYTTON ROAD, NEW DELHI.
TICKETS :
Rs. 5 Valid for Kamani Hall & Kala Kendra Grounds. Rs. 3 (Adults) & Re. 1 (Children) valid for Kala Kendra Grounds only.
AVAILABLE AT :
COTTAGE INDUSTRIES EMPORIUM, JANPATH; DELHI VANASPATI SYNDICATE, KHARI BAOLI; ASHOKA HOTEL, AND BHARATIYA KALA KENDRA BHAWAN.
Enquiries : 386428 & 29

JHANKAR
Presents

[illegible]n./Fri.	—	Harish Rawat (Kathak)
	—	Folk Dances (SBKK)
[illegible]e./Thu.	—	Vidyotma Sharma (Orissi)
	—	Folk Dances (SBKK)
[illegible]b. 6th	—	Aloka Panikar (Orissi)
[illegible]b. 9th	—	Jaishree (Kathak)

[illegible]ckets : Rs. 15, 10, 3.
[illegible]ailable at Shriram Bharatiya Kala [illegible]ndra, [illegible]a World Travel and Jhankar.
[illegible] 28[illegible]8.

Dhrupad & Dagars Go Together

[illegible]hriram Bharatiya [illegible]ala Kendra presents
KHAJURAHO
ballet in mayurbhanj chhau
[illegible]ance K C Naik
[illegible]usic Barun Gupta
[illegible]ighting Tapas Sen
[illegible]8, 29 & 30 March 7:00 pm
[illegible]amani Hall Copernicus Mg
[illegible]ickets Rs15,10,5,3 from
[illegible]ottage Empm.& site
[illegible]NQ: 386428

Shriram Bharatiya Kala Kendra
presents
Krishna Avatar
29th Aug.—8th Sept., at 7 p.m.
(2 shows on 6th, 7th & 8th Sept.— 3.30 p.m., 7 p.m.)
at Kamani Auditorium,
1 Copernicus Marg.
Tickets : Rs. 25/-, 15/-, 10/-, 5/-.
At Cottage Emporium
and venue.
ENQ : 386428, 388084
[illegible] SBKK 38[illegible]

SHRIRAM BHARATIYA KALA KENDRA presents
MASKS
a MODERN BALLET with CONTEMPORARY MUSIC
Choreography—Bhushan Lakhandri Music—Atul Desai
5th, 6th, 7th, 8th March, 7.00 p.m.
Kamani Hall, Copernicus Marg
Tickets.
Rs. 25/-, 15/-, 10/-, 5/- from Cottage Emporium & Site.
Enq: 386428, 388084
SBKK-2582R

Space Courtesy : INALSA, NEW DELHI.

CHANDRA MAKKAR

Daughter of noted choreographer, Bhagwandas Verma, Chandra joined the Shriram Bharatiya Kala Kendra in 1964 and performed important roles in its productions. She has adorned the roles of Sita, Mira Bai, Kaikeyi and Mandodari. Her stately stage presence lent a special stature and aura to her projection. An accomplished artist, she later served the Natya Ballet Centre where her father became the Director.

CHITRA VENUGOPAL

Younger sister of Maya Rao, the first Kathak product of the Shriram Bharatiya Kala Kendra, Chitra had her initial lessons from her sister. She is the second south Indian to be awarded a Government of India scholarship to learn Kathak at the Kendra under Guru Shambhu Maharaj. She also learnt under Pandit Birju Maharaj. She took leading roles in Kendra productions. Later she became the staff artist of Natya Saraswati in Bangalore.

DAGAR BANDHU

Distinguished brothers who helped dhrupad survive.

Sons of Ustad Nasiruddin Khan, the court musician of Indore and the grandsons of the celebrated Ustad Allah Bande Khan, the Dagar Bandhus—Nasir Moinuddin and Aminuddin—are illustrious representatives of a traditional family of musicians, among the most important in India. Their musical education began under their father, after whose death they shifted to Jaipur and later still to Udaipur where they learnt additionally from their uncles Ustad Riazuddin Khan and Ustad Ziauddin Khan.

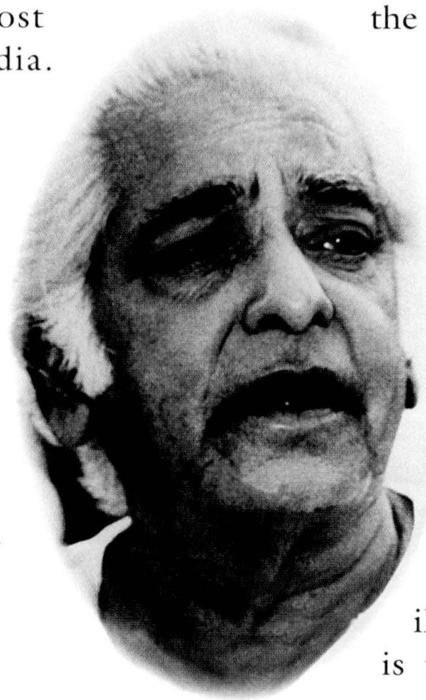

Ustad Nasir Moinuddin Khan was the greatest exponent of the style and his performance was characterised by dignified restraint and classical purity. He served as staff artist and a guru figure of the Shriram Bharatiya Kala Kendra for seven years in the sixties.

Ustad Nasir Aminuddin Khan Dagar, his brother, was born on October 20, 1923 in Indore. He continued the lineage and the form of Dhrupad, Dhamar and Alaap singing. His singing has purity of style and like his illustrious brother, he is the custodian of the tradition. He gave several performances and was among the first Indian vocalists to be recorded by the UNESCO for its Archives. The association of the Dagar Bandhus or brothers with the Kendra enriched the form, the performers and most certainly the institution. Ustad Aminuddin received the Sangeet Natak Akademi Award in 1985 and the Tansen Samman in 1990.

DEBU CHAUDHURY
(Born 1935)

A sitarist of repute.

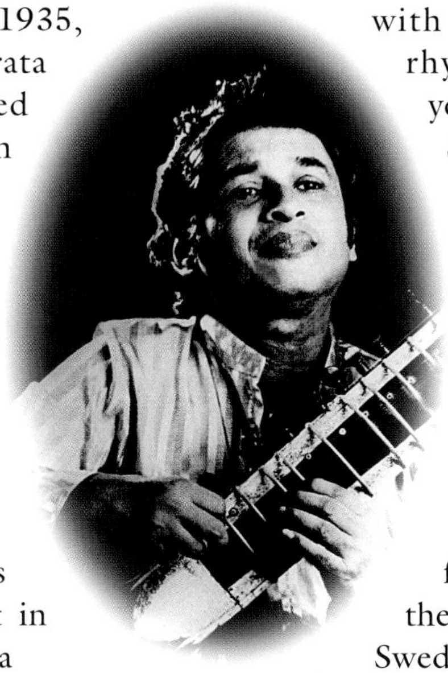

Born on May 30, 1935, in Bengal, Debabrata Chaudhury received his initial training in sitar under the late Panchu Gopal Dutta and later became a pupil of Ustad Mushtaq Ali Khan, the leading sitarist of the day.

Debu Chaudhury plays both aalap and gat in the traditional Senia style. His recitals are marked with a fine sense of rhythm. For several years he taught at the Shriram Bharatiya Kala Kendra and served as the Dean of the Music Faculty at the University of Delhi. A widely travelled artist, he has performed at all the major festivals, including the Festival of India in Sweden.

DEVENDRA SHANKAR

Brother of the illustrious Uday and Ravi Shankar, Devendra Shankar served the Shriram Bharatiya Kala Kendra as a choreographer in 1958. He learnt various dance styles at the Almora Studio and participated in several productions by Dada Uday Shankar. A knowledgeable stage expert, he was greatly instrumental in carrying forward the 'Ramlila' production after Narendra Sharma initially choreographed it.

Pandit DILIP CHANDRA VEDI
(1901-1977)

An eminent musicologist.

A descendant of Guru Nanak Dev, Pandit Dilip Chandra Vedi was born in 1901 at Anandpur Sahib in Punjab. He started learning music under Ustad Uttam Singh. Later he came under the tutelage of such learned and distinguished exponents as Pandit Bhaskar Rao Bhakle, Ustad Faiyaz Khan, Ustad Munir Khan and Ustad Haider Khan.

He was acknowledged as a master of Khayal and delighted audiences all over the world. He composed new ragas and was celebrated for his genius. He was made a Fellow of the Sangeet Natak Akademi. Earlier, he had taught for several years at the Shriram Bharatiya Kala Kendra where Dinesh Kumar Prabhakar, Asha Jain and several others came under his expert guidance.

DIBANKAR KHUNTIA

A former Jatra artist in rural Orissa, Dibankar joined the Shriram Bharatiya Kala Kendra as a trainee in the Ballet Unit in 1975. He worked in Orissi under his brother-in-law, Guru Mayadhar Raut at the Kendra and over the years was his supporting hand. He taught as a staff member of the Kendra, giving initial training to budding Orissi youngsters.

DINESH KUMAR PRABHAKAR

Inheriting his art from his father, the late Pandit Hussan Lal, Dinesh showed early promise and potential by winning the All India Radio music competition in 1968. He received training in music under his father and from Prof. Dilip Chandra Vedi at the Shriram Bharatiya Kala Kendra. He has given numerous performances throughout India and participated in all the major music festivals. He is presently working as a staff artist at All India Radio.

Guru DEVI LAL (1942-1976)

A devoted Kathak artist, musician and teacher.

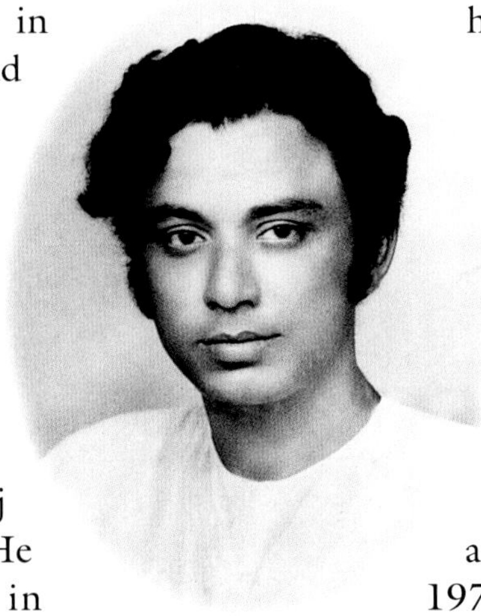

Renowned for his art of Kathak, Devi Lal came from a family of musicians in Rajasthan, having had his initial lessons under his father Pandit Omkar Lal. He studied the art of Kathak under Pandit Sunder Prasad and also under Pandit Shambhu Maharaj and Birju Maharaj. He then performed in productions and helped train several artists, including his younger brother Durga Lal. He toured extensively both as a dancer and as an instrumentalist. His untimely death robbed the world of art of a promising and accomplished Kathak artist. He died in 1976.

Pandit DURGA LAL (1948-1990)

A star of the Jaipur gharana of Kathak.

Born on September 9, 1948 at Mahendragarh in Rajasthan, Durga Lal was initiated into the arts by his father, Omkar Lal. He learnt the art of Kathak from the eminent gurus of the Jaipur gharana, Pandit Sunder Prasad and his own brother, Devi Lal. From Pandit Purushottam Das he learnt the pakhawaj.

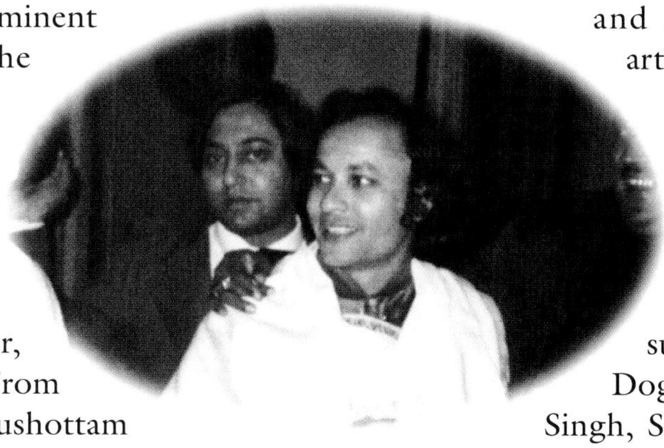

He charted a very rewarding course in the world of Kathak and was awarded the Rajasthan Sangeet Natak Akademi Award for the same in 1983 and the Sangeet Natak Akademi award in 1984. He had a long association with the Shriram Bharatiya Kala Kendra, first as a student and later as an artist. Later he taught at the Kathak Kendra and trained students such as Uma Dogra, Nandini Singh, Smriti Misra, Rakhi Dheer, Harish Rawat, Sharmistha Mukherjee and Jayant Kastuar. An untimely stroke claimed him on February 1, 1990.

FARIDUDDIN KHAN

A grandson of the late Ustad Mushtaq Hussain Khan Saheb of Rampur and a son of Ustad Mushtaq Khan, Fariduddin received training from both of them and continues their tradition through performance and teaching. He served the Shriram Bharatiya Kala Kendra for over a decade, training younger aspirants in the style.

FIRDOS AHMED KHAN

Son of Ustad Abdul Ghani Khan, he belongs to the Kirana gharana of the late Ustad Waheed Khan, Ustad Ghafoor Khan and Ustad Shakoor Khan. Firdos benefited from direct tutelage under the veteran Ustad Hafiz Ali Khan in sarod at the Shriram Bharatiya Kala Kendra.

GAURANGA CHAUDHURY

A percussion artist by training, Gauranga Chaudhury has had a long association with the Shriram Bharatiya Kala Kendra. His early training in tabla was under Ustad Inam Ali Khan and Ustad Latif

Ahmed Khan. He also trained under Pandit Purushottam Das. He has worked on a number of ballets, as a singer, actor and drummer. His two decades of work with the Kendra has vested him with an artistic continuity with the institution.

GHULAM SADIQ AND SIRAJ KHAN

The two Ghulam brothers received initial training from their father, Ustad Ghulam Jafar Khan, a sarangi player of eminence. Later, they came under the tutelage of Ustad Mushtaq Hussain Khan of Rampur and his son Ustad Ishtiaq Hussain Khan. Sadiq married the daughter of Ustad Mushtaq Hussain Khan. Both have performed extensively and recorded for radio and television. Their association with the Shriram Bharatiya Kala Kendra spans several decades.

GHULAM TAQI KHAN

Son of Ustad Mushtaq Hussain Khan, Taqi distinguished himself as a vocalist. In addition to having learnt from his father, he also learnt from his brother, Ustad Ishtiaq Hussain Khan. He got a Government of India scholarship to learn from them at the Shriram Bharatiya Kala Kendra. He performed on several occasions and has been recorded and broadcasted by All India Radio.

GURU GOPINATH (1908-1987)

A giant in the field of Kathakali and choreography.

A legend in his own lifetime, Guru Gopinath was born on June 24, 1908 in Champakulam village of Kerala. He learnt Kathakali and in 1934, the Maharaja of Travancore decorated him with the 'Veera Sringala' gold bracelet for his distinguished services to the art. He soon became the palace dancer of Travancore and performed extensively.

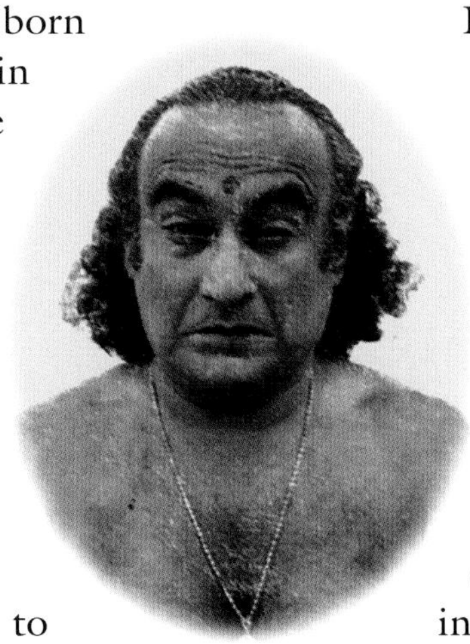

His art first found a partner in Ragini Devi, mother of Indrani Rehman. He later married Thangamani, well-known Mohini Attam dancer of the day and together they participated in several performances, including dance pieces for theatre and later cinema. He left Kerala and made

***Facing page:** Puppeteer Rehi who helped connect the* chaupies *for the script of 'Ramlila'.*

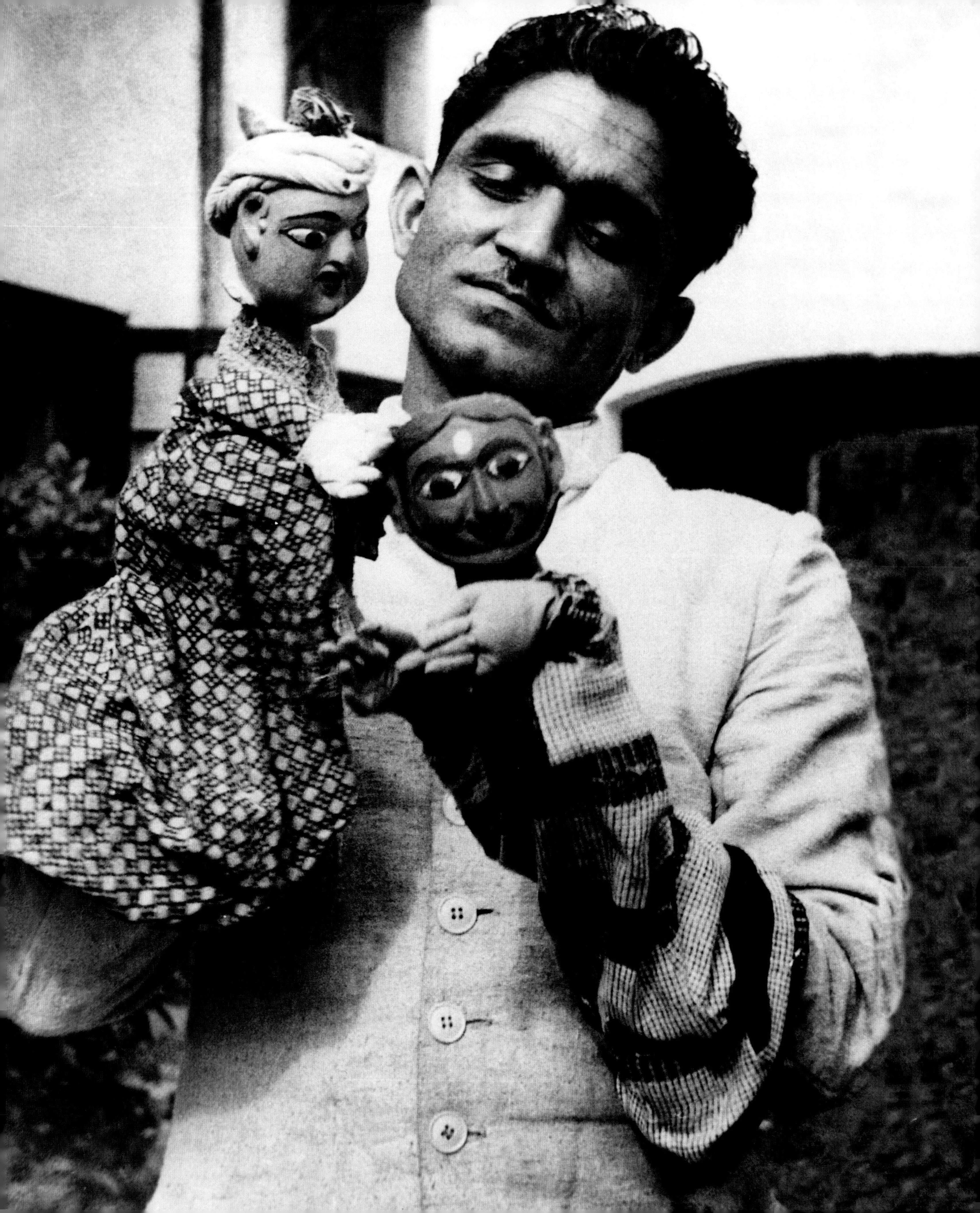

a home in Madras during his association with the cinema and dance world.

He travelled to USSR in 1954 as a member of an Indian cultural delegation, among the first such official visits from India. His association with the Shriram Bharatiya Kala Kendra started in 1959 when he choreographed the 'Ramlila' and added significant dimensions to it. As a trained Kathakali star-artiste, he brought in varied elements of the style and also introduced several younger artists such Krishnan Namboodri and K. Shekharan Panikar to the Kendra.

He continued his association with the Kendra for a number of years, even after his direct involvement was finished. He himself undertook the role of Hanuman in the Ramlila production. He was awarded the Sangeet Natak Akademi Award in 1965. He ran his own institution, the Viswa Kala Kendra in Trivandrum until his final years, and he died on stage enacting the role of Dasaratha on October 9, 1987.

Ustad HAFIZ ALI KHAN (1888-1972)

Veteran exponent of sarod.

Born in 1888, Ustad Hafiz Ali Khan served the Shriram Bharatiya Kala Kendra from its inception as a senior guru. He was a guru-in-residence when Naina Devi was the Director of the Kendra, then located on Pusa Road. He distinguished himself as a performer and a teacher of sarod. In his two sons, Rahmat Ali Khan and Amjad Ali Khan, he left the genius of the Senia gharana, descended directly from Tansen, the leading poet-composer at the court of Akbar. Ustad Hafiz Ali Khan was a giant in the arena of music both by the virtue of his talent and by the sheer stature of his standing in the art world. His long association with the Kendra enabled a younger generation of artists to learn under him and through their art his name continues. He received the Sangeet Natak Akademi Award in 1953 and was made a Fellow of the Akademi in 1954. He died in December 1972.

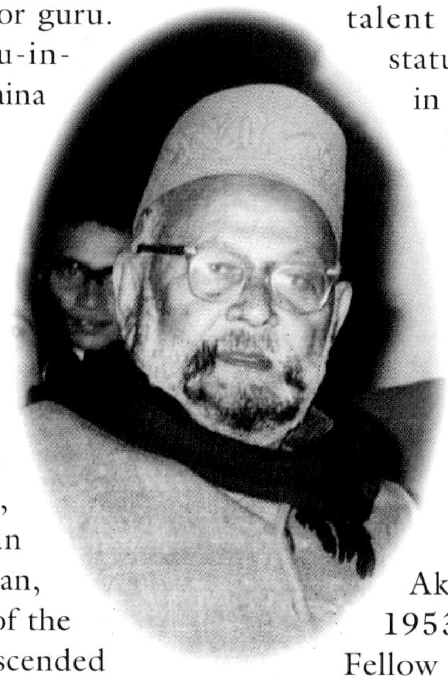

HARISH RAWAT

Born in 1954, Harish Chandra Rawat has had a close relationship with the family of the Shriram Bharatiya Kala Kendra. He joined as a trainee in the Ballet Unit in 1970, after his graduation from the Delhi University. He learnt Kathak and excelled in several roles of the 'Ramlila' production. He participated in many of the Kendra's ballets and then left the institution to chart an individual course as a solo artist and a teacher of dance.

HARSH LATA

Hailing from Gujarat, Harsh Lata had her initial training in Kathak from Guru Kanahiya Lal and Guru Gauri Shankar, of the Jaipur gharana. She acquired proficiency in Manipuri and Bharata Natyam as well. She gave several solo performances and came to Delhi at the invitation of the Shriram Bharatiya Kala Kendra. She took advanced training in Kathak from Pandit Birju Maharaj of the Lucknow gharana and learnt classical music from Ustad Ghulam Kadir Khan and the art of thumri from Siddheswari Devi. In addition to dance performances, she broadcasted several radio programmes.

Ustad HASHMAT ALI KHAN

He joined the Shriram Bharatiya Kala Kendra in 1957 as a tabla teacher and accompanist. In 1963, he received a Government of India scholarship for three years of intensive involvement with his chosen medium. He performed and travelled extensively and was sent to Guyana under a Government exchange programme. Upon returning to India in 1976, he joined the American International School as a teacher.

Ustad INAM ALI KHAN

A leading exponent of the Delhi gharana, Ustad Inam Ali Khan distinguished himself in the art of tabla playing and teaching. He served the Shriram Bharatiya Kala Kendra as an accomplished performer and teacher and among his exceptional disciples the name of the late Ustad Latif Ahmed Khan ranks high.

INDER RAZDAN

Among the senior-most associates of the Shriram Bharatiya Kala Kendra, Inder Razdan helped with the stage sets of the 'Ramlila' production in 1957. Since then, he has had a long innings and association with the institution. His ideas for the stage, sets and props have supported several productions. With Narendra Sharma, he devised the split-stage for a quick change of scenes in the 'Ramlila' presentation.

Since 1957, he has helped with several productions and events. His talent has been used for major cultural happenings and for many years now he has based himself at the Srinivas Mallah Theatre Crafts Museum, initiated by Kamladevi Chattopadhyaya.

IRENE ROY CHOUDHURY

A disciple of Ustad Bade Ghulam Ali Khan, she received exclusive training from him as she was his favourite pupil. She learnt Alaap from the Dagar Bandhu at the Shriram Bharatiya Kala Kendra on a Government scholarship. She also sang for some dance-drama productions. She represents the best of two important gharanas, the Patiala gharana and the Dagar.

Ustad ISHTIAQ HUSSAIN KHAN

The continuity of the Rampur gharana, as represented by Ustad Mushtaq Hussain Khan, is found in Ishtiaq Hussain Khan, his eldest son who embellished the art form with his repertoire and style. As a Khayal singer, the renditions of 'Tans' was his forte. He served as staff artist-teacher of the Shriram Bharatiya Kala Kendra for many years.

JAIDEVA CHATTERJEE
(Born 1930)

The seniormost ballet artist of the Kendra.

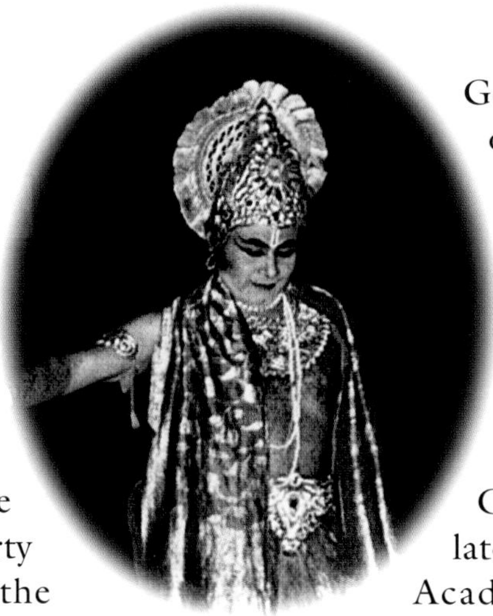

Born on August 8, 1930, at Chandorenagar in Bengal, he is the longest serving artist of the Shriram Bharatiya Kala Kendra. Jaideva Chatterjee's association with the institution spans forty years. Trained at the Government College of Art, his first appearance was in the ballet, 'Life of Buddha' in 1949. As a stage manager he worked for the All India Fine Arts and Crafts Society and later at the Lalit Kala Academi. He briefly studied under Nandlal Bose and has used his training in painting and sculpting. His enacting the role of Dasaratha and Vibhishana, in the 'Ramlila' production of the Kendra, has few parallels in terms of continuity and consistency. An able interpreter of scriptures and rituals, he has served the Kendra in several capacities, including as an in-house priest. A sculptor, he runs a Kali temple at home.

JUSTIN MCCARTHY

US born Justin McCarthy learnt Bharata-Natyam at Kalakshetra and later with Leela Samson. He is an accomplished pianist and composer. He also specialised in Tamil literature and Carnatic music. Adept in all these, he is a fine specimen of a complete artist, who also makes for an excellent teacher. He undertakes Bharata Natyam classes at the Kendra.

JYOTIRINDRA MOITRA

Trained under Vishmadev of the Badal Khan School of Music, Batukda, as Jyotirindra Moitra was popularly called, undertook additional grooming in the Rampur gharana in the mid-twenties. However, at the Shriram Bharatiya Kala Kendra he took classes in Rabindra Sangeet and collaborated with music composer, Sushil Das Gupta in creating the score for the 'Ramlila' and other productions. He later directed several dance-dramas and provided music for a number of films on Tagore directed by Satyajit Ray.

KAMLA JOSEPH

Decades of dedicated dance.

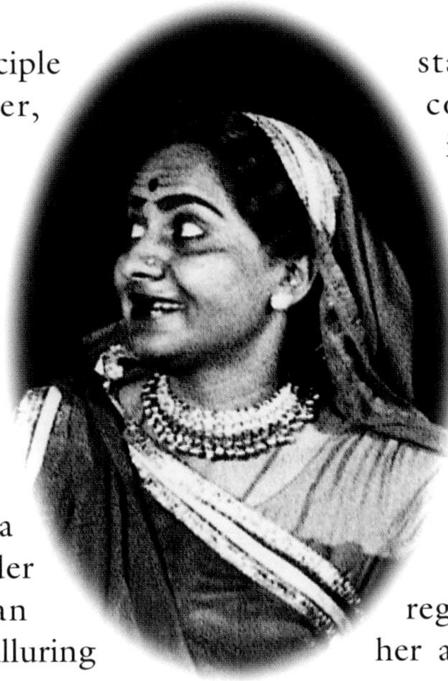

A student and disciple of Kathak teacher, Reba Vidyarthi, Kamla Joseph participated in stellar roles in the productions of the Shriram Bharatiya Kala Kendra, having worked under directors such as Narendra Sharma, Yog Sunder and Krishnan Namboodri. Her alluring stage appearance, combined with an in-depth understanding of music and mime made her infuse life even into ordinary roles or in group dances. Her association with the Kendra continued for decades and she regaled audiences with her artistic work.

KRISHAN AND RAM MOHAN

Sons of Shambhu Maharaj, the Kathak maestro.

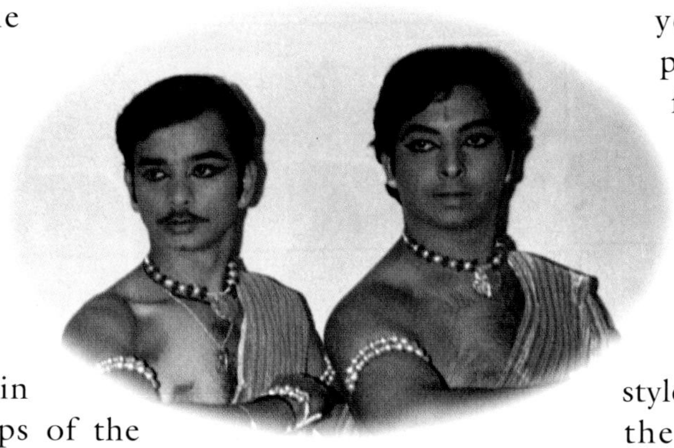

Sons of the legendary Shambhu Maharaj, Krishan Mohan and Ram Mohan have continued in the footsteps of the family tradition of Kathak. Both have been with the Shriram Bharatiya Kala Kendra at some point in time and have grown with the institution over the years. Of professional fabric, both have displayed an individuality without sacrificing style for which the Lucknow gharana of Kathak is known. After a long association with the Kendra, both are now on the staff of the Kathak Kendra.

KESHAV KOTHARI

Born in Rajasthan, Keshav Singh Kothari joined the Shriram Bharatiya Kala Kendra in 1956 on a Government scholarship as a student of Shambhu Maharaj. In 1958, he joined the Sangeet Natak Akademi and worked with the organisation for nearly four decades, serving also as the Director of Kathak Kendra and as the Secretary of the Akademi. Arts administration is his speciality and stage decoration and aesthetics his forte.

K. RAMACHANDRAN

With a desire to learn Kathakali, K. Ramachandran devoted himself to the task of acquiring the art form from Guru Gopinath. He served the Master with diligence and imbibed the finer nuances of the art. He joined the Shriram Bharatiya Kala Kendra in 1970 and remained its staff artist for long, playing several roles of which his persona of Laxmana in 'Ramlila' is most memorable. After years of association, he left the institution, to teach at school.

K. SHEKHARAN PANIKAR (1939-1986)

Senior choreographer who immortalised himself as 'Ravana'.

Born on December 11, 1939, K. Shekharan Panikar came under the influence of the native arts of Kerala as a child. He learnt the percussion instruments of Kerala and accompanied seasoned dancers like Indrani Rehman. He studied Kathakali under the renowned Guru Gopinath. He joined the Shriram Bharatiya Kala

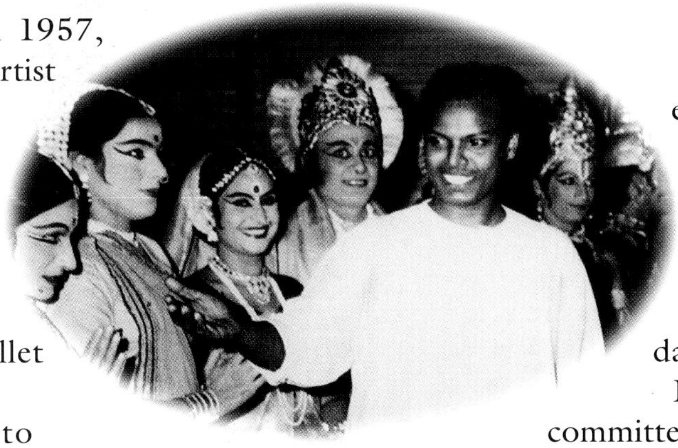

Kendra in 1957, as a staff artist and after decades of work became the Director of the Ballet Unit. In addition to performing the role of Ravana in the Kendra's 'Ramlila' production, he choreographed dance-dramas such as 'Keno Upanishad', 'Meghdoot', 'Dharti Ka Vivah', 'Krishnavtaar', 'Bahubali', 'Shakuntala' and 'Mahavir'. With the Kendra troupe he travelled extensively. He married fellow artist, Orissi dancer Aloka Panikar. A committed artist, he was also adept in the crafts of costume design and jewellery. An all rounder, his last years saw the choreographing of 'Valmiki Ramayanam'. He fought for artists' rights and lost to cancer, which claimed him in 1986.

KRISHNAN NAMBOODRI

An accomplished artist, Krishnan Namboodri absorbed the art of Kathakali from Guru Gopinath before going to Dada Uday Shankar. He joined the Shriram Bharatiya Kala Kendra in 1959. He undertook principal roles in the 'Ramlila' production of the Kendra and worked as Assistant Director in 1967. He directed 'Mira Bai' and helped with 'Sitayan'. He was involved with various aspects of the Kendra's productions and served it for several years.

Guru KRISHNA CHANDRA NAYAK (1920-1987)

A beacon of Mayurbhanj Chhau and a star choreographer who helped the Kendra platform this style through several dance-drama productions.

Born in 1920, Guru Krishna Chandra Nayak became a leading light of Mayurbhanj Chhau, which he learnt from Guru Jogendra Kumar Bhanj and Guru Bhagwandas. Others who helped and guided his work were Sadhona Bose, Mohammad Raja Khan and Vishweswar Bhanj. All this art was learnt in the confines of Raja Pratap Chandra Bhauj Deo's palace. The same Raja awarded him a medal for excellence in Chhau.

Guru Krishna Chandra Nayak left Mayurbhanj in 1943 and started teaching in Calcutta at the Adarsh Vidya Mandir. Later, he moved to Gwalior and worked with and taught at the Little Ballet Troupe. He travelled with them to Burma, Indonesia and

Thailand. He eventually left Gwalior and came to Delhi, where he joined the Shriram Bharatiya Kala Kendra in 1975. He had a productive time at the Kendra and choreographed and created several productions such as 'Jagdeo'; 'Konark'; 'Kalinga Vijaya'; 'Khajuraho'; 'Karna' and 'Chaitra Parva'. His association with the Kendra led to a focussing on Mayurbhanj Chhau and on the art of Guru K.C. Naik. He was given the Sangeet Natak Akademi Award in 1975.

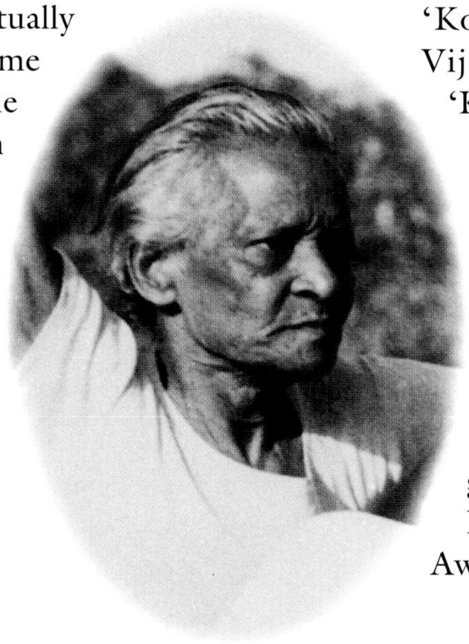

K.V. KANAN

Born in 1943, in Kerala, K.V. Kanan came to Delhi and joined the Shriram Bharatiya Kala Kendra in the mid-fifties. A founder-member of its Ballet Unit, K.V. Kanan was an accomplished stage in-charge, who as a dancer also understood the demands of the stage. He served the Kendra in various capacities and participated in most of its productions. He worked with director-choreographers such as Narendra Sharma, Guru Gopinath, Bhagwandas Verma, Yog Sunder, Krishnan Namboodri and K. Shekharan Panikar.

KUMUDINI LAKHIA
(Born 1930)

A leading Kathak artist who has distinguished herself as a contemporary choreographer.

Born on June 17, 1930, Kumudini Jayakar-Lakhia learnt Kathak from distinguished gurus like Shambhu Maharaj and Birju Maharaj of the Lucknow gharana; Pandit Sunder Prasad and Radha Lal of the Jaipur gharana and Vidwan Ashiq Hussain of the Benaras gharana. Despite varied schools, she charted an independent and individual course which is known for fine technique and high aesthetics.

She came to the Shriram Bharatiya Kala Kendra in the mid-fifties and took stellar roles in its initial productions of Kathak such as 'Malati Madhav' and 'Kumar Sambhav'. She impressed with her work and her teaming with Birju Maharaj led to a successful dance-partnership. Her association with the Kendra continued for many years.

In her capacity as a dancer, teacher and choreographer, she focussed her work on her institution, Kadamb, in Ahmedabad. She was the Vice President of the UNESCO

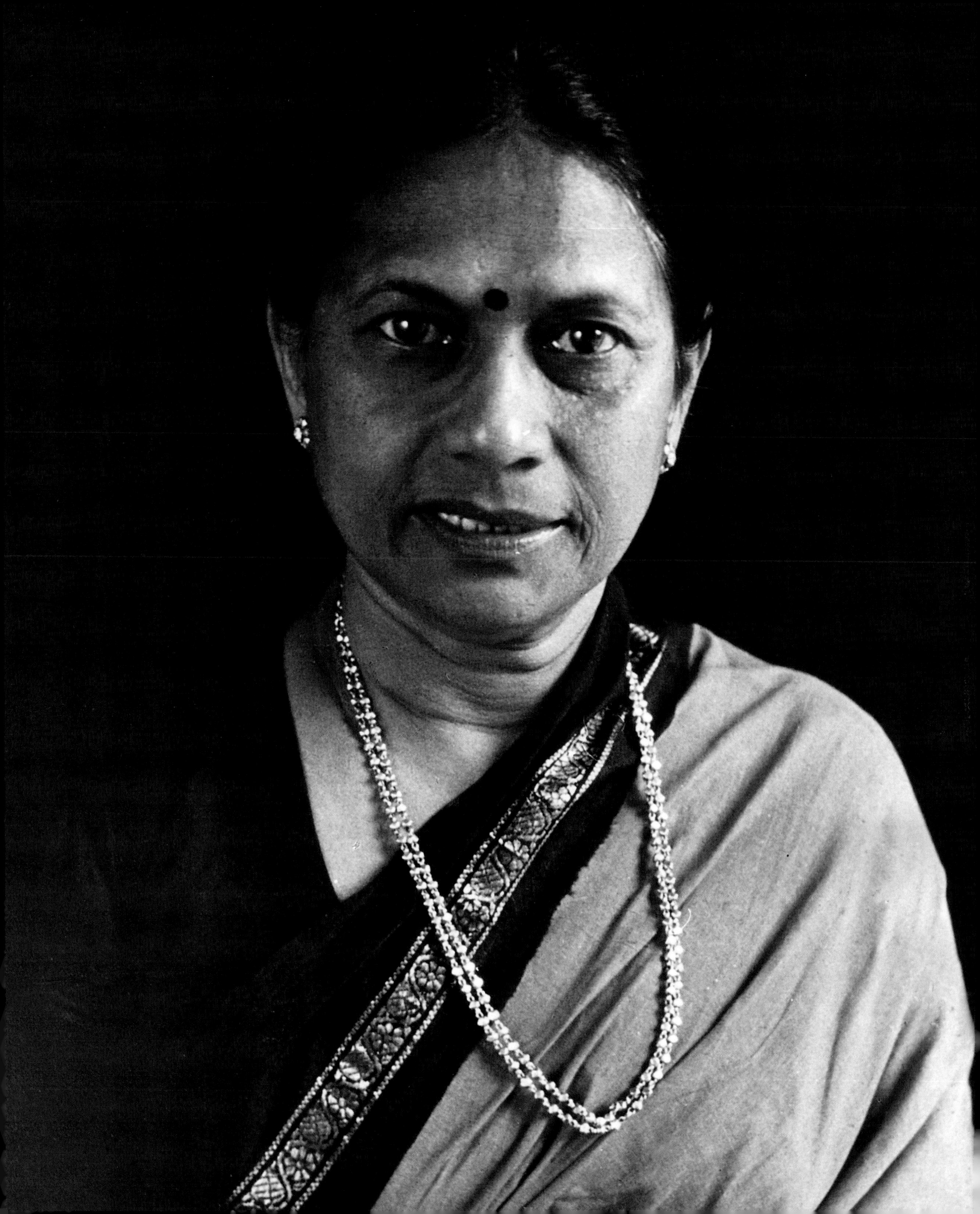

Dance Council and was given the Sangeet Natak Akademi Award in 1982. Among her known products are Daksha Seth, the Desai sisters, Aditi Mangaldas, Maulik Shah and Vaishali.

Guru KUNDANLAL GANGANI (1926-1984)

Senior Kathak guru of the Jaipur School.

Born on July 26 1926 in Jaipur, Kundanlal Gangani belongs to a traditional family of Kathakaars. With brother Sunderlal, his initial professional years were spent at Baroda and later he moved to Delhi. He learnt from his uncle, the legendary Guru Narayana Prasad. His association with the Shriram Bharatiya Kala Kendra started upon coming to Delhi in the early sixties. He had a long association with the Kathak world, having later taught also at the Kathak Kendra. Among his prominent disciples are Urmila Nagar, Urmila Goel, Vishnu Priya Pawar, Ashish Khokar, Prerna Shrimali and his son Rajendra Gangani, who continues his art after him.

LAXMAN BHATT TAILANG

Son of Pandit Gokul Chandra Bhatt, the famous devotee singer of the Dhrupad style of the Vallabh sampradaya, Laxman Bhatt was born on December 24, 1928 at Jaipur. He took his music education under Rajabhai Punchwale of Gwalior and was selected by the Education Ministry for specialised training in Dhrupad under the Dagar Bandhu, Nasir Moinuddin and Nasir Aminuddin Dagar at the Shriram Bharatiya Kala Kendra.

Laxman Bhatt has the experience of teaching music for over three decades and he has performed extensively in addition to having recorded for numerous radio stations.

LEELA SAMSON (Born 1951)

A sparkling specimen of the Kalakshetra mould of Bharata Natyam.

Born on May 6, 1951 Leela Samson learnt Bharata Natyam at Kalakshetra in Madras. Recognised for her sensitive involvement with the medium, she came to Delhi and in the mid-eighties was based at the Shriram Bharatiya Kala Kendra, where she groomed students in the art form. Among her principal products are Justin McCarthy, who now heads the

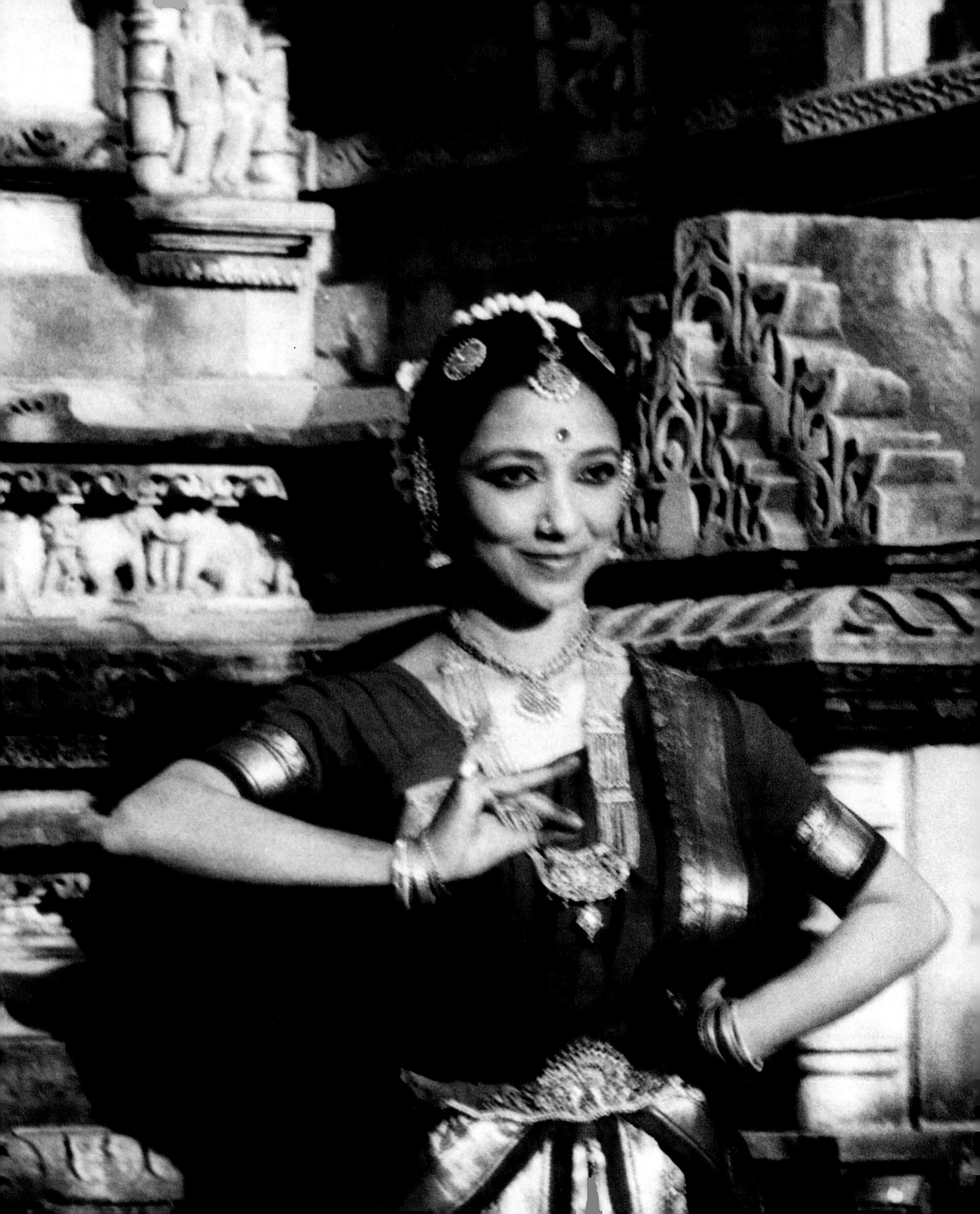

Bharata Natyam teaching section at the Kendra; Harish Rawat, the Kathak artist who learnt Bharata Natyam as well and Navtej Singh, Aditi Jaitly and Anusha Lal.

Her work has been recorded in a documentary film, *Sanchari,* and she has authored a book, *Rhythm in Joy*, in addition to writing articles on the arts. She received the Sanskriti Award in 1982 and the Padma Shri in 1990.

MAYA RAO
(Born 1928)

Principal disciple of Vidwan Shambhu Maharaj. She has distinguished herself as a complete artist—dancer, choreographer, teacher, devotee of dance.

Born in Bangalore in 1928, Maya Rao initially learnt Kathak from Pandit Sohan Lal of Jaipur and later under Guru Shambhu Maharaj and Guru Sundar Prasad at the Shriram Bharatiya Kala Kendra. She was the first student of the Kendra. She received a Government scholarship to learn under the Masters and after a successful initiation, she proved her professional credentials by presenting innumerable performances.

In 1961 she studied choreography in Moscow on a Soviet scholarship and on her return to India in 1964, founded the Natya Institute of Choreography in Delhi. She was also the Director of the Natya Ballet Centre for many years. She has choreographed over fifty dance-dramas, including works such as 'Krishna Lila', 'Vision of Amir Khusro', 'Tulsi Ke Ram' and 'Surdas'. She was a consultant choreographer to two Soviet productions on Indian themes: 'Shakuntala' and 'Ramayana'.

She received the Mysore State Akademi Award in 1968, the Sahitya Kala Parishad Samman in 1985 and the Sangeet Natak Akademi award in 1989. Maya Rao is presently based in Bangalore where she runs her Natya Institute of Kathak and Choreography.

MAYADHAR RAUT
(Born 1933)

One of the founding pillars of Orissi style of dance, he is a seasoned artist and guru.

Facing page: *'Parikrama'.*

Born in 1933, in the village Kanthapahara, near Banki in Orissa, Mayadhar entered the world of dance through theatre, serving at

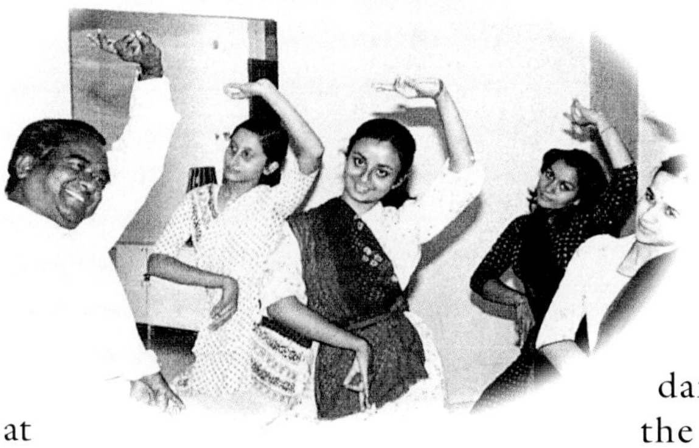

Kabichandra Kalicharan Pattnaik's Orissa Theatre. There he started the Gotipua dance under the guidance

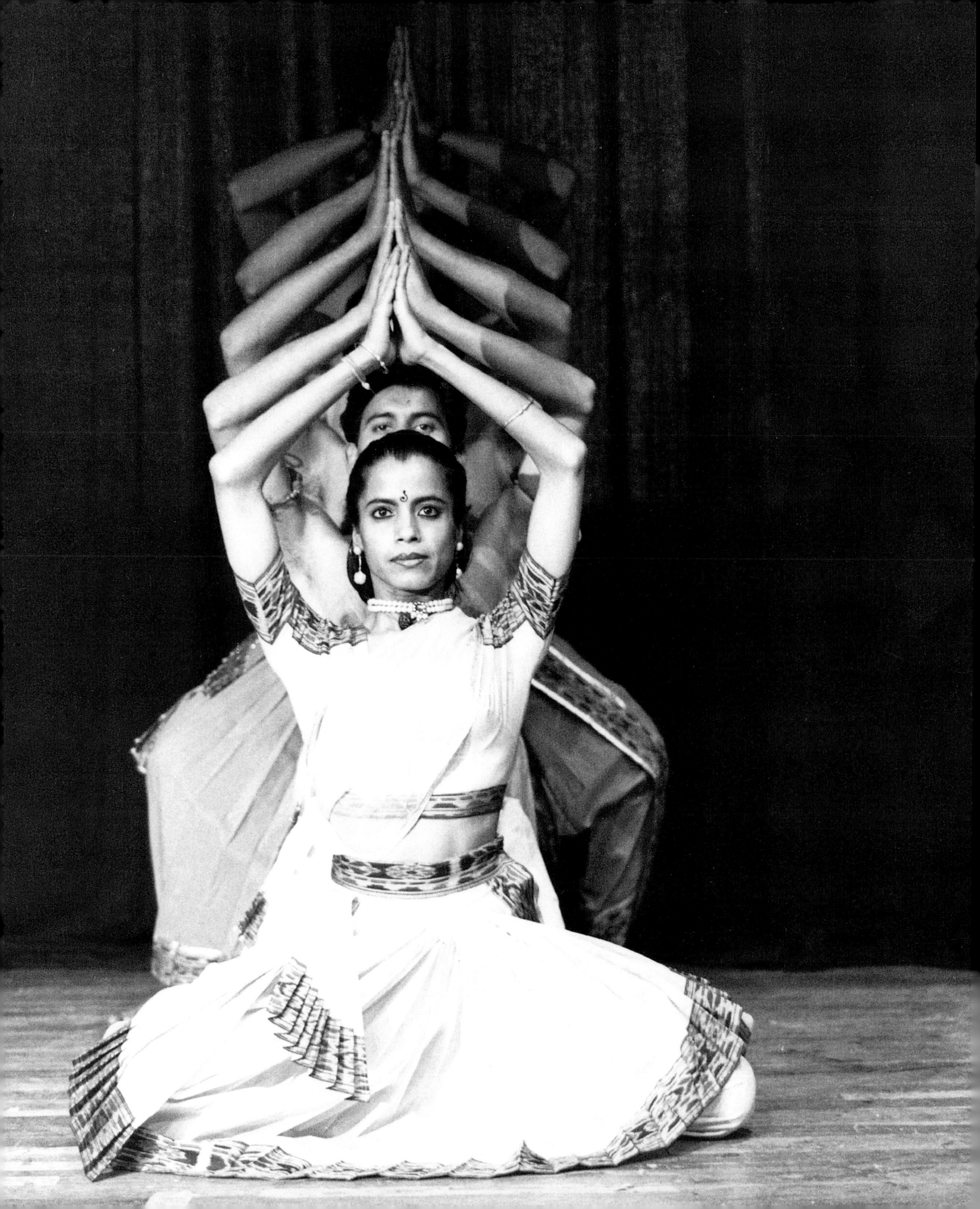

of Natyacharya Kalicharan Pattnaik and Mohan Mahapatra. In 1946, he learnt *abhinaya* from Goswami Mohan Sunder Deva. In 1947, he learnt Orissi from Guru Pankaj Charan Das and later modern dance from Dayal Sharan.

He then joined the Kala Vikas Kendra as the first guru of Orissi in 1952. In 1955, he was awarded a scholarship by Utkal Sangeeta Natyakala Parishad to learn Kathakali from Shri T.K. Chandu Panikar at Kalakshetra in Madras, where he came into contact with Rukmini Devi Arundale. It is this contact with Madras and Kalakshetra which made him evolve the sanchari in Orissi.

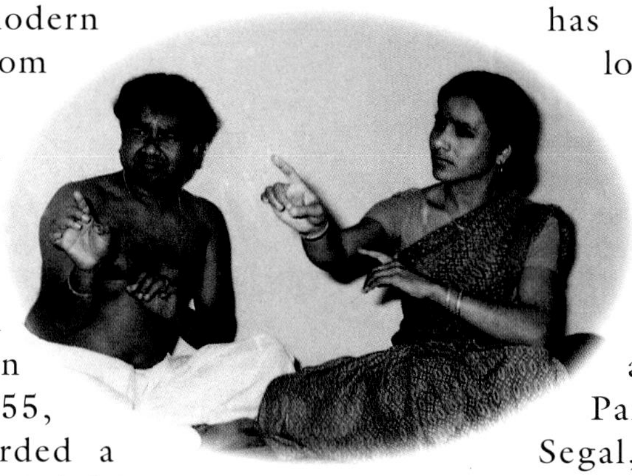

In 1960 he was in Delhi with the Natya Ballet Centre as an Orissi teacher and during that phase he learnt Kathak from Pandit Ramgopal Misra. In 1967 he joined Nritya Niketan. In 1970 he came to the Shriram Bharatiya Kala Kendra and has continued a long association of twenty-five years. His Kendra years gave him worthy disciples such as Aloka Panikar, Kiran Segal, Geeta Mahalik. Additionally, he took classes in the Jagganath Temple, Haus Khas, where he brought his brother-in-law, Dibankar Khuntia as an apprentice. Guru Mayadhar Raut today ranks as a pillar of Orissi and his work has won him the Sangeet Natak Akademi award in 1985 and the Sahitya Kala Parishad Samman in 1986.

MOHAN RAO KALYANPURKAR (1913-1985)

A Kathak talent who fused two styles—the Jaipur and the Lucknow.

Born in 1913, Mohan Rao Kalyanpurkar took intensive training under the guidance of Pandit Sundar Prasad of Jaipur. Later, he came under the tutelage of Kathak giants, Achchan Maharaj and Shambhu Maharaj. His training in two principal styles of Kathak equipped him with a firm understanding of the dance form, which he used in his professional life.

In Lucknow, he was spotted by the eminent musician Ratanjankar who selected Mohan Rao to serve the Marris College of Music, which later came to be called Bhatkhande Sangeet Vidyapeeth for several decades until 1971. After retirement, he joined the NCPA in Bombay as a Kathak teacher. Among his known products are Rohini Bhate, Raja Kelkar and Padma Kumari Sharma. He was awarded the Sangeet Natak Akademi Award in 1962.

MOHAN UPRETI (1928-1997)

A giant in the field of opera, theatre, music-composition and arts administration.

Born on July 6, 1928, Mohan Upreti imbibed the culture of Kumaon early in his childhood. While growing up, he absorbed leftist leanings for which he became a committed party worker. A patriot at heart, he was involved with the Freedom Struggle as a student activist, which brought him into contact with the IPTA (Indian People's Theatre Association).

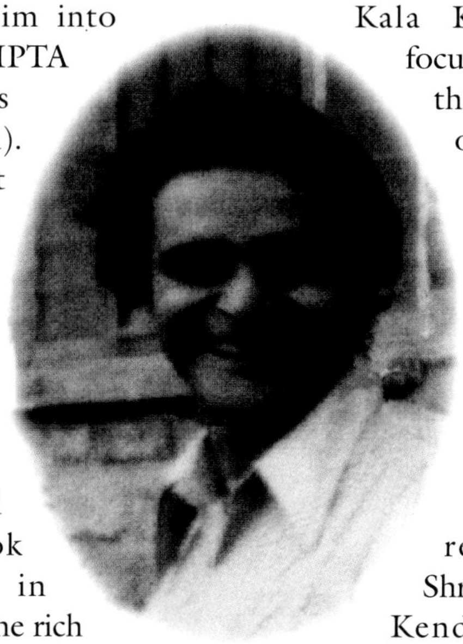

Having learnt classical music under Pandit C.S. Pant and V.S. Thakar, he did his advanced training in music from the Allahabad University and founded the Lok Kalakar Sangh in Almora, involving the rich folk traditions of the region. He composed music for dance-dramas, theatre productions, mimes, and travelled to various parts of India. His travels brought him several times to Delhi, where he served the Jamia Millia Islamia University as Professor of Music in 1962-63.

His association with the Shriram Bharatiya Kala Kendra started in 1964 when he joined as a Programme Officer. But at heart he was more interested in creative rather than administrative work. He was given the responsibility of organising major festivals, such as the Shankarlal, the Holi Utsav, the Basant Panchami celebrations and the opening of the Kamani Auditorium.

The National School of Drama requisitioned his expertise with folk music and operatic tradition and thus began a long creative association resulting in over fifty full length productions. The formation of his own Parvatiya Kala Kendra in 1968 focussed his energies on the collective talents of immigrants from Garhwal, who later settled in Delhi. To date, the group has done several productions on the tales and myths, lores and legends of the region. For the Shriram Bharatiya Kala Kendra he scripted several dance-dramas like 'Sitayan', 'Mira Bai', 'Surdas', 'Azadi-Ki-Ore', 'Krishna Avtar', 'Mahavir', 'Bahubali', 'Urvashi', 'Meghdoot' and 'Ganga'.

A prodigious output all through his creative years have vested him with a unique authority and scholarship, for which he is respected and recognised through countless awards, titles and honours. He has served on several committees, including the Governing Council of the Sangeet Natak Akademi and the Doordarshan as member in addition to becoming the Vice-President of the Uttar Pradesh Sangeet Natak Akademi. Married to Naima Devi, he continued with his work of propagating the varied cultural strains of India in general, and of Kumaon, in particular. He died in June of 1997.

Guru MUNNALAL SHUKLA (Born 1943)

A senior practitioner of the art of Kathak and a meritorious teacher.

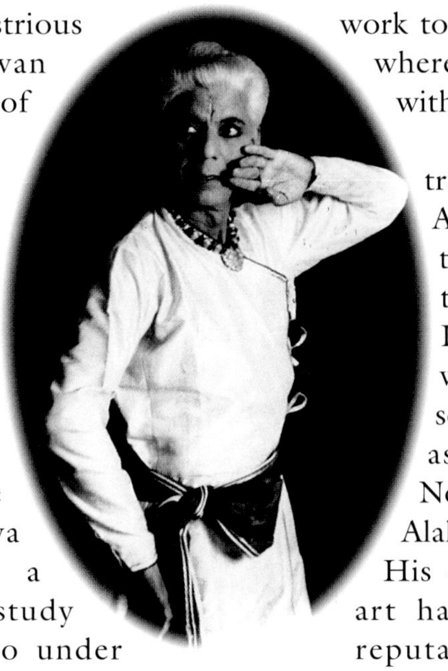

Born into the illustrious family of Vidwan Achchan Maharaj of the Lucknow gharana, Munnalal Shukla's mother Vidyavati was one of the daughters of Vidwan Achchan Maharaj. He came to Delhi in the mid-fifties and later joined the Shriram Bharatiya Kala Kendra on a scholarship to study Kathak. He did so under Birju Maharaj. His professional work took him to Poona, where he collaborated with Prabha Marathe in imparting training in Kathak. After 17 years there, he returned to the Kathak Kendra in Delhi where he trained several pupils such as Neera Batra, Neelima Azeem and Alaknanda Dasgupta. His dedication to his art has earned him a reputation which he continues to build upon.

Ustad MUNAWAR ALI KHAN (1930-1989)

Son and successor to the art of Ustad Bade Ghulam Ali Khan.

Son of the legendary Ustad Bade Ghulam Ali Khan of the Kasur Gharana was born on 15th August 1930 at Lahore in Punjab. One of the most talented musician of the Kasur form of Khayal Gayaki Thumri. He started his initial training under his uncle Ustad Mubarak Ali Khan, younger brother of Ustad Bade Ghulam Ali Khan and later with his father Ustad Bade Ghulam Ali Khan and his uncle Ustad Barkat Ali Khan. He blended styles of his grandfather Ustad Ali Bux Khan and his father Ustad Bade Ghulam Ali Khan and made for a new style in the field of classical music.

Ustad Munawar Ali Khan toured Europe a number of times and he was member of cultural delegations to number of countries representing his country. He taught at the Shriram Bharatiya Kala Kendra for almost a decade beginning the mid-seventies. He died on October 13, 1989.

Ustad MUSHTAQ HUSSAIN KHAN

Born in 1878, in the traditional family of musicians of Sahaswan, Mushtaq Hussain Khan was initiated in the art of music by his father Ustad Kallan Khan. His elder brother, Ashique Khan, too trained him in the family art of Gayaki. It was his tutelage under the renowned Haider Khan and ultimately under Ustad Enayat Hussain Khan Sahib that made him a court musician of Rampur.

He was given the Sangeet Natak Akademi Award in 1952. His scholarly command and his sonorous rendition won him acclaim, in addition to the President's Award in 1954. He was the first Indian to be so honoured. He joined the Shriram Bharatiya Kala Kendra in 1956 and trained several practitioners of his art form. He was given the title of Padma Bhushan in 1958. His principal products are Ishtiaq Hussain Khan, Naina Devi and Ghulam Taqi Khan, in addition to Ghulam Sadiq and Siraj Khan.

NAINA DEVI
(1919-1993)

Hailing from a family of educationists, she distinguished herself as a musician and an arts administrator.

Born on September 27, 1919, Nina Ripjit Singh, popularly known as Naina Devi, came from an illustrious musical family of Bengal, whose ancestry could be traced to Raja Ram Mohan Roy. She took initial lessons from Sangeetacharya Girija Shankar Chakravarty of Calcutta. Later she learnt from Ghulam Sabir Khan of Ambala and finally came to the great maestro Ustad Mushtaq Hussain Khan of Rampur and Rassolai Bai of Benaras. She married into the royal family of Kapurthala.

She came to Delhi in the early sixties and was appointed the first Director of the Shriram Bharatiya Kala Kendra. She served the Kendra at a time when the best musicians were involved with the institution and to a large extent her own musical background brought more musicians into the fold of the Kendra family. Her long association with the Kendra saw to the growth of the institution and later she created her own organisation, Raag Rang to focus on music. She was a leading musician of her time, having performed and recorded extensively. She specialised in Thumri and Ghazal, which dancers like Uma Sharma and Nandini Singh imbibed. For her work, she received the Padma Shri in 1974. Among her principal disciples are Shipra Bose, Shubha Mudgal, Madhumita Rai, Vidya Rao and Parul Banerjee. After a distinguished career, she passed away on November 1, 1993. The Naina Devi Foundation specifically set up to platform and project objectives dear to her heart, now serves the field of music and dance.

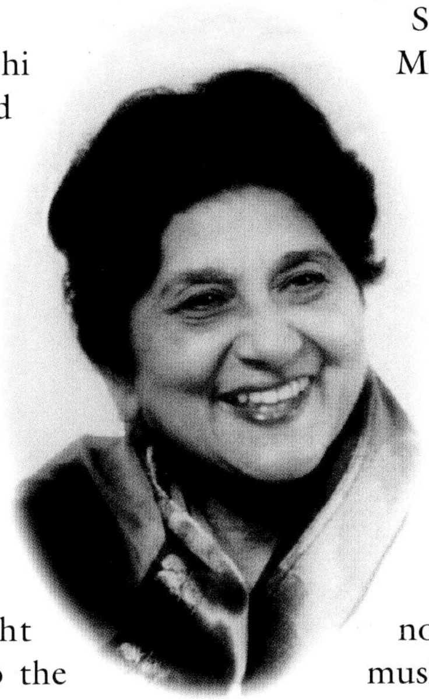

NAND KISHORE

Born on January 1, 1940 at Patna, Nand Kishore learnt dance from Shambhu Bhattacharya and joined the IPTA. He joined the Shriram Bharatiya Kala Kendra in 1964 as a staff artist and performed different roles in various productions. He also took an active interest in stage crafts, decor, props and making ornaments. Having served the Kendra for more than two decades, in which he travelled to many countries, Kishori, as he is fondly called, branched off on his own to teach at the DAV School.

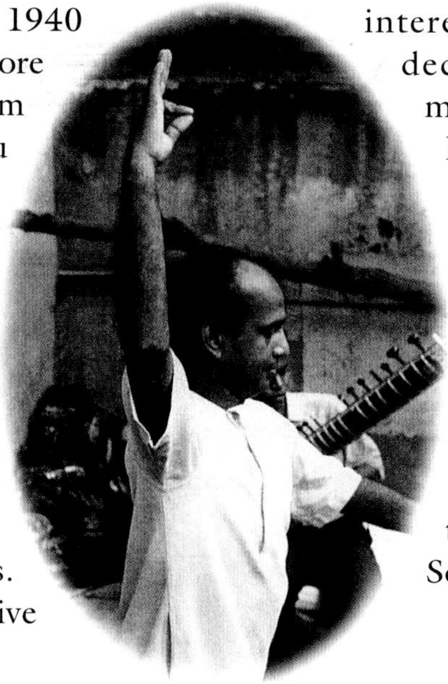

NEMAI CHAND BURAL

A disciple of the senior Dagar brothers, Ustad Nasir Moinuddin and Aminuddin, N.C. Bural joined the Shriram Bharatiya Kala Kendra as a student in 1957. His devotion to Dhrupad made him serve the form with commitment and his art took him to several countries where he performed. A leading Dhrupad singer, he wrote extensively and won several titles and honours. He headed the Hindustani Music Section of Santiniketan. A distinguished artist, he is a senior A-grade artist of All India Radio. He introduced a new methodology for notation and did his doctorate under Vidwan Suniti Chatterjee.

NIRMALA JOSHI (1928-1974)

The founding pillar of many a cultural institution of Delhi, she was the first Secretary of the National Academy—the Sangeet Natak.

Her name is synonymous with the founding of the art and cultural world of Delhi. Daughter of an eminent medical practitioner, Nirmala Joshi was actively involved with the music and dance world, having started the first society in this field, the All India Music Society. It was from this society that the Delhi School of Hindustani Music and Dancing arose to impart training to those interested in the arts. Later this school took the shape of the Sangeet Bharati in 1939, where such giants as Vidwan Achchan Maharaj and Devendra Shankar taught. The Nawab of Rampur was the chief patron. Pandit Jawaharlal Nehru supported her work and entrusted her with the task of organising the National Dance and Music Festivals. She was selected to head the newly formed National Academy of

Dance, Drama and Music, the Sangeet Natak Akademi. She was instrumental in starting many schemes connected with revival of the classical art forms and her role in resurrecting Kathak to its former glory remains unquestioned. She was also instrumental in starting and shaping the Shriram Bharatiya Kala Kendra with Sumitra Charat Ram. Her long years of association with the Kendra gave it direction, purpose, substance and strength. Nirmala Joshi's contribution to the enrichment of the cultural world of Delhi remains established long after her passing away.

NUPUR ROY CHOWDHURY

Having first learnt the art of music under stalwarts of the Agra gharana, Ustad Anwar Hussain Khan and Ustad Yunus Hussain Khan, Nupur Roy Chowdhury later came under the tutelage of Pandit Dilip Chandra Vedi. She specialised in Khayal under him and excelled in singing. Having made a mark in the professional world of music, she joined the Music Faculty of the Delhi University.

NARENDRA SHARMA
(Born 1924)

A pupil of Uday Shankar who continues the maestro's work.

Born on September 21, 1924, in Bulandshahar, Uttar Pradesh, Narendra Sharma came from a farmer's family to the world of dance. He ran away from home to enlist in the Uday Shankar School in Almora, where after a few years he went to Bombay to try his luck in films. In films and dance he had little success; in matters of the heart he won the hand of Jayanti, whom he married. As a member of IPTA, he participated in their presentations, including shows for soldiers in the war.

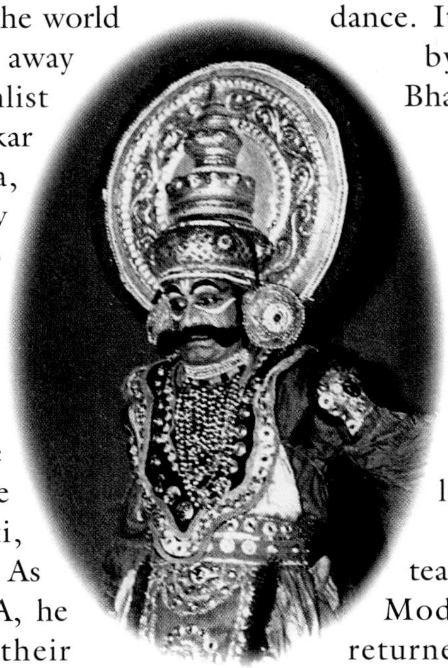

After this phase he came to Delhi to work in Modern School as a hobby teacher, teaching dance. It was his selection by the Shriram Bharatiya Kala Kendra as director of the 'Ramlila' production in 1957 that brought him centre stage in the world of the arts. Having mounted this production, he left the institution and continued teaching dance at the Modern School. He returned to the Kendra later for a short while. It was his association with the

Following pages 168-169: *Uma Sharma, Amjad Ali Khan with son and wife Subbulaxmi, Leela Samson in Holi Mela festivities with Sumitra Charat Ram and Shobha Deepak Singh.*

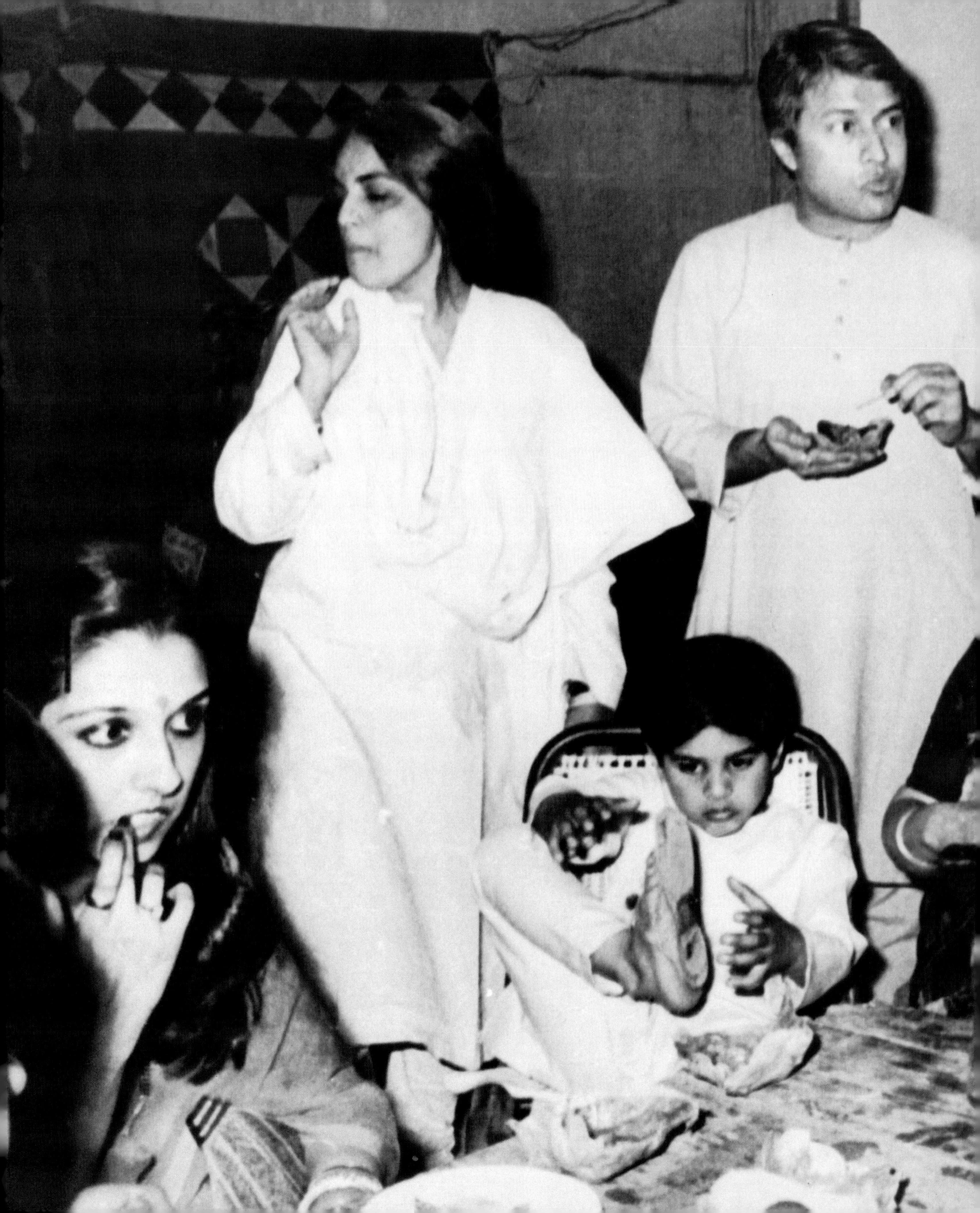

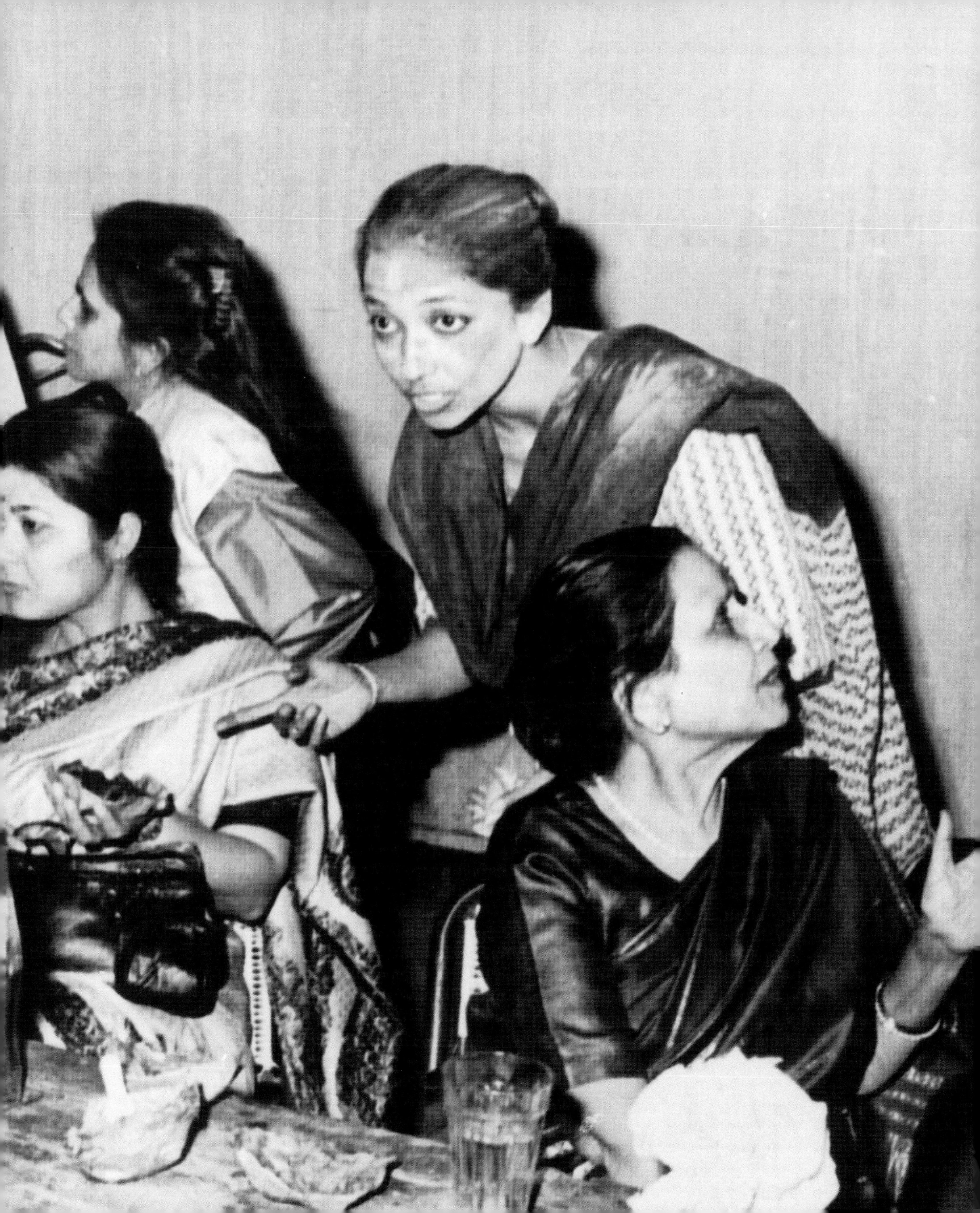

Modern School which brought him in contact with talented artists, who formed the Bhoomika Creative Dance Centre in 1972. Through Bhoomika, Narendra Sharma focussed on entertainment for children and did a few productions of lasting significance like 'The Wolf Boy'; 'Conference 79'; 'Hans Balaka'. For his work in the field of choreography, he was given awards and honours, including the Parishad Samman and the Sangeet Natak Akademi Award in 1976.

PRADEEP SHANKAR (1941-1998)

The Shaan of Oudh!

Born on May 3, 1941, he came into contact with Mumtaj Ali in 1955 and later, Sitara Devi. He was introduced to Lachchu Maharaj in 1956 and was trained by him. In 1959, he visited South Africa as one of Sitara Devi's troupe members. In 1960, he met Pandit Birju Maharaj and joined the Shriram Bharatiya Kala Kendra. He took stellar roles in the Kendra's productions and his role in 'Shane-e-Oudh' is particularly remembered. After several years of association with the institution, he served the Kathak Kendra and was sent by the ICCR to teach abroad. He died in the January of 1998.

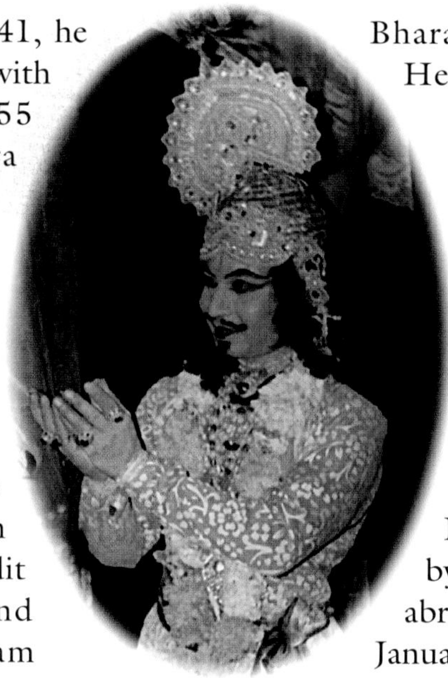

PARTHO DAS

A sitarist of repute, Partho Das joined the Shriram Bharatiya Kala Kendra in the eighties to serve in the Music Section and composed music for dance-dramas such as 'Shakuntala'; 'Chaitra Parv' and 'Buddha'. He left the Kendra to teach at the Bharatiya Vidya Bhawan. As a soloist he has made a mark but his contribution is recognised more as a composer.

PRABHA MARATHE

She joined the Ballet Unit of the Kendra in 1960, after graduating in Sanskrit and Marathi from Poona University. She participated in productions like 'Malati Madhav'; 'Kumar Sambhav' and 'Shane-e-Oudh'. She learnt under Pandit Birju Maharaj and later shifted to Poona to start her own institute, the Kala Chhaya. Guru Munnalal Shukla joined her institute and together they propagated Kathak for many years in the region.

Pandit PURUSHOTTAM DAS

Born on June 7, 1907, Pandit Purushottam Das learnt pakhawaj from his father Pandit Ghanshyam, who was a hereditary player at the Srinathji temple of Nathdwara. He came to Delhi and joined the Shriram Bharatiya Kala Kendra in 1957 at the invitation of the institution. He served the institution and his field of music with distinction until 1964. The Sangeet Natak Akademi bestowed him with its award in 1978. Thereafter he joined the Kathak Kendra and trained many aspirants in the art, until his retirement in 1981. He passed away on January 19, 1991.

PRATAP AND PRIYA PAWAR (Born 1942)

A Kathak dancing pair who served the form internationally.

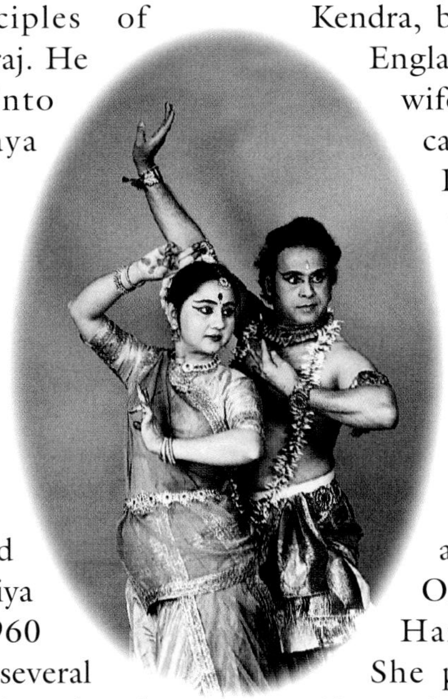

Born in Indore on May 20, 1942 Pratap Pawar is among the senior-most disciples of Pandit Birju Maharaj. He was initiated into Kathak by Maya Rao. His initial inspiration came from Vinod Chopra whose dance-items for Bombay films proved to be a major hit for youngsters like Pratap. He joined the Shriram Bharatiya Kala Kendra in 1960 and performed in several productions. He also played the role of Rama in the 'Ramlila' production of the Kendra. For Yog Sunder, he performed as Saleem to Asha Parekh's 'Anarkali'. After several performance tours and travels, he served as staff artist of the Kathak Kendra, before emigrating to England, where he, with wife Priya, served the cause of Kathak. Priya Pawar learnt Kathak under Mohan Rao Kalyanpurkar, Guru Kundanlal Gangani and Acharya Sundar Prasad.

In addition to Kathak, Priya acquired the art of Orissi through Guru Harikrishna Behera. She played the role of Sita in the Kendra production and is known for her sensitive portrayal and presentation. With her husband Pratap, Priya continues to serve the art of Kathak.

RAGHAVAN NAIR

The symbol of Ram in the evergreen production 'Ramlila'.

Trained and initiated into the world of dance by his elder brother, Krishnan Nair, Raghavan came under the tutelage of Krishnan Namboodri and Guru Gopinath. His stately personality lent itself well to the main roles of mythological characters and he portrayed Krishna for the Natya Ballet Centre's 'Krishnalila' and later joined the Shriram Bharatiya Kala Kendra as staff artist, undertaking the role of Rama in the 'Ramlila'. He served the Kendra for many years, becoming its Assistant Director. He collaborated with other dancers like Swapnasundari in the 'Om Shakti' production. An able dancer and teacher, he taught at the Modern School, before emigrating to Australia where he continues to serve the cause of the Indian arts.

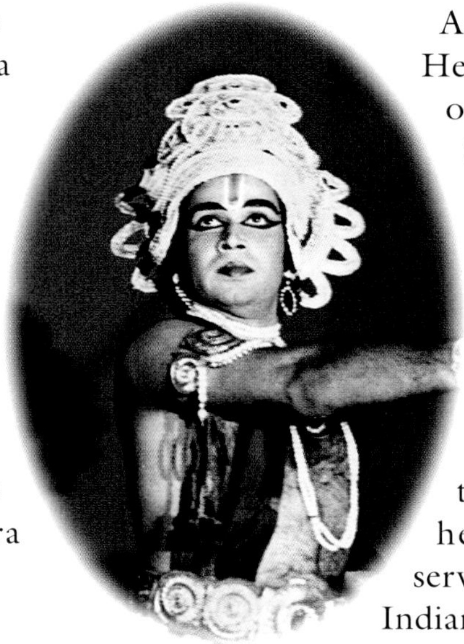

RANI KARNA

Born on March 3, 1939, in Hyderabad, Sind, Rani Karna learnt Kathak under Pandit Narayan Prasad, Pandit Sundar Prasad and Birju Maharaj. She served the Sangeet Bharati and was closely associated with the Shriram Bharatiya Kala Kendra, first as a student and later in a professional capacity. A seasoned Kathak artist, Rani Karna has carved a niche for herself in the world of Kathak by assimilating two divergent schools. She learnt Orissi in addition to Kathak and is regarded as a serious Orissi artist.

RASHMI JAIN VAJPEYI

Daughter of Nemi Chandra Jain, Drama Critic, and Rekha Jain, Children's Theatre Director, Rashmi Jain Vajpeyi was born on April 8, 1941 at Agra. Initially she learnt Manipuri in Allahabad, before coming to Delhi in 1957 to learn Kathak under Birju Maharaj for seven years at the Shriram Bharatiya Kala Kendra. A principal dancer of the Kendra, she participated in its productions such as 'Malti Madhav', 'Kumara Sambhava', 'Dali', 'Shan-e-Oudh' and 'Rasleela'. She gave solo recitals in several countries before settling down to domesticity having married the poet Ashok Vajpeyi.

RAM LAKHAN YADAV

A talented product of Guru Shambhu Maharaj, Ram Lakhan decided to dedicate his life to music after he learnt the art of pakhawaj from Pandit Purushottam Das. Although his association with the Shriram Bharatiya Kala Kendra started as a student, he has served the Kendra for several years and is now a staff artist of the Kathak Kendra. He has participated in various dance-dramas of both the Kendras and continues to delight with his control and command of pakhawaj.

Pandit RAVI SHANKAR (Born 1920)

Living legend of sitar.

Born on April 7, 1920, Ravi Shankar hailed from a family which gave the country eminent artists. Starting his career in elder brother Uday Shankar's troupe, Ravi Shankar decided to learn the sitar from Ustad Allaudin Khan Saheb, whose daughter Annapurna Devi, he later married. Presently, he is married to Sukanya and they have a daughter, Anoushka.

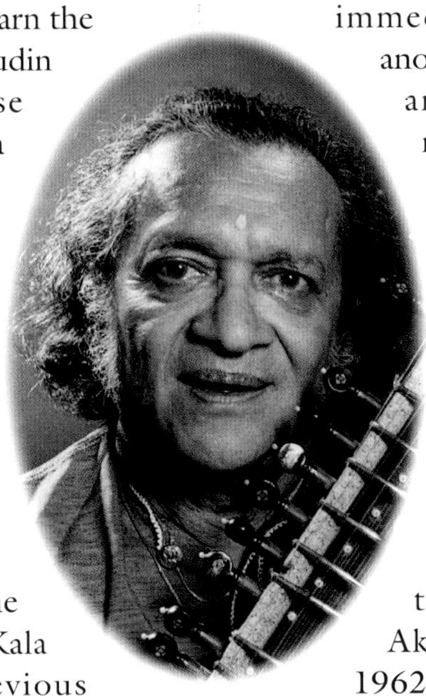

His career in music took off in the mid-forties. He was chiefly instrumental in shaping the Shriram Bharatiya Kala Kendra, in its previous incarnation as the Jhankar Music Society. He gave several special concerts for this society, teaming up with Annapurna Devi as well as with Ustad Ali Akbar Khan and Ustad Vilayat Khan.

He served as Director of Orchestra of the All India Radio. His biggest success came in promoting Indian classical music abroad, particularly in the USA and Europe. His teaming up with George Harrison established an immediate rapport with another generation, lost and in search of meaning. He started his school of music in Los Angeles and later in Benaras.

A highly individualistic artist, he has won every worthy award, honour and title, including the Padma Bhushan and the Sangeet Natak Akademi Award in 1962. He was also made a Fellow of the Akademi in 1975 as well as a nominated member of the Parliament's Upper House. His 75 years of service propagating Indian music remains celebrated not only as a highly acclaimed sitarist but as a composer and creator.

REBA AJMANI

Born in 1949, Reba pursued dance under Kelu Nair in Jamshedpur, before coming to Calcutta to perform professionally. In 1962, she came to Delhi and joined the Shriram Bharatiya Kala Kendra as a staff artist. Her association continued for years, while she learnt Orissi under Guru Hare Krishna Behera and later worked in Guru Mayadhar Raut's dance-drama productions. She acquired proficiency in Kathak under Guru Shambhu Maharaj and participated in many of the Kendra's productions before joining the Song and Drama Division in 1968, which she served until 1979. She was then sent on a teaching assignment by the ICCR to the Indian culture Centre in Surinam where she taught Orissi and returned to India in 1982 to proceed to Guyana in 1985. She is married to the well-known Kathak dancer Tirath Ajmani.

REHMAT ALI KHAN

Elder son of legendary sarod maestro, Ustad Hafiz Ali Khan, Rehmat is the elder brother of Amjad Ali Khan. He is steeped in the family tradition of playing the sarod and is reputed to be an artist of high originality with full command of the instrument. Trained at the Shriram Bharatiya Kala Kendra, Rehmat Ali Khan has performed for the radio and concerts. His involvement with the Kendra ushered in close relationships with several artists like dancer Uma Sharma. He is recognised as a sarodist of high repute even though he has maintained a low profile. He continues the Senia gharana by teaching and training aspirants based in Bhopal.

REKHA SHANKAR
(Born 1948)

A theatre and film actress, she remained a principal artist of the Kendra for decades.

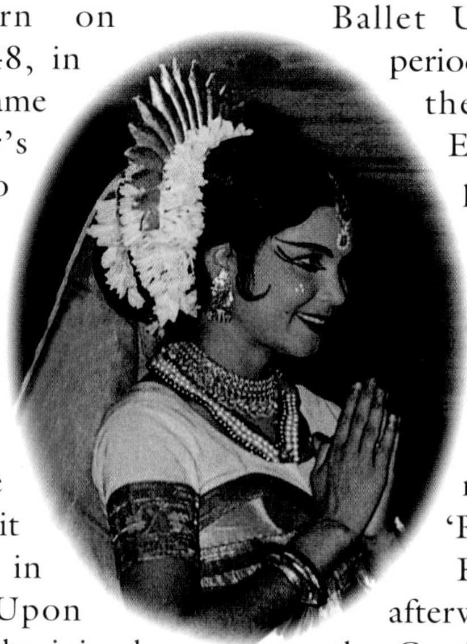

Elder sister of Reba Ajmani, Rekha was born on November 5, 1948, in Jamshedpur and came under Kelu Nair's tutelage. It was to the world of theatre that young Rekha was attracted and thus she made a professional career in Calcutta. She took roles in Satyajit Ray films, as also in Punjabi films. Upon coming to Delhi, she joined the Shriram Bharatiya Kala Kendra as a staff artist in 1960 and stayed until 1974 with its Ballet Unit. During this period, she travelled with the Kendra troupe. Earlier, she had the privilege of being groomed in Kathak by Guru Shambhu Maharaj and Pandit Birju Maharaj. She also enacted the role of Sita in the 'Ramlila' production. For several years afterwards she taught at the Cambridge School. She married the well known Kathak artist, Pradip Shankar.

RINA SINGHA

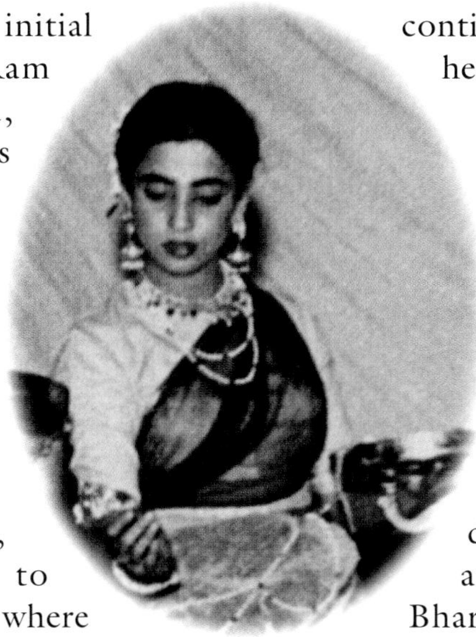

Having received initial training from Ram Krishna Shukla, Rina Singha was awarded a Government scholarship to study under Guru Shambhu Maharaj in 1958-60. After her professional training in India, she immigrated to England in 1961, where she taught and performed extensively. She moved to Canada in 1965 and formed her own dance company Jhankar, which continues to propagate her dance form. Since then she has contributed significantly to enriching the artistic life of Canada and has served on the Arts Council of Canada as an adviser on Indian dance. Her training at the Shriram Bharatiya Kala Kendra by renowned masters equipped her to chart this highly rewarding professional course.

RITA GANGULY KOTHARI

Having graduated from the Viswa Bharati University with honours in music and dance, Rita learnt from Siddheshwari Devi and claims to have learnt from Begum Akhtar, in her last years. She acquired proficiency in Thumri, Dadra, Tappa and Ghazal. She trained under Pandit Mani Prasad in Khayal. She performed and promoted the forms and married Keshav Kothari. After a long association with the Shriram Bharatiya Kala Kendra, she served the National School of Drama as a mime teacher, having had previous training in Kathakali. For her efforts in the field she was given the Sahitya Kala Parishad Samman.

SHAKUNTALA NAIR

A star ballet artist of the Kendra.

Daughter and disciple of Bhagwandas Verma, Shakuntala was trained by him before taking extensive lessons in Kathak from Pandit Sundar Prasad, Guru Kundanlal Gangani, Birju Maharaj and Devi Lal. She married Krishnan Nair, who was a senior staff artist of the Shriram Bharatiya Kala Kendra. She participated in principal roles of the Kendra productions and served the Kendra until she was sent by the ICCR to Fiji in 1972. Thereafter, she travelled and finally immigrated to Australia.

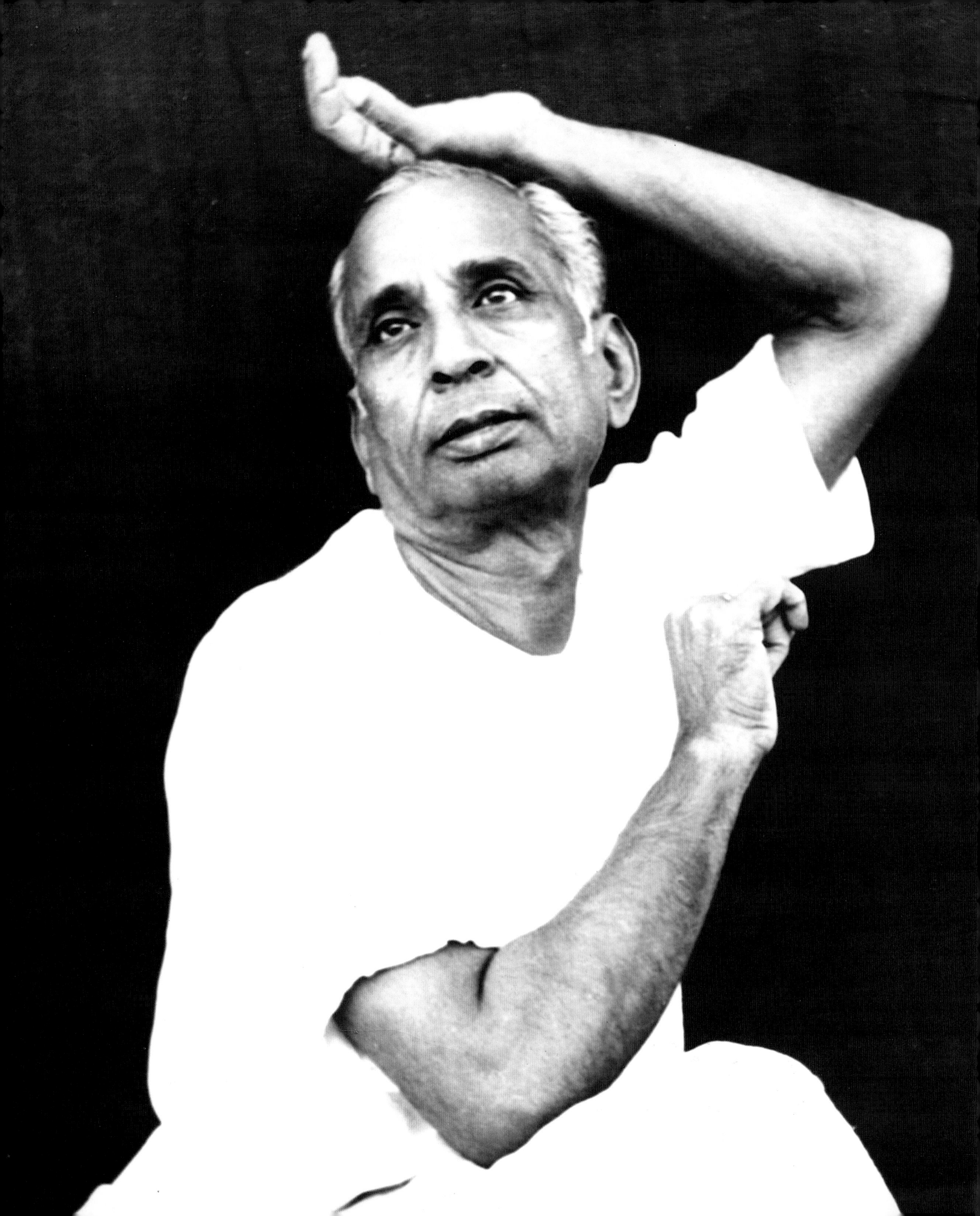

SHAMBHU MAHARAJ
(1912-1970)

Samrat of Kathak, who revived the art of the court and made it fit for the stage.

Son of the legendary Kalka Prasad and a nephew of Vidwan Bindadin, Shambhu Maharaj acquired the family art of Kathak from elder brother Vidwan Achchan Maharaj. A genius in his own right, he was brought to Delhi in the mid-fifties and became the first guru at the Bharatiya Kala Kendra. He trained just about every Kathak aspirant of that period and his fame as a performer, composer, and creator spread far. Countless tours and travels, awards and honours, titles and medals did not affect or alter his personality.

His association with the Kendra continued for many years and the Kathak section benefited immensely, as did the world of dance. He was awarded the Sangeet Natak Akademi award in 1955 and for enriching the Kathak form, later made a Fellow of the Akademi in 1967. Shambhu Maharaj strode high in his time and left an indelible mark on the cultural map of the country. He passed away on November 4, 1970.

SHANKAR YADAV

Born on August 15, 1919, Shankar Yadav was attracted to theatre and joined the Ariya Sangeet Natak Mandali in 1923. He spent a decade with the Mandali before going to Bombay to work as dance composer in films. He then joined the Sachin Shankar Ballet Unit before proceeding to Gwalior to become a member of the Little Ballet Troupe. In 1959 he came to Delhi to work with Begum Zaidi and later joined the Shriram Bharatiya Kala Kendra, with which he continued for years as a drummer and dancer, enacting the role of Sudamma in 'Krishnavtaar'.

SHANTI VAIDYANATHAN SHARMA
(Born 1956)

Senior disciple of Pandit Amarnath, her music has depth and devotion.

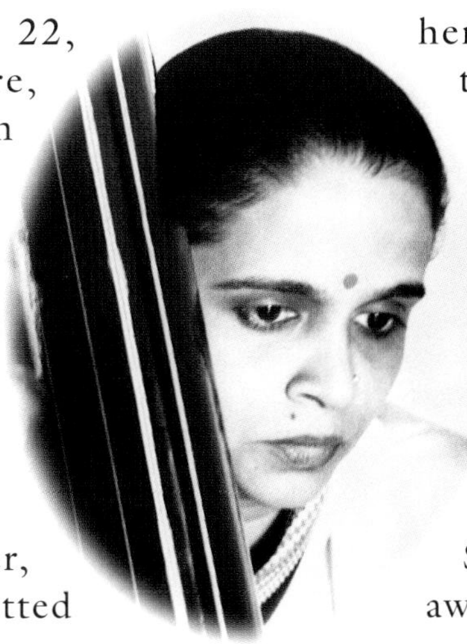

Born on August 22, 1956 at Tanjore, Shanti Vaidyanathan Sharma is the foremost disciple of Pandit Amarnath, the principal vocalist of the Indore gharana of the late Ustad Amir Khan. A dedicated singer, Shanti has committed her life to music and today ranks as a serious and senior practitioner of the form. Originally, an engineer by training, she left the field to pursue music full time. She performed at Kal Ke Kalakaar Sammelan and was awarded the Sur Mani

Dance-dramas produced by the Kendra '57–97

RAM LILA 1957
Choreography: Narendra Sharma

KATHAK-KI-KAHANI 1957
Choreography: Shambhu Maharaj

MALTI MAHADEV 1958
Choreography: Lacchu Maharaj & Birju Maharaj

KUMAR SAMBHAV 1958
Choreography: Birju Maharaj

DALIA 1961
Choreography: Birju Maharaj

SHAN-E-OUDH
Choreography: Birju Maharaj

GITOPADESH 1965
Choreography: Birju Maharaj

KRISHNAYAN 1966
Choreography: Birju Maharaj

TAJ-KI-KAHANI 1968
Choreography: Krishna Kumar

SITAYAN 1969
Choreography: Krishnan Namboodiri

MEERA BAI 1970
Choreography: Krishnan Namboodiri

GEET GOVIND 1971
Choreography: Krishnan Namboodiri

MEGHDOOT 1973
Choreography: K. Shekharan Panikar

AZADI-KI-ORE 1973
Choreography: Krishnan Namboodiri

URVASHI 1974
Choreography: Krishnan Namboodiri

RAMCHARITMANAS 1974
Choreography: Uma Sharma

KATHAK SEQUENCES 1974
Choreography: Uma Sharma

GLIMPSES FROM LORD KRISHNA'S LIFE 1975
Choreography: Guru Gopinath

DHARTI-KA-VIVAH 1975
Choreography: K. Shekharan Panikar

KENOPANISHAD 1975
Choreography: K. Shekharan Panikar

MAHABIR 1976
Choreography: K. Shekharan Panikar

SURDAS 1976
Choreography: Uma Sharma

KRISHNAVATAR 1977
Choreography: K. Shekharan Panikar

JAGDEV 1977
Choreography: Krishna Chandra Naik

KONARK 1978
Choreography: Krishna Chandra Naik

KATHAK SEQUENCES 1978
Choreography: Munna Shukla

KALING VIJAY 1979
Choreography: Krishna Chandra Naik

KHAJURAHO 1980
Choreography: Krishna Chandra Naik

SHAN-E-MUGHAL 1981
Choreography: Munna Shukla

YAYATI 1982
Choreography: Krishna Chandra Naik

BAHUBALI 1982
Choreography: K. Shekharan Panikar

MASKS 1983
Choreography: Bhushan Lakhandri

SHAKUNTALA 1983
Choreography: K. Shekharan Panikar

KARNA 1984
Choreography: Krishna Chandra Naik & Bhushan Lakhandri

ANARKALI 1985
Choreography: Uma Sharma, assisted by Vaswati Mishra

CHAITRA PARV 1986
Choreography: Krishna Chandra Naik, assisted by Madan Solanki, Rekha Sharma & Olek Niranjan Bisoi

KAMAYANI 1987
Choreography: Kumudini Lakhia

BUDDHA 1988

MAHADEV 1989
Choreography: Vaswati Mishra

HARIHAR 1990
Choreography: Olek Niranjan Bisoi, Leela Samson & Ram Mohan Mishra

TIRUPURANTAK 1991
Choreography: Shashidharan Nair

CHAKRAVYUHU 1993
Choreography: Shashidharan Nair

PARIKRAMA 1994
Choreography: Shashidharan Nair

MEERA 1995
Choreography: Shashidharan Nair & Papiha Desai

KRISHNA-KATHA 1996
Choreography: Shashidharan Nair & Papiha Desai

title. For about two decades now, she has been associated with the Shriram Bharatiya Kala Kendra, where she is a staff teacher imparting training to dedicated aspirants.

SHASHIDHARAN NAIR
(Born 1954)

Trained in Kathakali and Chhau, he now regales as a choreographer.

Born on March 17, 1954, Shashidharan Nair received training in Kathakali from Kalamandalam K. Padmanabhan Nair and the renowned Kavungal Sankaran Kutty Panicker. His professional career began with the Little Ballet Troupe of Gwalior before joining the Shriram Bharatiya Kala Kendra in the late seventies. He came under the care of choreographer-director, K. Shekharan Panikar and played stellar roles in the Kendra productions.

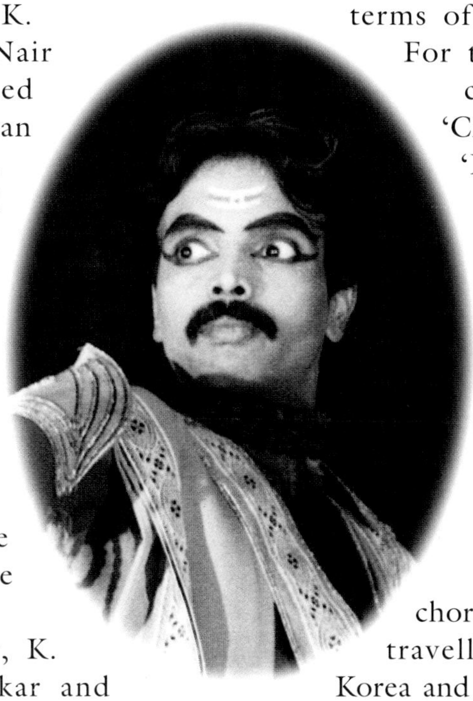

At about the same time, during his stay in the Kendra, he learnt Mayurbhanj Chhau from Guru Krishna Chandra Naik and today ranks as his successor in terms of choreography. For the Kendra, he choreographed 'Chakravyuhu' and 'Parikrama'. His earlier choreographic works include 'Sangharsh' for Yuva Mahotsava in 1989 and 'Tripurantak' for Hari Utsav in 1990. The latter choreographic piece travelled to Japan, Korea and Thailand under ICCR's patronage. He now teaches Chhau at the Kendra. He participated in *Taal-Mel*.

SUBHASH DUTTA

A trained musician, Subhash Dutta served the Shriram Bharatiya Kala Kendra as Manager. He took part in the Kendra orchestra and wrote lyrics, in addition to composing music. Occasionally, he broadcast light vocal music for the radio. His association was cut short when he organised a strike against the Kendra and left the Kendra with his wife Reba Dutta, who got a posting in Indonesia to teach Sanskrit.

SIDDHESHWARI DEVI

A legendary musician, she represents the essence of the Banarsi gharana.

Born in 1903, Siddheshwari Devi received early inspiration from her grandfather, himself a noted musician. It was her training under Guru Siyajee Maharaj of Kashi which gave her an initial grooming for the world of music, but it was her learning under Ustad Inayat Khan and Pandit Bade Ramdasji Maharaj which gave her music a life all of its own. She was soon renowned as an excellent singer, particularly of Thumri. Having inherited a vast repertoire, she was equally at home with Dadra, Tappa, Kajriand chaiti.

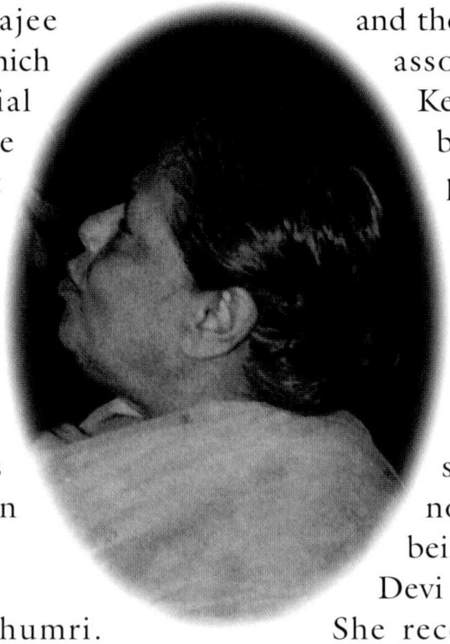

She came to the Shriram Bharatiya Kala Kendra in 1965 and thereby started a long association with the Kendra, of which she became an integral part. Thereafter, she joined the Kathak Kendra but her association with the parent body continued and she helped groom several disciples of note, the chief ones being Asha Jain, Savita Devi and several others. She received the Sangeet Natak Akademi Award in 1966 and the Padma Shri in 1967.

SHOVANA NARAYAN

Born on September 2, 1950 at Calcutta, Shovana Narayan trained in Kathak under Guru Kundanlal Gangani, Guru Sundar Prasad and Pandit Birju Maharaj. Her association with the Kendra started in the late sixties when she joined as a student learning Kathak.

She has progressed in her art of Kathak, given innumerable solo performances and created new compositions. Through her institution, Asavari, she teaches the art form to younger aspirants. A civil servant by profession, she has explored new avenues in Kathak and collaborated internationally with other forms to bring a commonality and cohesion to her work. In recognition of her work, she was awarded the Padma Shri in 1992, and the Parishad Samman in 1993. She has participated in *Taal-Mel*.

SHUBHA MUDGAL
(Born 1959)

Born on June 23, 1959, in Allahabad, Shubha Mudgal learnt Kathak from the Gangani family of the Jaipur gharana and later from Pandit Ramgopal Misra. Later, she came under the tutelage of Pandit Ram Ashray Jha in Allahabad. On moving to

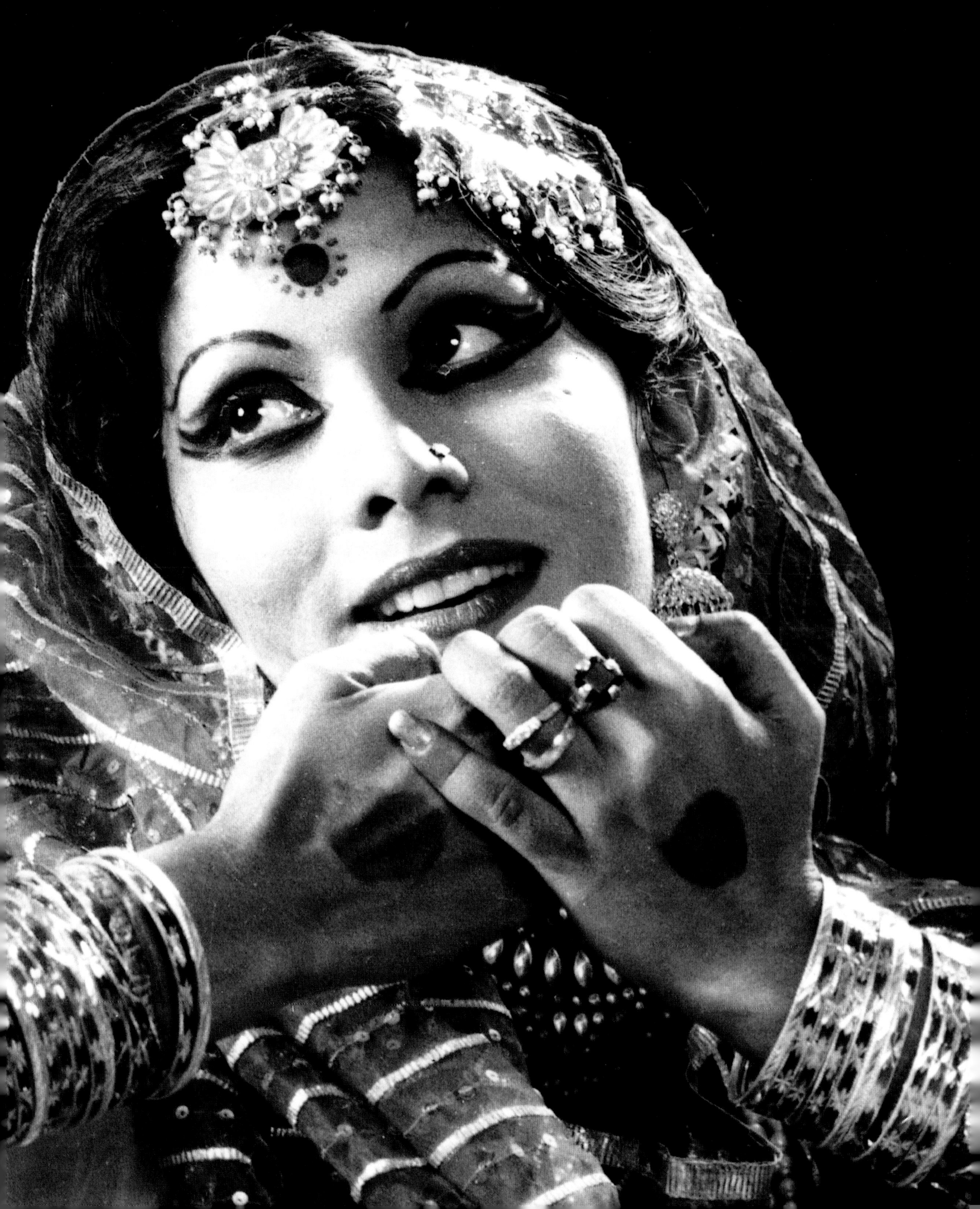

Talented musician and composer who has invited critical acclaim and wide outreach.

Delhi, she learnt from Pandit Vinay Chandra Maudgalya, Pandit Vasant Thakkar, Pandit Jitendar Abhisekhi and Kumar Gandharva. She also benefited by learning the art of Thumri and Dadra from Naina Devi.

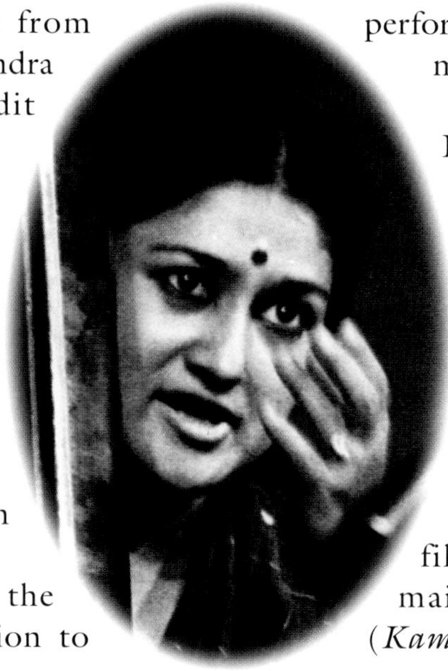

She is known for her deep involvement with the field and in addition to performing has composed music for Shriram Bharatiya Kala Kendra's production 'Parikrama', Sonal Mansingh's 'Draupadi' and compositions for Aditi Mangaldas, Astad Deboo and Neera Batra. She has also composed for documentary films and sung for mainstream cinema (*Kamasutra*).

Guru SUNDAR PRASAD (1891-1970)

A veteran Kathak artist-guru.

The younger brother of Jailal, Sundar Prasad was born in 1891 and trained in the art of Kathak by their father Chunnilal. He learnt the finer intricacies of the art from Maharaj Bindadin of Lucknow. He acquired insights into the twin schools of Kathak, the Jaipur gharana and the Lucknow gharana. In the thirties, he established the Bindadin School of Kathak in Bombay and spent over twenty years there during which he trained Mohanrao Kalyanpurkar, the Pooviah sisters, Shirin Vajifdar, Menaka, Sohanlal, Hiralal and Roshan Kumari. In 1958, he came to Delhi and joined the Shriram Bharatiya Kala Kendra and trained several dancers of the day such as Maya Rao, Uma Sharma, Urmila Nagar, Kumudini Lakhia, Durgalal and Shovana Narayan. His output and talent were widely recognised and he received the Sangeet Natak Akademi award in 1959. He passed away in 1970.

SUSHIL DAS GUPTA (Born 1922)

Music composer par excellence.

A music composer of great excellence, Sushil Das Gupta was born on November 20, 1922 and learnt from his brother, Abani Das Gupta before getting early and initial success in Bombay where he came under the guidance of Pandit Ravi Shankar, with whom he played and collaborated. His move to Delhi in the mid-fifties brought him in contact with the Shriram Bharatiya Kala Kendra, which he joined as the first music composer for its 'Ramlila' in 1957. He enlisted the help and

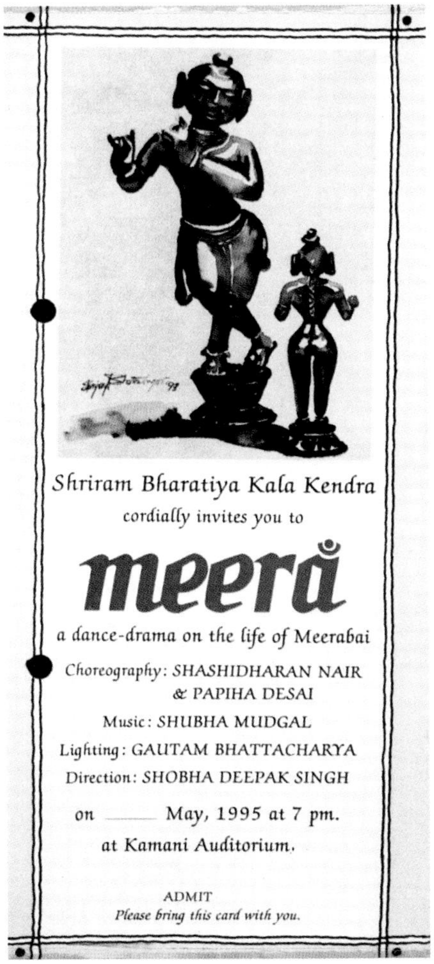
Shriram Bharatiya Kala Kendra
cordially invites you to
meera
a dance-drama on the life of Meerabai
Choreography: SHASHIDHARAN NAIR
& PAPIHA DESAI
Music: SHUBHA MUDGAL
Lighting: GAUTAM BHATTACHARYA
Direction: SHOBHA DEEPAK SINGH
on ______ May, 1995 at 7 pm.
at Kamani Auditorium.
ADMIT
Please bring this card with you.

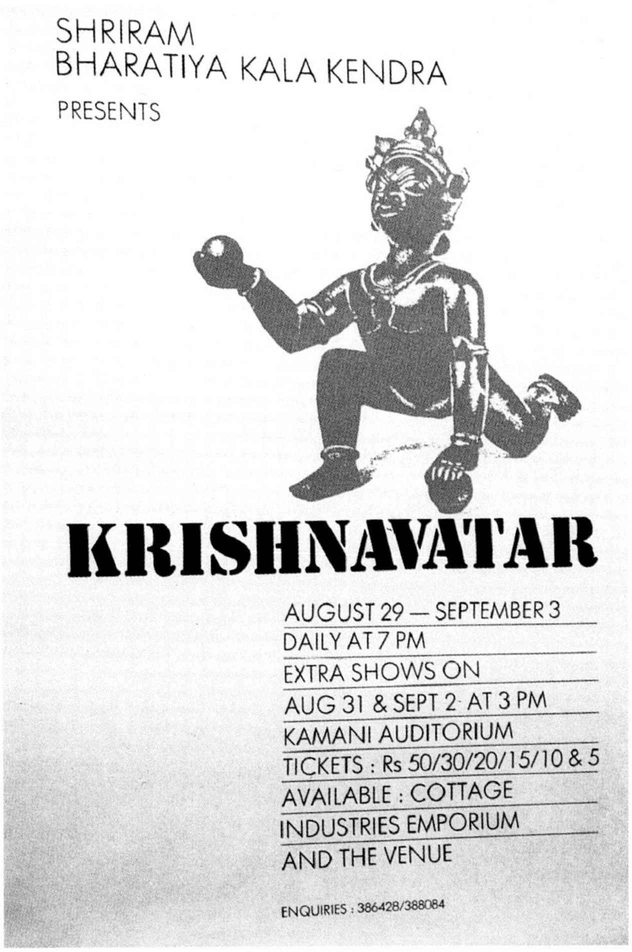
SHRIRAM
BHARATIYA KALA KENDRA
PRESENTS
KRISHNAVATAR
AUGUST 29 — SEPTEMBER 3
DAILY AT 7 PM
EXTRA SHOWS ON
AUG 31 & SEPT 2 AT 3 PM
KAMANI AUDITORIUM
TICKETS : Rs 50/30/20/15/10 & 5
AVAILABLE : COTTAGE
INDUSTRIES EMPORIUM
AND THE VENUE
ENQUIRIES : 386428/388084

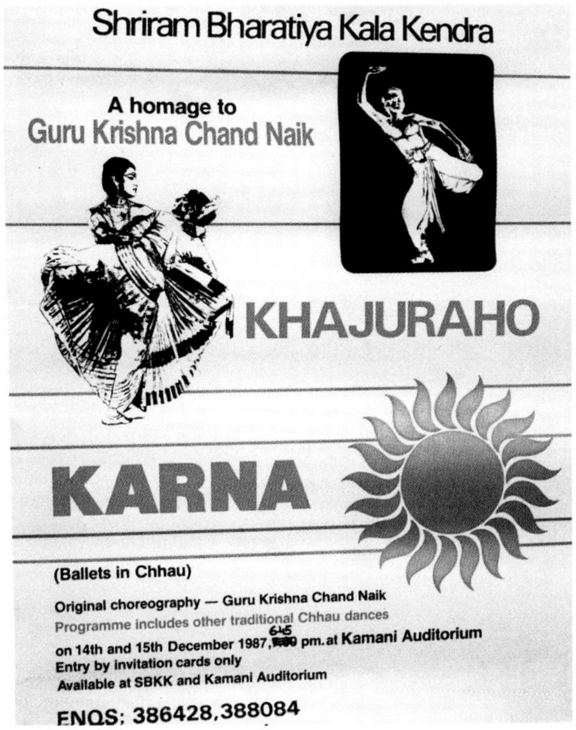
Shriram Bharatiya Kala Kendra
A homage to
Guru Krishna Chand Naik
KHAJURAHO
KARNA
(Ballets in Chhau)
Original choreography — Guru Krishna Chand Naik
Programme includes other traditional Chhau dances
on 14th and 15th December 1987, 6.15 pm. at Kamani Auditorium
Entry by invitation cards only
Available at SBKK and Kamani Auditorium
ENQS: 386428,388084

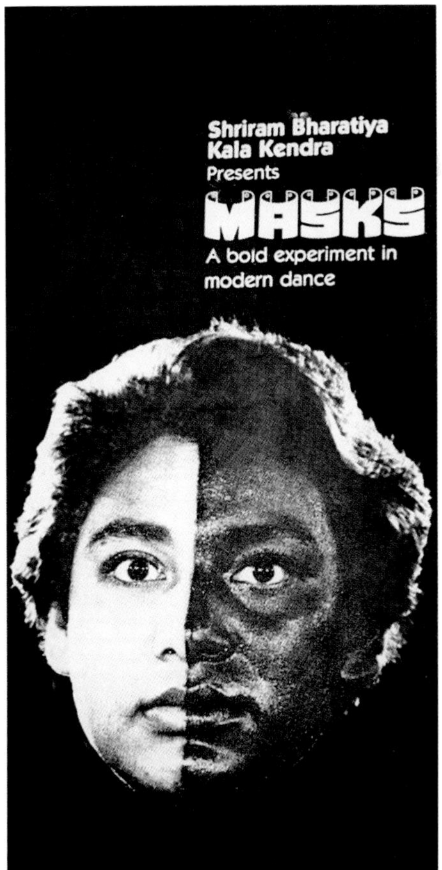
Shriram Bharatiya
Kala Kendra
Presents
MASKS
A bold experiment in
modern dance

collaboration of 'Batukda' Jyotirindra Moitra and together they created an everlasting score.

Guided by a patriotic spirit, a former Party member and an IPTA associate, he did several choirs and orchestra presentations. He also worked as the music director for the Natya Ballet Centre, composing music for its productions. For Bhagwandas Verma, he created the music for 'Amir Khusro'. In the seventies, he collaborated with Narendra Sharma's Bhoomika to compose music for most of its productions. He received the Sahitya Kala Parishad Samman in 1986 and is now concentrating on creating newer scores, including several discs.

SUNIL KUMAR BOSE

A disciple of Vidwan Girija Shankar Chakravarti, Sunil Bose served the Shriram Bharatiya Kala Kendra as its first Executive Director in the early sixties. As the Station Director of All India Radio, Delhi Kendra, he came into contact with fellow musicians whom he served and supported devotedly. He was associated with the Kendra for over three decades and his work was highly regarded.

TAPAS SEN
(Born 1924)

The lights wizard of India.

Born on September 11, 1924, Tapas Sen is acclaimed as the best light craftsman of India. Tapas started as a humble switch-board attendant of the then Electricity Board of Delhi. After initial experimentation and success, he tried his hand at lighting for films, first in Bombay and later in Calcutta. This brought him in contact with a host of film personalities like Harendranath Chattopadhya, Satyajit Ray, Hrishikesh Mukherjee, Mrinal Sen and Ritwick Ghatak. He also did stage lights for Sadhona Bose, the eminent dancer and Naina Devi's sister. He designed the lights for the 'Ramlila' production of the Shriram Bharatiya Kala Kendra and his association continues till date. He has provided light design for several events, openings, and halls such as the AIFACS, Kamani, Siri

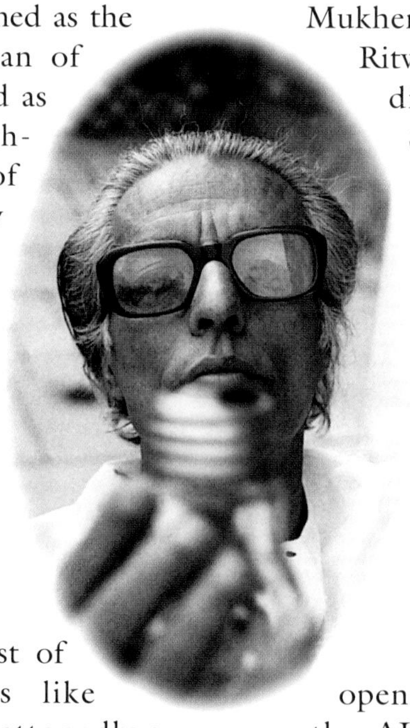

Fort, as well as the Son et Lumiere shows. He was awarded the Sangeet Natak Akademi Award in 1974.

SURINDER KAUR
(Born 1962)

A ballet artist who went to the world of Hindi films.

Trained in Kathak by Pandit Durgalal, Surinder Kaur acquitted herself well in stellar roles in the productions of the Kendra. She played Sita in 'Ramlila' and Sita in 'Krishnayan'. She left the Kendra to join the film world in Bombay, where she had some success.

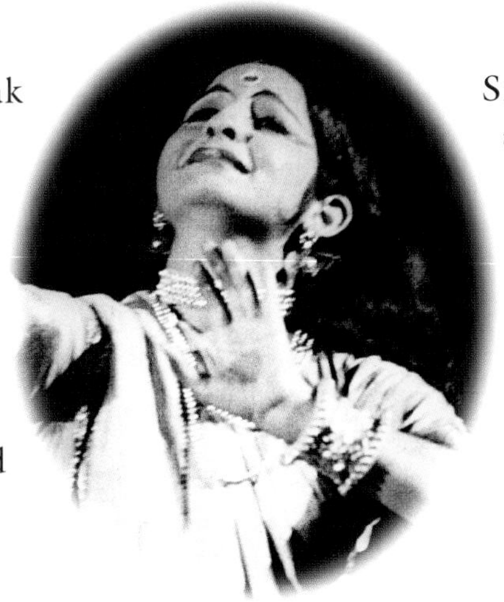

URMI B. GUPTA

Urmi Gupta learnt under the sarod maestro Ustad Hafiz Ali Khan and later from his son, Ustad Amjad Ali Khan, at the Shriram Bharatiya Kala Kendra from 1957-63. She also took part in Kendra productions and travelled abroad with the troupe, before settling down to a life of academics at the Birmingham University, England.

URMIL SHANKAR BHARGAVA

A devoted disciple of Ustad Mushtiaq Khan, Urmil Shankar Bhargava was also groomed by Pandit Dilip Chandra Vedi in the sixties. She specialised in Khayal and Thumri and was a committed disciple at the Shriram Bharatiya Kala Kendra.

URMILA GOEL

Born in Jaipur, Urmila Goel joined the Shriram Bharatiya Kala Kendra in the early sixties to learn Kathak from Pandit Sundar Prasad. She gave several performances with the Kendra before joining the Springdales School as dance teacher.

Vidushi UMA SHARMA
(Born 1942)

Queen of Kathak today.

Born on November 20, 1942, Uma Sharma learnt Kathak under the towering masters of the time, Guru Shambhu Maharaj, Guru Sundar Prasad and Pandit Birju Maharaj, after having joined the Shriram Bharatiya Kala Kendra to play the role of Sita in the 'Ramlila' production. The continued support of Naina Devi and Ustad Rehmat Ali Khan encouraged her to progress professionally.

A name to reckon with in the world of Kathak today, Uma Sharma has gone on to explore the roots of the Raas tradition of Braj and to include it in her repertoire. A seasoned practitioner of the art, she has composed and choreographed several individualistic pieces such as 'Stree', 'Madhushala' and 'Indra Sabha'. She runs her institution, Bharatiya Sangeet Sadan in Delhi. For her work she was awarded the Parishad Samman in 1985 and the Sangeet Natak Akademi Award in 1987. In 1996, she participated in *Taal-Mel.*

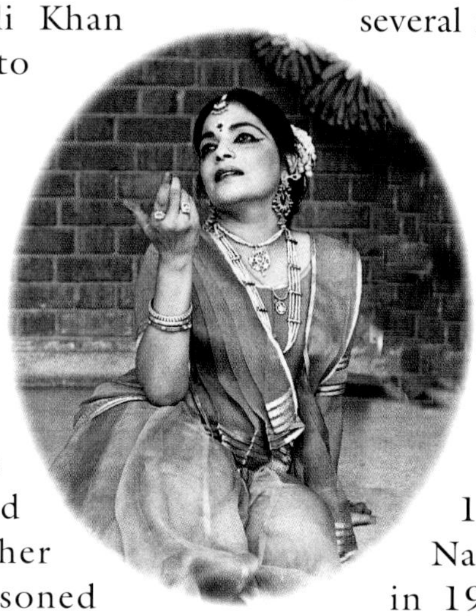

URMILA NAGAR

Urmila Nagar is held to be the principal product of Guru Kundanlal Gangani. She learnt from Pandit Sundar Prasad as well and studied classical music under Ustad Bashir Khan, Pandit Dilip Chandra Vedi and Siddheshwari Devi. An adept Kathak dancer, she is also a reputed ghazal singer. Her association with the Shriram Bharatiya Kala Kendra brought her to the Kathak Kendra, where she is now a staff teacher.

Ustad VILAYAT HUSSAIN KHAN

Son of Ustad Nathan Khan, the well-known Khayal singer of the Agra gharana, Ustad Vilayat Hussain Khan served the Shriram Bharatiya Kala Kendra in the early years and trained several aspirants in the tradition of Dhamar and Khayal singing. An accomplished musician, he gave several concerts at National Music Conferences.

VINOD NAGPAL

Actor and husband of theatre critic Kavita Nagpal, Vinod learnt music under Pandit Dilip Chandra Vedi and later Begum Akhtar. Over the years, he used his singing talent by lending his voice to theatre and opera productions, particularly those of Shiela Bhatia and Mohan Upreti. He is a well-known face on television and has undertaken character roles in mainstream cinema.

***Facing page:** Nirmala Joshi, the founding pillar of the Kendra and India's first cultocrat.*

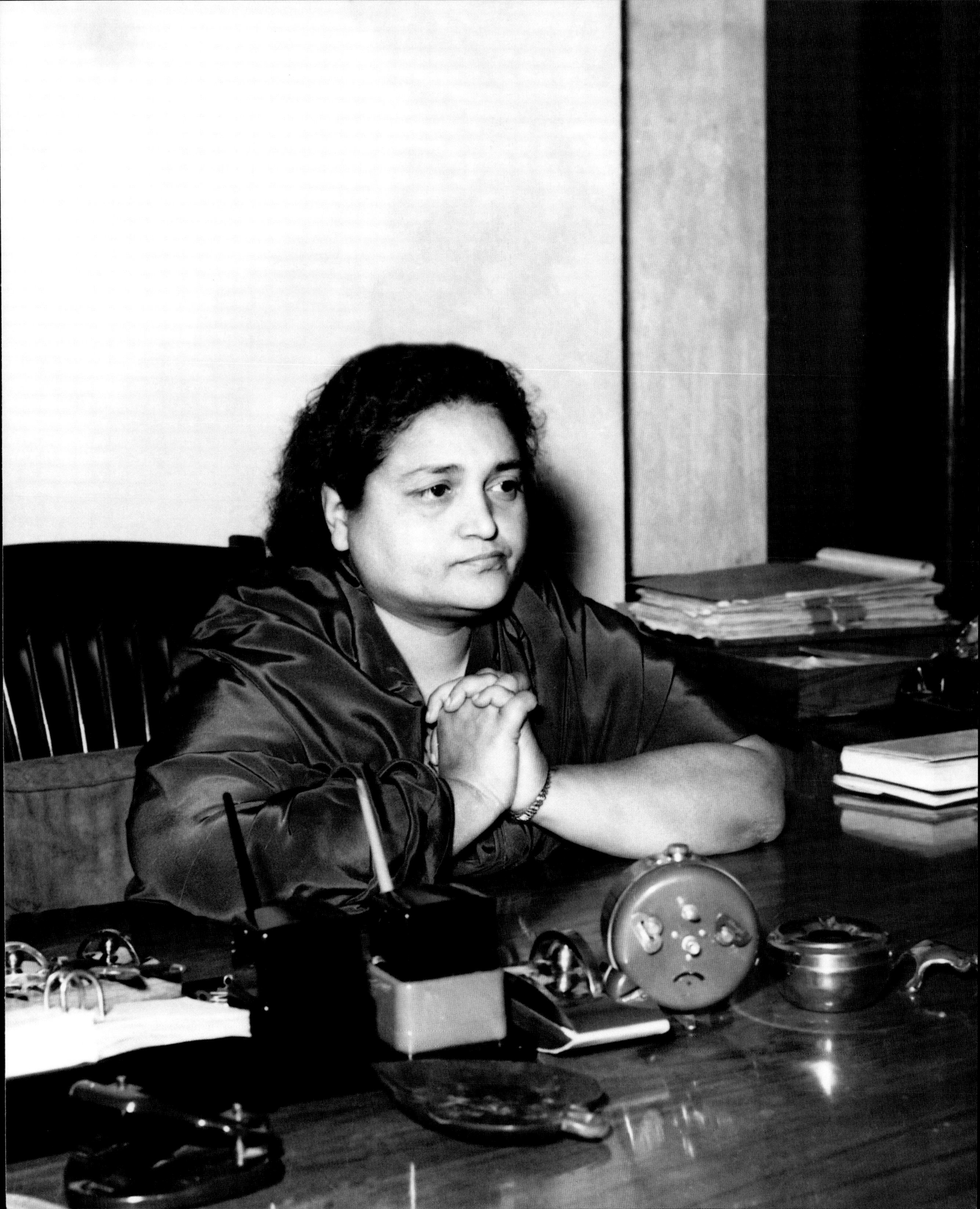

VASWATI MISRA

An accomplished artist of the Lucknow gharana of Kathak, Vaswati has married the form by marrying Krishan Mohan, son of Guru Shambhu Maharaj. She started her early training under Reba Vidyarthi and later under Pandit Birju Maharaj. She joined the Shriram Bharatiya Kala Kendra as a teacher of Kathak and served it for eight years. In that period, she also took stellar roles in Kendra productions. She has tried her hand at choreography and is presently a staff artist of the Kathak Kendra.

Ustad WAHEED KHAN

Son of Ustad Imdad Khan and the younger sibling of sitar wizard Ustad Inayat Khan, Ustad Waheed Khan served the Shriram Bharatiya Kala Kendra as a teacher of sitar. He trained several aspirants and was awarded the Sangeet Natak Akademi Award for his art.

YOGENDRA DESAI
(Born 1926)

A prince of Gujarat (and dance), a senior product of Santiniketan and Ram Gopal, a veteran choreographer.

Born on July 16, 1926, in Dhassa, Gujarat, Yog Sunder as he popularly came to be known, learnt first at Santiniketan before being trained by the legendary Ram Gopal in 1946. In 1948, he formed the Indian Revival Group and did innumerable performances for patriotic causes and for soldiers at war. His group was among the pioneers in presenting a variety of folk dances.

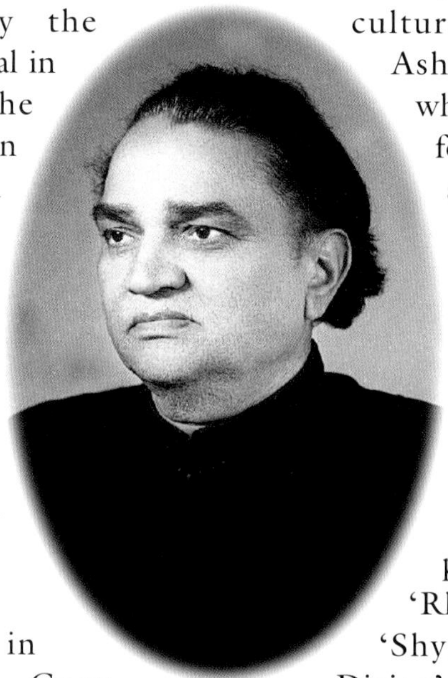

Having had previous training in Kathakali under Guru Kunchu Nair, Yog Sunder used it for creative work in composing dance dramas. Earlier in his career, he had danced with Nayana Jhaveri, Sadhona Bose and Tara Chaudhuri.

He came to Delhi on the advice of Jaspal Singh, the cultural chief of the Ashok Hotel group which was a platform for the arts, and did several shows for them before joining the Shriram Bharatiya Kala Kendra as Director. He continued his association and created new productions like 'Rhythms of India', 'Shyama', 'The Man Divine', and 'Darkness at Noon'. His daughter Papiha Desai, an Orissi dancer, continues in his footsteps. He has participated in *Taal-Mel*.

Index

ISBN: 81-7436-043-3

FIRST PUBLISHED BY
ROLI BOOKS (P) LTD
M-75, GREATER KAILASH-II MARKET
NEW DELHI-110 048, INDIA
PHONES: (011) 6442271, 6462782, 6460886
FAX: (011) 6467185

CONCEIVED AND DESIGNED BY
PRAMOD KAPOOR
AJOY KUMAR BISWAS
AT ROLI CAD CENTRE

COLOUR PHOTOGRAPHS:
SHOBHA DEEPAK SINGH: PGS. 113 (TOP),
116, 117, 120 (TOP), 122-123, 126-127, 128
AVINASH PASRICHA: PGS. 118-119
ASHISH KHOKAR: PGS. 113 (BOTTOM),
120 (BOTTOM), 124
MOHAN KHOKAR: PGS. 121, 125
RAVI PASRICHA: PGS. 113 (BOTTOM,
BHIMSEN JOSHI, 114-115

PRINTED AND BOUND AT
SINGAPORE